Children, youth, and families

Children, youth, and families
The action-research relationship

Edited by

ROBERT N. RAPOPORT

Institute of Family and Environmental Research, London

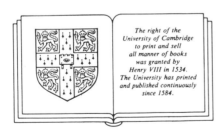

The right of the
University of Cambridge
to print and sell
all manner of books
was granted by
Henry VIII in 1534.
The University has printed
and published continuously
since 1584.

CAMBRIDGE UNIVERSITY PRESS

Cambridge
London   New York   New Rochelle
Melbourne   Sydney

Published by the Press Syndicate of the University of Cambridge
The Pitt Building, Trumpington Street, Cambridge CB2 1RP
32 East 57th Street, New York, NY 10022, USA
10 Stamford Road, Oakleigh, Melbourne 3166, Australia

First published 1985

Printed in the United States of America

Library of Congress Cataloging in Publication Data
Main entry under title:
Children, youth, and families.
Includes indexes.
1. Family policy – Research.   2. Family – Services for.
3.   Youth – Services for.   4. Child health services.
I. Rapoport, Robert Norman, 1924–
HV697.C42   1986   362.7′072   85–11643
ISBN 0 521 30143 2

British Library Cataloging-in-Publication applied for

Contents

v

Acknowledgments

Many people have helped with the development of thoughts and actions leading to the production of this book. I owe thanks for their constant support to Robert Haggerty, Linda Pickett, and the staff and board of the William T. Grant Foundation. Impetus for the line of work suggested in the book was sustained in a conference convened by the Foundation in June 1981, and thanks are due to the participants – Joan Aldous, Conrad Arensberg, Urie Bronfenbrenner, Michael Cohen, Leon Eisenberg, Sonia Jackson, Alfred Kahn, S. Michael Miller, Richard Price, Rhona Rapoport, Paul Schwarz, Eric Trist, Judy Weisbrod, and William Foote Whyte. Working with the contributors to this volume has been both pleasant and educational. Many other friends and colleagues, too numerous to name, have taken an interest in the topic, and I am grateful to them for sharing their thoughts and responding to mine. Marian Harrison provided competent administrative secretarial assistance. Rhona Rapoport has helped in every phase in many ways.

This book is dedicated to all our children, a glad offering in this International Year of Youth.

Robert N. Rapoport

1   Research and action

Robert N. Rapoport

This book is about the interplay between research and action in programs aiming to benefit children, youth, and families.

First we examine the interplay of research and action in other fields, particularly the science-technology relationship in the physical sciences. We then focus on the social sciences, where scientific knowledge is less developed and activities to which it might be applied less in the control of the experimenter. There are many lessons to be learned from recent attempts to develop a mutually beneficial interplay between policy, theory, and practice. The history of one such attempt – "action-research" – is described in some detail. In the contributed papers, instances of interplay between research and action are analyzed by authorities in different fields – child health, education, family life, social services, employment, juvenile justice, and community mental health.

The physical sciences

The mutually productive interplay between research and action in science and technology has been phenomenal. Both fields have developed exponentially, and cumulative achievements in each since World War II have proceeded beyond anything envisioned in earlier decades. Technological advances have dramatically increased our capacity to travel, to communicate, to combat disease and harness power. Similarly, dynamic advances in science have increased our knowledge of a range of phenomena, from outer space to the inner structure of matter.

Although both science and technology have grown in parallel lines, the nature of their interaction is complex. Various metaphors are employed to denote the way science and technology interact – mirror images, marriage mates, parts of a spectrum, or polarities in a continuum. Each is seen as distinct and necessary to the effective development of the other. However, criteria to distinguish one from the other and to characterize the relationship between them have been elusive. The quest for knowledge versus the quest for utility is not very satisfactory.

1

Many scientists, from Archimedes and Galileo to Gauss and Kelvin, have sought useful benefits from their work; and, conversely, many engineers have sought and achieved fame in science – from Leonardo da Vinci to James Watt. Nor is it satisfactory to characterize one as empirical-inductive, the other as logical-inductive; both styles are present in each field. Many advances in technology have come without direct interaction with science, for example, through the pragmatic problem solving of men like Thomas Edison and Isambard Kingdom Brunel; conversely, many advances in science have come without immediate technological tests or applications, for example, in the abstract reflections of such unworldly men as Einstein.

The operational definition by Derek de Sola Price is useful: Scientists have the primary immediate aim of producing published papers about their work, whereas technologists aim to produce other products – machines, drugs, or marketable objects. Price (1982) suggests the metaphor of dancers. Sometimes, as when the relationship is very close, they dance cheek to cheek, sometimes at arm's length or even turned away from one another. In the long run, as Price (1969) has argued: "Science without the by-play of technology becomes sterile, and in the several cases in which a materialistic society decided it would pay for the technology which gave economic gain, and neglect the science which was just a chess game, the technology became moribund."

The overall picture is one of discrete domains, each with its own professional training and credentials, its own characteristic modes of work, and its own distinctive products. Generally speaking, science is concerned with thoughts and ideas and its methods of work are curiosity-driven and center on the goal of increasing knowledge; technology is concerned with mastery, its methods of work are pragmatic and center on the goal of effective application of some kind of instrument, machine, or craft. Transfers between the two spheres occur in several ways: In the course of higher education, scientists learn something of the ambient technology as they study their own specialized subjects, and technologists learn something of the state-of-the-art science in their special fields. As networks of relationships accumulate in the course of building professional careers, personal relationships develop – in organizations, projects, and other structures engaging the efforts of both. Large-scale national programs such as the war effort or the NASA program generate such points of transfer. The two spheres, though often interacting only weakly at specific points, tend in the long run to be symbiotic, and at certain points their close interaction has sparked dramatic advances.

A classic sequence of interaction is described by Martin Rein (1983): "Theory generates the idea of a 'widget.' The 'widget' is invented, tried out in the real world, progressively debugged, and widely distributed."

Usually the interrelationships are more complex, with many false starts, blind alleys, confusions, and disappointments among which the brilliant achievements emerge. Peter Medawar (1984) describes one situation from which brilliant results arise – that of an interaction between contrasting individuals within the same field, biologists Alexander Fleming and Howard Florey: "The most important medical discovery of the 20th Century was made possible by the synergism between the talents and skills of two totally different people – the unhurried, rather unpractical Alexander Fleming and the energetic and capable Howard Florey, who did in tandem what neither could have done alone."

This synergism was catalyzed by wartime needs and by critical inputs from pharmaceutical industries aware of eventual economic benefits.

Wartime brought advances not only in weapons development but in radar, aircraft engineering, communications technology, and medicine. Some of these productive interactions have continued in peacetime, for instance, in the space program and in places like Silicon Valley. In this the galvanic interaction of individuals with contrasting skills – for instance, Hewlett and Packard – have frequently been conspicuous. Sometimes a single individual has forged integrative links between a research discovery and its practical exploitation. An example was Vladimir Dworkin, a poor immigrant from Russia with a polytechnic education, who invented the iconoscope that gave rise to modern television. RCA appointed him director of research, and in this post he not only rewarded his sponsors well but was given support for his own work, which won him many scientific honors.

Obviously there is no assurance that a specific collaboration between researcher and action agency will either lead to knowledge breakthroughs or will yield immediately profitable applications. Dael Wolfle (1959) illustrates this:

Last year the Nobel Prize in physics was awarded to two young Chinese-American physicists for their widely heralded work leading to the fall of parity. Physicists admire this work. It adds significantly to their thinking about the nature of the atom. But what does it mean to industry? So far, not much. But physicists are predicting, and history tells us that the prediction is probably correct, that the fall of parity will have far-ranging effects. [p. 23]

It often takes time for new information to be assimilated even within the same sphere. Freeman Dyson (1958), analyzing the assimilation of innovative ideas in the field of physics, concluded that it takes a generation for radically innovative ideas to be generally absorbed. James Clerk Maxwell's theory of the electromagnetic field, Rutherford's discovery of the nucleus, and Einstein's theory of gravitation are cases in point. Even the work of Yang and Lee, mentioned above, reflects this kind of time lag in that it answers a question posed thirty years earlier by Enrico Fermi.

On the other hand, there may be short-term as well as long-term benefits in fostering close linkages between people from science and those from action fields.

Industry spends billions annually on its own research and development, and government grants provide very large additional amounts to support research and development in fields considered in the public interest. The investment by industry in research is based on the conviction that it pays dividends. The economic value of federally sponsored research has also been affirmed. Analyses conducted in the period of the great expansion of federal funding in the 1950s concluded that for every dollar the nation invested in basic and applied research, the return to the country has averaged from one to two dollars a year for twenty-five years – or a total of twenty-five to fifty dollars in increased national wealth (Ewell, 1955). In other words, it has been demonstrated that government investment in research and its application has a payoff of between 100 and 200 percent over twenty-five years. Since these figures were compiled, there have been major shifts in government philosophy about how investments should be distributed. However, there is no question of the potential benefit of research – economic and otherwise.

The field of molecular biology has risen to prominence since the early post–World War II era. Advances in knowledge of genetic structures have generated a wide variety of potentially marketable products in agriculture, medicine, and other fields. Recent Nobelists Milstein and Koehler work on antibodies of immediate practical value estimated in market terms of billions of dollars. This is only one example in a burgeoning field.

Problems in the linkage

For a productive interplay between research and action several ingredients are necessary: financial support, an openness to new ways of thinking, competence, and public credibility.

Robert Oppenheimer in 1947 emphasized the importance of open-mindedness and its often surprising absence. Scientists frequently experience resistance to their findings or distortions in their application, by colleagues as well as by laymen.

Among the many reported examples from the lives of scientists, one of the most articulate is Max Planck's. In describing the resistance to the ideas he was advancing on the second law of thermodynamics in his doctoral dissertation, Planck (1949:18) wrote in his autobiography:

None of my professors at the University had any understanding for its contents. . . . I found no interest, let alone approval, even among the very physicists who were closely connected with the topic. Helmholtz probably did not even read my paper at all. Kirchoff expressly disapproved. . . . I did not succeed in reaching Claussius. He did not answer my letters, and I did not find him at home when I tried to see him in person at Bonn. I carried on a correspondence with Carl Neumann, of Leipzig, but it remained totally fruitless.

And among historians of science there are well-documented accounts of the resistance to theories now fundamental to modern thought – such as Pasteur's discovery of the biological nature of the fermentation process, Lister's germ theory, and Mendel's theory of genetic inheritance.

Bernard Barber (1961) has analyzed some of the reasons for resistance, other than the rational requirements for scientific demonstration. Barber notes that scientists, like other humans, experience a fear of newness. Long ago Francis Bacon indicated how preconceived ideas block the capacity to absorb innovations, even when there is an explicit value commitment to the quest for new knowledge. Thomas Kuhn (1957) has identified prevailing models of thinking, or "paradigms," as key elements in resistance to new ideas. Even after Copernicus published *De Revolutionibus,* most astronomers felt more comfortable with the assumption that the earth was stable and that it was the sun that revolved around the earth. Dael Wolfle observes that fundamental and sweeping innovations cannot be thoroughly grasped until a new generation grows up, until it is being used by a group of scientists who have the new idea in their bones, so to speak – who are thoroughly familiar with the new idea but not hampered by the old.

Other sources of resistance documented by Barber include methodological persuasion where some scientists reject the findings by others using different methodologies (e.g., in the quantitative-qualitative dissonances also described by Medawar); religious conviction (e.g., the stubborn resistance to Darwin's theories, persisting in some quarters to the present day); insider-outsider considerations, and the cleavages produced by professional and academic disciplines, "schools," and age-graded hierarchies.

Donald Schon (1966) notes organizational factors creating resistance to innovation in the costs of changing over from a tried-and-true operating procedure to one involving risks. In such instances the fear of newness is often quite reasonable, given the organizational requirements for system maintenance, and often it is only a threat to survival in a competitive world that induces a willingness to disrupt the stable state.

Nevertheless, as Robert Merton and others have shown, there has been a cumulative character in the growth of scientific knowledge and many examples of the interplay between scientists and men of action fostering this growth. But at any given point the interplay may be problematic or even lacking. One strategy to stimulate or improve it is to emphasize the potential benefits of fostering an interaction; another is to stress the potential harm of its absence.

Communication problems have often created barriers. Much of the work of scientists is oriented to their specialist colleagues and published in academic journals, and much of the work of technologists is conducted with little explicit interest in developing science. Though major governmental programs, such as the space program, have promoted interaction between science and technology, differences of *priority* become manifest and these affect the balance of investment. Scientists and technologists may be in communication with one another but nevertheless at odds in relation to resource allocation. This moves the decision process into a managerial stratum that is accountable to government rather than to academic or professional peers.

The social sciences

As in the physical sciences, there are various ways in which the researchers and the action agencies interact. Here, too, are examples of blurring and even merging of the two lines of development. Early anthropological data came, for example, from missionaries and colonial administrators; and some native anthropologists, such as Jomo Kenyatta, became political activists in the Third World.

Many advances in the social sciences have been made in the cloistered environment of the university. Conversely, many advances in the human services professions have arisen from pragmatic field experiences, or out of value commitments, without experimental evidence or demonstration of their validity. An example of the latter is the movement for universal suffrage and for equal rights. As in the physical sciences, there are intrafield variations, with some individuals in the fields of health, law, the social services, and education concentrating on the development of knowledge, and individuals in economics, sociology, anthropology, and psychology concerned with changing the world rather than merely understanding it.

Recently, some social workers are known primarily for their contributions to knowledge, while some "pure" sociologists have had a profound effect on policy or practice. Some psychoanalysts argue that their profession combines research and action. Nevertheless, as in the physical sciences, the distinction between research and practice is clearly institutionalized in training and in the goals and characteristic products of the work. The former aims to increase knowledge; the latter, to increase technical effectiveness.

Nevertheless, the image of dancers suggested by Price for the science-technology relationship seems also to be relevant in the social sciences. There have been periods of closeness and of distance between social scientists and social action agencies. When the movement has been toward close cooperation, the emphasis has been on the complementarities and mutual advantages of collaboration. When the movement has been toward separate development, the emphasis has been on the difficulties – the "unacceptable face" of some action enterprises, and the irrelevance of some research.

Overall, something like the "widget" model described by Rein has prevailed. Paul Schwarz (1981) describes this in terms of a circulation between the knowledge-producing centers in universities, think tanks, and research institutes on the one hand and the data-producing centers in the various applied fields. Theories and methodologies are worked out in academic settings and flow "downward" to the action settings, whence data is gathered and relayed "upward." The academic centers are supposedly value free, uninterested in biasing findings, and have the critical mass of resources necessary to analyze, reflect on, and develop information coming from the field.

Many leading social scientists follow a path in their careers that intermittently engages with matters of public interest. Raymond Firth, in his 1981 Malinowski lecture, notes the growing sense of appropriateness for academics to do this, supported as they are by public funds: "The intellectual climate of knowledge is changing perhaps irreversibly, moving from the assumption that scientific enquiry can be justified as an aesthetic pursuit for its own sake."

Firth observed an impressive growth of activity in the applied fields and their inventory of achievements. On the other hand, he describes the difficulty he has experienced when specific problems requiring action have been put to him. An anthropologist, however competent in the academic setting, finds himself faced with the task of "matching theory with practice; of coping with ignorance, apathy, distrust and hostility; of brooding over finance; of deciding where the line must fall between principle and expediency; and between dispassionate analysis and personal commitment" (Firth, 1981:200).

In many of the social science fields these difficulties have led to a disengagement from close relationships to action enterprises. After the flush of success of collaborations during World War II and in some of the postwar multidisciplinary programs of the 1960s, there were difficulties and a mutual withdrawal in the 1970s. Some of these experiences have been described in Moynihan's *Maximum Feasible Misunderstanding,* Pressman and Wildavsky's *Implementation: How Great Expectations in Washington Are Dashed in Oakland,* and Hall's *Great Planning Disasters.*

However, social science has also had examples of the kind of synergism described by Medawar for the Fleming-Florey relationship. Edward Zigler (1980) indicated in his inaugural essay for the *Journal of Applied Developmental Psychology* that this kind of synergism is a potential in the relationship between academic and applied behavioral science fields. Zigler notes that often there is a false polarization between basic and applied researchers, many responding with a mental image of their own best cases and the others' worst ones. If basic research is seen as "pure," applied research is by implication "dirty" or "sloppy" or dubious ethically. If the latter is "goal or mission oriented," the former is by implication sterile or trivial. Arguing for a dialectical process characterized by a creative tension between the two, Zigler cites several fields in which this is in fact manifested.

Kibbutz research has been useful as "a social experiment and child rearing laboratory'' for psychologists and anthropologists as well as a field for the application of research-based policies. Fruitful interplay is also seen in the work of Sarason, Bronfenbrenner, Campbell, Ainsworth, and Bowlby.

Action-research in history

In the early post–World War II years, a social science movement labeled ''action-research'' sought to develop this creative interplay between knowledge and action. Seen in historical perspective, this was a movement that evolved, went into eclipse, and may be emerging in a new form.

In the 1950s and 1960s there were many examples of enthusiastic collaboration between social scientists and action agencies. At the macroscopic level there were the Great Society programs, the War on Poverty, and a number of international programs, many of which continue – for example, the Peace Corps and the economic development programs directed toward Third World countries. Multidisciplinary social science programs were set up in major universities – among them the Human Relations Program at Yale, the Committee on Human Development at Chicago, the Department of Social Relations at Harvard, and the Institute of Social Research at Michigan. Links between applied social research programs and academic departments were encouraged – for example, at the Bureau of Applied Social Research at Columbia and the applied anthropology and social psychiatry programs at Cornell. Methods and concepts developed in wartime were applied to social problems in peacetime – for instance, Leighton's concepts of stress based on studies of Japanese internees were applied to social epidemiological research in Manhattan, Nova Scotia, and elsewhere (Leighton, 1984). The concept of the ''therapeutic community,'' first developed in relation to treating battle casualties, was applied to the reform of custodial mental hospitals (Jones, 1952). Anthropologists who had developed methods for studying ''culture at a distance'' during the war, set up area-studies programs such as the Russian Research Center at Harvard (Kluckhohn, 1959).

Among these programs, of particular interest here is the set of initiatives labeled ''action-research.''

The term ''action-research'' has meant various things to various people. *Webster's Third New International Dictionary* defines action-research as: ''The use of techniques of social and psychological research to identify social problems in a group or community coupled with active participation of the investigators to solve these problems.''

The definition we shall be using here is rather more ambitious, requiring the expectation of a *reciprocal* benefit – to scientific knowledge as well as to practical problem solving. This implies a relatively long-term commitment rather than a one-shot analysis or evaluation followed by disengagement. Though action-research involves analysis and evaluation, the characteristic way in which it is done is through an interactive cycle of engagement and temporary disengagement with the aim of contributing to a developmental process.

The definition we use is as follows: "Action research aims to contribute both to the practical concerns of people in an immediate problematic situation and to the goals of social science by joint collaboration within a mutually acceptable ethical framework" (Rapoport, 1970).

The term was used before World War II in two contexts, in anthropology and in social psychology. In anthropology it was promoted by John Collier, Commissioner for Indian Affairs under President Franklin D. Roosevelt. He used it to describe the kind of collaboration he envisioned between government agencies, such as the Indian Service, and anthropologists. The former could use the findings of the latter to develop knowledge-based policies, and the latter could benefit not only from the financial support of an interested government agency but from research opportunities opened to them through the backing of a government agency. Collier (1945) saw the Indian Service as a potential laboratory through which ethnic relations in America could be studied.

In the years following World War II, elements of this early conception were taken up in a set of studies sponsored by the Indian Service and conducted by anthropologists and psychologists in a number of settings. The studies were of cultural influences on children growing up in Navaho, Hopi, Papago, and Sioux tribes. Each study aimed to contribute both to the literature on socialization and to the administrative concerns of the Indian Service. As John Collier noted in his introduction to *The Hopi Way* (1947), the first volume in the series: "Through generations, the Indian Service pursued one or another special and decreed aim: to Christianize Indians, to substitute the individual Indian for the societal Indian, to make Indians into land individualists, to obliterate Indian superstitions, to make go-getters of Indians" (p. 6).

He cites such statements as the following, from reports of previous Indian commissioners: "[the aims are] to assist in the great work of redeeming these benighted children of nature from the darkness of their superstition and ignorance" (p. 6).

Collier argued that policy could and should be made by improving knowledge of actual Indian cultures, taking the view that "the Indian individual is part of a group, and the individual and the group are part of the ecological environment, each group within its particular world-field" (p. 7). He goes on to say that the goal of the Indian Service is to try to "understand more surely, predict more reliably, to act with knowledge more precise, so that we can know genuinely, what worth our Indian effort has and how it may be made significantly more realistic, and so that our good (which we presume) may not become the enemy of a better" (p. 7).

Others who participated in this program became key figures in the evolving field of culture-and-personality studies – W. Lloyd Warner, Edward Spicer, Dorothea Leighton, and Clyde Kluckhohn.

Though there were problems in the relationships with the Indian Service – for instance, over the ownership and publication of the data – the idea of action-research continued into the 1950s, and at Chicago a group emerged under the leadership of Sol Tax that called its work "action anthropology." Tax, on his early research visits to the Fox Indians in nearby Iowa, had felt the wish to do something to help them in their predicament vis-à-vis white society. His early interests in social work and in the therapeutic model had made him particularly sympathetic in this way. A group of mature graduate students, returned World War II servicemen, felt dissatisfied with not giving the Indians something for the demands placed on them by researchers. They wanted to do something tangible to help. The idea of action-anthropology – to combine research with a consultative kind of intervention – received some support from the Indian Service; and the university department was willing to support the idea as an interesting innovation in the methodology of studying social change, and as a convenient field laboratory for training anthropologists. The optimism that prevailed about what could be done is reflected in an essay by Fred Gearing, one of the graduate students at the time, when he subsequently wrote:

Infrequently, once in a decade perhaps, from somewhere in the social science community, an unusually powerful fact is discovered which seems to reach out in all directions and transform the many other facts and ideas it touches. A powerful fact of this kind has of late emerged, and one of the ideas touched is action anthropology. [Gearing, 1979]

Gearing expected that a synergistic effect would emerge by bringing together social research (in the form of the microscopic analysis of social interaction) and the action agenda being worked out with the Fox Indians. Tax and his group conceptualized the problem of the Fox in relation to the dominant white society as one of "social disarticulation." By studying the actual patterns of interaction and presenting these analyses to the actors, the hope was to reduce the disarticulation. Though the action-anthropology movement failed to thrive within the discipline, several members of the group made contributions in various applied settings – for example, Walter Miller in criminology, Lisa Peattie in planning, Robert Rietz in urban social service. We shall return to discuss some of the difficulties that may account for the inability of action anthropology to thrive as a field.

The other main strand of action research emerging after World War II is associated with Kurt Lewin. Lewin was primarily concerned with how social systems respond to authoritarian, compared with democratic, leadership, and the effect on social change. The relevance of these topics for events leading up to the war are apparent, and following the war Lewin was instrumental in establishing two organizations – the Committee on Community Inter-Relations (CCI), which became involved in problem-oriented social research projects, and the Center for Group Dynamics (CGD), which was more academic though still social problem-oriented. Two of Lewin's postwar publications set forth his conceptual model (1946 and 1947). Ketterer, Price, and Politser (1980) summarize the elements in Lewin's conception of action research as follows:

1. A cyclical process of fact-finding, action and evaluation, following which the process begins anew.
2. Feedback of information, even where the fact-finding is being conducted by an outside researcher.
3. Collaboration in reconciling the requirements of the research with those of the action organization.
4. Taking into account principles of group dynamics in conducting the research, as well as those of the theory associated with the problem being studied. This implies a recognition of the importance of system characteristics, power structure, values, the role of gatekeepers, opinion setters, and accepted experts.
5. The acceptance of the dual goal of practical problem solving and theoretical knowledge building.

In a much quoted statement of orientation, Lewin affirmed his belief that there is nothing so practical as a good theory. He also believed that many advances in theory occur by studying social systems in action, and that there is a danger of sterility in research oriented only to academic publication.

One of the strands of development emanating from the work of Lewin is identified with research at the University of Michigan's Institute for Social Research (ISR). The ISR was formed in the early 1950s when the Center for Group Dynamics moved from MIT to Michigan, joining forces with the Survey Research Center. Subsequent work, associated with such prominent social psychologists as French, Lippitt, Seashore – and more recently in the community mental health field, Price – has been particularly strong in its academic component and the insistence on rigorous quasi-experimental methodology.

A contrasting and complementary approach was taken by the group stemming from Lewin's other wing – the CCI. The National Training Laboratories (NTL) centered in Bethel, Maine, conducted its work through the use of group dynamics workshops. Although much of the interest in these groups – both practical and theoretical – was oriented to management development (stemming from the interests of Gordon McGregor and later Edgar Schein), it was also related to organizational change and development (e.g., in the work of Warren Bennis, 1969).

In Britain, the concept of action-research was used by the Tavistock Institute of Human Relations. This also built upon wartime experiences and evolved a set of guiding principles closely resembling those enunciated by Lewin. However, the Tavistock group was particularly oriented to psychoanalytic theory and methods.

The research component of the Tavistock group came from a range of social science and psychiatric disciplines. It was helped initially with foundation grants, but the eventual economic sources of support were linked to financially viable spheres of application, under the National Health Service (through the operation of the Tavistock Clinic) and in industry (through contracts with industrial organizations). Notable on the health service side was the work of John Bowlby and his associates; and in industry there was the work of Kenneth Rice on Indian weavers at Ahmedabad; Eric Trist and others' studies of coal mining (later to give rise to the concepts of "sociotechnical systems" and to the Quality of Working Life movement), and Elliott Jaques's studies of worker participation in decision making at the Glacier Metal Company, from which he evolved concepts such as "time span of discretion" as a yardstick for equitable pay differentials.

The Tavistock approach was clinical, and an early expression of the dual-goals ideal was "no research without therapy, and no therapy without research." The attention to group dynamics made a natural link with the NTL people in the United States, and a workshop similar in design evolved in the Tavistock setting. There were transatlantic exchanges of participants. As with some of the Americans in the organizational analysis mode, Tavistock personnel such as A. T. M. Wilson, Harold Bridger, and Elliott Jaques entered into sustained consultancy relationships with organizations. This was sometimes rationalized in terms of the importance of the cyclical model, working through the feedback and absorption of research findings in specific settings. The titles of some of their works give the flavor: for example, Jaques's *Changing Culture of the Factory* (1951) and Sofer's *The Organization from Within* (1961) – to be followed later by Emery and Trist's *Towards a Social Ecology* (1973).

There was a move in the 1960s to balance the Tavistock penchant for qualitative modes by forming a link with the Institute for Operational Research. This group, also born in wartime experience of applied social research, had a complementary penchant – being primarily oriented to mathematical models. The joint functioning of the Institute for Operational Research and the Tavistock Institute produced a number of studies in the planning field linking with American counterparts such as Russell Ackoff and West Churchman (see Lawrence, 1966).

The 1970s brought difficulties and attrition to the Tavistock efforts in the field, as in the United States. However, the action-research approach persists and some of the recent work was described in a volume edited by Alfred Clark (1976).

In both Britain and the United States, action-research programs were developed in the 1960s in relation to large-scale community development programs associated with government agencies. In both countries there were optimistic

rhetoric but mixed experiences. Gardner Murphy wrote an introduction to Louis
Zurcher's book on a project in the poverty program. He wrote:

Action research . . . has offered huge promise to the social sciences . . . this conception
is quite different from that of applied social research. . . . It is not enough to provide a
"research aspect" for a huge integration program, or after an expensive study has been
completed to conduct a brief "evaluation" of its outcome. Rather, it is essential that as
intervention comes to be conceptualized the requisite feed-back can be provided by which
the intervention itself can be understood. [Murphy, 1970]

Daniel Patrick Moynihan, in a speech to the British Social Science Research
Council (1970), described the relation between action-research and policymaking in America as follows:

Action research . . . is going on in the United States at an enormous rate. . . . In fiscal
year '70, we were spending 345 million dollars a year on social science research and
development right out of the Federal Treasury. . . . It is a lot of money, and we don't
expect to get much without this kind of expenditure. Carl Deutsch and John Platt have
been doing a study of the major "inventions" in social science in the twentieth century.
. . . They found that since 1930, a characteristic of the great majority is that they involved
lots of capital and lots of people . . . [and] between 1919 and 1929, Europe produced
three-quarters of the "inventions" and since 1930 the United States produced more than
three-quarters . . . [this] probably reflects investment. . . . Action research is a big enterprise in America – a growing one which is not likely to diminish. [Moynihan, 1970:3]

The new programs were accepted by the academic mainstream more than were
many earlier efforts. But they experienced other difficulties. Moynihan indicated
that there were changes in the audience. Action-research in the social sciences
has been "comfortably symbiotic" with liberal political groups. These groups
remained interested but began to clamor for results. Conservatives, in contrast,
often did not wish to know because they operated on the basis of received opinions. There were problems with both audiences, but the problems were different.

In Britain there was also an initial enthusiasm for collaboration by a liberal
government. A. H. Halsey (1972) describes the Education Priority Area Program
(EPA) as having "an experimental or quasi-experimental design. . . . Ends are
stated together with means to their achievement. . . . Ends and means are modified and explicated in a program of action, and relations between them are analyzed by research monitoring of the action program."

Goals were set up by political policy groups, based to some extent on recommendations by expert committees including social scientists. Government departments accepted the policies as part of their mission and commissioned research to evaluate program effectiveness. Halsey called this "experimental social
administration."

Program evaluation grew as an autonomous field in the United States. Carol Weiss (1972) acknowledged the relevance of the action-research tradition in the rapid growth of the program-evaluation field. Donald Campbell (1974) also noted the association. Program evaluation, being a more limited conception than action-research, tailored its work to the requirements of the sponsors of action programs. Researchers in this field use such concepts as "monitoring and accountability," "impact assessment," "efficiency," and "cost effectiveness" (Lichfield, 1975; Rossi and Freeman, 1982). It has been beyond the scope of most program evaluation to participate in the cycle of program design, implementation, feedback, and dissemination. And it has been the unusual evaluation study that has gone beyond a summative analysis of outcomes to identify processes involved.

The eclipse of action-research

Nevitt Sanford entitled a paper written in the late 1970s "Whatever Happened to Action-research?" He pointed out that much that could have passed as action-research continued to be done in the 1970s, but under other labels. He considered that action-research as a distinctive multidisciplinary approach was eclipsed by the growth of the specialized academic disciplines. But there were other problems that made for the eclipse.

Some of the issues are analyzed in Robert Rubinstein's (1984) paper on the failure of action-anthropology to flourish. There was the loss of the charismatic leader. Sol Tax became absorbed in a new enterprise that diverted his attention, a world journal for the profession, *Current Anthropology*. His followers reverted to more classical disciplinary approaches or became increasingly marginal to the academic field. There were also problematic elements in the collaborations undertaken. The issue of ownership and control of the data has already been mentioned in relation to the Indian Service. There were changes in the administration of the Indian Service also and in the political priority attached to helping Indians as a distinctive ethnic group. This made for difficulties in funding projects. In some situations where financial support was forthcoming, as in the ill-fated "Project Camelot," anthropologists found it difficult to reconcile their personal and professional values with those of the military and covert-intelligence agencies. The Vietnam War exacerbated this values issue, and eventually the Department of Anthropology at the University of Chicago, as did others around the country, asserted the need to maintain a distinction between basic academic research and what was called "mission-oriented" activity (Stocking, 1979). The latter, associated with government-controlled activity, had become suspect.

Another issue was that of identifying the specific action agent for partnership. Action-anthropologists considered themselves as collaborating with native peoples rather than with government agencies. But the Fox experience raised the question of which natives. In Fox society some factions favored assimilation with white society (as did the Indian Service), whereas others favored separate development. Lisa Peattie (1968) developed an advocacy model according to which action-anthropologists were seen to be like lawyers, acting as advocates for their clients regardless of the client's power position. Theoretically there could be anthropologists on different sides of a social-values issue. Stephen Polgar (1979), another of Tax's students, argued that action-anthropologists should represent the deprived and inarticulate subgroups. The question of which deprived groups and under what conditions was never fully engaged.

The action-anthropology group became aware that they were in difficult and politically highly charged areas, requiring, as Firth (1981) later noted, skills that were different from those for which they had been trained in the academic setting. Competence in an academic setting might not be directly related to an anthropologist's capacity to negotiate a viable role in what Cora DuBois (1980) called the "power, managerial administration" world.

Even where there was backing and support of the power structure, it was not always found to be beneficial for anthropological research. Tom Sasaki, an American anthropologist of Japanese descent, conducted a study of Navaho Indians, among whom he might have been expected to be accepted in a friendly manner because of his Mongoloid appearance. However, Sasaki's project was undertaken in the period following World War II during which Navaho scouts had achieved a celebrated success against the Japanese, communicating with one another by radio with no need to encode their messages because no one on the other side understood Navaho. Sasaki noted that when he said, as most anthropologists do, that he wished to learn the language, it aroused considerable suspicion that he might be an enemy spy. He found himself avoiding any explicit study of the language (Sasaki, 1960:8). More germane to action-anthropology, the project was conducted with the full cooperation of the Bureau of Indian Affairs, local representatives of which offered much guidance and practical help including the provision of housing. The aim of the action agency was to settle Navahos, who had been migratory people from time immemorial, onto a stable ecological base of irrigation agriculture. The research was a disinterested analysis of social, technological, and economic factors in an experiment in planned change. The government support on the site stimulated the fantasy that the researchers had something to do with getting the Indians to adopt the agency's formula for the number of horses that could be allowed to graze on agricultural lands. Too close collaboration came to be seen as sometimes counterproductive, reflecting adversely in some people's minds on the action-research model itself.

In the field of urban studies, Peter Szanton (1981) analyzed a number of consultation projects that have relevance for action-research, although the nature of

the enterprise is somewhat different. He observed that the traditional source of
consultative advice, the universities, were not generally well placed to help urban governments. They were often located in rural settings, and their work was
organized around the concerns of the separate disciplines. To counter this, there
was the growth of independent institutes with multidisciplinary capability and
competence in urban issues, for instance, Arthur D. Little, McKinsey, and the
RAND Corporation. These organizations did not suffer from some of the shortcomings of the academics – for example, the overconcern with academic peers'
opinions, the "solo" style of work with an elastic time scale, the lack of famil-
iarity with client perspectives, the preoccupation with originality rather than reliability, and so on. Szanton found that though the specialist consulting organizations avoided some of the pitfalls of the academics, they were prone to others
– such as producing reports that were conceptually weak. This led to the difficulty that their conclusions, although sensible from the point of view of a specific
setting, sometimes proved not to be feasible in other settings. The urban governments were not well advised by their consultants not only because of the characteristics of the consultants (as both university consultants and specialist organizational consultants presented difficulties); there were also the intrinsic difficulties
in collaborating with an urban government. The complexities and different lines
of power and expertise involved present daunting challenges to any outsider,
even an invited consultant.

Szanton concluded that successful collaboration requires effective clarification
of several sets of issues.

One set of issues has to do with the *client*. Identification of the client is a more
complex matter than it may appear, and the necessary work must be done, once
the client bodies are identified, to form relationships and develop trust. This may
involve several subsets within the client body.

Another set of issues has to do with management of the consultation. It is
important to: find internal champions in the client organization; watch out for
discontent, to be careful in the use of program evaluation (and be aware of its
potential abuses); pay attention to keeping alive an interest in the product – that
is, feed back some data and opinions early but not too much or too early; avoid
overpromising and giving unfeasible advice.

Szanton gives special attention to lessons for academics who would involve
themselves in urban consultation. He observes that they should give realistic
thought to "whether you can do the job, why you want the job, and what it
will really cost". He also draws lessons for producers, for university administrators and for third parties. As consultative work concentrates on *advice,* rather
than research, he observes that the highest duty of consultants is not to solve a
problem but to produce a stronger client – "a client better able to manage his or
her or its own problems . . . to so involve, stimulate, educate, and encourage

his clients as to make them less fearful of further innovation and better equipped to make it work'' (p. 160).

In another setting where there has been interaction between researchers and action agencies, educational research, a different set of problems has been highlighted. An outstanding example is seen in James Coleman's report on school segregation. This was based on a mathematical analysis that was difficult even for behavioral scientists to understand, let alone schoolteachers, government administrators, and legislators. The argument was highly politicized and the researcher found himself to be at a disadvantage in trying to relate his data to the polemic. It was for this reason that Fred Hechinger (1981) argued that researchers like Coleman do better by keeping a little distance, concentrating on the data analysis.

It is one thing for a researcher to go into a community and make a study that he publishes in a remote place many years later, but quite another to give evidence or publish reports in live situations where people have high stakes.

Frequently social research comes up with findings and ideas that are new and unfamiliar, giving rise to dissonance. Often social scientists have been unprepared with reliable data to answer searching policy questions. Riecken (1983) and Moynihan (1970) have noted that negative results can develop in such situations if a social scientist produces a lot of new ideas without solid data to back them up.

The American Social Science Research Council recommended that in the face of massive social problems such as poverty, crime, drug abuse, and family discord, the best approach in developing new solutions is to try them on a small scale, to evaluate the field trials to improve them, and only if they are confirmed at this level, to recommend bringing them into practice on a large scale. But the pressures of political action make for a sense of urgency and social scientists have sometimes colluded in short-circuiting the process.

Pressman and Wildavsky argue that this was part of what went wrong in the urban poverty program. They call the more grandiose strategy a "recipe for violence": "promise a lot; deliver a little"; "lead people to believe they will be much better off, but let there be no dramatic improvement"; "try a variety of small programs, each interesting but marginal in impact and severely underfinanced."

Harold Gerard (1983) suggests that this was also part of what went wrong with the school desegregation program. He writes that the historic Supreme Court decision to desegregate the schools (*Brown* v. *Board of Education,* 1954) was surrounded with top social scientist participation. Gerard views its outcome as the result of a collusion between the rhetoric of politicians and the utopianism of social scientists.

There was consensus in academic circles that segregation was psychologically harmful and that it produced inequalities of opportunity. By hypothesis, merging would remove the psychological stigmatization that went with separation – in which blacks were defined as a "pariah" group. In addition, hypothetically the merger would foster a "lateral transmission of values." In other words, whites' achievement orientation would rub off onto blacks, providing the motivation to help overcome inequalities. However, data to support the idea that merging racially segregated school populations would remedy these deficiencies was very thin. The results did not vindicate the hypotheses: School desegregation has neither increased minority interaction nor improved minority achievement values and self-esteem.

Gerard's analysis emerges with the identification of flaws in the experts' assumptions, namely that (1) there would be firm and consistent endorsement of the program by those in authority; (2) there would be an absence of competition among the representatives of the different groups; (3) equivalence of positions and functions would exist in the desegregated setting; and (4) interracial contacts would be of the type that fostered learning about one another as individuals (p. 870). In fact, this set of conditions was nonexistent as a total package and was often contravened by conditions operating in the opposite direction. For example, black self-esteem was found to diminish in many desegregated classrooms because of a range of situations from teacher prejudice to unfavorable experiences of direct competition with whites. After a detailed dissection of flaws in the underlying assumptions, Gerard concludes that

social scientists were wrong in the belief that change would come easily. There were so many resistances to overcome, many of which should have been anticipated, but many of us were blinded by our ideology into thinking that we could have Utopia in one fell swoop of mandated bussing. Simply mixing children in the classroom and trusting to benign human nature could never have done the trick. . . . What I am questioning here are the assumptions underlying the belief that school desegregation as implemented in the typical school district will be an instrument to achieve that end. [p. 875]

Gerard further observed that when Stuart Cook, one of the social scientists who influenced the original conceptualization of the program, wrote about what had gone wrong, he defended himself and his colleagues by "blaming the system." However, Gerard notes, "it was the self-same system about which the predictions were made, a system with which the framers were intimately acquainted." Therefore, he concludes, "Excuse not accepted" (p. 872). He argues that the social science participation was shortsighted, unsophisticated, and based on rhetoric rather than research.

Stuart Cook, in a closely argued rejoinder (1984), notes that the 1954 statement was based on what was known then, not now, and that more recent research on desegregation negates Gerard's earlier findings. Gerard's studies discrediting the prediction of advantage in desegregation were based on populations originally in segregated schools. Cook argues that Gerard's observations were of too limited duration to support his generalizations. Subsequent studies of students who experienced desegregation for their entire school lives show more positive outcomes, particularly where effective intervention strategies accompanied the structural change. There is, Cook notes, a great and growing interest from teachers and policy-makers in developing classroom experiments to improve further the results for student self-esteem, school achievement, and race relations.

Both Cook and Gerard agree on the importance of encouraging the kind of collaborative research and development work broadly considered to be action-research.

Several points emerge about the interface problems between high-caliber research and urgent action programs:

1. Action people often expect that the research will produce results that will be comprehensive, persuasive, and quick. While they might endorse the idea that the results should also be validated scientifically, they tend to feel that the scientific goals should not be pursued at the cost of being slow, technically complex, or expensive. One of the tricky issues in action-research is how to build in the scientists' requirements without losing the opportunity altogether by making demands the action partner will not accept.

2. There has been increased recognition of the costs and risks of social research, particularly in complex and changing situations. This contributes to mutual withdrawal – researchers back to their academic settings, the action people to traditional wisdom.

As Moynihan indicated, there was a comfortable relationship between researchers and ''liberal'' government agencies in the era following World War II. This allowed many problems of collaboration to be confronted constructively. But more recently not only has there been a backlash following the kinds of difficulties described, but there have come to power governments openly hostile to social science. This has put the entire federal basis for supporting social research at risk, and it has only been through the effective mobilization of pro–social science persons within government and the formation of an effective consortium of social science agencies (COSSA) that continuities have been maintained. In Britain, where almost the entire academic system is publicly funded, the assault on social research has been even more drastic, and the defense of social research less effective. The mutual hostility has been virulent: many Conservative politicians see social scientists as ''pink'' and many social scientists see Conservative politicians as atavistic.

None of these conflicts need be disastrous. Using the Head Start program as an example, antagonistic elements took the negative findings in the early research as counterindicating the value of the intervention. Subsequent research has vindicated the initial idea, though in a more sophisticated form – not as a simple quasi-inoculation. Zigler (1980) has indicated how the research-and-development approach was crucial in sustaining the continuity of effort that eventually resulted in successful development of the program. Critical commentaries were used to improve selection biases, statistical techniques, the formulation of outcome variables, the mixture of methodologies, and so on. In the end there was general recognition that the improved indications of outcome were a consequence of research coupled constructively with the action program (Zigler and Valentine, 1979).

The critical style and quasi-experimental model underlying most evaluation studies make them prone to what might be called "false negative" conclusions. If a significant correlation is not forthcoming in aggregated data, the conclusion may be stated that "there is no effect." Zigler notes that this not only is dubious scientifically but can provide ammunition to those who feel that any government money spent to help with the life problems of the disadvantaged is wasted.

Research and action: the state of the art

Action-research, in both name and conception, has not actually died out in the two decades since its most vigorous period. There have been a number of organizations, such as the Center for Action Research associated with the University of Colorado, the Institute for Social Research at the University of Michigan, (Ketterer et al., 1980), and the Tavistock Institute, (Clark, 1976), that have "kept the flame alive." On the other hand, the specific approach has been indubitably eclipsed by the growth of a number of specialized disciplines and new approaches to making the linkage between research and action.

Many of those who supported one or another form of action-research acknowledge that there have been fiascos. They tend nevertheless to emerge optimistically, implying the eventual resilience of rational attempts to link research and action. Francis Sutton, for example, describes how the Ford Foundation backed action-research programs in international development programs in the 1960s. Two decades and $1.5 billion later, he and many of his colleagues see as naive both the technical knowledge and the social assumptions that had guided their earlier efforts. At the time, little was known about foreign areas – both in terms of how technology could be incorporated into economic programs and in terms of political processes of developing countries. Now there are a number of important and productive area-study programs and an accumulation of both knowledge and wisdom in these fields. However, the initial cynicism following some disappointing experiences with regimes lacking integrity has given way to a more balanced perspective. First, many action-research programs have been successful, even in difficult Third World settings (see, for example, Korten, D., 1980; Korten, F., 1982; and Partridge, 1984). There is a perception that though "well laid plans go wrong [there have arisen] new needs and receptivity for [continued] analysis'' (Sutton, 1982:55).

Similarly, though Peter Hall in his *Great Planning Disasters* (1980) details the incredible miscalculations, blind spots, disappointing side effects, and so on of such great planning enterprises as the Sydney Opera House, the Bay Area Transit Authority, the Fourth London Airport at Stansted, and the like, he does not reject the relevance of a systematic research input. On the contrary, he concludes that we are now in a better position than ever to generate mutually beneficial relationships between research and planning.

In relation to this, the kindred multidisciplinary approaches are relevant – policy analysis (Weiss, 1980); operational research (Lawrence, 1966); action-learning (Morgan, 1983); participatory research (Brown and Tandon, 1983); program evaluation (Rossi and Freeman, 1982); social experimentation (Campbell, 1974; Riecken and Boruch, 1974); social intervention (Seidman, 1984); social ecology (Emery and Trist, 1973); Bronfenbrenner's concept of "experiments by nature and design'' (1979); and the field of community psychology (Rappaport, 1977).

These various approaches to linking research and action represent different disciplines' responses to segments of the overall problem, and taken together they present a very rich inventory of methods and skills (see D'Aunno and Price, 1984). In terms of Price's metaphor, the dance has been on between the two partners – but perhaps they have been dancing in different rooms and with different steps to different music. This is not necessarily bad. Different approaches are required in different situations, and various ways of communicating may be effective in different relationships. The old action-research did not, in Nevitt Sanford's terms, "get off the ground.'' Paul Schwarz (1981) considers that this may have been due to incomplete application of the model rather than to its fundamental deficiency. Some of the colossal efforts fell short because they did *not* break up the long sequence from input to desired results into manageable chunks, conceptualized as part of a cycle; they did *not* provide sufficiently for negotiating the collaborative approach, essential for cycle continuity; and they did *not* incorporate what they were learning from research to help across bridges and hurdles along the way. Much has been learned from analysis of paradoxical elements in attempting to approximate the ideal action-research model (Marris and Rein, 1974), and creative efforts are being developed to reconcile some of the dilemmas, for example, between sponsors' requirement of summative evaluations and action-researchers' need for formative evaluation, particularly in relation to innovations (Room, 1983).

William Bevan (1980) added his voice to that of leading figures in other social science fields to call for an increased sensitization by academic scientists to matters of social and political action. Though this is likened to asking the lamb to get into bed with the lion, it is nevertheless recommended both so that the scientific enterprise can be supported and thrive, and so that the action fields may benefit.

Robert Haggerty (1984) sums it up:

We believe that the needs which originally prompted the collaboration between action personnel and researchers are still present – perhaps more so. We believe that we have learned from past difficulties how to overcome some of them and that a great deal of benefit can occur from properly conducted action research. Many innovative service programs have developed in the crucible of the community. But, their creators rarely have time or training to conduct research related to their programs. . . .

Dissemination of results is also difficult for service personnel, but essential for replicating and influencing public policy. . . . Action research seeks to marry the creativity and commitment of innovative service personnel to the theoretical and research skills of the academic, to produce better results for both. [p. 7]

To help the enterprise of promoting a mutually beneficial interplay between research and action, authorities in eight fields bearing on children, youth, and families examine what of relevance has been learned in their own fields. In considering what they write, we shall seek answers to ten questions that are apparent from what has been said:

1. What is action-research today?
2. What is the relation between action-research and kindred approaches seeking to link research and action?
3. What conditions give rise to action-research collaboration?
4. What should be the form of collaboration between researchers and action agents?
5. How can collaboration between such diverse personnel be manageable?
6. How can continuity be maintained given the limitations of the "project" framework?
7. How can generic as well as specific issues be addressed in particular research/action situations?
8. How can an action-research project achieve maximum impact?
9. What conditions favor successful action-research?
10. What is the future of action-research?

References

Barber, B. Resistance by scientists to scientific discovery. *Science,* 1961, *134*(3479).
Bennis, W. *Organizational development: Its nature, origin and prospects.* Reading, Mass.: Addison-Wesley, 1969.
Bevan, W. On getting in bed with a lion. *American Psychologist,* 1980, *35*(9), 779–89.
Boruch, R., and Shadish, W. Design issues in community intervention. In E. Seidman (Ed.), *Handbook of social intervention.* Beverly Hills, Calif.: Sage, 1983.
Bronfenbrenner, U. *The ecology of human development: Experiments by nature and design.* Cambridge, Mass.: Harvard University Press, 1979.
Brown, L. D., and Tandon, R. Ideology and political economy in inquiry: Action research and participatory research. *Journal of Applied Behavioral Science,* 1983, *19*(3), 270–294.

Campbell, D. T. Qualitative knowing in action research. Kurt Lewin Award Address, Society for the Psychological Study of Social Issues. New Orleans, 1974.

Campbell, D. T. Getting ready for the experimenting society. Introduction to L. Saxe and M. Fine, *Social experiments: Methods for design and evaluation.* Vol. 131, Sage Library of Social Research. Beverly Hills, Calif.: Sage, 1981.

Clark, A. *Experimenting with organizational life.* New York: Plenum, 1976.

Collier, J. The United States Indian Service as a laboratory of ethnic relations. *Social Research,* 1945, *12,* 275–76.

Collier, J. Introduction to L. Thompson and A. Joseph, *The Hopi Way.* Chicago: University of Chicago Press, 1947.

Cook, S. The 1954 Social Science Statement on School Desegregation: A reply to Gerard. *The American Psychologist,* 1984, *39*(8), 819–31.

D'Aunno, T., and Price, R. H. The context and objectives of community research. In K. Heller, R. H. Price, S. Reinharz, S. Riger, and A. Wandersman (Eds.), *Psychology and Community Change.* Homewood, Ill.: Dorsey Press, 1984.

DuBois, C. Some anthropological hindsights. *Annual Review of Anthropology* (Vol. 9). Palo Alto, Calif., 1980.

Dyson, F. Innovation in physics. *Scientific American,* 1958, *199,* 74.

Emery, F., and Trist, E. L. *Towards a social ecology: Contextual appreciation of the future in the present.* New York: Plenum, 1973.

Ewell, R. Role of research in economic growth. *Chemical and Engineering News,* 1955, *33,* 2980.

Firth, R. Engagement and detachment: Reflections on applying social anthropology to social affairs. *Human Organization,* 1981, *40*(3), 193–201.

Freeman, H. E., Dynes, R. R., Rossi, P. H., and Whyte, W. F. (Eds.). *Applied sociology.* San Francisco: Jossey-Bass, 1983.

Gearing, F., Netting, R. McC., and Peattie, L. *Documentary history of the Fox project, 1948–1959.* University of Chicago, Department of Anthropology, 1960.

Gerard, H. B. School desegregation: The social science role. *American Psychologist,* 1983, *38*(8), 869–77.

Haggerty, R. Annual report of the president, William T. Grant Foundation. New York, 1984.

Hall, P. *Great planning disasters.* New York: Penguin Books, 1980.

Halsey, A. H. *Educational priority.* London: HMSO, 1972.

Hechinger, F. Editorial, *The New York Times,* May 10, 1981.

Jaques, E. *Changing culture of the factory.* London: Tavistock, 1951.

Jones, M. *Social psychiatry: A study of therapeutic communities.* London: Tavistock, 1952. (Published in the United States as *The therapeutic community: A new treatment method in psychiatry.* New York: Basic Books, 1953.)

Ketterer, R. F., Price, R. H., and Politser, E. The action research paradigm. In R. H. Price and P. E. Politser, *Evaluation and action in the social environment.* New York: Academic Press, 1980.

Kluckhohn, C. *Mirror for man.* New York: McGraw-Hill, 1959.

Korten, D. C. Community organization and rural development: A learning process approach. *Public Administration Review,* 1980, *40,* 480–511.

Korten, F. F. Building national capacity to develop water users' associations. World Bank Staff Working Papers, No. 528, 1982.

Kuhn, T. S. *The Copernican revolution.* Cambridge, Mass.: Harvard University Press, 1957.

Lawrence, J. R. (Ed.). *Operational research and the social sciences.* London: Tavistock, 1966.

Lees, R., and Smith, G. *Action research in community development.* Boston: Routledge & Kegan Paul, 1975.

Leighton, A. Malinowski Award lecture, Society for Applied Anthropology. Toronto, 1984. (To be published in *Human Organization.*)

Lewin, K. Action research and minority problems. *Journal of Social Issues,* 1946, 2(4), 34–46.
Lewin, K. Frontiers in group dynamics: Social planning and action research. *Human Relations,* 1947, *1,* 143–53.
Lichfield, N., et al. *Evaluation in the planning process.* Elmsford, N.Y.: Pergamon Press, 1975.
Marris, P., and Rein, M. *Dilemmas of social reform.* New York: Penguin Books, 1974.
Medawar, P. The penicillin men. Review of G. Macfarlane, *Alexander Fleming: The man and the myth. The Sunday Times* (London), February 12, 1984.
Morgan, G., and Ramirez, R. Action learning: A holographic metaphor for guiding social change. *Human Relations,* 1983, *37*(1), 28.
Moynihan, D. P. *Maximum feasible misunderstanding.* New York: Free Press, 1969.
Moynihan, D. P. The role of the social scientist in action research. British Social Science Research Council Newsletter, November 1970, pp. 2–5.
Murphy, G. Introduction to L. A. Zurcher and C. M. Bonjean, *Planned social intervention.* San Francisco: Chandler, 1970.
Partridge, W. L. (Ed.). *Training manual in development anthropology.* Washington, D.C.: American Anthropological Association, 1984.
Peattie, L. Reflections on advocacy planning. *American Institute of Planners,* 1968, *44,* 80–88.
Planck, M. *Scientific autobiography* (Trans. F. Gaynor). New York: Philosophical Library, 1949.
Polgar, S. Applied, action, radical, and committed anthropology. In R. Hinshaw (Ed.), *Currents in Anthropology.* The Hague: Mouton, 1979.
Pressman, J., and Wildavsky, A. *Implementation: How great expectations in Washington are dashed in Oakland.* Berkeley: University of California Press, 1973.
Price, D. de Sola. The structures of publication in science and technology. In W. H. Gruber and D. G. Marquis (Eds.), *Factors in the Transfer of Technology.* Cambridge, Mass.: MIT Press, 1969.
Price, D. de Sola. The parallel structures of science and technology. In B. Barnes and D. Edge (Eds.), *Science in context.* Milton Keynes: The Open University Press, 1982.
Rapoport, R. N. Three dilemmas in action research. *Human Relations,* 1970, *23*(6), 499–513.
Rappaport, J. *Community psychology: Values, research and action.* New York: Holt, Rinehart & Winston, 1977.
Rein, M. *From policy to practice.* New York: Macmillan, 1983.
Rice, K. *Productivity and social organization: The Ahmedabad experiment.* London: Tavistock, 1958.
Riecken, H. W. The National Science Foundation and the social sciences. *Social Science Research Council Items.* New York, 1983.
Riecken, H. W., and Boruch, R. F. *Social experimentation: A method for planning and evaluating social intervention.* New York: Academic Press, 1974.
Room, G. The politics of evaluation: The European poverty program. *Journal of Social Policy,* 1983, *12* (Part 2), 145–63.
Rossi, P. H., and Freeman, H. E. *Evaluation.* Beverly Hills, Calif.: Sage, 1982.
Rubinstein, R. Reflection on Action Anthropology. Paper presented at the annual meeting of the Society for Applied Anthropology. Toronto, March 14–18, 1984.
Sanford, N. Whatever happened to action–research? In A. W. Clark, (Ed.), *Experimenting with organizational life.* New York: Plenum, 1976.
Sarason, S. B. *Psychology misdirected.* New York: Free Press, 1981.
Sasaki, T. T. *Fruitland, New Mexico: A Navaho community in transition.* Ithaca, N.Y.: Cornell University Press, 1960.
Schon, D. The fear of innovation. In R. M. Hainer, S. Kingsbury, and D. B. Gleicher (Eds.), *Uncertainty in research, management and new product development.* New York: Conover-Mast, 1966.

Schwarz, P. Throwing science at problems. Paper prepared for the William T. Grant Foundation Conference on Action Research. New York, June 8, 1981.

Seidman, E. *Handbook of social interventions.* Beverly Hills, Calif.: Sage, 1984.

Sofer, C. *The organization from within: A comparative study of social institutions based on a socio-therapeutic approach.* London: Tavistock, 1961.

Stocking, G. Anthropology at Chicago: Tradition, discipline, department. Chicago: University of Chicago Library, 1979.

Sutton, F. X. Rationality, development and scholarship. *Items, 36*(4). New York: The Social Science Research Council, 1982.

Szanton, P. *Not well advised.* New York: Russell Sage Foundation, 1981.

Weiss, C. *Evaluating action programs.* Boston: Allyn & Bacon, 1972.

Weiss, C. *Social science research and decision-making.* New York: Columbia University Press, 1980.

Whyte, W. F. Social inventions for solving human problems. *American Sociological Review,* February 1982, *47,* 1–12.

Wolfle, D. *Science and public policy.* Lincoln: University of Nebraska Press, 1959.

Zigler, E. Introductory essay for the inaugural issue of *Journal of Applied Developmental Psychology,* 1980.

Zigler, E., and Valentine, J. (Eds.). *Project Head Start.* New York: Free Press, 1979.

2 Education: improving practice through increasing understanding

Barbara Maughan and Michael Rutter

"To change the world by understanding it." So Halsey (1972) characterized one of the strong impulses drawing action and research together into collaborative work. Equally compelling has been the desire to understand the world better through the study of change. These constitute the twin concerns of action research: the improvement of services through increased knowledge, and the development of knowledge through the study of innovatory practice.

In education, the range and volume of innovation in the last two decades has been immense. House and Mathison (1983) have recently discussed the American experience, encompassing as it has the development of preschool programs, curriculum reform, school improvement efforts, the establishment of regional R and D (research and development) centers, and, most recently, minimum competency testing. Much of this intervention has also been federally funded; the private foundations have also supported major change efforts, and educational practice has been strongly influenced by legislative decisions and court rulings. In the British context, typically less well funded and with a greater degree of local autonomy, innovations have also been widespread. The government and research councils sponsored the Educational Priority Areas, the Schools Council promoted curriculum reform, comprehensive schooling largely replaced selection at the secondary stage, and there have been growing moves toward in-school evaluation and the preparation of long-term reviews at the school level.

The history of collaboration between social scientists, practitioners, and policymakers in each of these areas has been checkered. The heady enthusiasm of the 1960s gave way to disappointment and disillusion as many early programs failed to live up to their initial promise. Innovations were dogged by false starts, shifting goals, inadequate evaluations, and much-contested conclusions. Major revisions have been required in both innovation strategies and research methodology, and we have learned perhaps as much about what not to do as about roads to successful change. If more realistic mutual expectations have developed as a result, the process has been an expensive and often painful one.

26

Action-research in education

By no means do all educational interventions with research components fall within our definition of action-research. The action-research model, as we conceive it, involves more than evaluating program effects, the "spot the winner" approach to assessing outcomes for children. This is, of course, often an essential element of action-research strategies but rarely in itself adequate to the furthering of either practice or theory that we see at the core of the action-research approach. This in addition requires the study of *how* and *why* things happen, a focus on process as well as outcome. Only in this way can we gain useful understandings of how to improve educational provision that, in their turn, can enrich our knowledge of theoretical concerns. To achieve these ends, collaboration must take place at the level of goals and aims, and research and action should be more than simply parallel but separate elements of innovative programs.

The first chapter in this volume has outlined the general features of action-research. Certain special issues and problems arise in the educational context. First, we are concerned here with a universal service, whose effects are intended to have long-term consequences for children. Though in some cases we may wish to assess outcomes on the basis of short-term individual effects, in general our emphasis will be on long-term implications for groups. Programs designed to improve children's skills in the early years of schooling will aim to boost their attainments throughout their school careers; more widespread efforts at school improvement will be concerned to provide all children with a firmer foundation for their subsequent learning. The design of much educational research is thus inevitably more complex than evaluations in many other fields.

Second, one of the major contributions of research has been to underline the multiplicity of influences outside the school that bear on children's progress within it. Isolating and charting the effects of educational interventions is no simple matter. It is rarely possible to "control" the effects of these external influences, but attempts must at least be made to take them adequately into account.

Third, the hoped-for outcomes of education are both diverse and often disputed. Many programs are designed to affect social as well as intellectual development, either as a primary goal or in the hope that increased motivation and self-confidence will influence cognitive performance. The assessment of cognitive development alone is rarely adequate, but wider evaluations have been hampered not only by the lack of appropriate measures in many areas, but also by limitations in our understanding of the processes by which such developments take place.

Finally, we must acknowledge that much educational action has been undertaken without research. Practice has been affected at the classroom level as much by movements – such as "progressive" education – as by the detailed findings generated by empirical research, and at the policy level by political as much as theoretical considerations. With a relatively "soft" technology, and a heavy reliance on professional skill and expertise, teachers' response to materials developed outside the field has characteristically been ambivalent. The professional attitudes of teachers have played an important part in the take-up of new methods and provide a further influential set of issues to be considered in any collaborative enterprise.

Many different styles of collaboration are illustrated in the educational literature. At one end of the spectrum there are experimental programs, designed and mounted specifically for research purposes, and often outside the mainstream school system. Many preschool programs were of this kind, set up to explore, in conditions approximating as closely as possible to classical experimental designs, the implications in practice of different theories of child development and learning. Even under these relatively auspicious conditions, the paths for research have not always been smooth, nor its implications for practice clear.

Moving to the more turbulent context of the school, the picture becomes more complex. Interventions here range from the introduction of prepackaged curriculum materials in individual subject areas to attempts at organizational development, and major system-wide changes such as desegregation in the United States, or the change to comprehensive schooling in the United Kingdom. These differ widely in their demands on the teacher and the school for change, the strategies likely to promote or support that change, and the methods most adequate to evaluate its effects. Research must attempt to disentangle the impact of particular innovations amid a complex interaction of influences, and often against a background of incomplete or changing implementation and lack of clearly defined goals. Further still on our spectrum, we find more explicitly exploratory efforts, where collaborations are designed to develop emergent solutions rather than to apply preexisting ones. Finally, at the farthest extreme from research control, there is the movement toward the teacher as his or her own action-researcher, attempting to break free from paternalistic domination by research and to develop skills in the classroom by exploring practice with the support of external consultants, but in a largely self-directed way.

The field thus presents us with a family of possible action-research approaches rather than any single or dominant style. Each has its own characteristic problems and tensions. The examples we have chosen represent a number of different modes but are by no means exhaustive. They illustrate some of the recurrent issues to be faced, and some of the solutions that might be proposed. We have drawn on programs from both U.S. and U.K. experience and, to provide some coherence in terms of the educational issues involved, have focused on two main areas: early childhood education, and issues of school effectiveness and improvement. Major developments have occurred in both of these fields in the last two decades, and our examples draw on different stages in those developments. We begin by considering some of the earliest large-scale experiments in the preschool education field.

Preschool education

On both sides of the Atlantic, the early 1960s saw a reawakening of interest in early childhood education as a measure of social reform, a means of counteracting the effects of poverty on young children and even, in some formulations, of spearheading an attack on poverty itself. Several powerful lines of thinking converged to support this view. Within psychology, hereditarian theories of intellectual development were challenged by evidence on the influence of the environment (Hunt, 1961) and the possibility of the first four or five years as a "critical period" in human development (Bloom, 1964). Large-scale surveys of school attainment demonstrated the links between children's social and economic conditions and educational achievement (Douglas, 1964; Coleman, 1966). Explanations for the low attainments of poor children were found in the cultural-deficit models of writers such as Lewis (1968); habituation to poverty was seen as generating a subculture of values, adaptive in their own setting but with damaging effects on progress at school. The logic of all these positions coalesced to point to early educational intervention as the most powerful means of breaking into this cycle, providing "compensatory" experiences for children from low-income families, and preparing them to enter the formal school system on a more equal basis with their peers. Individual experimental programs had reported encouraging results (e.g., Bereiter and Engelmann, 1966), and the American War on Poverty provided the political support for nationwide preschool developments in Head Start.

Head Start

The era was one of immense optimism over the benefits that could accrue from collaboration between social scientists and policy-makers in the resolution of social problems. Head Start was closely bound into the political process from the outset: The wider War on Poverty might have lost much public support had it not included a preschool element, and the need to maintain political impetus had a profound effect on the shape of the initial preschool programs. Pleas from advisory psychologists that pilot projects be evaluated before any nationwide launch were disregarded, and the first summer programs, mounted in 1965 after only three months' planning, reached some half a million children.

Accounts of the launch of Head Start emphasize both the enthusiasm and excitement it generated, and the lack of real knowledge of what early enrichment programs might achieve for low-income children, or how they should best be designed (Zigler and Valentine, 1979). The planning committee set up to guide the programs proposed a comprehensive model, with the wide aims of promoting the social, emotional, motivational, and intellectual development of young children. Parental and community involvement were seen as essential elements from the outset, and basic health care a further important theme. Within these general aims and guidelines, flexibility of provision in each local area was crucial. There was no one typical Head Start program but instead a wide range of differing patterns of provision across the country as a whole.

The difficulties of evaluating a program of such vast scope and broad goals were immense. Methods and measures had to be developed and administered in a limited span of time, and Gordon (1979) concluded that, despite the range of quantitative measures collected on the first summer's program, the most productive effort at that stage may well have been the least structured: ethnographic reports of the workings of the programs themselves.

Subsequent evaluations concentrated more heavily on quantifiable outcomes, and indeed were later criticized for their lack of attention to information that could have helped improve the working of the programs in practice. The results of early studies mirrored the optimism of the initial launch. Immediate gains were found in children's social development and motivation, and in their cognitive skills. Perhaps the most influential evaluation, however, published by the Westinghouse Learning Corporation in 1969, concluded that these gains were not sustained: By the second and third grades, children who had participated in the first summer and full-year programs achieved no higher scores on school achievement tests than low-income children without preschool experience of this kind. Soon after their entry into the ordinary school system, any immediate advantages from the Head Start experience had apparently "washed out."

These data have been subject to numerous reanalyses and the Westinghouse study criticized for its limited focus on intellectual development, and its failure to take account of differences between different program models. It nevertheless attracted widespread public attention. It was taken as a signal that preschool interventions had "failed" and that, along with them, the social science formulations on which they had rested were seriously discredited. An inevitable backlash ensued: The proper role for social science in the policy process was at the stage of evaluation rather than, as had occurred here, in its development.

In more recent years, it has been recognized that many of the initial premises on which these early programs were based were both ill-conceived and naively optimistic. In retrospect, it was clearly implausible that major social disadvantage could be eradicated by an eight-week enrichment program, or even by the more sustained preschool provision that developed in later years. A weakness of many of the early evaluations, however, was that they were not designed to illuminate the reasons for the negative findings and were open to a wide variety of interpretation as a result. Jensen (1969) used the results to reopen the nature-nurture controversy, arguing that environmental interventions would inevitably prove fruitless because intelligence was influenced primarily by genetic factors; Clarke and Clarke (1976) concluded that the critical-period hypothesis was mis-guided; and Bronfenbrenner (1974) contended that the form of the initial inter-ventions was not optimal. Closer attention to the design of the evaluations might have at least ensured that choices could be made between these differing inter-pretations.

Educational Priority Areas

We shall return later to some subsequent developments in action-research collab-oration in more recent U.S. preschool programs. At this stage, however, we move on to consider the first large-scale British experiment of this kind, the Educational Priority Areas (EPA). This program, launched in 1970, had much in common with the early American work; the focus was once again on the development of preschool provision, parental and community involvement, and the enrichment of primary school curricula to offset the effects of social disad-vantage. The project had its roots in the recommendations of the Plowden Com-mittee (1967) for positive discrimination for disadvantaged schools and areas. It was designed as an action-research program from the outset, jointly funded by government and the Social Science Research Council as an innovative approach to what was variously described as "experimental social administration" or "fu-turology as design." Action and research teams worked together, under a uni-versity-based national director, in four areas in England and one in Scotland. The program was funded for a three-year period, during which time the teams aimed, with only limited resources at their disposal, to develop, implement, and evaluate strategies toward "the production of a working policy for EPA practice which would, at least in principle, be national in its scope" (Halsey, 1972).

Within a short period the project succeeded in promoting an impressive variety of initiatives, some highly innovative. These are described in the various reports of the research, but formal evaluations were disappointingly limited. Despite the program's wide-ranging aims, quantitative evaluations were largely focused on tests of reading and language skills, mostly immediately on completion of the various program elements, and on relatively small numbers of children. Assess-ments of success in other areas – in stimulating community involvement, en-couraging parental interest, and raising teacher morale – rested largely on im-pressionistic accounts. The test score data that were available showed some short-term gains from the use of structured preschool language development materials, but more equivocal results where longer follow-ups were feasible. Primary school curriculum developments showed only limited and unreliable gains, and their success appeared heavily dependent on the attitudes of the teachers involved. Where they were uncommitted, the interventions failed; even among the majority of enthusiastic teachers, measurable gains were few. Halsey (1972) suggested that there may have been improvements in other, less easily measurable areas, such as social relationships or communication, but no data were available to support these conclusions.

The EPAs were designed specifically as demonstration projects from which national policy directions could be developed. An immediate tension arose, however, between the long-term aim of national policy relevance and the short-term need for locally appropriate action. Few specific guidelines for action had been developed before the program began. The problems of each local area were pressing, and the action teams were often concerned first and foremost to "get something done." The diverse characters and needs of the four project areas meant that such responses were inevitably varied. The dilemma was largely resolved in favor of local autonomy and action: It was recognized at an early stage that "local autonomy and initiative could not and should not be subjugated to . . . the rigorous constraints of a national experimental design" (p. viii).

This set major limitations on the extent to which broader policy conclusions could eventually be drawn. Some of the earliest criticisms of the program centered on the overambitious recommendations made on the evidence available (Town, 1972). In turn, this experience has frequently been cited as illustrating an inherent limitation in the applicability of action-research methods to large-scale policy issues. The responsive nature of the action-research model is seen as best suited to resolving problems specific to particular local circumstances, and so of necessity less valuable in illuminating wider policy concerns. This view rests in part on a conception of the relationship between research and policy – the one providing specific and sufficient prescriptions for the other – that rarely operates in practice in social policy fields. As Halsey pointed out, research can provide "an aid to intelligent decision making, not a substitute for it," relevant information rather than uniquely exclusive conclusions. Rigorously evaluated and well-documented local evidence can make a useful contribution to the wider debate, provided its limitations are appropriately acknowledged. A more serious difficulty with EPA design, however, was the attempt to encompass the development and evaluation of intervention strategies, and the formulation of wider policy conclusions, within the span of a single project. Quite different research designs are needed to test new intervention programs in optimal circumstances – or at least, as here, with considerable additional support – from those to assess the feasibility of large-scale implementation (Rutter, 1977). In the EPA program, what might perhaps more reasonably have been regarded as a pilot for a national experiment served as the experiment itself.

Many other issues arose. One of particular interest here was the role of teachers in the EPA program. They were to some extent "third parties" in the project as a whole, the primary collaboration with the education service being at central rather than local level. Their impact was nonetheless considerable. We have already seen that teacher enthusiasm played a part in affecting children's responses to a number of the curriculum innovations. In addition, it was clear that teachers' concepts of the experimental nature of the action differed markedly from those of the project staff. In the London area, for example, despite the apparent advantages of a structured approach to language development, nursery teachers rejected the experimental materials a priori because they conflicted with current teaching principles of free play and child-initiated activities. Conversely, other curriculum developments in the London primary schools were enthusiastically accepted, and continued in use after the formal conclusion of the research, despite the lack of any demonstrable effects. Barnes (1975) suggested that teacher concepts of acceptability differed widely from those of the social scientist. Teachers in the London schools were not prepared to "experiment" with new materials in a spirit of open-minded inquiry, but instead made their evaluations pretrial. Their criteria for adopting or continuing innovatory approaches turned less on their merit as assessed by external evaluations, more on questions of relevance, interest, and perceived congruence with current styles of work.

Some of these problems might have been avoided if local teachers had been more closely involved in joint planning of the experimental programs from the start. Inadequate appreciation of differing value systems has bedeviled many attempts at curriculum reform; it is perhaps not insignificant that many of the most successful experimental innovations in the educational field have taken place outside mainstream institutional structures, where staff could be specifically recruited and trained in the desired approaches. In an important sense, however, this is only to sidestep the issue. More fundamentally, collaborative styles of working require the development of a mutually acceptable framework, where the expectations and needs of both parties are recognized and neither becomes too dominant nor subservient to those of the other.

Parent Child Development Centers

Our next example – the Parent Child Development Center (PCDC) program – was one of a series of U.S. initiatives, designed in the years following the first Head Start programs to overcome some of their perceived weaknesses and to incorporate more recent theoretical advances in the child development field.

Negative findings from the early preschool experiments prompted widespread debate on both the focus and the age most appropriate for future interventions. More recent research had drawn attention to the importance of the infancy period (e.g., Ainsworth, 1969) and of the central role of parents in mediating environmental influences (Hess and Shipman, 1965; Bronfenbrenner, 1969). This implied a different focus for intervention, involving both parents and children, and an extension of the age range of such efforts down to the infant years. Parent and Child Centers (PCC) designed to provide education in child development for mothers as well as direct educational and support services to children, were set up in response to these trends.

A number of differing solutions were proposed to strengthen research methodology. The planned variation and Follow Through programs (Rhine, 1981) were designed to contrast a series of differing program models, each with a clearly articulated relationship to particular theories of children's learning and development. A conference at the Brookings Institution, reviewing this and other experiences, proposed further refinements for future experiments (Rivlin and Timpane, 1975). These explicitly recognized the differing stages – of development, initial testing, and wider application – considered necessary in the implementation of innovatory programs. These stages could not all be accomplished concurrently: Each raised distinct and separate issues, demanding different research designs and evaluation questions. The Brookings formulation proposed that (1) programs be developed from clear theoretical bases, to allow for the most illuminating tests of intervention – outcome links; (2) evaluation be made only when models were fully developed and personnel trained; (3) agreement be reached in advance as to what constituted successful outcomes; (4) measures of implementation – the extent to which practice actually reflected stated intentions – should also be included; and (5) the process of development should proceed from controlled experiments in a limited number of sites, through replication, to wider dissemination in a variety of different settings. It was recognized that this full cycle might take some ten to twelve years.

The PCDC experiment, launched in 1970, was planned along these lines (Andrews et al., 1982). The first, five-year, phase of the program was to be devoted to the development, documentation, and evaluation of differing theoretically based models of parent education, designed to help mothers become more effective agents in their young children's development. Three of the existing PCC sites were chosen for this phase. The evaluations, involving random assignment of mother-child pairs to program and control conditions, were seen as developmental in this first phase; they would be used to assess short-term effects, be internal to each site, and involve the development of a range of new assessment instruments. No definitive guidelines for policy were expected to emerge from this phase.

A second five-year phase would then test the feasibility of replicating success-ful models in other sites. A cross-model, external evaluation would now be in-troduced, allowing for comparisons between programs and assessment of effects for new groups of participants; the possibility of differential effects for differing target populations was an important element of the design throughout. This sec-ond phase would also allow for longer-term assessments of effects for mothers and children involved in the first phase. Wider-scale dissemination was envis-aged as a third, and again separate, stage.

The rationality of this design had strong intellectual appeal; it seemed ideally suited to meeting the joint action-research aims of testing theoretical proposi-tions, and to developing well-defined guidelines for policy. It was also recog-nized as ambitious, and demanding of both time and resources. In the event, the very features conceived as its main strengths proved insuperable barriers to its implementation. Phase I, federally funded, proceeded as planned, and demon-strated positive effects at the three original sites. Over the five years of its oper-ation, however, major changes had occurred in the economic and political cli-mate. By the mid-1970s, when the second phase was to be mounted, support was being withdrawn from many social programs, and there was a growing dis-inclination on the part of federal authorities to fund the replication stage. Foun-dation funds were secured to support the replication sites; each site continued to collect internal evaluation data, but support for the proposed cross-site evaluation came "too little and too late." By 1980, two of the replication sites had been forced to close entirely for lack of funding, and the Education Testing Service, originally commissioned to develop the external evaluation, was directed to fo-cus only on internal data collected at each separate site during phase II.

The precise direction and effects of these trends could not have been foreseen at the outset, but the experience underlines the potential vulnerability of many long-term programs to changes of social and political climate. Sustained funding was not the only difficulty: The decade spanned by the experiment saw major shifts in theory, public attitudes and policy, all of which limited the applicability of the findings that did emerge. Theoretical concerns had extended beyond the mother-child dyad toward a wider conception of family, school, and community influences on children's development. Changes in social attitudes combined with economic pressures to orient many of the mothers in the program to roles and needs apart from those of promoting their children's development. The notion of "critical periods" in development was seriously challenged, and both parent education and other compensatory strategies were rejected in some quarters as based on an inappropriate view of poverty, blaming the victim and so diverting attention from underlying structural inequalities. The issues central to the PCDC's theoretical and policy interests at the outset had been eclipsed, if not actively rejected, ten years later. The evaluators concluded that "While the notion of a carefully designed longitudinal experiment of this kind has great intellectual appeal, in practice it is unlikely to reach completion'' (p. 76).

As a collaborative research program, and a parent education endeavor, the experiment was more successful. Evaluators and curriculum developers worked harmoniously throughout, and innovative observational procedures were developed to assess the programs' effects on maternal behavior. Clear effects were found, on both maternal and child measures, after some two years of participation in the program, and follow-up data one year after graduation continued to show advantages to program participants, although less marked. Perhaps the major limitation of the evaluation design was the lack of measures to assess which aspects of the programs contributed most importantly to these effects, or what processes might mediate influences on the children's development. Once again, the desire to mount multifaceted programs to ensure maximum impact outran the ability to assess specific program components.

The Head Start, EPA, and PCDC studies are only examples of an extensive range of preschool experiments begun in this early period. We have focused on their difficulties as much as their achievements; in the field of early educational interventions as a whole, these achievements have been considerable, but many issues still remain to be resolved. Perhaps the most pressing of these is the question of long-term effects. We have already seen some of the difficulties in the way of the necessary long-term evaluations. Where such evaluations have been possible, however, it has become clear that immediate and more delayed effects may be quite different, and the processes linking them complex. A collaborative venture between some of the initial investigators in eleven early research and demonstration programs, the Consortium for Longitudinal Studies (Lazar and Darlington, 1982), has recently produced encouraging findings from an eight-to-eighteen year follow-up of early participants. Despite the loss of any sustained advantage over controls on tests of ability after some three to four years (and indeed very depressed scores in absolute terms), these children were less likely to have been assigned to special education placements later in their school careers, or to have been retained in grade. There was also some evidence of attitudinal change among the children and their mothers. These are perhaps modest, but by no means unimportant, gains. The results of this Consortium effort are open to some criticism, on grounds of attrition rates, and the extent to which teachers in later grades may have known about the children's earlier experiences. It is also unclear how far results from these well-resourced demonstration programs may generalize to more widely disseminated models. Nevertheless, collaborative efforts of this kind – between researchers in the same field – provide an important means of capitalizing on otherwise potentially disparate research findings. If individual programs are likely to be vulnerable, in the short or long term, eventual contributions to both theory and policy may depend on the possibility of integrating findings from a variety of sources to bear on the issues involved. For too long, the values of the academic community have done little to encourage the cumulative development of knowledge in this way. A broader conception of action-research could profitably encompass collaborative efforts of this kind on a wider scale.

Perry Preschool Program

One of the most carefully designed individual studies included in the Consortium analyses was the Perry Preschool Program (Berrueta-Clement et al., 1984). Begun in 1962, this experiment involved random allocation of severely disadvantaged black children in a two-year preschool program. The 58 children in the experimental group (comprising five successive years' intakes) attended the preschool for two and a half hours daily over the period, and received a weekly home visit from a teacher. Their progress – assessed annually between the ages of 3 and 11, then at 14, 15, and 19 – was compared with that of 65 control children. High contact rates were maintained throughout the follow-up, and later evaluations increasingly focused on "real world" measures of progress.

Early findings followed the pattern familiar from many other studies. At the end of the preschool, experimental children had a 12-point advantage in IQ over controls. By the end of the second grade, this had been lost; at 14, each group had a mean WISC IQ of 81, almost exactly comparable with their 3-year-old scores. Despite this, the experimental groups maintained some gains on standardized attainment tests, and by the end of their schooling were significantly less likely to have been placed in special classes. Instead, they were *more* likely to have received remedial help within the mainstream: The authors suggest that teachers perceived these children as having greater potential to succeed – with help – in the ordinary school setting. By age 19, there was evidence that preschool participants had been less involved in crime and delinquency than controls, were less likely to use welfare services, and had a lower incidence of teenage pregnancy. Their high school graduation rates were higher, and they were more likely to be involved in post-secondary education, or to be in work. Despite the apparent "washout" of early IQ gains, these young people had been more successful in their scholastic progress, and in their adjustment outside and after school. How could these later findings be explained?

Over the period of the study, the researchers have developed a transactional model of the processes involved, positing a dynamic relationship between influences at each stage. Rather than "sleeper effects" – suggested by some commentators to account for similar findings from other studies – they propose that the initial intervention set off a chain of developments, some self-reinforcing, that were manifest in different ways at different stages. Although early IQ gains were not sustained, their timing – coinciding with the first years in school – may have provided a crucial link with later progress. They enabled the children to carry out their first scholastic tasks better, so increasing their own sense of mastery and commitment to school, and prompting higher expectations from their teachers. These in turn were likely to have been central in later decisions on school placement. Improved adaptive functioning in the school setting seems likely to have generated a more positive social dynamic, which both sustained and supported later developments. Where, in earlier formulations, cognitive gains had been assumed to be the mediating link between immediate program effects and later progress, this model points to improvements in adaptive functioning and commitment to schooling as the more important processes involved – a conclusion in line with the findings from other research (Rutter, 1985).

The project's findings, as well as illuminating theoretical concerns, have had a major impact on policy. Cost-benefit analyses suggest that by age 19, the intervention had yielded economic benefits to the participants and the community over seven times the cost of one year of the program. The results have been used to support the expansion of educational and child-care facilities in many local areas, to reinforce moves toward the provision of public education at the age of 4, especially for disadvantaged children, in a number of states, and to support the preservation and expansion of the national Head Start program. Over time, this particular collaboration between action and research seems likely to impact on social policy in ways undreamed of by its initial developers.

Parent-teacher collaboration

Our final example of interventions focusing on young children comes from a recent small-scale British study of parent-teacher collaboration in the early years of primary schooling (Tizard, Schofield, and Hewison, 1982). Within its chosen compass, it illustrates many of the advantages of the action-research approach, involving close collaboration between researchers and teachers in ordinary schools to test a specific hypothesis derived from previous empirical findings. The research design was both manageable and imaginative, and, though many of the issues underlying the research require further investigation, the studies conducted to date have already had valuable implications for both theory and practice.

The intervention in this case was planned as a direct test of findings from earlier surveys (Hewison and Tizard, 1980). These had been designed to explore home-based influences on children's early reading skills within a largely working-class population. The influence of social factors on children's school achievement has been widely documented in studies *between* different social class groups. Here, the aim was to identify whether any similar processes might operate *within* a generally disadvantaged population, where children were at serious risk of reading failure. Among the range of aspects of upbringing explored, one emerged as clearly, and somewhat unexpectedly, related to children's reading levels. Children whose mothers heard them read regularly at home had markedly higher test scores than their peers. This finding was replicated in different samples, and could not be accounted for by variations in maternal language behavior, the children's ability levels, or other aspects of their upbringing at home. Parental ''coaching'' of this kind appeared strikingly important, accounting for over a third of the variance in children's reading skills by the age of 7 to 8 years. Just under half the mothers in the survey samples heard their children read in this way. The action phase of the research was planned to test whether other mothers could also be encouraged to become involved in their children's learning, and if so, whether similar beneficial effects would be found.

The experimental work took place in six primary schools in disadvantaged inner-city areas. The design of the project involved comparisons between three different approaches to the teaching of reading: the parent-teacher home collaboration scheme; extra reading tuition in school provided by an experienced teacher seconded to the research; and the schools' own usual methods serving as a control. In the home collaboration scheme, teachers and researchers worked together to encourage all parents – including those for whom English was not their own first language – to hear their children read at home on a regular basis. Teachers selected materials suited to their ongoing work with the children in school, and record cards were exchanged between teachers and parents to monitor what was read. The researchers visited each child's home at regular intervals to advise on ''good practice.''

The authors describe the design of the research as ''a compromise between the strict requirements of an experiment and judgements about real-world feasibility'' (p. 12). The main problems centered on the most appropriate unit of randomization to different treatment groups. Choices between the assignment of individuals or classes to differing intervention programs pose recurrent problems in educational research: The use of intact groups, such as classes, creates potential biases and difficulties in analysis (Cook and Campbell, 1979) but is often the only feasible and acceptable solution from the teacher's point of view. In addition, randomization by class may provide a more appropriate basis for later generalization of findings. With a recognition that strict experimental conditions could only be achieved at the expense of policy relevance of this kind, the investigators in this project opted for the random allocation of classes to differing treatment groups, and a concurrent replication of each treatment in two different schools.

The results unequivocally favored the home reading scheme. Parents responded positively, and the children's test scores showed that the program had beneficial effects at all levels of initial reading ability. At the end of the two-year experiment, proportions of poor readers in the home collaboration groups were reduced, and proportions of able readers increased. Gains by comparison with the control group were maintained at a one-year follow-up. Extra help with reading within school produced some improvements, but these were less reliable and least marked for children with initially low scores. The home collaboration scheme was of greater benefit than a practically feasible alternative, and, perhaps most encouragingly, was likely to be of value to children at greatest risk of reading failure. Informal observations suggested that the children's attitudes had also improved, and that the project had provided a basis for the development of many other home-school links.

Projects of this kind offer some of the clearest examples of the advantages of a collaborative approach to research. The main strengths in this instance lay in the direct development of the intervention work from previous naturalistic epidemiological findings, and in the use of a design appropriately planned to provide interpretable answers to specific and relatively limited questions. This particular project represents only one step in a series of studies that would be needed to understand the full implications of the initial survey findings: From a theoretical perspective, further work is still required to illuminate *why* parental coaching should be effective, and whether the benefits of the home-based scheme lay primarily in increased parental involvement and interest, increases in the children's motivation, or other factors. These issues could not easily have been encompassed within a single study, but instead needed to be addressed in a series of incremental stages, each requiring different designs. Although progress of this kind is inevitably slow, it is essential if we are to derive clearly interpretable results from intervention-based research.

One further element critical to the success of the project was that cooperation between researchers and teachers was maintained at a high level throughout. In a literature containing all too many examples of misunderstandings and failures of communication between action and research staff, this in itself was a considerable achievement. The salience, specificity, and clarity of the intervention were doubtless helpful here, but in addition the researchers went to considerable pains to ensure that both the design and the conduct of the program were acceptable to the schools involved, and fitted satisfactorily with their current ways of working. The direct involvement of the researcher may also have been important. Although there are clear risks in the immediate combination of action and research roles, there are also benefits. Direct involvement provides additional opportunities for ensuring that programs are being implemented as intended, and may have the further advantage of diffusing potentially damaging teacher anxieties about involvement in research.

In many areas of human service provision, the more so where the "technology'' is relatively soft and practitioner skill and expertise consequently of greater importance, evaluations of services become, to a greater or lesser extent, evaluations of practitioners. Much educational research is explicitly or implicitly critical in this way. Although a stance of this kind is in many instances scientifically justified and indeed responsible, it is unlikely to provide fertile ground for collaboration. A number of different solutions could be envisaged, the active involvement and commitment of researchers being only one. Whatever the chosen solution, however, it is clearly crucial that relationships of trust and openness be maintained in any work of this kind. The numerous examples of failed communications between practitioners and research staff in intervention projects are too frequent to dismiss, but equally clearly need not be inevitable. Real attention to the implications of participation for practitioners must be among the cornerstones of any such attempt.

School influences and school improvement

We turn now to examples of collaboration drawn from our own work in schools. This has largely focused on older children, and on more general issues: of school differences, effects and effectiveness, and, more recently, school improvement. We have been involved in studies in these areas for almost two decades, in a programmatic development of research that has included both naturalistic studies and experimental interventions, each building directly from the findings and issues raised in preceding phases of the work. The program has depended heavily on the support of local teachers, and indeed many of its developments have occurred as much as a result of their promptings as of our own. The work has not been without its difficulties, but has nonetheless convinced us of the potential of collaboration of this kind, and of a flexible, staged approach to the exploration of research questions.

Our interest in school effects and school differences arose in the first instance almost by chance, as a spin-off from an epidemiological survey in one area of inner London. This was designed to explore the prevalence and correlates of learning and behavioral disorders in childhood, and had its prime focus on family-based factors (Rutter et al., 1975).

The results showed, as anticipated, high rates of learning and behavior problems in this inner-city population. Individually focused psychological and remedial services could not hope to reach the large numbers of children involved. Instead, much would depend on the skills of their classroom teachers. The immediate response of some of our colleagues at this stage was to set up action-research workshops for local teachers, involving training and experimentation work with behavioral techniques in the classroom. These in turn developed into the Teacher-Child Interaction Project, a collaborative research and in-service training program maintained over a number of years (Yule, Berger, and Wigley, 1984).

The survey findings also suggested, however, that both educational and behavior problems clustered by school. Some primary schools had much higher rates of such difficulties than others, and it seemed unlikely – though we could say no more than this on the basis of the survey findings – that this was entirely accounted for by family and neighborhood factors. Instead, it seemed possible that some school-based influences were involved. These findings emerged early in the 1970s. The climate of ideas at this stage, at least in the academic community, was by no means favorable to the notion of school influences. The apparent failures of early intervention programs, together with widespread evidence of the effects of social factors on educational attainment, coincided to fuel something of a deterministic view, largely negative in its assumptions about the school system as anything other than an agent of social and cultural reproduction. Some more locally based studies, including our own, suggested that this might be an overreaction. Although the school system almost certainly could not, as the liberal optimists had hoped, "compensate for society," school influences might nevertheless have an impact, and by no means an unimportant one, for the individual child. Our local steering committee of teachers urged us to explore the question of school differences and influences further.

The ideal test of school effects, like other social programs, would require random allocation of children to different types of school provision. This is rarely likely to be ethically acceptable or practically feasible in real-world settings. Instead, alternative approaches need to be found. Longitudinal studies, capitalizing as far as possible on naturally occurring variations in school provision, offer perhaps some of the best alternative possibilities of teasing out the issues involved. Our own survey provided the basis for a follow-up of this kind as the children entered secondary school: The survey data could act as intake measures against which the children's subsequent progress could be assessed.

We approached the next stages of the study in a number of different phases. First, we needed to confirm whether school effects were indeed evident in the children's progress in early adolescence. A preliminary follow-up suggested that this was the case: We found marked differences in rates of progress at different schools, and could not account for these in terms of differences in resource levels or administrative characteristics. Instead, it seemed likely that they reflected more subtle internal features of the schools and their functioning, which could not be satisfactorily assessed by survey-type techniques alone. A more detailed study of the internal social organization of the schools would be required to take these issues further.

We recognized that this was potentially both threatening and intrusive to the schools: It would involve an explicitly comparative study between schools all in close proximity to one another, and a detailed focus on their day-to-day modes of operation. It would almost certainly have been impossible to mount a study of this kind without the basis of cooperative relationships we had established over previous years, and the farsighted and open commitment of the teachers to the need to explore the issues involved. With their agreement, however, we planned a continued study in twelve local schools, combining a further follow-up of the pupils' progress with a detailed study of the schools themselves.

This phase of the work took us into a closer involvement with the schools. At the outset, we had few guidelines as to which features of the complex range of interactions that make up a child's experiences at school were likely to be most influential. We thus began with a period of unstructured, informal pilot work, supplementing such guidance as could be derived from the existing literature with our own observations and the views of teachers themselves. Throughout this period of development work, and the more formal phases of data collection that followed, we needed also to develop and maintain a new form of relationships with the schools. This involved a number of features: the need to be accepted in the schools and yet retain some independence from them; the need to show understanding of their problems and modes of working without endorsing any particular style of approach; and the need to be accepted by both teachers and pupils alike, and avoid overidentification with any particular group. The research role always poses problems and challenges in action settings, and these are perhaps most marked in studies requiring long-term involvement in organizational contexts comprising many different "client" groups. At the outset, we found our energies as researchers engaged as much in developing appropriate ways of working with the schools, and preparing the way for formal data collection, as in the more technical issues usually assumed to be the central preoccupation of the social scientist.

At the close of this phase of the work, the analysis of our findings took us some considerable way forward in understanding school effects (Rutter et al., 1979). First, as we had anticipated, we found that the schools indeed differed markedly in their outcomes for pupils by the end of the period of compulsory schooling. These differences were apparent in measures of both attainment and behavior, and were not simply reflections of initial variations in intakes. Second, our measures of the schools as social institutions, their process and ethos, revealed equally striking variations in climate and culture. Third, these two sets of factors were closely related. Different patterns of internal school functioning characterized the more and less successful schools. Since the publication of these findings, a number of other studies – using a variety of different methodologies – have reported similar results. We are now beginning, on the basis of a range of different types of evidence, to have a clearer picture of the extent of school effects and some of their correlates (Purkey and Smith, 1983; Rutter, 1983). The great majority of this evidence is still, however, correlational. Though strongly suggesting causal links, studies of this kind cannot entirely rule out other possible interpretations of school effects. The next logical step would involve a further change of focus: To test whether improvements in school practice would indeed result in predicted improvements in pupil progress, we needed to move on to a study of change.

This has been our concern in recent years. Our initial approach involved an intervention study in three schools, whereby we worked with them, in a characteristic action-research way, to change their practice in selected areas. The extensive literature on attempts to introduce change in schools, whether at the level of specific curriculum innovations or broader attempts at organizational development, attests to the many difficulties facing an enterprise of this kind. Early strategies modeling school improvement efforts on the research, development, and diffusion methods used in other fields are now seen as largely inappropriate in the school context (Berman, 1981). This style of work took inadequate account of the professional value systems of teachers, and the organizational characteristics of schools (Baldridge, 1975). Since the mid-1970s, a range of differing organizational theories and guiding metaphors have been explored in an attempt to provide a more appropriate basis for the promotion of change. No satisfactory new synthesis has yet emerged.

Our own initial approach, working with schools each facing different but relatively pressing problems, was a pragmatic one: We would work in flexible ways, focusing on the problems each school identified as of major current concern. Surveys of teacher attitudes, together with some of our findings from the earlier research, formed the basis for our initial joint planning. Each school selected areas for attention, and we worked with them in projects ranging from classroom management workshops to surveys to highlight the causes of pupil disaffection.

Some successes were achieved in each of these areas, but as the project progressed, we became increasingly aware of one of the classic difficulties faced in action-research of this kind: The problems the schools had selected for initial attention were not always those that we perceived as most central to achieving schoolwide change. We then faced the dilemma of whether, and in what ways, to make our analyses of the situations clear. To fail to do so ran the risk that the project would proceed with only piecemeal and almost inevitably insufficient change. To go ahead, however, risked the Charybdis of complete rejection and the possibility of compromising our working relationships with the schools. As external researchers, with no power in the schools, and only such authority as they chose to extend to us, we could do little to enforce our interpretations. Conscious of the low morale already existing in some areas, we had no wish or right to undermine it further.

Our solution to this dilemma was to move forward in two different ways. In our continuing work with the intervention schools, we took a middle course, selectively emphasizing proposals for change that seemed to us most likely to contribute to our central aims. In addition, we added a new and complementary element to the research: a retrospective naturalistic study of change in schools with recent changes in key senior personnel. Together, these two approaches have added greatly to our understanding of the process of change in schools. The retrospective study demonstrated that it is possible for schools in disadvantaged areas to improve their pupil outcomes over time. Attendance and attainments improved markedly in schools adopting coherent strategies for change, even though pupil intakes remained essentially unchanged. These findings strengthen the causal inferences on the impact of school effects from the earlier, comparative study. Interviews with staff pointed to some of the factors involved here: the importance of consistent and clear goals, a staged and cumulative approach to change, attention to the total environment and ethos of the school, and the involvement of staff and pupils in a focused program to develop new relationships and modes of working.

We have also learned a good deal about the contributions that external agents can make in school improvement efforts. Recent reviews in this area (Fullan, Miles, and Taylor, 1980; Louis, 1981) have concluded that although such externally induced efforts can be effective, this is by no means always the case. Studies of Organization Development (OD) have suggested that the likelihood of success is perhaps .5 probability or less. The "readiness" of schools for change, and the styles of work of external agents, both emerge as important determining features. Our own experience suggests both that we might have paid greater attention to the necessary preconditions for change in the schools, and that our own style of work might have included a more constructive element of challenge from the outset.

The final problems we highlight from this experience concern the state of our knowledge at the start of the study. Our previous research had provided a series of correlational findings on aspects of school process associated with differing pupil outcomes. Neither these findings, nor any other work in similar fields, could provide more specific guidelines at the outset as to whether changes in any one of these areas might be needed as a basis for developments in others, or have the best chance of generating multiplier effects. With hindsight, we concluded that we had attempted to move forward to an action phase too soon, and had chosen perhaps some of the most difficult conditions in which to mount our intervention. In retrospect, we might have been better advised to delay attempts at change until fuller evidence was available from naturalistic studies to provide more detailed guidelines on the nature of the processes involved.

Conclusions

"But when it is performed well, problem focused research requires not only high levels of dedication, sustained energy, tolerance for ambiguity, and a thick skin, but also expertise in conceptual and methodological areas and political sophistication."

So Rhine (1981) summed up experience from the Follow Through program. These are demanding requirements, but as we have seen, action-research is a demanding approach, subject to a variety of vicissitudes. We have dwelt on these, we hope not excessively, because they clearly require forethought if collaborative work of this kind is to succeed.

The experience of the last decades has provided us with many useful guidelines for future collaborations, and an awareness of some of the pitfalls that can arise. Reviewing these briefly, we must begin at the heart of the matter, with the collaborative relationship itself. Writers on action-research have dealt extensively with the difficulties apparently inherent in this relationship, whether between policy-makers and social scientists, or practitioners and field researchers. The principles, perspectives, and time frames of these groups have been seen as so essentially different that stumbling blocks and tensions, sometimes insurmountable, will inevitably arise in sustained attempts at collaboration.

The examples we have reviewed here suggest that this is by no means necessarily the case. Mutually productive relationships can be developed, but cannot be taken for granted. They require flexibility – and often some compromise – on both sides, a willingness to adapt to the demands of a new style of work. As we have seen, this can be achieved most satisfactorily when all the parties are involved in joint planning from the outset, and when research and action form part of an integrated whole, with neither element too dominant or subservient.

A second series of issues turns on questions of pace. The desire to improve provision, and the commitment to create a better world, can tempt researchers to move forward to action too hastily, or to promise more than can realistically be expected. At the least, precipitate action based on only partially articulated theory is likely to produce inappropriate interventions or uninterpretable findings. At the worst, it can have more seriously deleterious consequences. To be productive, action-research requires some tempering of idealism with an awareness of the art of the possible.

This is perhaps most obvious in the development of new programs eventually intended for large-scale dissemination. Developing, evaluating, and testing the replicability of new action strategies are each discrete and separate problems. Each poses different questions for practice and research, and requires a staged, incremental approach. Cumulative and flexible developments are needed here, whether through a programmatic approach to the evolution of individual projects, or collaboration between researchers in related fields. Much of this work is inevitably long-term. Although long-term funding is increasingly difficult to secure, part of the social science role must be to argue the case for sustained support, and to point to the impossibility of developing our understanding in crucial areas of service provision in isolated short-term projects.

Concern for wider policy relevance adds an extra dimension to action-research in human service fields. To date, large-scale initiatives of political origin have faced severe difficulties. We are inclined to the view that policy interests can perhaps be better served by more locally based studies, developing organically from epidemiological or clinical research, or from the more immediate concerns of practice. Experience suggests that research affects policy in unpredictable ways, as much by changing the climate of ideas, and raising new issues for debate, as through the application of specific empirical findings. In this context, well-designed locally based studies have a valuable role to play.

Our examples provide many other pointers to the conditions under which action and research collaboration can best succeed. It is our conviction that it *must* succeed, and for a number of different reasons. First, services for children are too important to go without investigations of their success and effects. Experimental studies outside the mainstream can make valuable contributions here, but much of the necessary work must be done in the ordinary school and classroom if it is to tackle the most pressing practical concerns. Second, the essentially social nature of human development demands that it be studied and understood within its social context. Both naturalistic and intervention studies are of importance here. Each, in different ways, depends upon the maintenance of constructive collaborative relationships between practice and research.

References

Ainsworth, M. D. S. Object relations, dependency and attachment: A theoretical review of the infant-mother relationship. *Child Development,* 1969, *40,* 969–1025.

Andrews, S. R., Blumenthal, J. B., Johnson, D. L., Kahn, A. J., Ferguson, C. J., Lasater, T. M., Malone, P. E., and Wallace, D. B. The skills of mothering: A study of Parent Child Development Centers. *Monographs of the Society for Research in Child Development,* 1982, *47*(198), 6.

Baldridge, J. V. Organizational innovation: Individual, structural and environmental impacts. In J. V. Baldridge and T. E. Deal (Eds.), *Managing change in educational organizations.* Berkeley, Calif.: McCutchan, 1975.

Barnes, J. (Ed.). *Educational priority.* Vol 3: *Curriculum innovation in London's E.P.As.* London: HMSO, 1975.

Bereiter, C., and Engelmann, S. *Teaching disadvantaged children in the preschool.* Englewood Cliffs, N.J.: Prentice-Hall, 1966.

Berman, P., and McLaughlin, M. W. *Federal programs supporting educational change.* Vol VIII: *Implementing and sustaining innovations.* Santa Monica, Calif.: RAND Corporation R-1589/8-HEW, 1979.

Berman, P. Educational change: An implementation paradigm. In R. Lehming and M. Kane (Eds.), *Improving schools*. Beverly Hills, Calif.: Sage, 1981.

Berrueta-Clement, J. R., Schweinhart, L. J., Barnett, W. S., Epstein, A. S., and Weikart, D. P. Changed lives: The effects of the Perry Preschool Program on youths through age 19. *Monographs of the High/Scope Educational Research Foundation, 8*. Ypsilanti, Mich.: High/Scope Press, 1984.

Bloom, B. S. *Stability and change in human characteristics*. New York: Wiley, 1964.

Bronfenbrenner, U. Motivational and social components in compensatory education programs: Suggested principles, practices and research designs. In E. Grotberg (Ed.), *Critical issues in research related to disadvantaged children*. Princeton, N.J.: Educational Testing Service, 1969.

Bronfenbrenner, U. *Is early intervention effective? A report on the longitudinal evaluations of Head Start*. Office of Child Development, U.S. Department of Health, Education and Welfare. Washington, D.C.: U.S. Government Printing Office, 1974.

Clarke, A. M., and Clarke, A. D. B. *Early experience: Myth and evidence*. New York: Free Press, 1976.

Coleman, J. S., et al. *Equality of educational opportunity*. Washington, D.C.: U.S. Government Printing Office, 1966.

Cook, T. D., and Campbell, D. T. *Quasi-experimentation*. Chicago: Rand McNally, 1979.

Douglas, J. W. E. *The home and the school*. London: MacGibbon and Kee, 1964.

Fullan, M., Miles, M. B., and Taylor, G. Organization development in schools: The state of the art. *Review of Educational Research*, 1980, *50*(1), 121–83.

Gordon, E. W. Evaluation during the early years of Head Start. In E. Zigler and J. Valentine (Eds.), *Project Head Start*. New York: Free Press, 1979.

Gross, N. Basic issues in the management of educational change efforts. In R. Herriott and N. Gross (Eds.), *The dynamics of planned educational change*. Berkeley, Calif.: McCutchan, 1979.

Halsey, A. H. *Educational priority*. Vol. 1: *E.P.A. problems and policies*. London: HMSO, 1972.

Hess, R. D., and Shipman, V. C. Early experience and the socialization of cognitive modes in children. *Child Development*, 1965, *36*, 869–86.

Hewison, J., and Tizard, J. Parental involvement and reading attainment. *British Journal of Educational Psychology*, 1980, *50*, 209–15.

House, E. R., and Mathison, S. Educational intervention. In E. Seidman (Ed.), *Handbook of social intervention*. Beverly Hills, Calif.: Sage, 1983.

Hunt, J. McV. *Intelligence and experience*. New York: Ronald, 1961.

Jensen, A. R. How much can we boost IQ and scholastic achievement? *Harvard Educational Review*, 1969, *39*, 1–123.

Lazar, I., and Darlington, R. Lasting effects of early education: A report from the Consortium for Longitudinal Studies. *Monographs of the Society for Research in Child Development*, 1982, *47*(195), 2–3.

Lewis, O. The culture of poverty. In D. P. Moynihan (Ed.), *On understanding poverty*. New York: Basic Books, 1968.

Louis, K. S. External agents and knowledge utilization dimensions for analysis and action. In R. Lehming and M. Kane (Eds.), *Improving Schools*. Beverly Hills, Calif.: Sage, 1981.

Plowden Report. *Children and their primary schools*. London: HMSO, 1967.

Purkey, S. C., and Smith, M. S. Effective schools: A review. *The Elementary School Journal*, 1983, *83*, 427–52.

Rhine, W. R. (Ed.). *Making schools more effective: New directions from follow through*. New York: Academic Press, 1981.

Rivlin, A. M., and Timpane, P. M. (Eds.). *Planned variation in education: Should we give up or try harder?* Washington, D.C.: The Brookings Institution, 1975.

Rutter, M. Research and prevention of psychosocial disorders in childhood. In J. Barnes and N. Connelly (Eds.), *Social care research*. London: Policy Studies Institute, 1977.

Rutter, M. School effects on pupil progress: Research findings and policy implications. *Child Development*, 1983, *54*(1), 1–29.

Rutter, M. Family and school influences on cognitive development. *Journal of Child Psychology and Psychiatry*, in press.

Rutter, M., Yule, B., Quinton, D., Rowlands, O., Yule, W., and Berger, M. Attainment and adjustment in two geographical areas. III: Some factors accounting for area differences. *British Journal of Psychiatry*, 1975, *126*, 520–33.

Rutter, M., Maughan, B., Mortimore, P., and Ouston, J., with Smith, A. *Fifteen thousand hours: Secondary schools and their effects on children*. London: Open Books, 1979.

Tizard, J., Schofield, W. N., and Hewison, J. Collaboration between teachers and parents in assisting children's reading. *British Journal of Educational Psychology*, 1982, *52*, 1–15.

Town, S. W. Action research and social policy: Some recent British experience. *Sociological Review*, 1972, *21*(4), 573–98.

Westinghouse Learning Corporation. *The impact of Head Start on children's cognitive and affective development: Executive summary*. Ohio University report to the Office of Economic Opportunity. Washington, D.C.: Clearing House for Federal Scientific and Technical Information, June 1969. (EDO 36321)

Yule, W., Berger, M., and Wigley, V. Behaviour modification classroom management. In N. Frude and H. Gault (Eds.), *Disruptive behaviour in schools*. Chichester: Wiley, 1984.

Zigler, E., and Valentine, J. *Project Head Start*. New York: Free Press, 1979.

3 Youth employment: managing tensions in collaborative research

Richard H. Price and Anna Celeste Burke

In the United States the employment prospects and problems of youth have generally been regarded with both ambivalence about whether or not to intervene on behalf of youth in the area of employment and ambivalence about how to do so. As Hahn (1979) has put it, "youth, like old people, are alternatively seen by society as economic assets or liabilities, as worthy of social investment or as an undeserving stratum of society" (p. 245). Thus, the visibility of youth and the priority placed on their employment needs have varied considerably over time.

In part, this ambivalence toward the employment problems of youth is rooted in contradictory sets of societal objectives for and notions about youth. Traditional notions about the work ethic and the importance of transmitting these values to young people have tended to encourage a positive view of early employment. Admonitions about the dangers of idleness have generated concern about high rates of unemployment among young people. This is especially true for those who have dropped out of or completed high school. From this perspective, youth is a critical period in which young people take on the responsibilities of adults and establish a commitment to work.

In contrast to this view is the somewhat idealized conception of adolescence and young adulthood as a period of carefree exploration and experimentation. From this perspective, young people are widely perceived to be in need of protection from premature or too rapid exposure to the responsibilities and activities of the adult world. Within this framework, the employment of youth is often considered to be more problematic than unemployment.

Both employment and unemployment of youth have ranked among the concerns of researchers and policymakers. But determining how seriously to consider employment or unemployment of youth has been difficult. Despite a general increase in emphasis on the employment problems of youth in recent years, there continues to be a great deal of inertia from past policies and practices that

Preparation of this manuscript was supported in part by grant No. MH38330 from the National Institute of Mental Health in support of the Michigan Prevention Research Center.

have relied on the "natural" maturation process to ensure the transition of youth from school to work. Such beliefs about the "naturalness" of the transition from student to worker have tended to mitigate against intervention efforts.

Moreover, research efforts to establish the impact of employment and unemployment on youth have been inadequate and inconclusive. The literature is marked by disagreement about the consequences of employment and unemployment for individual development, school performance, career preparation and selection, and subsequent labor market performance. Thus, the inconsistency of existing research has contributed to the ambivalence of policy and program initiatives for youth.

Hidden in the disagreement about the value and importance of employment for youth is the fact that concern about the employment of youth varies with age. Those who study youth employment refer to the problems confronting 14- to 24-year-olds – generally the span of time covering the period from entry into high school to completion of college and acquisition of a first serious job commitment. The target age of public and private initiatives varies greatly, but most government youth programs are aimed at minors in the 16- to 21-year-old age group. For some programs, though, this age bracket may extend downward to include 14- to 16-year-olds and upward to include everyone under 30.

The emphasis tends to shift as researchers and policymakers focus on one end or the other of this age group. At the lower end of this age spectrum there is greater interest in educational and vocational preparation and less commitment to immediate employment as the most appropriate outcome of intervention efforts. As the focus shifts upward, though, attempts at intervention move more directly to secure an attachment to the labor market. For the bottom of this age group, then, employment may be viewed as deviant and unemployment as acceptable, whereas just the opposite tends to be true for those at the upper end of this age distribution.

Issues of gender, class, and ethnicity have also contributed to the difference in perception of employment issues. Typically, unemployment has been considered a more serious problem for poor, minority males. Females have been perceived as less in need of employment or employment preparation and more in need of protection than male youth. Together, crosscutting factors of age, ethnicity, gender, and class contribute further to the ambivalent evaluations of youth employment issues.

Because of continued ambivalence about youth employment issues we continue to find the following disagreements about U.S. policy on the employment and training of youth. First, there is widespread disagreement about whether or not to intervene on behalf of youth concerning employment or unemployment issues. Second, there is serious disagreement about the nature and intensity of any intervention efforts to be made. Such disagreements have resulted in alternating waves of interest and neglect, producing ambitious initiatives followed by severe reversals and numerous changes of direction around interventions aimed at youth.

The field: youth employment and unemployment

What follows is a brief review of the literature on the effects of employment and unemployment on youth. It is meant not to be a comprehensive review of the field but to provide an overview highlighting major issues in this literature. After this review of the research literature, the range of intervention options with youth will be described with a closer look at the role of action-research in resolving the practical problems of intervening with youth and providing researchers and policymakers with adequate feedback on the merits of such interventions.

Youth employment

Certainly, making a "normal" transition to adulthood depends on establishing and maintaining a stable attachment to the labor market. But at what point young people should be introduced to the work world and how they should go about preparing for this transition are not at all clear from scholarly research or practical experience (Barton and Fraser, 1978; Hamilton and Crouter, 1980).

Individual development. Those who consider the employment of youth to be advantageous to adolescent development (Panel on Youth, 1974; Task Force, 1975; Wirtz, 1975; Work-Education Consortium, 1978; Tyler, 1978; Conrad and Hedin, 1977; Hedin and Conrad, 1980) argue that work experience provides youth with a number of benefits. Hamilton and Crouter (1980) place these benefits into three categories:

1) Most broadly, work is expected to socialize adolescents to adult attitudes, values and behavior; independence and responsibility are particularly stressed. 2) Realistic career directions, knowledge of career possibilities and related educational requirements, and commitment to meeting these requirements may be considered a part of socialization to adulthood, but are specific to work. 3) A third benefit, also a subset of adult socialization, is that it teaches job related attitudes, behavior, and skills such as punctuality and "good work habits." [1980:325]

In opposition to these views are those who suggest that early employment may be detrimental to normal development. Based on the notion of adolescence and youth as periods of "moratorium" from adult responsibility (Erikson, 1968; Keniston, 1971), they suggest that premature introduction to the adult responsibilities of the workplace may interfere with identity formation and psychosocial adjustment (Hamilton and Crouter, 1980).

Others who actually oppose work experience as an option for young people do so on the grounds that much of the work available to young workers is alienating in many ways. Behn et al. (1974) question the value to youth of early exposure to the boredom and dissatisfaction reported to be widespread among adult workers (Work-Education Consortium, 1973). Evidence from Greenberger and Steinberg's (1981) survey of high school students with jobs indicates that although these students do seem to have a greater sense of responsibility about money and more opportunities to be helpful to others at work, many demonstrate little attachment to their work or co-workers. Furthermore, working students were more likely than nonworking students to be cynical about work, viewing it as essentially an unrewarding and meaningless activity (Steinberg et al., 1982). This discussion has prompted researchers to call for more caution in advocating employment for youth and for more attention to and research on the quality and amount of the work experience (Hamilton and Crouter, 1980; Steinberg, 1982; Stern, 1984).

Career development and labor market outcomes. Research on the relation of employment to subsequent labor market performance has raised a number of unresolved questions about the merits of employment. These questions have led to growing skepticism about the value of work experience to youth. At the same time, policy guidelines have stressed the benefits of gaining some work experience as a way of easing the transition from school to work.

Advocates of youth employment have emphasized the value of work experience in making more realistic career decisions. Such decisions are supposed to be based on more accurate information about work derived from contact with the "real" world (Bucknam, 1976; Panel on Youth, 1974; Work-Education Consortium, 1978). In addition, work experience is supposed to increase motivation to continue in school as a means to achieving realistic career goals. Hamilton and Crouter (1980) and others have argued that employment generally has little to do with providing information on the range of career alternatives available to youth. They cite evidence regarding the limited kind of employment most often available to young people. These authors express concern that early employment might, in fact, cut off career exploration. Steinberg et al. (1982) contend that employment may act to depress school performance, which runs counter to the idea that work can enhance students' attachment to continued education. Stern (1984) stresses the importance of the "quality" of work experience as a mediator of positive consequences to employment.

Hamilton and Crouter (1980) also challenge the idea that employment necessarily teaches young workers job-related skills such as punctuality, responsibility, dependability, and so forth. The impact of early employment on later employment prospects for youth is also somewhat equivocal. Walther (1976), for example, found that employment experience by itself does not improve the employment prospects of youth. In opposition to these findings, others have demonstrated that a positive relationship does exist between youth employment and adult employment (Stevenson, 1978; Stephenson, 1979). Of course, these findings need not contradict one another entirely. It may be that employers perceive workers with early employment experience as more likely to possess desired job-related skills regardless of whether or not they acquired such skills as young workers.

Youth employment and delinquency. Theories of delinquency have made conflicting claims for and against the employment of youth. Both control theories (Hirschi, 1969) and strain theories (Cloward and Ohlin, 1960; Merton, 1968) have provided support for the idea that employment acts as a deterrent to increased involvement with crime and delinquency. For control theorists the deterrence is tied to the fact that employment binds youth more closely to conventional activities. Similarly, strain theorists argue that employment enhances conformity to socially acceptable attitudes and behaviors by reducing strains that push young people into delinquent activities. In particular, employment provides youth with the socially acceptable means to acquisition of legitimate goals, such as possessions, prestige, achievement, and so forth.

The relationship between work and delinquency surely seems to be more complicated than these theories would suggest. Evidence exists to indicate that working is associated with a higher incidence of some delinquent behaviors among young people (Hirschi, 1969). In particular, working youth may be more likely to engage in status offenses. Part of exposure to the adult world encountered in the workplace may include experimentation with or adoption of behaviors proscribed to youth but acceptable for adults. Thus, working youth may display, for example, higher rates of smoking, alcohol use, and sexual activity than nonworking youth. Moreover, employment may increase the opportunity for young workers to engage in some kinds of delinquent or criminal activities. Ruggiero, Greenberger, and Steinberg (1982) found that 60 percent of the young workers they studied had committed a theft or some other "improper" act such as going to work while intoxicated. In part, the findings of higher alcohol and drug use among working youth may be due to the fact that employment provides youth with the income needed to purchase these substances (Borus, 1984). Although the benefits of employment may ultimately outweigh the costs, it is clear that employment is not a panacea for the problems confronting young people. Although it may solve some problems for youth, it inevitably poses new challenges for them.

Unemployment among youth

Regardless of the eventual outcome of the debate about the advantages or disadvantages to youth of employment, many young people in the United States and other Western industrialized countries either want to work or must work for one reason or another. From their point of view (Nuttal et al., 1977) and from the point of view of researchers and policymakers concerned about them, not being able to find work is a serious problem.

Although unemployment has generally been higher for young workers than older workers, statistics indicate that the rates of unemployment among young people in the United States and elsewhere rose sharply in the 1970s and 1980s (Hahn, 1979). This dramatic increase in unemployment created speculation that the circumstances of young workers had shifted, so that large numbers of youth could no longer be expected to make the transitions from school to work without assistance (Taggart, 1981).

Current estimates are that about half of all persons counted as unemployed by the U.S. government are between the ages of 16 and 24. Teenage workers (16 to 19) represent about one fourth of those currently unemployed. These unemployed youth are concentrated in minority groups and low-income households. Joblessness among low-income and minority youth has exceeded 40 percent in the years following the recessions in the 1970s (Hahn, 1979). Overall, unemployment among youth still stands at about 20 percent, despite the effect of the "recovery" in the United States.

These statistics actually underestimate the problem because these figures do not include the large numbers of young workers who would like to be working but have become "discouraged," have stopped looking for work, and are no longer counted among the unemployed. Bowers (1982) and others have demonstrated that young workers – especially those belonging to minority groups, females, and those from low-income sectors – are likely to become discouraged and quit searching for work.

Social impacts on youth. Much of the recent interest in the plight of young unemployed workers comes from concern about the social costs of high rates of unemployment. This includes, but goes beyond, the costs due to lost productive capacity resulting from underutilization of young workers. In addition to this foregone contribution from young workers, there are other costs associated with providing income maintenance and other welfare services to unemployed youth (Bresnick, 1983). Moreover, unemployment has been associated with higher rates of criminal and/or delinquent activity (Phillips, Votey, and Maxwell, 1972; Ehrlich, 1973; Greenberg, 1977). The urban riots among young people in the 1960s have been attributed by some observers, in large part, to high unemployment (Glaser, 1978; Boone, 1982) among this group. Thus, calculation of unemployment "costs" have included consideration of large-scale social unrest resulting in extensive damage to persons and property.

Personal "costs" of unemployment. Research on the psychosocial costs of unemployment indicates that unemployment is associated with the loss of self-respect (Smith, 1977; Turtle, 1978), an increased sense of helplessness, and a loss of competence (Barrington, 1976; Smith, 1977; Casson, 1979; Hartley, 1980). Other signs of psychological distress associated with unemployment include anxiety (Tseng, 1972; Jahoda, 1979; Brewer, 1980), anger and depression (Jahoda, 1979), unhappiness and despair (Barrington, 1976), and alienation (Rapoport and Rapoport, 1975; Brewer, 1980; Hartley, 1980; Rapoport, 1981).

Besides these mental health consequences, Becker and Hills (1980) have found evidence of a "scarring effect" on unemployed youth. That is, youth who experience unemployment are likely to experience additional bouts of unemployment. In addition, Bowers (1982) identified a clear association between the extent of past joblessness and the likelihood of subsequent unemployment.

Despite ambivalence and disagreement about the consequences of employment and unemployment for youth, a number of policy initiatives and action programs have been developed in recent years to aid young people entering the labor market. In the next section we present a conceptual scheme to classify these action programs. We will then consider specific examples of each approach, emphasizing the issues of collaborative action-research that emerge in each case.

Intervention strategies for youth employment: an organizing framework

The range of intervention options developed to deal with youth employment issues can be classified in terms of the main thrust or aim of the intervention. The policies and programs developed to intercede for youth can be categorized along the following lines:

1. Interventions aimed at changing the distribution of positions available to youth;
2. Interventions aimed at changing the distribution of youth available to fill positions in the social structure; and
3. Interventions designed to alter the allocation rules or matching process to produce a different "fit" between the existing distributions.

These goals are not mutually exclusive and particular interventions or programs have more than one aim. Nevertheless, most programs focus primarily on one of these approaches.

Changing the distribution of positions

By and large, intervention strategies that have focused on changing the distribution of positions in the social structure have relied on various "job creation" schemes. Where there are too few jobs available to youth, one strategy has been to develop or create additional positions. The most typical interventions in this category are governmental job programs designed to put young people to work. Job development schemes have generally provided incentives to employers to make jobs available to youth. Ideally, subsidies to these employers are intended to create new positions in various firms. But often such subsidies simply increase the likelihood that existing jobs will go to young people. Of course, such schemes are exceedingly vulnerable to the changes in political climate and public interest in providing direct employment opportunities to youth. Jobs created or developed by such schemes are routinely done away with by changing political administrations. The variable size and scope of recent job programs in the United States, such as Comprehensive Education and Training Act (CETA) jobs, demonstrate this sort of instability. Thus, job creation schemes in the United States have not usually been created with the notion that they would provide individuals with long-term employment. To the extent that work experience is useful to young people and for the duration of the time they receive support, such schemes do serve a purpose.

Altering the distribution of youth available for jobs

These intervention strategies are directed not at changing the social structure but at changing young people in some way. Programs may include basic or remedial education as well as vocational education courses and, in some cases, higher education. This strategy includes the full range of "employability development and training" programs. The major rationale for such interventions is to shift the distribution of young workers by changing the frequency of particular skills or other attributes. Such programs are plagued by the difficulty inherent in making accurate forecasts about the distribution of positions available to youth, thus, placing limits on the ability of education and training programs to prepare youth adequately for entry into the labor market. These difficulties will probably continue given existing conditions of high turnover in the structure of the labor market.

Altering allocation rules and facilitating matching

The main goal of this group of interventions is to facilitate the "match" between the distribution of youth and existing positions. These programs help youth iden-

Table 3.1. *Interventions with youth*

Intervention Strategy	Policy/Program Initiatives
To change the distribution of positions available to youth	Job creation schemes Job development
To change the distribution of youth available to fill positions in the social structure	Basic and vocational education employability development and training programs
To change the allocation rules or the process of matching the distribution of people to positions	Affirmative action/quota systems Job search assistance

tify, locate, and secure appropriate employment. Such programs may teach young people allocation principles and provide information about employer decision-making regarding hiring. These programs frequently provide "job search" assistance of a variety of different kinds.

Another kind of intervention within this category seeks to alter allocation practices that provide youth with unequal access to positions in the job structure. Policies and programs like affirmative action and various quota systems have sought to change the fit between the distribution of positions and people by reworking allocation guidelines and producing a different match than would otherwise be made.

Table 3.1 summarizes these intervention strategies and program initiatives. In the pages that follow, a particular program falling within each of the three categories will be selected for more detailed discussion of the role of action-research. We have not only chosen specific projects to reflect these various policy alternatives and themes, we have also chosen projects that reflect different problems or issues in the conduct of collaborative action-research. Issues such as the conflict between local and national perspectives, the problems of program implementation, and questions about the degree to which research can guide program action are all raised.

In reviewing these programs we observed that many of the broader themes in the field of youth employment that we described earlier emerge again in specific contexts. For example, some of the apparent ambivalence about the meaning and importance of youth employment takes specific form in the implementation of some of the program initiatives we will describe.

The first two programs we discuss will be considered only briefly, and we will highlight only a single issue in the collaborative action-research process. But the third project, which we think nicely illustrates the collaborative potential of action-research, will be considered in more detail.

Changing the distribution of jobs: the Youth Entitlement Demonstration

We suggested earlier that a major strategy for coping with youth unemployment involves intervention efforts aimed at changing the distribution of positions or jobs available to youth. The Youth Entitlement Demonstration, mandated by Congress in the Youth Employment and Demonstration Act of 1977, is a clear example. This project was undertaken collaboratively between the federal government employees under the authority of the Comprehensive Education and Training Act and the Manpower Demonstration Research Corporation (MDRC), a nonprofit publicly supported corporation formed to develop, manage, and evaluate large-scale innovative social programs.

The Youth Entitlement Demonstration was designed to establish a guarantee, or "entitlement," to a job for any youth who met eligibility criteria for economically disadvantaged youth. Approximately 37,000 low-income youth between the ages of 16 and 19 were enrolled in programs in seventeen competitively selected communities across the country. The program guaranteed them a part-time job during the school year and a full-time job during the summer months on the condition that they remain in, or return to, a secondary school or obtain an equivalent educational experience. Thus, in effect, youths in the program were guaranteed a job if they maintained acceptable academic performance standards and remained in school until graduation.

The role of the Manpower Demonstration Research Corporation was to oversee the research on this program, focusing on impact, implementation, and cost. Their relationship to the local programs that carried out the Youth Entitlement Demonstration appears to be somewhat less collaborative and interactive than other examples we shall examine, but this may in part be because of the size of the project. We will focus on issues of implementation in this example because they reveal both unexpected implementation problems that can arise in such projects, and some of the cultural and ideological conflicts that can underlie implementation difficulties. These problems of implementation have been effectively summarized by Ball and his colleagues (1979).

Issues of implementation

As we suggested, the congressional act and program design for the Youth Entitlement Demonstration require that jobs be available to youth once they have enrolled in the program and demonstrated their eligibility and willingness to continue in school. But CETA program staff found themselves confronted with problems in making jobs accessible to youth. For example, in some cases jobs identified in the private sector required participants to commute out of the central city to suburban areas. Even where bus transportation was available, travel time decreased the attractiveness of the jobs for participants. Geography was even a larger problem in rural areas, where connecting jobs and youth often involved elaborate arrangements.

Another major problem encountered in the development of the program was coordination between CETA program personnel and the school systems. The school became a major agency involved in the program because information about youth school attendance and performance was an important requirement of the program, and some flexibility in class schedules to allow youth to work was expected. School systems, Ball and his colleagues (1979) argue, are large, bureaucratic, slow-moving, and reluctant to adapt to new programs. Program personnel, on the other hand, needed rapid changes because of the time-limited nature of the project. Many delays and disruptions in the project were due to the lack of historical relationship and the organizational dissimilarity between the program and the school systems.

Perhaps the most interesting dilemmas associated with the Youth Entitlement Demonstration had to do with local program implementers' views about the nature of the program itself, particularly its entitlement aspects. Ball et al. (1979) note that in many program sites the attitude toward the idea of a job "guarantee" affected the way in which advertising was conducted for the program and youths were recruited. For example, in Baltimore program developers wanted to avoid any emphasis on the guarantee feature. "A job guarantee means these kids are owed," one prime sponsor spokesman commented. "We didn't want to project this image. . . . We didn't want to sell this thing as a giveaway" (Ball et al., 1979:39). Thus, the program implementers' own values and ideologies became critical elements in the implementation process. Discomfort with the underlying assumptions of the program may have led to an unwillingness to recruit vigorously for it.

A related issue had to do with how the program was viewed in generally conservative rural areas. Ball and his colleagues suggest that a general rural mistrust of government "handouts" and the idea that entitlement was a program for "shiftless misfits" may have inhibited potential participants from applying to the program.

This brief account of the Youth Entitlement Demonstration suggests that program implementation may be thought of as interconnections or transactions between a variety of individuals, groups, and organizations. Effective implementation requires not only an understanding of the practical barriers to weaving the web, but an awareness of value and ideological conflicts that may make cooperation less likely.

Changing the distribution of youth: "work maturity" programs

Programs that attempt to change the distribution of youth available for employment are usually called employment development programs. The rationale behind employment development projects for youth is the idea of "work maturity." Interviews with large numbers of employers revealed that employers of youth complained of a variety of problems including: absenteeism, tardiness, lack of interest in the job, tendency to ignore instructions, and unwillingness to learn. Employers wanted productivity, dependability, good work habits, and high motivation among youth.

Johnson (1981) suggests that willingness and ability to accommodate workplace expectations about rules and authority, standards of work, cooperation, adaptability, and learning, are the cornerstones of the idea of work maturity. The various programs designed to improve the chances of youth in the labor market are aimed at these goals. There is some indication, however (Mangum and Seninger, 1978), that what it takes for youth to win the respect of and acceptance by employers may be just the opposite of what is required to win peer respect. Thus, there may be underlying tensions in the goals of employability development projects and the goals of participants.

A typical employee development project is the "Jobs for Delaware's Graduates" (JDG program), which is an effort to identify high school youth who are likely to have difficulty making the transition from school to full-time employment. Aspects of the program include participation in career clubs and one-to-one counseling to improve youth attitudes and motivation (Mangum, 1982).

Two major modes of training exist in employability development. One relies heavily on work experience to improve "work maturity." The other focuses heavily on classroom-based training and skill development. It is to decisions about which of these alternative program approaches is most appropriate and how local and national perspectives may affect those judgments that we now turn.

Local versus national research perspectives

In an insightful analysis of the dilemmas created by local involvement in action-research, Taggart (1981) raises questions about the value of local evaluations in judging program effectiveness. He argues that local program developers and researchers may make very different judgments because of their local involvement.

A convincing case in point has to do with the relative value of work experience versus classroom-based training. Taggart notes that long-term national follow-up data clearly indicate that work experience has no impact on postprogram earnings, whereas classroom training can substantially increase earnings relative to controls. But at the point when participants leave each kind of program, a much higher percentage of work-experience clients as opposed to classroom-training participants are employed. It is not until approximately half a year after termination from the program that gains for classroom trainees exceed those of work-experience participants. If local researchers and program developers judge the effectiveness of programs primarily by termination results, they would be led to prefer work-experience programs. Longer-term national research makes it clear, however, that initial advantages for work experience are reversed in approximately one year.

There are other important considerations for local program developers and researchers that may also affect decisions to implement work-experience rather than classroom-based programs. Taggart (1981) observes that, from a local budgetary perspective, the work-experience approach seems to make more sense. Classroom training is initially more expensive. Furthermore, from the local program developer's point of view, classroom trainees do not produce a social product, whereas work-experience participants are gainfully employed and may return resources to the local jurisdiction and tax base. Thus, from the local program developer's point of view, there are strong incentives to prefer work experience–based programs.

It seems clear that action-research that relies solely on local perceptions may seem more "valid" because the experiences of local actors seem more vivid and immediate. But local perceptions are, by definition, limited, certainly geographically and also temporally. Getting closer to a program does not always mean seeing it better.

Matching youth and jobs: collaborative research in job search programs

We suggested earlier that the third intervention option available in reducing unemployment is to improve the match between available jobs and youth by aiding youth in the job search process. Some results from the national longitudinal study of the high school class of 1972 indicate that long-term unemployment among youth may be prevented by immediate movement into the labor force (Griffin, Kallenberg, and Alexander, 1981). Wegmann (1983) suggests that these findings argue for approaches that facilitate immediate entry into the labor market at the conclusion of schooling, particularly for those youth most likely to experience lengthy unemployment. The overall goal of such efforts is to intensify the job search effort, to reduce search time, and to prevent discouragement and long-term unemployment.

Typically, programs designed to assist youth in job search have four major components (Wegmann, 1983). First, they teach youthful job searchers that direct approach to potential employers is much more effective than searching through published lists or classified ads. Second, these programs provide a script or a guide to aid participants as they contact employers, seeking interviews and openings. Third, these programs typically provide material support for job searchers including typing, answering services, photocopying, and desk space. Fourth, and perhaps most important, these programs provide youth a place to check in every morning where they will find sympathetic support and guidance of counselors and other participants.

Let us now turn to a specific example of such an action-research based intervention program. We will describe the program itself and the action-research process associated with it in some detail because it provides a useful example of the cyclical, iterative, collaborative, and self-correcting problem of action-research (Ketterer, Price, and Politser, 1980). As we follow the story of a particular program, "Job Track," we will see a process of problem identification, diagnosis, intervention, evaluation, and rediagnosis unfold. The self-correcting nature of the action-research process reveals itself, in this example. Later we identify principles that appear to underlie the self-correction in the process.

Job Track I: the initial action research cycle

Job Track is a job search assistance program developed and designed jointly by Olympus Research Centers (ORC), a nonprofit research organization, and the Mayor's Youth Services Office of San Francisco Job Service (Johnson, 1982a). The staff running the program were employees of the San Francisco Job Service trained by Olympus Research Center staff. The program design consisted of two days of classroom instruction in job search techniques followed by three days of supervised job search activity in the course of a single week. Job Track had many of the generic features of job search assistance programs described above. An initial evaluation of the program, which occurred during 1980, revealed that participants obtained work in 50 percent less time than a comparison group. Furthermore, the job-finding rate was higher for Job Track participants, approximately 66 percent as opposed to 53 percent for a comparison group. Furthermore, Wegmann (1983) suggests that the program probably helped some individuals find employment who would have been discouraged and given up had they been left to their own devices.

Despite the apparent success of Job Track, Johnson (1982a) reports that Job Track was not recommended for replication because it was not able to recruit enough youth to make the program cost-effective. New participants averaged less than six a week. This meant that the cost per "obtained employment" was six hundred seventy-two dollars, far exceeding the cost of placing youth in jobs through the usual public employment service.

Although Olympus Research Center had been responsible for the design and research of Job Track in this initial phase, their role shifted in the second period to a diagnosis of the reasons for low levels of recruitment and to redesigning and revitalizing the program based on their diagnosis.

Development of Job Track II: diagnosis, implementation and evaluation

Olympus Research Center staff set about doing a diagnosis of the problems associated with underutilization. They used two basic strategies. First, they interviewed a number of program operators to identify explanations for the lack of program use. Although a number of informal theories emerged from these interviews, a much more practical strategy involved examining those programs that *did not* appear to have problems of utilization. Johnson (1982b) reports at least five major characteristics of programs that were effective in recruiting. First, they had developed a wide word-of-mouth base, and former participants often referred clients to such programs. Second, they were well publicized and had developed high levels of community awareness and a strong constituency. Third, they provided services to a mix of clients rather than to a narrowly defined target group. Fourth, programs with an attractive environment and physical facilities seemed to be more heavily used. And, finally, consistent attention to all processes of recruitment, including maintaining contact with the referral staff, was an important aspect of the recruitment process.

Armed with this information, Olympus Research Center staff redesigned the program. A publicity program was designed to draw participants from the wider youth population in the community. The Job Track staff, with ORC's assistance, developed a marketing plan to publicize the program. The Private Industry Council of San Francisco donated funds to support this public-information campaign, and bus poster displays with information tear-off slips were installed in 275 municipal buses, particularly in lines running in depressed areas that are widely used by young people. Johnson (1982b) reports, "almost immediately, the phones at Job Track began to ring incessantly" (p. 93). An evaluation of the revitalized program indicated that Job Track had increased enrollment fivefold without a loss in effectiveness (Wegmann, 1983).

Although Job Track II appears to be a success story in action-research, the important question is not so much the fact of the success, but how the process actually worked. A revealing discussion of the collaborative research process in Job Track is offered by Johnson (1982b).

Making it work: three principles

Johnson (1982b) tells us a great deal about the nature of the collaborative relationship between the San Francisco Employment Development Department (EDD) and the Olympus Research Center in making it work. She suggests that three principles *shared by both groups* informed most decisions in developing Job Track II. The first of these was an agreement to make Job Track II *replicable* by regular employment service staff rather than by highly trained or especially enthusiastic trainers. This included, among other things, developing a program that could operate within the agency's own support system with a defensible cost and an approach that was consistent with the reporting requirements of federal and state agencies. Johnson says "the curriculum, the ambience, the leaders and the leader training processes would have to be relatively free of charismatic inspirers, exotic innovations, costly gimmicks, or hard-sell approaches" (p. 77).

The second principle shared again by EDD and ORC staff was, in Johnson's words, *a search for balance* on nearly every dimension of the program. For example, the development of an expense allowance for job-searching youth could be threatened by either of two extremes. An expense allowance that is too large tends to corrupt the intent of the program and draw youth into searching for more stipends rather than a job. On the other hand, an expense account that is too little does not facilitate job hunting. Similarly, the length of the program had to be balanced between the need to impart information and the need to retain youth in the program. Still another area of balance had to do with the composition of groups. They were not designed to consist solely of disadvantaged minority youth nor of a "creamed" youth population whose chances of getting a job were far better than those of others. Similar principles of balance and consistency were reflected in the recruiting strategies developed.

Johnson suggests that the third guiding principle that governed their work related to the *decision-making process* and the partnership between ORC and EDD. She describes two alternative models for decision making that can be used in such circumstances. One model implies prior planning by a higher authority, which is then carried out by an operating staff. This is essentially a "top down, two-stage model." In contrast, a second model is one in which implementation is iterative and people at all levels in the planning and delivering process react and modify original program intentions in a learning-by-doing process. This "bottom up" strategy involves considerable improvisation. Johnson (1982) notes, "in the last analysis, it was ORC's responsibility to design and evaluate the . . . demonstration. However, each institution – ORC and EDD – continuously made adaptations to accommodate the requirements and constraints of the other partner" (p. 81). Johnson observes that this iterative process is an excellent model for program development and produces no problems in evaluating *processes*. However, it produces serious problems for the evaluation of *outcome*.

Most outcome evaluations view programs in static terms, as finished products, blobs, which are then opened, dissected, and examined. The dynamic changes in the nature and content of Job Track during and since the . . . demonstration period presented ORC with a moving target, or, to retain the metaphor, the blob was constantly changing shape, a factor which is sometimes obscured by aggregates and averages. In ORC's view, a more comprehensive picture of a program is attained by both types of analysis – process and outcomes. [Johnson, 1982b:82]

Johnson's interpretation goes a considerable distance in explaining the successful improvement of Job Track II. The principles were *shared* principles in the collaboration, not merely held or implemented by one party. Second, they emphasized "robustness" of program content and style. The expectation that the program must be designed so that it could be delivered by the average staff member rules out certain possible program elements, but at the same time guarantees that those that are ultimately included can actually be carried out. The concern with balance and realism, although seemingly obvious, reflects an inherent tension in many of the day-to-day implementation decisions that must be made by researchers and program personnel. Too much or too little of a program element can be equally handicapping, and these apparently innocuous details are crucial for both successful research and implementation. Finally, the idea of an iterative collaboration and mutual adjustment between researchers and service delivery personnel allows alterations in the program in small incremental steps, enhancing the process of program improvement but making it unclear when outcome evaluation is appropriate. Perhaps this suggests that after an initial period of incremental improvement, programs will indeed need to experience a period of "refreezing" (Lewin, 1946, 1947) before a rigorous outcome valuation can be conducted.

Conclusions

We have now examined three major approaches to developing programs for youth employment. One focuses on altering the distribution of available jobs; a second, on altering the distribution of available youth; and a third, on improving the match between the two.

Points of tension in collaborative research

Reflecting on these three collaborative research approaches to youth employment, we can discern a number of interesting points of tension in the collaborative research process. We do not believe that these points of tension are easily resolved or removed from collaborative research. Indeed, these tensions may be both characteristic of and the greatest strength of the collaborative research process. Let us examine each of these tensions briefly in turn and then ask about the implications for future research in the field of youth employment.

Value and ideological differences. At a number of points in examining our case histories, we noted implicit, and sometimes explicit, differences in values and ideological orientations between researchers and practitioners or between policymakers and implementers. Because action and change may often challenge closely held beliefs and values, collaborative action-research will often uncover value differences previously unacknowledged or latent. The discovery of these differences is in itself instructive, and an understanding of them is crucial to the effective implementation of an action program.

Differences in time perspective. At several points in our discussion, we noted that different actors in the collaborative research process had strikingly different time perspectives on the action being undertaken. Schools and program developers experienced different time perspectives and different pressures for change and consequently could not always collaborate effectively. Local program developers with a limited time perspective on the measurement of outcome data drew quite different conclusions than national researchers with the luxury of longitudinal studies and large samples. It is likely that researchers and practitioners will also have different time perspectives, with practitioners feeling the urgency for rapid action and researchers needing time for reflection. This tension, too, we expect, frequently manifests itself in collaborative action and research projects.

Broad policy perspectives versus local knowledge. Frequently, researchers and policymakers will seek broad generalizations about the effect of policies and program initiatives, whereas local practitioners will be sensitive to local values and geographical constraints or opportunities. Parochialism is, of course, both a strength and a weakness. Local knowledge is frequently critical for local implementation, but may have little to do with broad generalizations and national policies.

Replicability versus "model" programs. Frequently, "model programs" are developed by researchers in special circumstances with a substantial research budget and support staff. These model programs often have features that are extremely difficult to duplicate in local circumstances where there are fewer resources. There will exist, we expect, a tension between what is ideal and what is repeatable and possible to accomplish at the local level. Collaborative action-research may begin with an ideal program, but researchers will be wise to settle for one that is repeatable and, in that sense, robust.

Program balance and trade-offs. Most programs are multifaceted and require decisions about the extent to which each aspect will be emphasized. As we've seen in a number of examples thus far, programs that survive and accomplish their goals appear to be programs that are willing to strike a balance on each crucial program dimension, and between action and research.

Mutual adaptation: planners versus doers. Our examples also offer ample evidence that "top down" strategies in collaborative research have less to recommend them than do attempts at mutual adaptation between researchers and program providers. The compromises that are reached in such circumstances may not be ideal from either group's point of view, but appear to be the best course to accomplishing anything at all.

Measuring process versus measuring outcome. Collaborative research, if it retains its features of iteration, adaptation, and nearly constant change, places real limits on the possibility of measuring outcome. Holding a program in a steady state long enough to measure outcome effectively is no easy task, and yet the demand for evidence of effective outcome remains. This tension, like the others we have mentioned, appears inherent in the collaborative research process and may require some movement back and forth between "process" and "outcome" approaches to evaluation.

Collaborative research and youth employment programs in the future

Each of the tensions is quite real and reflects the conflict inherent in the collaborative research process. These tensions are the product of conflicting demands of action and contemplation and between efforts at implementation and attempts at analysis. Despite these tensions, or perhaps because of them, we think action-research has much to offer the youth employment field. It is from the creative use of the tensions produced by collaborative research that insight and knowledge can be gained to facilitate the transitions from school to work for youth. Realistic confrontation of the conflicts identified through the action-research process holds the key to the development of innovative and effective intervention strategies.

Specifically, we think action-research can aid the youth employment field in several important ways. First, of course, it can continue to point to areas of conflict and disagreement at various junctures in the processes of research, policy formation, planning, program development, implementation, and evaluation. For example, action-research can provide opportunities to promote and sustain dialogue between federal policy objectives and local needs and capacities. Elmore (1983) has raised doubts about our ability to use policy as a tool for problem solving. He challenges the traditional notion of a "top down" approach to the solution of social problems generally advocated in the implementation of social policy. He suggests instead that the solution is to "tip social problem solving on its head" using "backward mapping" to deal with problems from the ground up. But both "top down" and "bottom up" strategies have advantages and disadvantages. We think the real potential for action-research is to foster a dialectic and interactive approach to problem solving by facilitating interaction between knowledgeable collaborators with both kinds of viewpoints. In the long run, such an interaction may produce a better-integrated, more stable framework for dealing with youth employment issues.

Until that happens, though, action-research can assist those concerned with youth employment issues in other ways. Collaborative action-research can anchor programs securely in local settings. D'Aunno and Price (1984) have described the importance of collaborative research in meeting the needs of communities. Programs that are designed to meet the needs of such communities and prove to be effective will have greater flexibility in dealing with the vagaries and volatility of federal policy. Collaboration at the local level may provide effective interventions with some insulation from shifting national priorities and initiatives.

Levin (1983) has pointed to the importance of increased participation in solving employment problems by various sectors of the community. This is especially true for the employment field where effective intervention is contingent on voluntary participation and cooperation among groups with seemingly divergent interests. He argues that economic stability, employment opportunity, and the quality of work life depend on greater participation by all members of the community. Action-research may play a key role in what appears to be a major trend in the United States in the area of youth employment and elsewhere. The trend is in fostering new kinds of partnerships among a wide range of organizations and groups. When it comes to developing and working within the framework of such collaborative arrangements, action-researchers have an advantage of long experience in making such partnerships productive ones.

In sum, then, the action-research perspective could be useful to the youth employment field in a number of ways. By facilitating dialogue and interaction among various parties to the youth employment field, there is the possibility for more stable planning and preparation. Action-research can add flexibility and security to programs providing services to youth and can lead the way in developing new and effective partnerships among various organizations and groups. Finally, we would hope that action-research could provide insight into some of the enduring research questions about the meaning and impact of work on youth.

References

Ball, J., Diaz, W., Leiman, J., Mandel, S., and McNutt, K. *The youth entitlement demonstration: An interim report on program implementation.* New York: Manpower Demonstration Research Corporation, April 1979.

Barrington, J. Young and unemployed. *Australian Journal of Social Issues,* 1976, 2, 27–33.

Barton, P. E., and Fraser, B. S. *Between two worlds: Youth transition from school to work.* Washington, D.C.: National Manpower Institute, 1978.

Becker, B., and Hills, S. M. Teenage unemployment: Some evidence of the long run effects on wages. *Journal of Human Resources*, Summer 1980, 354–72.

Behn, W. H., Carnoy, M., Carter, M. H., Crain, J. C., and Levin, H. M. School is bad, work is worse. *School Review*, 1974, *83*, 49–68.

Boone, C. W. Creating jobs for minority youth. *Social Policy*, 1982, *12*(4), 29–36.

Borus, M. E. *Youth and the labor market*. Kalamazoo, Mich.: The W. E. Upjohn Institute for Employment Research, 1984.

Bowers, N. Tracking youth joblessness: Persistent or fleeting? *Monthly Labor Review*, February 1982, *105*(2).

Bresnick, D. Youth jobs. *Social Policy*, 1983, *14*(2), 37–40.

Brewer, G. *Out of work, out of sight*. Melbourne: Brotherhood of St. Laurence, 1980.

Bucknam, R. B. The impact of EBCE: An evaluator's viewpoint. *Career Education Journal*, 1976, *33*(3), 32–37.

Casson, M. *Youth unemployment*. London: Macmillan, 1979.

Cloward, R. A., and Ohlin, L. E. *Opportunity*. New York: Macmillan, 1960.

Conrad, D., and Hedin, D. Learning and earning citizenship through participation. *National Council for the Social Studies Bulletin*, 1977, *52*, 48–73.

D'Aunno, T., and Price, R. H. The context and objectives of community research. In K. Heller, R. H. Price, S. Reinharz, S. Riger, and A. Wandersman (Eds.), *Psychology and community change*. Homewood, Ill.: Dorsey Press, 1984.

Ehrlich, I. Participation in illegitimate activities: A theoretical and empirical investigation. *Journal of Political Economy*, May/June 1973, *1*, 521–65.

Elmore, R. F. Social policymaking as strategic intervention. In E. Seidman (Ed.), *Handbook of social intervention*. Beverly Hills, Calif.: Sage, 1983, pp. 212–36.

Erikson, E. H. *Identity: Youth and crisis*. New York: Norton, 1968.

Glaser, D. Economic and sociocultural variables affecting rates of youth unemployment, delinquency and crime. Paper presented to the conference on youth unemployment: Its measurement and meaning, Department of Labor, Washington, D.C., 1978.

Greenberg, D. F. The dynamics of oscillating punishment. *Journal of Criminal Law and Criminology*, December 1977, *68*, 643–51.

Greenberger, E., and Steinberg, L. D. The workplace as a context for the socialization of youth. *Journal of Youth and Adolescence*, 1981, *10*, 185–210.

Griffin, L., Kallenberg, A., and Alexander, K. Determinants of early labor market entry and attainment: A study of labor market segmentation. *Sociology of Education*, 1981, *54*, 206–21.

Hahn, A. B. Taking stock of YEDPA: The federal youth employment initiatives, Part 1. *Youth and Society*, 1979, *11*, 237–61.

Hamilton, S. F., and Crouter, A. C. Work and growth: A review of research on the impact of work experience on adolescent development. *Journal of Youth and Adolescence*, 1980, *9*, 323–38.

Hartley, J. Psychological approaches to unemployment. *Bulletin of the British Psychological Society*, 1980, *33*, 412–14.

Hedin, D., and Conrad, D. Study proves hypotheses – and more. *Synergist*, 1980, 8–14.

Hirschi, T. *Causes of delinquency*. Berkeley: University of California Press, 1969.

Jahoda, M. The impact of unemployment in the 1930's and 1970's. *The Bulletin of the British Psychological Society*, 1979, *32*, 309–14.

Johnson, J. N. *Work orientation project: A report of progress and current status*. San Francisco: Far West Laboratory for Educational Research and Development, March 31, 1981.

Johnson, M. *The state of the art in job search training*. Salt Lake City: Olympus Research Centers, 1982a.

Johnson, M. *Getting youth on the job track*. Salt Lake City: Olympus Research Centers, 1982b.

Keniston, K. *Youth and dissent: The rise of the new opposition*. New York: Harcourt Brace Jovanovich, 1971.

Ketterer, R. F., Price, R. H., and Politser, P. E. The action research paradigm. In R. H. Price and P. E. Politser (Eds.), *Evaluation and action in the social environment*. New York: Academic Press, 1980.

Levin, H. M. The workplace: Employment and business interventions. In E. Seidman (Ed.), *Handbook of social intervention*. Beverly Hills, Calif.: Sage, 1983.

Lewin, K. Action research and minority problems. *Journal of Social Issues*, 1946, *2*(4), 34–46.

Lewin, K. Frontiers in group dynamics: Part 2, Social planning and action research. *Human Relations*, 1947, *1*, 143–53.

Mangum, G. L. *The processes of employability development: Theory, practice and curricula*. Salt Lake City: Olympus Publishing Co., June 1982.

Mangum, G. L., and Seninger, S. F. *Coming of age in the ghetto*. Baltimore: Johns Hopkins University Press, 1978.

Merton, R. K. *Social structure and social theory*. New York: Free Press, 1968.

Nuttal, E. V., Nuttal, R. L., Polit, D., and Clark, K. Assessing adolescent mental health needs: The views of consumers, providers and others. *Adolescence*, 1977, *12*, 277–85.

Panel on Youth of the President's Advisory Committee. *Youth: Transition to adulthood*. Chicago: University of Chicago Press, 1974.

Phillips, L., Votey, H. L., and Maxwell, D. Crime, youth and the labor market: An economic study. *Journal of Political Economy*, May/June 1972, *80*, 491–504.

Rapoport, R. Unemployment and the family. The Loch Memorial Lecture. London, The Family Welfare Association, 1981.

Rapoport, R., and Rapoport, R. N. *Leisure and the family life cycle*. Boston: Routledge & Kegan Paul, 1975.

Ruggiero, M., Greenberger, E., and Steinberg, L. D. (1982). Occupational deviance among adolescent workers. *Youth and Society*, 1982, *13*, 423–48.

Smith, P. *Unemployment: Its costs and casualties*. Sydney: Australian Council of Social Sciences, 1977.

Steinberg, L. D. Jumping off the work experience bandwagon. *Journal of Youth and Adolescence*, 1982, *11*, 183–206.

Steinberg, L. D., Greenberger, E., Garduque, L., and McAuliffe, S. High school students in the labor force: Some costs and benefits to schooling and learning. *Educational Evaluation and Policy Analysis*, 1982, *4*, 363–72.

Stephenson, S. P., Jr. From school to work: A transition with job search implications. *Youth and Society*, 1979, *11*, 114–32.

Stern, D. School based enterprise and the quality of work experience. *Youth and Society*, 1984, *15*(4), 401–27.

Stevenson, W. The relationship between early work experience and future employability. In A. V. Adams, G. L. Mangum, W. Stevenson, S. F. Donagey, and S. Mangum (Eds.), *The lingering crisis of youth unemployment*. Kalamazoo, Mich.: W. E. Upjohn Institute for Employment Research, 1978.

Taggart, R. *A fisherman's guide: An assessment of training and remediation strategies*. Kalamazoo, Mich.: W. E. Upjohn Institute for Employment Research, 1981.

Task Force 1974. *The adolescent, other citizens, and their high schools*. New York: McGraw-Hill, 1975.

Tseng, M. S. Self-perception and employability: A vocational rehabilitation problem. *Journal of Counseling Psychology*, 1972, *19*, 314–17.

Turtle, A. Life – not in it: A psychological comparison of employed and unemployed Sydney youth. *Vocational Guidance Bulletin*, 1978, *4*.

Tyler, R. W. (Ed.). *From youth to constructive adult life: The role of the public school.* Berkeley, Calif.: McCutchan, 1978.

Viney, L. L. Psychological reactions of young people to unemployment. *Youth and Society,* 1983, *14*(4), 457–74.

Walther, R. H. *Analysis and synthesis of DOL experience in youth transition to work programs.* Springfield, Va: National Technical Information Service, 1976.

Wegmann, R. G. Group job search training for youth. *Youth and Society,* March 1983, *14*(3), 320–34.

Wirtz, W. *The boundless resource: A prospectus for an education/work policy.* Washington, D.C.: New Republic Book Co., 1975.

Work-Education Consortium. *Work and service experience of youth.* Washington, D.C.: National Manpower Institute, 1978.

Work-Education Consortium. *Work in America: Report of a special task force to the Secretary of Health, Education and Welfare.* Washington, D.C.: U.S. Government Printing Office, 1973.

Leslie T. Wilkins

The law, both criminal and civil, impacts upon young persons, as with adults, at a very large number of levels. Juveniles have rights of protection from abuse that may extend beyond the similar protections for older persons, or they may have reduced rights by reason of the fact that they are assumed not to be capable of making certain determinations for themselves. Much of civil law and tort does not apply to young persons because until they attain a certain age (determined by the law), they are assumed to be unable to make contracts, but they are often regarded as covered by contractual assumptions in respect of the behavior of others. The law and the concept of justice for young persons is as extensive as law, if not life, itself, and most of the social agencies of government are involved to greater or lesser degrees in specific ways with young persons. Other chapters will deal with the concerns of agencies as they relate to welfare, education, health, and other matters. In this chapter we will confine our attention to the field more usually considered under the heading of "juvenile delinquency," though it is recognized that all aspects of law, welfare, age and sex, race, and many other differentiations interact with legal constructs. That is to say, the concept of justice discussed in this chapter is not that of "social justice" but rather that of "criminal justice."

Juvenile delinquency

From the commencement of recorded history, adult populations have expressed strong disapproval of certain behaviors among their youth. The variety of terms by which these disapproved behaviors have been known over the several thousands of years may give the impression of considerable change in both the behavior of young persons and adult public attitudes. However, any reader of early writings may well be impressed more by similarities than differences in the frictions in youth's interactions with older generations. Certainly, as social life became more complex and regulated, so adult populations sought to use new tech-

73

niques of social administration to address "youth problems" in the light of contemporary beliefs.

Dominant religions, myths, and magics of the time and place had considerable impact upon how the "problem" was perceived and consequently on the action prescribed. One has only to take a superficial look at the philosophical literature currently fashionable in the field of jurisprudence to see that this remains true at the present time. The recent revival among philosophers and jurists of the idea of retribution and the doctrines of Kant and Hegel provides a current example. There may be trends in the historical and philosophical development, but at any time there will be those who adhere to viewpoints of the past, so that trends tend to be obscured by persisting conflicts.

Research and values

Few would claim that social research is "value free"; the belief systems, value choices, and personal philosophical perspectives of those concerned in research are usually recognized as of importance. In addition to difficulties in the interpretation of research findings that result from value orientation, the layman's information as to the contributions of social research are influenced by another factor. Once a piece of research is completed, the scientist wishes to tell the significant things that were done and to put across his conclusions in a convincing manner. The sidetracks, misunderstandings, confusions, and the hand of chance that will have played a large part in the work will be glossed over or omitted. Discussions of politics, interpersonal tensions, and managerial difficulties are generally regarded as superfluous by editors of journals concerned with the furtherance of science and technology. Thus, research students tend to get the impression that research is a straightforward matter of developing hypotheses from theory and putting selected hypotheses to the test. It is not this way in the best-run laboratories; it is not that way in social action-research in any of the applied areas; and it has certainly not been the prevailing mode in the juvenile justice field.

Those whose concerns relate to child health, education, or employment avoid some of the difficulties experienced by research workers, social reformers, and administrators in the field of "behavior disorders" of the young. In these former areas there appears to be less confusion or doubt as to the ends to be sought, and the specifications of problems tend to be characterized by more clear-cut philosophy and methods. Although the concept of health may be debated and the content of educational courses give occasion for disagreement, there is a greater degree of consensus about the ends that are responsibly advocated, and also the value of the scientific approach is more generally accepted with less troublesome intrusion of intractable ethical issues.

Some historical notes on action-research in juvenile justice

It seems safe to assert that in times of conflict of basic beliefs about human nature and the universe, there also proliferate conflicting attitudes toward children in general and toward deviant youth in particular. Confused and conflicting views still proliferate.

In the period since the concept "action-research" was developed, it seems that investment in action-research projects in the juvenile justice area has followed much the same pattern as in other action-research fields. Analysis of published materials indicates that action-research projects reached a peak in 1972, though many of these projects were doubtless commenced some time previously. An earlier trend showed a monotonic increase from pre–World War II to the early 1960s, followed by a period of little growth until 1965, when there began a rapid rise until the peak of 1972. Since 1972 the rate of publication has dropped dramatically (Romig, 1978).

Most of the significant points that can be made in a short chapter are perhaps best made by a few selected "case studies." Before we turn to this approach, however, it may be helpful if some general overview is attempted. Any such classification is essentially simplistic, and this attempt is made with apprehension. Nonetheless, others have previously proposed systems of classification for other purposes (e.g., Rutter and Giller, 1983), and it may be reasonable to put forward one that relates to our present analysis. From this perspective it may be suggested that there are three periods of development, or perhaps we might say "fashions," in the recent history of the field. The initial period we illustrate by the underpinning philosophy and operational techniques of the Cambridge-Sommerville project. This may be seen as the period of the popularity of action based on theories of individual personality. The Cambridge-Sommerville project was begun in 1935 and the casework terminated in 1945. Data from follow-up studies continued to be published until 1981. There are, of course, many articles and references during this period (see, for example, McCord, 1981).

The second phase began in the mid-1960s and continued to the early 1970s. This emphasized sociological or socioeconomic theories. Around this time there began a trend away from the use of micro models (based on reductionist theories) toward the use of macro models (based on structural theories). A concurrent trend undermined the research element in action-research: Much support was diverted to "demonstration projects." The action side of action-research was based on the conviction that certain procedures that were either more effective or cheaper (or both) could be put into effect without radical change and possibly with political benefits. The research element in this period, as is illustrated later in our case material, tended to show that beliefs as to effectiveness did not stand up well to rigorous testing. It is doubtful that the abandonment of the research element was wholly or even mainly related to these kinds of findings; rather, action-orientated humanitarians believed *so* strongly that the treatment they advocated was desirable, that the clients needed what was being offered, and that there were no better alternatives, that they should put it into effect if at all possible. There was little or no regard to research in any formal sense. Despite the absence of research or the disjunction between the logic of the system and its activities, some of the projects doubtless did have beneficial outcomes. Perhaps the most noteworthy case under this category is the Vera Institute bail project. In such instances, demonstration that it could be done was all that was necessary. Adding costs for research merely reduced the effort that could be given to advocacy and publicity.

The third period, which is continuing at the present time, emphasized "rights" and "justice." It is characterized as having a "systemic" orientation, taking account of the fact that different subsystems are involved in "doing justice" – the individual, the police, the courts, and so on. Focus shifted from exclusive concern with the individual who was seen as needing "treatment" or reeducation and turned to the larger systems and to decision makers who function in relation to "referrals" to which the individual is subject within the total system. Questions of fairness, equity, human rights, individual dignity, social justice, and, for the individual, "just deserts," began to gain currency and to conflict with the medical model, which required identification of an ailment and the provision of an appropriate remedy, or the social model, which required fundamental structural change.

This latter change, although probably not caused by, was certainly fueled by the outcome of much research that had failed to show any certain success in the prior methods of dealing with offenders. Perhaps the first publication to put forward this perspective in popular terms was the report of the Society of Friends Service Committee, published in 1971 by Hill and Wang under the title *Struggle for Justice*. That same year also saw the first meeting of the very influential Committee on Incarceration under the chairmanship of Charles Goodell. The publication *Doing Justice* (von Hirsch, 1976) is the report of the deliberations of this committee.

These studies faced questions of value choice directly and separately from the idea of the scientific method. The test of moral action, it was suggested, is not how the individual may react in the future to the prescribed "treatment," but how appropriate is the disposition to his past behavior. As the report of the Committee on Incarceration states: "We conclude that . . . the sentence should depend on the seriousness of the defendent's crime . . . on what he *did* (their italics) rather than on what the sentencer expects he will do if treated in a certain fashion" (p. xvii).

This change is, of course, of fundamental significance in two ways: (1) it does not discuss the efficiency of the disposition so much as its morality; and hence (2) it takes as its reference the past ("what he did"). Previously the criteria had related to "what he might do." In brief, the one justifies action in terms of information about the past, whereas the other claims legitimacy in terms of expected beneficial outcomes. The consequences of this change are still taking effect. In particular, the shift from the construct of juvenile delinquency to the concept of "juvenile justice" is being implemented at various levels. The committees set up by the American Bar Association to consider issues in juvenile justice provide an example of the impact of this philosophical change upon professional opinion and subsequently on official action.

Though we have referred to three periods, the three themes have been present throughout. The incompatibility of a forward reference with a backward reference does not seem to have been realized or accepted, with the result that we find various attempts at the blending or mixing of different basic constructs, which some would characterize as little more than muddle. However, throughout the first period the moral justification in our society was focused on the individual – did he "get better," "stay out of trouble," or "learn to cope constructively." Though this was the kind of moral justification for the action, it does not follow that beliefs about "causes" of delinquency were always taken to be within the personal sphere of individual growth.

In the mid-1960s a confluence of social factors – some of which were expressed in the "student riots," such as those at the University of California at Berkeley – raised questions as to the validity of the assumption that an individual's "maladjustment" was the problem. As one of the slogans put it at that time, "Do not adjust your mind, it's society that is distorted." (Odd, perhaps, that many who advocated this approach sought to modify their minds by the use of various hallucinogens.) Among the "structural" theories were many that were, to a greater or lesser degree, related to Marxian arguments, as is reflected, for example, in the articles that made up much of the content of the Berkeley-based journal *Issues in Criminology*. Some workers in this tradition were much involved with youth demonstrations in the late 1960s (cf. Platt, 1969).

There were other theories, which may have been inspired by an interest in cybernetics and information theory, such as the theory of "deviance amplification." Deviance amplification theory (often considered to have arisen in England) drew attention to the ways in which the processes of social control could be responsible for escalation of the very problems they were supposed to alleviate. There are common elements in labeling theory and the theory of deviance amplification that make it difficult to assign priority. However, a statement of a form of deviance amplification theory that owed much to cybernetics and information theory was separately developed (Wilkins, 1964).

In the discussion that follows, consideration is focused on projects having an essential and concurrent research element. Many other projects that may have had a research-based idea or certain research elements are excluded if research was not an integral part of the design. In this definition, not only the two words but also the hyphen in "action-research" are given meaning. This excludes, for example, the most notable, early projects of the Vera Institute.

Within this limited interpretation of the scope of action-research, in our first period the preponderance of research designs were based on the unit of the individual. Later there was a move toward the larger unit of the family. But in this phase, whether it was the family or a larger unit of reference, it was the client or the person(s)-in-need who were the focus of study and remedial action. Slowly a change began to take place in the perception of an appropriate or acceptable focus. As we noted, issues of "rights" and fairness became more dominant. Studies began to appear that looked at the decisions made by those in authority – the "transmission end" was seen as at least equally as important, if not more important, than the "receiving end" – and theories of social and organizational change were developed.

Prevailing explanations of unacceptable behaviors tend to divide into two, often characterized as "bad" or "mad." If the individual's behavior is traced to the latter category, the argument moves to suggest the need for pity or "help" rather than blame or "punishment," furthermore, the case is then seen as within the ambit of science and technology, and especially of medicine.

If the first category is invoked, the individual "deserves" punishment, indeed – it has been argued, as had Marx, Kant and Hegel previously – has a basic *right* to appropriate punishment. The combination of rehabilitative, welfare, or similarly based activities with that of punishment (though widely advocated) is logically unacceptable. It is probably true that where treatment is involuntary, not only will it be highly likely to fail, but such forced treatment may indeed *constitute* a form of punishment. Volumes have been written on the problem of the justification of punishment, and the question will not be resolved here; a passing note of awareness is all that can be given.

The concept of "juvenile"

The term "juvenile" used in the title of this chapter is more a legal term of art than descriptive of an individual. It often refers to the age of majority, which varies from country to country, from time to time, and even by class of action (e.g., drinking, driving, military service, property ownership, etc.). A juvenile is, by definition, not an adult – that is to say, is not a *complete person*. Thus there is a similarity between an adult who is "not responsible" (or, in some countries' law, of "diminished responsibility") and a person who is not responsible by reason of age. We do not propose to explore this jungle of tangled concepts and constructs, but it is important to recognize the significance of this shadowy analogy.

Perhaps the fact that certain of the helping professions (particularly social work and psychiatry) have been much involved in action-research in the juvenile justice field owes something to the potential similarities of concepts regarding young persons who, by reason of age, are deemed to be not "fully responsible" and concepts regarding adults who for other reasons are regarded as not "fully responsible" for their actions. The latter was a recognized domain for these professions and the former a reasonable extension to that valid domain.

More than half a century ago humanitarian reformers began to point out that whatever was being done did not do that which society required of it – it neither reformed the individual nor reduced the incidence of reprehensible behavior. So, why not try something new? To support the new kinds of action, a different theoretical base seemed to be required, and in large measure (particularly for juveniles) this was found in the existing and currently fashionable techniques used in the treatment of persons who were seen as "mentally disturbed." Perhaps to accommodate this viewpoint, juvenile delinquency was linked with a larger category of child and youth problems under the term "behavioral disorders."

Using the framework described above – of three stages of development with different conceptual orientations dominant in each – we can consider selected examples of action-research in each stage.

It seems appropriate not only to note one or two of the action-research projects in each stage but also to provide an example of cases that are on the borderline of the definition of action-research. We shall attempt to draw inferences from the projects described. These lessons from the work will relate to either the area of application or the methodology of the study, or both.

Some cases of social action-research in juvenile justice

The roots of action-research in juvenile justice

The history of social action-research in this area has not developed in a straightforward linear fashion. One reason is that action-research projects requiring many stages of formulation, investigation, and feedback often take form in various stages, sometimes with a patchwork of diverse funding and successive episodes of start-up and termination. One project, for example, was begun in 1935, continued through 1945, was resurrected again in 1980 with a further follow-up, and terminated in 1981, with the results published a year later (McCord, 1981). Many action-research projects defy classification by date because they are ongoing.

Counseling in community settings

Cambridge-Sommerville. This project represents the preventative orientation to individuals at risk – a concept linked to research in child development fields. In this it represents one of the most important, extensive, and powerful action-research projects.

The Cambridge-Sommerville project (1939–80) predates the widespread use of the term "action-research," but it fits the definition more closely than many more recent projects that lay claim to be within this category. The project followed as closely as possible the requirements of the experimental method. It involved an "experimental" and a "control" group of vulnerable young males – the former being given the best treatment indicated at the time (and still widely believed in), the latter being subject only to the collection of comparable data. As McCord (1981) reports, the study was designed with the hope that it would reduce or prevent delinquency. The program terminated in 1945.

Over a period of years, each youth in the experimental/treatment group received two visits a month from a trained social worker as well as both educational support and psychological counseling; furthermore, if it was assessed that there were family problems, these were not ignored. The staff, in addition to the ten social workers, included tutors, a shop instructor, consulting psychiatrists, medical doctors. There is no doubt as to the level of effort and money invested in the project. Short-term follow-up provided rather inconclusive results. By 1942, however, 253 matched pairs of boys remained in the program. Thirty years later a follow-up of these 506 participants was carried out. This study reported that "as measured by objective criteria, men in the treatment group were more likely than men in the control group to have had undesirable outcomes" (McCord, 1981). Furthermore, the report continues, "since the differential between treatment and control groups was greatest among those subsets who had been given more treatment, the relationship appears to be causal" (p. 405).

Various explanations were suggested for this unexpected and disturbing result. Among those proposed, only one obtained much support. This noted that, "The Cambridge-Sommerville Youth Study seems to have raised the expectations of its clients without providing the means for increasing satisfactions. The resulting disillusionment seems to have contributed to the probability of having an undesirable outcome" (McCord, 1981). But suppose that "means for increasing satisfactions" had been provided? Would this not have increased the dependence of the clients? How can it be assumed that the outcomes would then have been reversed?

Something went wrong, but there is little to indicate what it was unless it was a "treatment effect."

It is interesting and challenging to note not only that there was a strong positive correlation between delinquent behavior and the amount of intervention, but that among the treated group fewer (half) graduated from college, although the groups were matched on IQ. Other social indicators that were assessed also showed relationships with treatments that were in the ''wrong'' direction.

Inferences from Cambridge-Sommerville example. The results of long-term follow-up studies can always be challenged on the grounds that the situation has changed since they were completed and hence the results cannot apply today. It is then thought plausible to go on to claim that if repeated under present-day conditions, the outcomes would be quite different. But, of course, such studies cannot, by their very nature, be repeated at the present time. The time required for the results to be revealed means that any results can be questioned on grounds of being out-of-date. By this argument all long-term follow-up studies are a waste of money. This may be a valid administrative position, but it is not likely to commend itself to social scientists. It is not so much the particular point in time when whatever is done is in fact done that is of importance, but *what precisely it is* that is done. If the same procedures were to be followed again, there is little hope for different results beyond the range of chance. If, and only if, differences between current practice and the practice at the time can be stated clearly and these descriptions supported by collateral evidence to the effect that the revised methods operate in a different manner, may it be reasonable to have some doubts as to the results of long-term follow-up studies.

Whatever the reason for the negative results of the very considerable and well-intentioned activity and expenditure in the Cambridge-Sommerville project, it would be reasonable to think that similar methods tried today would have similar results. Of course, there is no evidence that *different* methods based on similar or even on different premises would work any better, but it may be possible to develop sound arguments in favor of trying methods of intervention that are based on *different* sets of assumptions. If the assumptions are changed, then there will be consequential changes in the methods used. If any similar attempts are proposed with a view to effecting reductions in delinquency, it would appear necessary to examine both assumptions and methods with the strong presumption that unless both are significantly different from those of the Cambridge-Sommerville project, the outcomes will be similar.

The Massachusetts Alternative. We have said that much action-research in the juvenile justice field derives from the work and thinking of those concerned with ''mentally disturbed'' adults. This was particularly true in the earlier projects, but a substantial proportion of later projects also came from this orientation. In particular, it was the newer methods for dealing with mental patients that were seen as adaptable to behavior problems of the young. Among the specific techniques that originated in mental hospitals was one that was consciously invoked by those concerned with juvenile justice, namely Maxwell Jones's approach termed the "therapeutic community."

A project that the originators acknowledge owes its philosophical and practical basis to the therapeutic community model became known as the "Massachusetts Alternative." This project is an exemplar of the entanglement of serendipity (even pure chance) and the planned. Even muddle may have played a positive role.

Between 1970 and 1972, Massachusetts closed down most of its youth correction institutions. Jerome Miller is quoted by Patterson (1984) as saying that "the whole punitive system has no meaning for violent kids other than to make them more violent." Miller was appointed as Director of Youth Services in 1970. In a broadcast interview, Miller suggested that the Alternative developed in his thinking when one of his directives was misinterpreted by institution staff. He further stated that in his view this "misunderstanding" was a feature of a campaign to discredit his management of the Authority. However, the "misinterpretation" resulted in institutionalized youth being discharged within less than three months after reception – hardly time for any treatment regimen to take effect. Miller says that he did not intend this outcome, which only came to his notice at a later date because of a complaint. Surprised that only one complaint arose from a large number of discharges (and hence potential complaints), he intensified his measures of reform, in the course of which he invoked the assistance of Maxwell Jones, who had opened the wards of his hospital in south London and developed the concepts of therapeutic community.

The Massachusetts Alternative is an excellent example of action linked with research and illustrates some of the basic features of this kind of enterprise, but it does not fit precisely with the strict definition of action-research because the policy changes and the research that assessed the results of those changes were not integrated into a single project. If the constraint of contemporary and combined involvement of "doers" and "thinkers" is required to qualify for inclusion in the record of action-research, there are few pure cases in juvenile justice. However, Maxwell Jones had conducted a form of action-research at his original therapeutic community base that served to clarify concepts and methods (cf. Rapoport, 1959). The evaluation of these reforms and other alternative methods of dealing with young offenders in the community, rather than in incarceration, was carried out later by Lloyd Ohlin (1984). Ohlin summarized his findings: "Juvenile arrest rates are down, court appearances are down – faster than the fall in the juvenile population." However, it was not demonstrated that the desirable situation was directly due to the changes in the ways young persons were behaving or in ways of dealing with young offenders.

Inferences from the Massachusetts Alternative example. The idea of closing the juvenile institutions in Massachusetts was, according to oral evidence from the central actor, influenced by the chance (or mischance) that a memorandum was incorrectly read. This illustrates that "muddle" is often a factor in the background of innovation. Muddle is not the same as serendipity, but it may occasionally graduate to serendipity, through the scientific approach. I recall being told of an experiment that led to a breakthrough in semiconductor development that makes the distinction briefly and pointedly. The scientist had some material "cooking." If left switched on overnight, it would overheat and burn out the apparatus or worse. However, he wanted it to reach the highest temperature possible, and when he left to attend a meeting in the afternoon, he told the lab assistant to switch off before he went home. Soon after the scientist left, so did the lab assistant. The apparatus was not switched off. The next morning the scientist found the apparatus burned out – fortunately no more than a burnout – but rather a mess. There were two kinds of responses when the scientist found out what had happened: (1) Send for the cleaners to clear up the mess and discharge the lab assistant. (2) Take a careful look at what has happened in the overcooking. (The former is said to characterize the "administrative approach" and the latter the "scientific approach.") The result of this "accident" was that it revealed the need to obtain higher temperatures, but next time, under adequate control.

But we cannot give credit to the "accident" for the idea; serendipity involved both the event and the kind of attitude, which did not react adversely and precipitately to an unforeseen and even unwelcome event. It seems safe to say that extremely few of the memos that are are misread (intentionally or not) result in the production of a new idea. Perhaps the unexpected, unplanned, and untidy is all too unwelcome and therefore too frequently goes unexplored?

Highfields. An early example of a "true" action-research design – a comparison at Highfields of two modes of dealing with juveniles who had been "dealt with" by the courts – shared the fate of many of the early projects (Weeks, 1958). Those concerned with the implementation of social policy quickly began to depart from the constraints of the research design, thus prejudicing the validity of any inferences that might be drawn from the outcomes. It may be useful to take a little time to summarize this example.

The objective of the project was to ascertain whether a new, cheaper, and more relaxed treatment for youthful offenders in a center known as Highfields resulted in more or fewer recidivists than the existing treatment in the "reformatory" known as Annandale. It was proposed to have matched groups disposed by the courts to each institution so that the groups were precisely similar in all respects except in the treatment methods of the institutions. The attempt to match did not succeed.

Apart from the technical difficulty of putting matching designs into practice in any procedures involving human subjects, Weeks (1958) reports, "there is some evidence that the juvenile court judges did, in fact, send boys to Highfields because they thought them better prospects for successful treatment" (p. 69).

The research workers at Highfields were also hampered by incomplete information. Nonetheless they seem to have tended to make their inferences on the basis of the information available. It seems to be thought that the amount and qualities of information required for administrative or even court decisions need not meet the same criteria of acceptability as information for research. Judges who are unable to obtain information on one factor may be more prepared to assume the equivalence of a proxy item of information than should research workers, for whom it is unacceptable to assume that any one item of data, if not available, may be substituted by another: Substitution requires proof of adequate similarity.

In this specific case, the age of onset of criminality was known in respect of more of the Highfields boys than of those who went to Annandale. Now it is known that one of the strongest correlates of recidivism is the age of first recognized "crime." It is also known from research published as early as 1955 that the presence or absence of information is itself a factor of considerable significance in assessments of the probability of reconviction (Mannheim and Wilkins, 1955). Those individuals who have more data recorded about them are different from individuals whose records are not so complete – perhaps the latter have better strategies for escaping the attention of those in authority. If this is so, we might expect verbal therapies to have less of an impact upon them.

Inferences from the Highfields example. The research workers were convinced that matched allocation to the two different available treatment modalities was ethically justified because both were, initially and in the absence of the information they hoped to obtain, equally valuable, indicated dispositions. The juvenile court judges, however, believed that they could improve upon the matching by subjective selection. Perhaps they were right in two ways: They could do it, and their action was justified. The latter kind of argument cannot be tested by research methods, but it seemed to the research workers in this project that it might be salvaged if the former argument were thoroughly examined. The question at issue was whether the better recidivism rate observed at Highfields was due to the selection of "better" (i.e. more suitable) cases by the courts.

Before we consider whether correction might be made for the possible selection bias that upset the matching design of this action-research, it is essential to point out a serious omission in the logic of both the Massachusetts Alternative project and that at Highfields. Let it be assumed that Highfields and Massachusetts both show a considerable benefit from the alternative or "experimental" treatments. May we then, as the authors do, infer that the Highfields and the Massachusetts Alternative treatments possess essential elements of therapy (or social work) that are proving effective in "reaching" the young offenders? It is not that simple.

It too often occurs that research designers take note only of the elements that they modify and assume that any significant outcomes must be due to the controlled variables. This is, of course, a fallacy but one that is all too often unrecognized throughout policy-research.

A feature common in both the Highfields and Massachusetts projects was that the alternative/experimental procedures were cheaper than those with which they were compared. It is cheaper to keep youth incarcerated for shorter periods than for longer; the cost of security is a major factor in institutional care and it is cheaper to operate institutions at lower levels of security. The outcome of the alternative forms of treatment may be better just because it is cheaper. That is to say, the cheaper methods involve less intervention by authorities in the lives of the clients. It cannot be accepted without proof that the more the intended "good" that is done, the better is the result. Perhaps the more that is done, the more the autonomy of the individual is threatened?

In the justice area it is not feasible to test the likely rate of spontaneous recovery or the benefits of "benign neglect": If an individual is found guilty, then "something has to be done about it," and "something" is always done. It cannot be said, as a popular text suggests, that *Nothing Works,* because "nothing" has not been tried. (The title of the book is, of course, not intended to be interpreted this way.) The essential consequences of being "found out" will, it may be assumed, be somewhat traumatic in themselves for the inexperienced offender. Thus, as a necessary consequence of the offending act "becoming known" to the authorities, some concomitant events of considerable significance for the actor simultaneously occur. Hence a base rate for inaction, as in other fields, cannot be established here.

One conclusion emerges fairly clearly from both projects and is usually well demonstrated in any social action program. In Massachusetts it was proved that considerably shorter periods of removal from the community were possible without the system breaking down and without trouble developing for the administration. It demonstrated the political feasibility of a modified procedure, hence it might be argued that because it was "known" that the new methods were superior (in any event, they were cheaper), they ought to be put into effect. In the Highfields project it was demonstrated that, provided no constraints were placed upon the dispositions of the judiciary, a proportion of offenders would be selected for the "preferable" (cheaper) treatment. In both cases, ways of saving money were derived from action-research procedures.

As we noted when we discussed our general classification, some ten years after Highfields the "practical approach" gained currency. Those involved with social welfare policy came to believe that the benefits from implementing action-research owed nothing to the research element. Thus the research element was soon to be omitted and we saw the development of what came to be called "demonstration projects." Both Highfields and the Massachusetts Alternative were most successful as "demonstration projects" – they showed that the new modalities could be put into effect.

Highfields: The research salvage operation. Projects such as Highfields are costly. Despite the value of the demonstration element, the research workers who were involved with its origin wished to remedy the problem of bias in the selection of cases so that it might be possible to say something about the new treatment modality other than that it was possible to do it. Attention was turned to ways whereby the damage to the matching design (caused by the subjective determinations of some allocations) might be repaired. The fact that funds were available for a "salvage" project after completion of the original study indicates that the research element was, *at that time,* given considerable importance.

It is in the design of the research of a follow-on project intended to resolve the problem of bias (due to noncompliance with the original plan) that Highfields was a child of its age. Statistical methods that enabled the "prediction of recidivism" (assessments of the prior probabilities of risk) had been developing for some thirty years, particularly in relation to the determination of parole. Accordingly, it was hoped to examine and to attach a probability to the "better risks" who had apparently been selected by the judges to go to the Highfields center. It might then be possible to say whether the greater level of success was more than expected in view of the better "material" available to the new treatment. Even this did not work out too well, largely because of problems with the availability of information regarding the offenders placed in the two treatments. No analysis, no matter how sophisticated, can substitute for missing data.

The influence of Highfields. Highfields, despite its defects, was most influential. Discussion of the problems of proof of the superiority of the new, desirable methods was particularly important. For a while some popularity attended action-research that was intended to compare programs designed to deal with individuals whose behavior had, through the medium of its social institutions, attracted the intervention of agents of the community. It seems to have been particularly appealing to invent and try out systems that were "better" (i.e., more humanitarian or more powerful?) in bringing about change in behavior and that, at the same time, were cheaper to administer. Such programs were, of course, always open to criticism in that they did nothing until there had developed a situation it would have been most desirable to prevent. On the other hand, some argued that any measures that impinge on the autonomy of an individual require a justification – the individual must have "done something" in order to be liable for the treatment. The medical model did not fit too well because persons with behavioral disorders, particularly those about whom the community felt most apprehensive, did not often voluntarily seek treatment. Thus the new treatments could be tried only on "captive audiences" or persons who had "qualified."

Treatment, many thought, came too late because of the protection afforded by the law. Furthermore, the law that provided the necessary qualifications for therapeutic intervention had other undesirable consequences, many of which were subsumed under the term "labeling."

The dual problems of treatment being "too late" and "contamination" of treatment with undesirable consequences involving the legal status of those treated led to suggestions that attention might be given to young persons whose circumstances placed them in vulnerable groups, and hence who, as individuals, were seen as *potential delinquents* or as likely to have multiple social problems in later life. The early action-research project that fits this class of endeavor is that already mentioned, namely, the Cambridge-Sommerville project, which unfortunately did not prove of individual help to those who received its ministrations, nor, by the same token, did society benefit, except in terms of increase in knowledge in the field. Despite the evidence, the call for action to prevent delinquency – some intervention before an individual has caused harm – remained, and is still strong today. There are, however, serious problems of human rights in dealing with a person in terms of probability of future acts as the grounds for selection for intervention, unless the individual voluntarily seeks such intervention. Some, partly for these reasons, sought to develop approaches that did not specifically involve the individual but sought to change the environment. It was thought that the problems of intervention in relation to "human dignity" and "personal autonomy" can be avoided if the intervention is beneficial to all recipients, whether potentially delinquent or not. Much of the action-research that was developed through the commission of the Kennedy administration would claim this justification. Among the most important were a collection of projects under the general heading of Mobilization for Youth.

Often the clients (the potential delinquents) were not directly identified, such as with those projects that sought to enhance the resources of the educational system (e.g., the "Teacher Resources" program refers to "teachers," although the intent was, wholly or mainly, to reduce youth problems, that is to say, criminal activity). The connection was made through the theoretical concept of frustration, or specifically of "blocked opportunities" put forward by Cloward and Ohlin (1960), both of whom were involved directly in the work of the President's Commission. Although this theory (i.e., that of blocked opportunities) could not be claimed to be a "scientific law," it certainly became a kind of "case law."

Numerous ways were tried (mainly by the selection of a title or format) whereby it was hoped to avoid ethical problems of treating the juveniles as though they were already delinquent. In addition to the Teacher Resources project, many other major projects of action-research were based on the blocked-opportunity theory. The Chicago Area project identified a geographic region for a variety of support for ongoing social projects, and the Mobilization for Youth focused on providing legitimate economic opportunities for those who were more likely to find illegitimate opportunities for gain. These series of projects amounted almost to a "movement" with the purpose of bringing about changes in attitude, feelings, ideals, and respect for the law, and of creating a style of life in the poorer districts that was "more acceptable." It is difficult to assess the outcome of this investment. The larger, the more diffuse, the projects, the less convincing was any analysis that claimed direct results. Smaller projects, although within the general framework of the theory, did seem to have beneficial results, some of which may have been quite robust and long-lasting (see Wilkins and Gottfredson, 1969).

The Probation Subsidy project – a critical path. The three projects we have dealt with in some detail above (Massachusetts Alternative, Highfields, and Cambridge-Sommerville) provide useful indications of some important points regarding the definition, origins, and political involvement of social action-research in the juvenile justice field. However, the research reports do not provide much information as to how they came to be put into effect in the first place. We have identified only one project for which a detailed "trace" of events is possible. This study makes it clear that a sound project is not sufficient of itself to ensure that it is put into operation; the environment of the proposal plays an important role, and much of this is under the control of neither the research nor the social action persons interested in getting it started.

The California Probation Subsidy project passed through two phases – at the end of the first it seemed lost forever, but later it was restarted and the environment was such that it enabled it to survive and to be successful. The project involved all age groups, but it was mainly concerned with youth: It required legislation to put it into effect because it involved the budgetary process.

The history of the California Probation Subsidy project has been traced from its first phase to implementation in legislation. For few, if any, other projects is there such a detailed record, but insofar as information is available, this study seems to embody many features that commonly characterize action-research.

The Probation Subsidy took several years to reach implementation. Prior to its being legislated there had been some incentive for courts to give imprisonment rather than probation, since the costs of probation were on local taxes whereas imprisonment was on state taxes. Adjustment of this bias would provide an incentive to use probation. The financial provisions were straightforward but sophisticated and technical.

To describe the development and history in words would be tedious and too complex, and we must refer the reader to our diagram, which represents a form of "critical path." (Critical path analysis is, of course, not intended as a method of historical analysis but rather should serve the planning function.) Usually diagrams supplement the text, but in this case our text will supplement the basic presentation, which must be diagrammatic. The analytical diagram is presented in Figure 4.1.

Convergence counts. It is interesting that the first chain of events stopped without trace. The only event that may remotely provide some explanation for this discontinuity may be the coincidence of the Giants game. This fact reduced publicity to zero. Public support was not obtained because the public were, in the main, uninformed. The passing of the bill, on the other hand, was associated with a diverse array of supporting interests. Both the number and the diversity were, probably, of importance.

In practical situations it is unusual for any "pure type" model to tell the whole story. There are dynamic elements and interests and there are "static" elements and interests. External interests may have more influence than it is possible to identify after the event. Those within the organization may "feel" that there is pressure for change from external organizations, although they themselves are unaware that they also exert pressures, and there is always the chance event and natural inertia.

The range of action-research

It is not possible, nor perhaps is it necessary, to describe more projects in even the limited detail of the four selected case studies presented above. The range of topics covered by action-research is as wide as the field itself.

Earlier, when discussing the historical background, we noted that although there was evidence of changing fashions in both the subject matter and the methods, all features seemed to be present at all times in greater or lesser degree. Some evidence for this claim may now be given and some further inferences

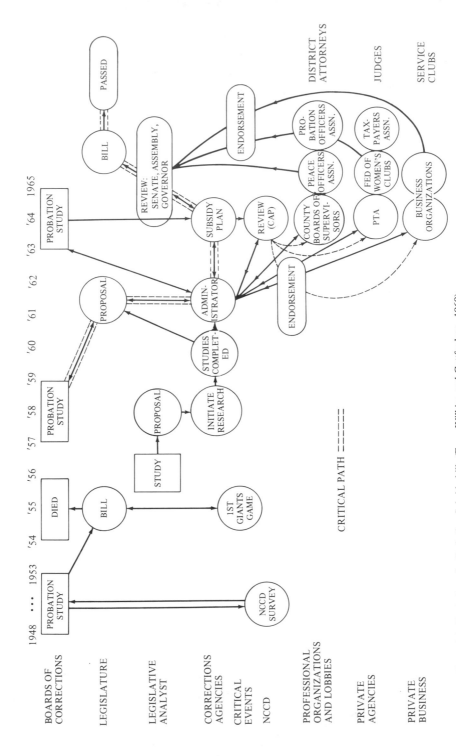

Figure 4.1. Evolution of a Probation Subsidy bill. (From Wilkins and Gottfredson, 1969)

drawn from a more general viewpoint on the field over the recent decade or two.

A risk with case history methods of presentation is that the general nature of problems may be lost sight of in the specific. To offset this tendency, we must stress that the specific points, especially those taken up in our notes on inferences from each project, had elements common to many projects in the juvenile justice field. Furthermore, though the case materials may have indicated the depth, it seems essential also to illustrate the issues in action-research generally. By this means we hope to show the relevance of issues of the 1960s and 1970s both for problems in the juvenile justice field and for action-research in the late 1980s.

In the mid-1960s, in the United States and in some other countries, there developed a general public concern for the behavior of young persons. Though not a new phenomenon, it was notable in that at that time the climate was not unfavorable to the employment of the scientific method. Hence, many persons whose reputations rested upon their research rather than on their political or other status became involved in situations of power where they could make their opinions felt. There were appeals to "facts," statistical data, and research measurement of problems. But the facts were depressing.

The President's Commission (1967), for example, stated: "Many Americans take comfort in the view that crime is the vice of a handful of people. This view is inaccurate. In the United States today, one boy in six is referred to the juvenile court."

Since that observation there has been no reduction in the rate of juvenile crime. In England in the mid-1980s and to a lesser degree in the United States, the misbehavior of young people has again become a matter of "public concern" – or perhaps we might dare to say, a useful political theme. There is one large difference in the expression of contemporary "concern" and that of the mid-1960s. Then (but not now) there was a call for research, as the previously quoted report continued: "A small fraction of 1 percent of the criminal justice system's total budget is spent on research. This figure could be multiplied many times without approaching the 3 percent industry spends on research, much less the 15 percent the Defense Department spends."

The boom in action-research, demonstration projects, and technological transfer, which, as we noted, reached a peak in 1972, doubtless owes much to the work of the commission and statements of the kind quoted above. It seems useful to refer to two studies that listed and classified some of the juvenile justice action-research and related projects. Romig (1978) sampled from a total of 829 studies that he was able to find in the English language literature and to learn about by writing to agencies. He classified this sample into kinds of "action" or "intervention." His classifications were:

1. Casework
2. Behavior modification

   3. Educational
   4. Vocational and work programs
   5. Group counseling
   6. Individual psychotherapy
   7. Family therapy
   8. Therapeutic camping
   9. "Ideal" (by which he seems to mean need-goal oriented)
  10. Diversion from justice system of various forms
  11. Juvenile probation
  12. Community residential programs
  13. Institutional
  14. The Massachusetts program (noted above)
  15. Parole

The reported outcomes of all the cases he abstracted under each of his categories make gloomy reading. Some seem to offer some hope of reduced recidivism, but there is no one category that promises unreserved success. There may be elements within one or two kinds of activity that might lead to more frequent satisfactory outcomes, but it is not easy to identify them.

Romig's classification does not indicate the types of problems addressed but rather relates to the methods of intervention employed. In 1968–69, with the purpose of assessing "payoff," another sample of federally funded action-research was carried out (Wilkins and Gottfredson, 1969).

Their sample provides a useful indication of the kinds of individual problems receiving attention at that time:

   1. Probation subsidy projects in California, Indiana, and other states (as case history above)
   2. Community-level institutions (Ohio)
   3. Group homes for boys and girls (Oregon)
   4. Youth Development Center (Philadelphia)
   5. Halfway houses (Michigan)
   6. Vocational rehabilitation projects (Tennessee)
   7. Furlough from penal institutions (federal)
   8. Work passes for institutionalized individuals (Michigan)
   9. Bail reform (including young persons) (Massachusetts)
  10. Police-community relations (Kansas)
  11. Probation mental hygiene unit (New York)
  12. State family court established (New York)
  13. Glue-sniffing project (Denver)
  14. Volunteer demonstration project (Boulder)

Some of the projects may better be classed as "demonstration" rather than "action-research." For example, the Vera Institute approach to bail reform had some appearance of being based on a predictive score, but the score was set up on "face validity" and, when later tested, did not correlate with the likelihood of "jumping bail." Nonetheless the work of the institute persuaded the courts to place far higher proportions on bail with "own recognisances" and the outcome was "satisfactory" – many would say commendable.

There is no need to list more – the scope, in terms of both topics and geography, is sufficiently evident from the above. It may surprise some to note how current and topical are some of the problems in this mid-1960s listing (e.g., glue-sniffing, police relations with youth, particularly minority groups, etc.).

In addition to the many hundreds of projects addressing more or less specific problems similar in type to those listed, there were general or packages of projects, such as Mobilization for Youth (as noted above) and others. Perhaps there was more social research activity at that time than at any time since.

The current position

As we move toward the mid-1980s the trend has again begun to swing back toward emphasis on the individual. There is now less demand for social research; indeed, political figures currently in power scorn social research and claim that all that is needed is to give the offending individuals a "short sharp shock" or for the courts to "get tough." The problems seem much the same, but research, it is suggested, has had its day: It was tried and, being associated with gentle approaches, has failed. A "moral panic" is generated by publicity about the mugging of old people, abuse of drugs, particularly among the younger juvenile age groups, and other dramatic materials. There is a demand for the identification of the potentially serious or violent offender and for his "incapacitation." The patterns of concern and political pronouncement are much the same in Britain as in the United States and some other "Western democracies." The guiding principle in the United States in late 1984 was that of "selective incapacitation," and the focus of attention was on the "career criminal." It should be noted, however, that in Britain today the problem of crime is not so likely to be simplified to the problem of the criminal. It is recognized that in addition to the actor, there is need to consider the "acted upon" (usually the victim), and also the environment and the type of offense. A reasonable proportion of research effort has been directed toward making crime more difficult. The Home Office Research and Planning Unit – the official government agency concerned with criminological research – has taken a strong lead in projects designed to reduce temptation and opportunities to commit crime (see, for example, Clarke, 1984). Despite this official concern with structural analysis, this approach remains generally unpopular; indeed, Dr. Clarke, the Director of Research of Home Office Research and Planning, who was identified with this approach to the reduction of crime, resigned in late 1984 to take an academic appointment in the United States.

Doubtless many theories owe much to thinking in other areas of scientific inquiry. The idea of symmetry in physics – of equal and opposite forces – has had considerable influence in social theory. The fact that the theory is now under revision in the field of physics will, in time, doubtless have an impact on the development of social theory. Doubtless there are fashions in scientific thought, but it is unsafe to conclude that fashion alone provides the explanation of the switches in the kinds of preferable models, though these forces are not well understood.

Disillusionment with treatment began to take effect in the mid-1960s. Despite this, there was a persistence of some to claim that an acceptable approach was to identify and work with "potential delinquents." Eventually it had to be admitted that it was unlikely that methods that had failed to make much impact upon the criminal careers of those who had been identified by "due process of law" would succeed with those identified by any other means. Moreover, the "other" means whereby delinquents or potential delinquents could be identified had proved inefficient and many also saw them as objectionable on moral grounds.

The second spinoff from disillusionment was a tendency to face up to the concept of punishment for crimes. By definition, crimes are officially punishable acts. But the acceptance of the idea of punishment was possible only if punishment was "just" – it was commensurate with the seriousness of the crime. Thus the "just deserts" school of thought made much of the concepts of individual rights and personal responsibility. In the juvenile field the emphasis on "rights" calls for detailed attention to the making available of appropriate information and representation for children. One lesson we have learned from the past action-research is that even the best of well-intentioned expert intervention on behalf of the juvenile can be counterproductive if it detracts from the empowerment of the individual to cope with his or her own stresses and challenges. The role of research in relation to the advocacy of children's rights is important, and it would seem that researchers involved in this area should take an active part in seeing that the uses of research do not become abuses. This calls for a greater degree of involvement than typical for purely academic research workers.

Action-research, at its peak of methodological sophistication, was well informed in systems theory. Commenting on one impact of this perspective, Wilkins and Gottfredson (1969) note that the location and definition of the problem and the situation in need of change

are seen as functions of the internal flow of information. Action is not imposed upon the system by an external agency; rather it arises from the internal tension of the system itself. Unlike "social engineering" the solutions are sought in relation to the definition of the problem as it emerges from the system. Under these circumstances the implementation of social action depends upon the extent to which correctly coded information about the problem and its solution reaches all decision points in the system.

The climate of social research

Social research, particularly research or action concerning acts classified as "crimes," cannot avoid association with politics, if not with politicians. As political preference has swung from "progressive" to "conservative," preferences also have changed from dynamic, change-oriented models, to models emphasizing the value of traditional forms and the desirability of stabilizing them. The most devoted social reformer must recognize that the man in the street makes demands for punishment for those seen as deserving it. Indeed, no act is defined as a crime unless it is believed that it is morally justified to administer punishment to those who commit it. In the sociopolitical environment it is important to see that it is reasonable to assume important similarities between the public demand for punishment for offenders, and the demand for any other public services. Public punishment has public costs. Public expenditures, on health and welfare and no less expenditure on means of punishment, require allocation rules. In this framework the demand for punishment is a demand function similar to any other recognized in economic theory (cf. Wilkins, 1984). Punishment is a "commodity" (a scarce social resource), the distribution of which is a task of the criminal justice machinery of government. Whereas the actual operation of the criminal justice system, as with any other public service, is subject to political and other value considerations, research has a role in providing accurate information and in contributing to concept formulation and the specification of problems that need attention.

The earlier phases of action-research reflected their environments, and the same is true today. Furthermore, the present phase and philosophy of action-research owes much to the earlier emphasis on systems theory. A perspective gradually has emerged that has turned research workers' attention away from the individual delinquent or potential delinquent (the actors) as the central elements of analysis, toward other factors in the total systemic situation, namely, the decision makers and the environment in which the criminal act took place. This has revealed a need for further analysis of the act itself.

The initial disillusionment was, perhaps, amplified when it came to be accepted that even had the medical analogue been successful and treated offenders responsive in that they reduced or ceased their criminal activity, the amount of crime in society would be only minimally reduced. Surveys of complaints of criminal activities (rather inappropriately called "victim surveys") showed that only a small proportion of crime was reported to the police and of that, only a small fraction was "cleared up." Thus, very few crimes (acts) could be traced to offenders (actors). If dealing with potential delinquents would not work, and the problem of crime was to be attended to, some elements in the situations other than the perpetrators would need to be modified. This meant that research into crime and delinquency had to consider four different kinds of data, namely, data generated by: (1) the actor; (2) the qualities of the act itself; (3) the environment in which the act took place; and, perhaps less obviously, (4) data generated by the system set up to deal with the other three elements, in particular the decisions of those in authority in the field.

We have already reported on the Probation Subsidy project, and it will be noted that it fits well into the last category. Also in this category are projects such as the bail reform of the Vera Institute. But more closely involving research activity was the development of policy control systems through computer-assisted decision making in relation to the granting of parole and, most recently, to sentencing in some states in the United States. The original work involved close cooperation between the United States Parole Commission and a research team at Albany. The degree of cooperation may be assessed by the fact that the action impact of the research was put into operation before the research report could be written, and this, in turn, was due to the integration of personnel from action and research sectors in the work. A visitor to a steering committee meeting remarked that he could not distinguish the research team members from members of the board, except that the former were perhaps slightly younger (see Wilkins, 1972).

The construction of living environments that will make delinquent behavior less probable will require the collaboration of many disciplines and applied skills. We now know that the prevention of crime through environmental modification is not possible in any general way. Each form of crime is different and needs to be considered separately and specifically. The design of shops can be made to render shoplifting less attractive and less probable – particularly by young children. But the modifications in the locations of products that will serve this specific purpose will serve none other. Vandalism cannot be prevented while it is thought of in that way: Rather it must be specified as to what precisely a "vandaling act" involves, such as writing "political" comment on public toilet walls with "marker" pens, or paint spraying, or other. When this degree of specification is made, it is possible to identify points of intervention that relate not to individual offenders but to all potential offenders. This is because by this means specific acts are rendered less attractive and more difficult to carry out, or are more likely to be observed or are for other reasons less probable. These methods would seem to provide a very rich field for the revival of action-research thinking and doing.

Thus, current approaches tend to emphasize the need for modification of actions or decisions by those in authority in order to effect changes in the behavior of potential offenders. Such changes, however, are not revolutionary changes in the total social system but rather are piecemeal changes in detailed activities, concrete constructions, modes of movement, and the like. These changes are neither dramatic, nor grandiose, nor, indeed, particularly interesting; rather they are niggling, multiple, detailed, and highly specific. Only shopkeepers can modify displays to reduce shoplifting, vandalism can be reduced by using building materials of certain kinds, burglary can be reduced in high-rise dwellings by modifications of the layout of public access, bus robbery can be reduced by use of tokens and sealed coin drops. The necessary detail seems endless. In a word, specific crimes can be made marginally more difficult, less attractive, or more risky.

Doubtless the "habitual" offender will either expend the necessary greater effort or change the style of his activities. However, there are relatively few habitual offenders, and at least one third of "crimes known" are due to juvenile activities. If current correlations are at all stable, and if the age at which a young person commits the first crime is (by these means or others) delayed by one or two years, the total volume of crime would be reduced by an extremely large percentage. How much reduction may be effected is not possible to predict because much depends upon estimates of the rates of offending for which existing data are most suspect. Estimates of 50 percent can be obtained from quite reasonable assumptions. Nearly all habitual offenders begin in small ways as juveniles, and the earlier they begin, the longer and more dangerous their criminal career.

In addition to crime prevention, justice' has to do with the ways in which accused and offenders are dealt with, and the quality of justice is improved by such procedures as the provision of reasons by parole boards, and the control of disparity in sentencing by the use of guidelines and other applications of computer-assisted decision making.

The future of action-research in the juvenile justice field

From an examination of the accomplishments of and the difficulties experienced in action-research in the juvenile justice field, we are better able to appreciate the tasks involved.

In most early action-research, the research worker was oriented to the action agency in a service relationship. The tendency was to seek to please, and often there were instances of unrealistic promises of payoff or a "product" that would satisfy the agency. There were bound to be misunderstandings, disagreements, and disappointments. Sometimes these were due to the tendency for researchers to be too optimistic as to the outcome of their proposed work. Sometimes it was a matter of interference from political, bureaucratic, or other factors external to specific projects. In any case, there has undoubtedly been a reaction that has, in the short run, brought about the recession of interest in and support for new ventures in this field.

Some of the problems experienced in action-research have been common to social research generally and to the policy sciences. Lawrence Tribe (1972) for example, makes the following observations:

. . . insofar as the policy sciences have too passively accepted as given the decision-maker's formulation of what he wishes to accomplish, one would call for more sustained attention to the problem of how to frame questions, greater efforts in modelling and simulation aimed at yielding alternatives not yet conceived by the decision-maker and even a willingness to challenge the values that the decision-makers posit.

Policy scientists, like program evaluators, have something in common with action-researchers. But action-researchers have a more specialized role in their responsibility for the management of the research component of the collaboration. It is important to take this into account.

One conclusion that seems warranted from this is to change the role in the research/action–agency relationship from that of vendor of services to a purchaser, to that of colleague with colleague. While preserving separate responsibilities and separate positions in the different systems involved, each member of the collaborative team should ideally participate in the planning and execution of the project and in the discussion of implications.

Applying this thinking to the 1980s, the likelihood is that projects will be on a smaller scale with more modest goals than in the 1960s and 1970s. We now view individuals in a systems framework, as linked to roles, organizations, and larger social structures, rather than as collections of specimens to be sampled or "referred." This implies a greater awareness of how any particular project fits with others and a sensitivity to contextual elements. This, in turn, affects the way a project is formulated and how its results are interpreted.

It is difficult to make projections as to the content of future work in the juvenile justice field, or to assess which of the various social concerns will give rise to a call for research collaboration as distinct from a simple call for reform. Research thrives where there is curiosity and an acceptance of areas of ignorance. There is no problem of sustaining this atmosphere in academic settings, and in the world of action (where there arises much of the impetus for action-research) there are several fronts that present challenges to which action-research might make a useful contribution. One is in finding new ways for dealing with the delinquent without reference to the courts – by techniques of "diversion" or by the use of community mediation procedures. Innovative experiments have been carried out using these methods (see Vorenberg, 1982). Collaboration in these kinds of projects will be as much with social service agencies as with the legal system. The area of sentencing is very important and promising, and the emphasis on "rights" calls for detailed attention to appropriate information and representation for children. Perhaps the emphasis on juvenile delinquency will diminish and the problems now classified under this heading will be sorted into other categories? Perhaps punishment will become more distinguished from treatment? Perhaps "rights" will extend to the provision of information and the greater level of participation in decisions on the part of those decided about?

One lesson we have learned from the past action-research is that even the best of well-intentioned expert intervention on behalf of the juvenile can be counter-productive if it detracts from the empowerment of the individual to cope with his or her own stresses and challenges.

In the field of juvenile justice any reasonable policy requires assessments along two dimensions – the desirability of a particular outcome, and the probability of achieving it. At the present time there is no agreed hierarchy of desirable goals, indeed, there are few, if any, statements of goals in a language of sufficient precision and detail even to contemplate the idea of attaching a probability estimate to the outcome. When goals can be specified in concise communicable terms, research techniques should be capable of providing estimates of the likelihood of achievement. With the aid of a "map" of desirabilities and the probabilities, a more powerful, rational strategy of action-research could emerge in the field of juvenile justice. This will require cooperation between research and policy, between science, technology, and administration: Perhaps we might say it will require the revival of "action-research."

References

Clarke, R. V. Opportunity-based crime rates. *British Journal of Criminology,* 1984, *24*(1), 74–83.

Cloward, R. A., and Ohlin, L. E. *Delinquency and opportunity.* Glencoe, Ill.: Free Press, 1960.

McCord, J. Consideration of some effects of a counseling program. In National Research Council, *New directions in the rehabilitation of criminal offenders.* Washington, D.C.: National Academic Press, 1981.

Mannheim, H. and Wilkins, L. *Prediction methods in relation to Borstal training.* London: HMSO, 1955.

Mayhew, P. M. et al. *Crime as opportunity.* Home Office Research Study No. 34. London, HMSO, 1983.

Ohlin, L. As quoted in Patterson, noted below, 1984.

Patterson, M. *The Massachusetts Alternative. Radio Times,* 1984, *243*(3155), 3.

Platt, A. *The child savers: The invention of delinquency.* Chicago: University of Chicago Press, 1969.

Rapoport, R. N. *Community as doctor.* London, Tavistock, 1959.

Romig, D. A. *Justice for our children.* Lexington, Mass.: Lexington Books, 1978.

Rutter, M., and Giller, H. *Juvenile delinquency.* New York: Penguin Books, 1983.

Society of Friends Service Committee. *Struggle for justice.* New York: Hill & Wang, 1971.

Tribe, L. H. Police sciences: analysis or ideology. *Philosophy and Public Affairs,* 1972, *2*(i), 66–110.

von Hirsch, A. *Doing Justice.* New York: Hill & Wang, 1976.

Vorenberg, E. W. *A State of the art survey of dispute resolution programs involving juveniles.* Washington, D.C.: American Bar Association, 1982.

Weeks, A. *Youthful offenders at Highfields.* Chicago: University of Chicago Press, 1958.

Wilkins, L. T. *Social deviance: Social policy, action and research*. London: Tavistock, 1964.
Wilkins, L. T., and Gottfredson, D. *Research, demonstration and social action*. Davis, Calif.: NCCD, 1969.
Wilkins, L. T. *Guidelines for parole and sentencing*. Lexington, Mass.: Heath, 1972, 1978.
Wilkins, L. T. *Consumerist criminology*. London: Heinemann, 1984.

5   Personal social service and income transfer experiments: the research and action connections

Alfred J. Kahn and Sheila B. Kamerman

Introduction

Our focus is the relationship between research and action – or knowledge and practice – in two social policy domains: the personal social services and income transfers (income maintenance). We have chosen to look at projects in two fields, since we find comparative perspectives to be generally enriching.

We pay attention here to two aspects of the research-action nexus. First is "action-research" as discussed in Chapter 1. At its point of major accomplishment such research contributes simultaneously to scientific theory (knowledge) and to intervention strategies (practice). Second is the research on knowledge utilization (Weiss, 1977; Lynn, 1978; Hayes, 1981). The focus here is on the relationship between research and public policy development and on the relative importance of knowledge as contrasted with politics, organizational dynamics, preferences, and many other factors on public policy and public administration. These two aspects of the research-action connection may, on occasion, be kept separate when assessing small, locally based experiments and "demonstrations" in which behavioral and social science research assesses and contributes to specific testing and improvement of practice interventions and, in turn, learns something itself. However, maintaining a distinction between the two is impossible when referring to multiproject studies or research at the macro level, when the "practice" is not only a matter of individuals acting in direct relation to other individuals but rather a matter of large-scale interventions. New programmatic initiatives and professional practices require new resources and, thus, policy change or new policy development.

Knowledge, therefore, may produce policy change – or vice versa. In each case the cycle includes knowledge-policy-program specifics, but does not always start at step one. Practice may be derived directly from social science principles or social science knowledge; practice may be empirically based, and social science knowledge derived from it; practice may be intertwined with social science knowledge. *And practice knowledge may develop independently of the social*

101

science base and derive from its own experience. All these relationships are viewed here as relevant to consideration of action-research.

The two fields chosen for illustration are at extremes of public social expenditures.

Income transfers make the largest claims on public budgets in modern industrial societies, except in wartime. The field covers social insurance, public (social) assistance, the use of the tax system to increase or decrease individual disposable income, as well as those in-kind and service benefits, such as food stamps and health insurance, that may be an integral part of the income transfer system.

The *personal social services,* such as the field of public housing and housing policy, are a minor budgetary item, however important to social workers, clinical psychologists, and related staffs, or to users. They cover such developmental, socialization, helping, treatment, and rehabilitation programs as family and child welfare, social services for the aged, adolescent and youth social services, children's institutions, community centers, family day-care and some day-care centers (but not preschools in the educational stream), a variety of mutual aid and self-help efforts, and so forth.

The income transfers tend to reach public attention around issues of expenditures and funding – because of the large sums involved – and with regard to the stigmatized subgroups that benefit from income-tested ''welfare'' programs. For the former, the issue often is ''Can we afford it?'' and for the latter, ''Are they cheating us?'' The personal social services have been visible in recent years as newly discovered, highlighted, or increased social problems have come to the fore: child, spouse, or elderly abuse and neglect; runaways; problems of the deinstitutionalized; the need for community care of the frail elderly. In general, services designed to respond to problem situations – case services – get most attention; socialization and developmental services to meet ''normal'' life-style needs get less attention, although child-care services and leisure-time services for the elderly (senior centers) have become increasingly important in recent years.

In our exploration of the research-action axis, we begin with the personal social services. We have chosen one group of currently active projects focused on client-level interventions (Project Redirection) and another, earlier series concerned with service delivery and administration (Services Integration). We forgo attention to the hundreds of small, locally based ''demonstrations,'' ''studies,'' ''experiments,'' in child welfare, family services, runaway youth programs, or of services to the aged in institutions or senior citizen centers. These, too, are relevant to our charge. Many, by virtue of their isolation, size, limited durations, or limited reports – if any – do not enter into the knowledge or practice mainstream. Others are accumulated into larger reports similar to the projects here reviewed, or may inspire or contribute to such projects. At the single- or small-project level they are best for hypothesis generation or refinement of new practice approaches. This is of no minor significance. We have earlier reported on neighborhood service centers (Kahn, 1976).

Project Redirection (PR)

Project Redirection, guided by the Manpower Demonstration Research Corporation (MDRC), is a national-scope effort to assist teenage women who are either pregnant or young mothers to achieve self-sufficiency. Its initial five-site demonstration and research undertaking in the 1980–83 period (Boston, Detroit, New York, Phoenix, and Riverside, California) was sufficiently encouraging to sponsors and observers that a seven-site replication effort was launched (1983) and is still under way. The initial sites and the subsequent ones were chosen in an applicant ''competition.''

The initial project has produced six published reports: an interim report on program implementation, baseline data on the population, an ethnographic study on a subsample, and an interim report on impacts covering the first twelve months after enrollment, a final report on implementation, and a final impact report. There is as yet no analytic published report on the replication. Nonetheless, the above offer enough about the process so that, along with documentation about and discussion of current activity, it is possible to discern the nature of the contribution. The project's visibility, obvious value, and popularity, and the significance of its objectives, make it important for discussion.

Since the MDRC and sponsors are inevitably focused on implementation success and impact, the available reports do not specify many aspects of project and research staffing (disciplines, theoretical preoccupations), intervention process, and unanticipated effects relevant to this paper's central concerns. We deal here only with what was deliberate, manifest, and centrally important, in the knowledge that much else has probably occurred.

Project Redirection was launched as an attack on adolescent motherhood, a response to the concern that ''early child-bearing frequently truncates opportunities for educational and occupational advancement and leads to long-term welfare dependence. Adolescent mothers constitute a long-term drain on the public fisc, as indicated by the fact that over 60 percent of all mothers who received AFDC payments in 1975 first gave birth as teenagers'' (Branch and Quint, 1981:v).

Through a process not specified in the published reports, the PR ''response,'' as it evolved and was formulated as implementation began, was to link teenage mothers and pregnant teens ''with a variety of services aimed at helping them to complete schooling, acquire employment skills, and ultimately, attain personal and economic self-sufficiency'' (Branch and Quint, 1981).

The target population consisted of young women aged 17 and under. There were, in the initial sample, 250 young women who were worked with in four experimental sites and another 264 in four comparison sites. Later, a fifth experimental site was added, raising the experimental population total to 350. At the height of the activity the quota was 300, because Detroit had been lost. Operations began in July 1980. Final impact analyses covered two years of operation.

The interventions* were carried out by established community-based organizations, funded by several Department of Labor grant programs and the Ford Foundation. Almost all participants received Aid to Families with Dependent Children (AFDC), or "welfare," either as independent recipients or as members of eligible families. One Department of Labor connection was via the work-incentive (WIN) program, with a representative making available to eligible participants child care, employability services, a thirty-dollar monthly stipend, and related services. The city funding levels, mostly Department of Labor and Ford funds, but some local match also, ranged from approximately $254,000 to approximately $540,000, the difference being the maximum number of local program participants. The projects concentrated variously on Hispanic, black, Chicano, and white project populations and the sponsoring community agencies had corresponding ethnic connections. There were some differences in the local staffing patterns.

The specific objectives were listed as follows: continuation of education, delay of subsequent pregnancies, acquisition of employability and job skills, improved maternal and child health, acquisition of life management skills, and eventual reduction in welfare dependency.

How was this to be achieved? The initial reports all describe the strategy in very concrete, practical terms, using the languages of social work practice, public administration, and counseling. There are no abstract, theoretical, social science conceptualizations. (This does not mean that these may not have existed for some of the staff.) There is some attempt to summarize the strategy as one of educating the participants to "invest" in themselves and their futures, but this would appear to have been a verbal summing-up, not a guiding theory from which much derived. Initially, the sites were provided with the outlines of a program derived by central leadership and advisors from the fund of experience in this field, their observations, and their own ideas. The local community agencies were to translate the outlines into program specifics. There was obviously some influence from the interaction among them, and between each site and the group as a whole, with those researchers who studied implementation success

---

*   Our description here deals with the initial five-city experiment that became four and then three cities by the end. There is as yet no replication report.

and those researchers who focused on client impacts. This is not reported but is inferred. The final implementation report (Branch, Riccio, and Quint, 1984) is the first full picture of the "treatment" as it emerged. In the early phases it was conceptualized as an offer of six types of service: maternal and child health; education; employability (counseling, job training, and/or placement orientation seminars); life management (family planning, nutrition education, parenting education, counseling); transportation; child care.

The final executive summary states: "The treatment in Project Redirection is a combination of services and close relationships in which the teens participate with caring adults. In the provision of these services and supports, Project Redirection seeks both to bring immediate benefits to the participants and their children, and to influence participants to adopt the attitudes and behaviors essential to meeting program objectives" (Branch, Riccio, and Quint, 1984:xiii).

The local community agencies were expected to ensure access to most of the standard services through a "broker" role, based on their own coordination or networking activities. Where necessary, however, they could themselves fill a local service gap. (It proved necessary in several instances.) The broker staff was made up largely of social workers.

PR's major innovative intervention elements were three specific, uniform service delivery components: an Individual Participant Plan (IPP), a Peer Support program, and a Community Woman component. The IPP combined a social worker case assessment with planning in a team conference, and reshaping and completion of the plan in interaction with the Community Woman. It also had elements of "contracting" between client and helpers. The peer support activities brought participants together at the site: It combined instruction and administrative control with mutual aid. The Community Woman, a new idea, concerned with modeling, support, and control, was gradually shaped and standardized through training activity conducted by the National Council of Negro Women.

Not analyzed conceptually in the initial or intermediate reports, but recognized in the final reports as affecting participation by the young women in the various activities, was the thirty-dollar monthly WIN stipend, for many their only cash income. Similarly, whereas the Community Women had been thought of as volunteers, the ones who "took hold" all earned up to seventy-five dollars (fifteen dollars per teen) – and for many it was part-time work, not subsidized volunteering.

We shall forgo detail, despite the availability of an interesting report on the backgrounds, attitudes, and training of the "mentors" (Community Women), merely to state that each of the components was shaped by trial and error, that the sites never were all the same, and that the project concept did not call for similarity – since the purpose was to fit the strategy to varied community service networks, different target populations, different labor markets, and somewhat different mentor populations. It was an empirical and quite pragmatic undertaking.

What kinds of evaluative questions were therefore asked? The first implementation report dealt with the ability to recruit sites and go operational, recruit target populations and Community Women, mobilize and coordinate needed services, develop the IPPs and monitor services. The early finding was that necessary elements were "solidly in place" (Branch, Quint, et al., 1981:v). Sufficient detail is offered to be very useful to others who might wish to move in similar directions, with or without research. There also seemed to be early success in much of the sought-after program involvement (school enrollment, family planning participation, use of pediatric care, etc.). The evaluation plans were described as covering implementation, participant impact, and cost. Of interest, implementation and impact were to be explored by different teams.

The subsequent baseline report on both the study group and the comparison group was essential to the ultimate impact analysis. It led to a characterization of the participants as "a multi-problem group" with severe economic, educational, and social deficits. Their problems ". . . far exceed their ability to deal with them" (Polit, 1982:vi). At the time of enrollment in PR, half were not in school, yet there were strong education and vocational interests in the group upon which the program could build. Indeed, the work aspirations appeared strong.

In short, the baseline report provided strong support for the various program elements. A reader concludes that those who designed the interventions had this group of young women in mind and successfully recruited the participants they meant to serve. The report is also independently useful to a broader community of professionals and scholars who want to consider etiology and intervention in this sphere. It is buttressed in this role by a specialized ethnographic study reported by a team of anthropologists (Levy and Grinker, 1983). The intensive study of eighteen of the teenagers provides depth and dynamics to the statistical studies. Both the complexity of the intervention task and the basis for hope that "progress is possible" are documented in rich descriptions of these cases. Inevitably, as is inherent in such efforts, there is a limitation to generalizability.

The final implementation report concludes that this was an enterprise successfully carried off. The loss of Detroit in 1981 is said to have been related to situational factors and not believed to reflect on the model. Boston carried out the program but withdrew at the end of 1982, apparently over differences in regard to the educational component and wind-down plans. Significant proportions of the young women were enrolled in or participated in the various types of programs listed above, services were mobilized, the individual program plans guided what was done, peer group support was modified as needed and implemented, the mentors functioned actively (Branch, Riccio, and Quint, 1984). Attrition, although considerable, was not regarded as excessive. Now there could be a more complete formulation of the nature of the "treatment." In short, the final implementation report gives a picture of a living program, largely carried out but not for all participants, not the same everywhere, described largely with the data from a management information system fully operative in its final year. No site did everything fully. High proportions of young women were exposed to most program components. Some took part far more than others. The mentor program, with not insignificant turnover, was gradually shaped and carried out. Each component grew, developed, learned, and was better described and more sharply defined in the final year than the year before. And the full (two-year) implementation report states that the program is "do-able"; assessing or establishing specific impact is a different question.

The final impact analysis (Polit, Kahn, and Stevens, in press), is less encouraging or definitive than the implementation assessment. To quote the authors in their concluding chapter:

The underlying question to which an answer was sought was whether these teens' lives were improved after enrolling in the program relative to what their lives would have been like had Project Redirection never existed. The question that many readers may well be asking is whether teen parent programs in general are a worthwhile social investment. Unfortunately, neither question can be answered unambiguously.

Among the problems discovered during the final analysis was that "Comparison groups were more different from experimental groups than expected with respect to important background variables and less different than expected with regard to service receipt." Indeed, community services had expanded so that, although not in PR, comparison teens received a considerable amount of service. This also was evidence that through an unexpected self-selection process, many were highly motivated.

The PR "treatment" groups had shown positive impact after twelve months, but after two years, when they were no longer enrolled, the evidence of impact was gone: They looked like the comparison group.

Within the "treated" group positive impacts remained for those who were most deprived at the start: the school dropouts, those in AFDC households, those who had a pregnancy after enrollment. But overall program results "were not overly encouraging," given the "absolute level of continuing disadvantage." Only one-fourth had earned diplomas, nearly one-half had second and third children.

The analyst could guide future targeting and suggest useful program improvements. There was no euphoria, nor was there a sense of waste in this field of many failures.

The overall judgment of the sponsors and of other foundations, made well before the final impact analysis was carried out, was that the first-year results were good enough to be captured and built on, given the importance and complexity of the problem and earlier failures elsewhere. The one-year report had shown that services with useful modest effects could reach these young women. The two-year report reinforced this. The seven new sites are not studying impact. Their focus is on whether and how a diversity of sponsors (especially schools) can adopt this "model," shaped originally in community-based organizations. They are interested, as well, in whether and how new community interventions of this kind can move from special project to "institutionalization." Ford Foundation and community foundations are the major funders. They have met to coordinate their efforts.

Clearly, the PR reports and studies are full of valuable help for those who would program for this target group. Several foundations find evidence of reasonable research and development payoff with respect to an intractable problem. There are caveats and limitations – and we have omitted much essential detail, yet PR offers mild encouragement and some experience on which to build. This is the type of record out of which good services have grown and developed historically. Practice improves out of intelligent building on the past, imagination, commitment, and much trial and error.

What does this project contribute to the "research and action" discussion?

One can find in professional journals and some publications in the behavioral and social sciences evidence that research and demonstrations in the personal social services do at times start with behavioral and social science theory, which is then operationalized into interventions that are evaluated. Head Start, the "opportunity" programs of the antipoverty war, cognitive therapies for dealing with child abuse, psychodynamic theories as to parental neglect, all come to mind. PR, however, reflects another and a more prevalent mode. Professionals, managers, and administrators, often together with public officials, assemble to cope with problems requiring policy response or new services. They pull together the available experience that they or their advisors and staffs know about. They may build upon innovative agency work and pilot projects. They also may tap experience in the literature or by bringing in experts. They sometimes may even formally survey experience or visit operating models. They then decide what to do. The solution adopted is described in operational terms and sometimes may be an incomplete framework – as is here the case. Depending on the identities of participants and the nature of the process, the formulations can be experiential and practical, or social science–theoretical. In the present situation, the former was the case. Administrative, professional, and "paraprofessional" experience from many places was pulled together around problems of creating services, coordination, case management, case assessment, client "contracting," and support groups. Some new ideas about "mentoring" were added because there had been very positive assessment of the results of a Ford Foundation project with the Sisterhood of Black Single Mothers in Brooklyn. It would all be worked out in further detail en route and tested. There was a more complete "treatment" description in the final year than earlier – and it was in the language of line staff and participants, not of social scientists or practice scholars. There were no comprehensive social science formulations at the start or at the end. A potential, if unexplored, tie-in to professional theories (the connection between "hard" services and creating a supportive relationship) emerged during the impact analysis (Polit, Tanner, and Kahn, 1983:125–26). Perhaps more would follow. The objective was improved services, and insight into service models that could be standardized and that would come from the experience and the evaluation. In this sense PR worked very well.

Services Integration

The frustration of generalizing from the small local-level project is the lack of replicability, its possible atypicality, inability in a one-case "study" to know which elements of context are relevant and which not. Case numbers (client totals) are apt to be small. The services integration story is at the other end of the continuum.

In the early 1970s, federal officials, especially the then Secretary of Health, Education and Welfare (HEW), Elliot Richardson, became aware of two problems in the social services, which they saw as interrelated. First, many federal programs overlapped with each other and with programs in other departments, a consequence of a complex federal grant-in-aid program to states and localities, categorical legislation, historical baggage, and competing programmatic concepts. Moreover, states and localities suffered even greater fragmentation because their delivery systems encompassed public and private agencies, the latter subdivided in many ways. For example, family service agencies were in one network, child welfare agencies in another, and they were almost routinely subdivided along sectarian (and, perhaps, ethnic) lines as well as by function (abuse reporting, residential treatment, etc.).

The other troublesome aspect of the fragmentation, a consequence in part of the first but also of discipline specialization and competition, was the general lack of holistic case intervention approaches. A single person could be served by several specialized social workers; members in a given family could be on the active caseloads of several different agencies. Often, no one had responsibility for the "whole" case.

The twofold fragmentation was not confined to the elements of a single social welfare field: income transfers, medicine, education, personal social services, housing, or employment. It generally spanned several, since agency operations impinged on one another and individual or family problems did not confine themselves to one field. After all, the dynamics of boundary setting for fields, of program development for public agencies, and of needs experienced by families and individuals, all follow quite independent – and little understood – principles.

"Services integration," defined as "reduction of fragmentation at the point of delivery" (Richardson, in Lynn, 1975) was one of several initiatives planned for the Department of Health, Education and Welfare. Although much of the "Mega-Proposal," an effort to restructure many of the income maintenance, health, and education planning systems programs and policies of the department, did not lead very far (Lynn, 1975), the efforts to reduce service fragmentation did get considerable attention. There were activities in many cities and states. Several summations and evaluations were produced.

Of interest, there was never a legislative mandate or a budget, despite a series of failed attempts to pass what was known as "allied services" legislation. The secretary, however, was able to assign funds from existing programs whose research, evaluation, demonstration, training, and innovation mandates allowed flexibility. Although there is no estimate of total expenditures because there were often state and local "matches" and expenditures in addition to federal grants, the total was very large by social service research and demonstration standards.

In the period 1973–76 the efforts were expressed in a number of initiatives variously known as "Services Integration" or "Services Integration, Targets of Opportunity" (SITO), "Capacity Building" projects, or "Partnerships to Improve Delivery of Services." Guided by the Office of the Assistant Secretary, Planning and Evaluation, DHEW staff in several units prepared guidelines, processed applications, made grants, and also contracted with agencies and organizations for evaluations and technical assistance, in the fashion of that period.

For example, in fiscal 1974 there were thirty-one active SITO projects, of which twenty-six were operating at state, substate, regional, county, municipal, or neighborhood levels (Kamerman and Kahn, 1976:453–54). Eventually there were probably fifty projects at the peak of activity. We rely on our own 1974 and 1975 explorations of these projects as well as on the commissioned reports and evaluations and several subsequent studies to summarize what occurred. Clearly there was funding, commitment of competent personnel, a sense of urgency and indeed a mission, and no lack of imagination.

One review of twenty local projects (John, 1977) speaks for many: The projects tried many different things, few tried precisely the same thing, and there was uneven provision for learning from them. More specifically, "services integration projects attempted a variety of linkage activities with such goals as greater accessibility and availability of services, greater responsiveness of service providers to clients, and enhanced efficiency and accountability. . . . These findings must be regarded as guides for further research rather than as proven conclusions" (John, 1977:63).

The projects adopted a number of strategies as they sought to deal with the uncoordinated and fragmented delivery system and the lack of a holistic approach to individuals and families. Several concentrated on "pooled funding" for operations or capital investment out of different funding streams; the achievements were modest. Others followed a pattern that was popular in many initiatives during the 1960s and 1970s (a strategy that had been popular in the 1920s) as units of different services "co-located" in order to simplify cooperation and client access to several programs. Results were mixed and reception hardly enthusiastic (John, 1977:63–64).

Almost all the projects reported by John made efforts at planning and programming linkages; although there were some enthusiastic reports, there also were problems of turf and confused lines of authority. Success seemed to depend on the presence of sufficient authority to enforce cooperative work. And, not surprising, the greatest successes came where joint planning by several agencies was undertaken to create new programs to fill gaps in the system. Nobody's turf was invaded.

The only widespread new administrative linkage created in many places was the multi-agency client information system. Many positive results were found, but these systems never seemed to make a duplicative intake process completely unnecessary (e.g., determining eligibility in programs other than the agency that does the initial study). Such systems do sometimes improve interagency referrals and have uses in planning and resource allocation. Nor were agencies generally prevailed upon to give up presumably duplicative core services: outreach, diagnosis, referral, follow-up. Nonetheless, in the course of the several services integration initiatives, many agencies were found to have strengthened their own core services, thus making a contribution to improved accessibility and accountability – often through a "case management" function or what we have called case integration (Kahn, 1979:150–51).

There is little evidence (John, 1977:66) that increased case conferencing among agencies paid off. In short, most of the devices seemed to add to service accessibility and availability – but not to efficiency, economy, system simplification. The evidence on the holistic case emphasis is mixed. As indicated, there are no useful data on client-level effectiveness as one goes from individual projects to the system of experiments and demonstrations.

John concludes that services integration can move only incrementally and requires political skill. Service delivery may be improved but will be costly. After all, he notes, "the evidence is fragmentary and difficult to assess. There was no consistent definition of the problems addressed . . . and many projects developed their own language . . . the available data . . . are primarily descriptive" (p. 69).

He might have added that although many sociologists, psychologists, economists, political scientists, and scholars of public administration were involved in these efforts, along with social workers, civil servants, and paraprofessionals, the enterprise was essentially atheoretical. If there was fragmentation, one would coordinate and integrate. If clients were lost, there would be information systems. If clients had to go to too many different places, one would bring the services together. There was no guiding intelligence for the separate projects and thus there really was no research capable of theory building or theory testing. Some individual projects were exceptions, but such efforts were not across the board. And because the federal and the state efforts were essentially ad hoc, using "assembled" funds, there generally were no control or "contrast" locales, so results were not definite. For large public enterprises, most were short-lived. Many were pulled in new directions en route by virtue of developments on the public scene.

We have summarized and commented on John. Other reviews modify this picture in specifics but do not change the essential conclusions. Lynn, for example, conducted case studies of services integration in six states and found that the political environment was very important to what occurred. In short, he illustrated some fundamental political science without discovering new practice or social science principles (Lynn, 1983). Gardner, examining what general purpose governments can do in services integration, concluded that "it takes time." (The usual two- or three-year funding cycle for federal demonstration projects is so inadequate as to make one suspicious of the intent.) Gardner also concluded that "it takes talent," that consensus building is an important part of the process – particularly because states and localities do not have the same agenda as the federal government. He cautioned that general government executives must be free to challenge all assumptions, avoiding the specialist's tendency to retreat to technology (Gardner, 1976). All interesting, but not very far down Richardson's road.

Exploring "services integration from categorical bases," Horton and others looked in detail at projects in Kansas (a mental health center), Brooklyn (a family reception center), Pennsylvania (a community education project), and Atlanta (evaluation and employment services for the handicapped). (This, after all, is what PR is. Yet no connection is made by those who designed PR.) Each of these projects had adopted the goal of integrating a diversity of services and facilities, the better to respond to client needs. The report focuses on factors most conducive to services integration, as derived from the four cases. Stable, adequate funding is found to be most important. Also stressed are a strong project director, community receptivity, a supporting administrative structure, a committed staff, and long-term planning (Horton, Carr, and Corcoran, 1976). No surprises here for the readers of public administration texts and 1984 confirmation by PR. No mention of basic knowledge or theory, either.

Earlier, the Human Ecology Institute had reported on sixteen SITO projects; Marshall Kaplan, Gans, and Kahn had reported on thirty; an ABT three-report series documented twelve (Abt, 1971; Gans and Horton, 1975; Human Ecology Institute, 1975).

For present purposes we need not differentiate, but it is useful to summarize several additional bits of insight relevant to our "action and research" exploration from these and similar sources. First, only some of the projects really reached the point of developing and testing new service delivery approaches, the payoffs for the Richardson initiative. Many of the others were confined to "capacity building," creating management information systems, computerized records, and the like. Much of the work in the early years was devoted to discovering or rediscovering the possible techniques and technologies for services integration: co-location, shared core functions, information/referral/follow-up mechanisms, case management (assignment of primary responsibility for the case to one staff person), agreements to provide complementary services, joint funding, advocacy for targeted groups, noncategorical administration, coordinated planning, general purpose government in a leadership role, administrative devices to facilitate waivers of federal categorical legislative requirements.

The summing up by Marshall Kaplan and his collaborators in 1973 was not very different from what was to be said three years and many millions of dollars later: Integration of services was not extensive; integration results in (should one say "is evidenced by"?) improved accessibility, continuity, and efficiency; there is no single best model; a wide range of factors facilitate and inhibit the process (Marshall Kaplan, Gans, and Kahn, 1973, included in Gans and Horton, 1975).

In retrospect, it seems obvious: A major federal initiative on an intergovernmental level, in an era in which ideologies – including those of the initiators – favored more devolution, and without federal legislative mandate or specific appropriations. No wonder that under the banner of services integration many different things were intended and occurred, but the package was not standardized – and most of the efforts were short-lived or evolved from one focus to another. The initiators were public officials and their "pundits," policy analysts and planners who adopted commonsense administrative solutions to the problems of concern to Elliot Richardson – and many others – or who merely saw ways to use federal funds for local administrative reforms or capacity building that they considered desirable. Thus, there was some R and D in "capacity building" (how to create management information systems or information services), but it did not predate the large-scale operational efforts. Ultimately the payoff was to be at the client service level, but no one asked about the operational-practice requirements of improved service delivery that was to end fragmentation. Would the management reform be truly supportive? What of new service techniques, training methods? Did they not need formulation and testing? Moreover, the heavy investment in reporting and evaluation overwhelmed the investment in service delivery per se and came very early in a project's history. The evaluators were often better trained and/or of higher status. The results were inevitable: Sometimes evaluating staffs, defining their report needs, determined the intervention "reforms."

Nowhere in the literature of the era is there a major theoretical tract – or even a major conceptual memorandum – explaining what was to be tested and the hypotheses as to how it would work – in sociological, social psychological, or political science terms. The administrative writing was more elaborate, most of it empirical and ad hoc. One should not underestimate this, however. A careful review of reports, articles, research reviews, and texts was to yield a number of very useful descriptions of varied service integration concepts, service delivery activities, experience with program linkages and case management, policy management approaches, and learning about organizational structures. The contributions of those "catalogues" of what was being done were to affect practice in public administration and management (Agranoff and Pattakos, 1979). Practitioners were offered leads, guides, models, manuals, and suggestions.

What remains of all this? Causation cannot, of course, be attributed, but we can observe the following:

1. Most states have created human resource or human services agencies, or super-agencies, with many or most of the relevant jurisdictions in the social services. These serve in budgeting, resource allocation, planning, and coordination roles at the state level, some more so than others. Almost all have "core" income maintenance and service jurisdiction. After that, they differ as to which other of the major service sectors are "integrated" (Hager and Hansan, 1978).
2. A few states have permitted or encouraged integration at the local social service delivery level, most have not. Three or four have sustained innovations in local service delivery planning – whether as a result of the initiatives of the mid-1970s or other local considerations.
3. The "case management" role developed and used in many local service delivery projects has been refined further and used in many other programs (including PR), but with no acknowledgment of these earlier efforts.
4. Federal block granting has simplified the situation for states that want to break out of the constraints imposed by earlier categorical grants-in-aid – and the cumbersome procedures required to coordinate and pool efforts among the categories.
5. The central concepts developed in the 1970s are visible in the literature – as are the relevant operations in the field: information services, case advocacy, case management, ombudsmen, management information systems. These are now tools of the trade in many places.
6. Much of what occurred is not directly traceable to the services integration initiatives. Some clearly had other roots. There is little obvious coherent learning in public administration, political science, or social work practice out of all this.

Individual projects may have had systematic "theory-focused" findings, but not these multiproject efforts.

7. If anything, increased – or at least undiminished – categorical legislation and funding at all governmental levels (abuse, neglect, homelessness, hunger, etc.) have added to the problems that troubled Richardson in 1973. In a basic sense, there was no "impact."

In 1983, a multidisciplinary team in Florida concluded that despite some fifty SITO projects at the local level, and top-level state reorganization of health and social service agencies in half the states, researchers had not yet developed clear ideas about the most important factors contributing to successful functional integration; "moreover, after ten years of intense investigation, there are still few outcome studies that show how integration affects clients, workers, managers, or the structure itself of public or publicly-supported agencies at the local level" (Imershein et al., 1983:21).

Examining eight years of experience in Florida against this backdrop, the authors, who are trained in sociology, public administration, and social work, develop the hypothesis that

when formal structure is principally responsive to the demands of the political environment and intensive day to day monitoring does not occur, then some decoupling between formal structure and service delivery activities will occur. Furthermore, following decoupling, participants providing direct service to clients become more responsive to them than to demands from the organization's formal structure or political environment . . . under these conditions the decoupling process will actually enhance the organization's effectiveness in meeting client needs. [Imershein et al., 1983:27]

A suitable paraphrase of the above could be quite funny. It may well be that the Richardson initiatives did everything that was needed except free practitioners to work with clients. The focus on capacity building and structure for coordination and integration, and the development of a corps of nonpractitioner case managers, apparently frequently had a contrary effect. Perhaps it was too much to expect one series of initiatives adequately to encompass client-level practice and interorganizational relations. There are organizational theorists who do try to bridge the relationship, but they clearly were not in command. Commonsense public administration let top-level structure dominate, and little was achieved long run, despite some local successes.

The social experiment in income transfers

In her 1970 discussion of the prospects and strategies for "systematic thinking for social action" (Rivlin, 1971), Alice Rivlin concentrates on the substance, not the process, of decision making. She concludes that many "education, health, and other social services are not effectively produced now," but that "some techniques or forms of organization or combination of resources now in use are probably more effective than others if we could find out what they are.'' Most efforts to find out are unsuccessful. Rivlin would encourage ''natural experiments'' and, especially, large-scale social experiments. The systematic, large-scale social program experiment becomes the equivalent of the controlled experiment of basic research. It is, in short, large-scale action-research that is planned, scientifically controlled, carefully analyzed. It has specificity and precision not attempted in the two projects discussed earlier. It is more costly, by far.

Over the past decade there has been large-scale social experimentation in income maintenance and labor market intervention, housing vouchers, and health maintenance organizations (Kershaw and Fair, 1976; Watts and Reese, 1977; Bradbury and Downs, 1981; SRI, 1983). Here we look specifically at one of a series of income maintenance experiments, the Seattle-Denver experiments generally known as SIME-DIME (SRI International, 1983).

We draw heavily on an analytic essay by Burtless and Haverman (1984).

Unlike the services integration efforts, SIME-DIME was a true experiment, conceptualized in social science terms, carefully designed and piloted, producing masses of data that were analyzed, reanalyzed, and debated by a large group of scholars from the field of economics and related disciplines. Substudies were carried out by disciplinary specialists. Other social experiments in the income maintenance series that reported earlier could be drawn upon for operational and analytic experience, particularly the well-analyzed New Jersey Negative Income Maintenance Experiment and the Rural Income Maintenance Experiment (IRP, 1976; Kershaw and Fair, 1976; Watts and Reese, 1977).

The SIME-DIME effort began in Seattle in 1970, was extended to Denver in 1972; the experimental period continued to 1978. It was the largest of the income maintenance projects by far, since its sample totaled almost 5,000 families.

This series of experiments should be seen in the context of efforts to reform what was seen as the U.S. ''welfare'' problem. Assistance levels for Aid to Families with Dependent Children varied by state and were too low in most places. Most of the working and nonworking poor two-parent families were not eligible, despite the poverty level at which many lived. Administration was costly, inefficient, and believed to be inequitable. There was interest in creating incentives to work where once these were seen simply as support programs. It was believed that AFDC eligibility rules encouraged men to desert their wives and children.

The experiments tested variations of a negative income tax (NIT) income guarantee as an alternative, sometimes associated with education, training, counseling, and day-care subsidies. Although the several studies collected a very wide range of outcome data, it would be correct to note that given the issues in the public policy debate, the main criteria had to relate to: income sufficiency of the schemes tested; the creation of work incentives or disincentives as measured by total work effort; and family structural impacts. Because the participating scientists and agencies had other interests as well, the project structures and research plan accommodated exploration of impacts on health and fertility, consumption, mobility, children's school performance, and family life. These other social and economic outcomes were also seen as possibly having indirect effects on the labor supply response or to have long-term impact for both the labor supply response and earnings. Several of these studies also replicated studies in the other negative income maintenance experiments.

For present purposes we need say little more than that these were true experiments, with carefully selected control groups. About 60 percent of the sample received NIT grants, if eligible, and 40 percent were regularly interviewed controls, some of whom were eligible for counseling and training. A sophisticated sample model governed family assignment to treatment or control groups and to specific treatment subgroups. The treatment population received one of three guaranteed support levels (potential eligibility was for three to five years), and were assigned one of two rates at which benefit payments were reduced as family earnings increased ("tax rates"). The counseling-education-training was meant to test the human capital theory that labor market participants choose to increase their human capital investments to the extent that in so doing they improve their economic circumstances. The counseling sought to ensure relevant information and vouchers for education and training and tested two levels of subsidy.

It should be noted that the specific NIT plans tested grew out of public proposals and debate at the end of the Johnson and the beginning of the Nixon presidential terms. Rigorous research required that the intervention alternatives be defined and fixed. And it required a considerable period of time for the programs to generate the behavioral responses of interest. The specific results (guarantees, tax rates) could not therefore specifically apply to the Ford or Carter eras or today's circumstances, and their value therefore had to depend on their more basic contributions to relevant theory with regard to impacts of guarantees on behavior.

This brief summary does not do justice to the theoretical underpinnings, design sophistication, and complex but highly effective research and demonstration administration of SIME-DIME. Full disclosure of results has permitted debate as to implications. For present purposes we merely suggest the types of findings:

1. A "small book" (SRI International, 1983:Vol. 1, Part 3) reports findings of labor supply response in policy and theoretical terms. There is here a significant contribution to the theoretical discipline and to policy. To summarize selectively: A universal NIT at 110 percent of the poverty line and a mean tax rate of 50 percent "would lead to significant reductions in virtually every major dimension of labor supply." The main difference is more frequent and longer spells of nonemployment rather than full labor force withdrawal; given the in-

come guarantee, males in particular spend more time looking for work; the less generous NIT programs make single female family heads worse off – as they do many dual-family heads receiving welfare. The policy conclusion is that only an NIT coupled with a rigorously supervised job search and strong penalties for underreporting could satisfy three goals: adequate minimum benefits, desirable economic incentives, and reasonable cost. Here, of course, the research confirms long-standing conventional wisdom. Probably more important, SIME-DIME, as do the other three experiments, shows that at the levels tested, income guarantees above poverty do not cause "massive withdrawal from the labor force" (p. 169). The decreases in labor supply were small and confirmed considerable economic theory about substitution and income effects.

Of some interest, too, is the finding that raising the tax rate (cutting the guarantee) actually increases work effort. Although those who continue to receive transfers work less, those who lose benefits work more. Here, tough politicians were closer to the reality than economists and reformers (Burtless and Haverman, 1984:6–7).

2. The counseling-training programs had startling and unexpected results. Participation was considerable, but the programs seemed in the long run to erode the labor market position of all but single women who took part in a counseling-only option. The analysis suggests that open-ended, nondirective counseling led many participants to develop unrealistic expectations and ultimately to worsening circumstances. It was the single women with fewest skills, unemployed at enrollment, who made progress. Of course, a deteriorating labor market probably contributed as well. The findings, nonetheless, elevated the importance of program targeting as opposed to nondirective counseling and widened opportunities.

3. A number of the administrative experiences in the research (choosing an accounting period that most accurately reflects applicant income) were to contribute to reforms in public assistance.

4. The most publicized findings and the ultimate downfall of the endeavor related to marital stability: "The negative income tax (NIT) plan tested in SIME-DIME dramatically increased the rates at which marriages dissolved among white and black couples, and decreased the rate at which Chicano women entered marriages" (p. 259). The detailed analysis finds that these generalizations, although accurate, obscure a great deal: There is less dissolution at the most generous NIT levels, the presence of children matters but differs by race (Chap. 10), the relative amount of time at home of husbands and wives – as mediated by labor supply effects – matters. Nonetheless, the effects remain.*

5. It proved possible to contract with a highly qualified, well-staffed organization, Mathematica Policy Research, to administer the grants and services and with others, especially the Stanford Research Institute, to conceptualize and implement the ongoing experimental research. Highly qualified scholars took part in the analytic work and a series of independent assessments.

It should be noted that this and other income maintenance experiments focused on what the public required by way of information before enacting welfare re-

---

* An unpublished debate persists here, however. A review committee noted that the breakup effect was concentrated where women had job counseling, and wondered whether it was a true family effect or an artifact. There is some debate as to why the issue has not been pursued analytically. It may yet be.

form; would it create work incentives or disincentives, would it strengthen families, would it be very costly? Despite secondary studies in the fields of health, consumption, and child care, there was no substantial study of the success of these programs in providing adequate income.

Pondering this and related experiments in labor market programs, Burtless and Haverman note that subsequently neither Nixon nor Carter initiatives were advanced by the results. The latter was burdened, at the least, by higher cost estimates. The subtleties and moral dilemmas of the marital instability story in all its complexity was lost on the floor of the Senate and in the press, and the "guaranteed income" cause was doomed – as was any major welfare reform.

These authors note that expensive social experiments tend to be undertaken with reference to program and policy proposals about which there is strong controversy. The ambitious program testing subjects proposed initiatives "to critical examination of a type that is rarely imposed on existing programs." "Experimentation does not and probably could not shed light on the main points at issue – the demands of equity, the nature of a fair distribution, and the limits of a society's obligation to help those who are at least partly able to help themselves." The moral would appear to be: "If you advocate a particular policy reform or innovation, do not press to have it tested" (Burtless and Haverman, 1984:25, 26, 27). However, the testing can be useful social science, in any case, if well done.

Conclusions

The story, if long, is interesting. *Services integration* was initiated by public officials who defined a problem and used "common sense" in addition to accumulated experience to suggest practical solutions. In retrospect it is clear that they were addressing not one but many problems. They assumed that case integration (addressing fragmentation of clients) and agency program and operational coordination (addressing system fragmentation) can be solved in one initiative. But they drew upon no body of clearly relevant behavioral, organizational, or political science knowledge, or direct-practice principles. They developed no coordinated intelligence or operational capacity. Early surveys yielded possible initiatives ranging from co-location and pooled funding to case management and computerized information systems. These were disseminated, subsidized, reported. State-level reorganization was encouraged. Changes occurred, but it is not known whether client-level improvement resulted. A decade later it was a fact that fragmentation on the program level and the case level had, if anything, increased. The initiative itself was fragmented, unified only in its funding and evaluation reporting. Moreover, subsequent policy developments added still further to fragmentation at every level. There was no evidence that basic knowledge had improved or insights or professional skill levels had been raised. Many of the ideas they had promoted in these projects remain active and influential, but there is little indication that systematic learning has occurred. Thus, in 1985 the services integration theme is being raised once again in discussions and recommendations concerning needed improvements in the delivery of mental health services. Case management is a major strategy in another series of demonstration prospects on long-term care. The wheel is being reinvented again.

SIME-DIME, on the other hand, was a research and social science success: rigor, sufficient time, clarity of design, technical competence, successful implementation and data collection, superb analysis. However, its main experimental innovation was an NIT model that was not quite the Nixon proposal, and even more distant from subsequent Ford and Carter proposals. How else field an intervention that takes three, five, or ten years to test? How else remain focused on basic scientific questions and on the demands of the research design than to fix an intervention – and shape it with the theoretical issues in mind? Such studies cannot adapt proposals to changing social, economic, and political currents every year or two.

The results – interesting with regard to labor market theory and the family economy and human capital theory (in short, good research for economics) – were a disaster for welfare reform advocates: The programs have high costs, there are some negative family stability and labor market effects. Counseling-education-training may not pay off as hoped. Counterintuitive findings are obviously to be valued in all research, but observers note that we subject only difficult proposals to this kind of intense scrutiny, which inevitably will uncover costs and side effects of public policy, whereas most public policies are adopted and continue unexamined.

In any case, the payoff must then be assessed in social science terms. Was enough learned from SIME-DIME in a basic sense? Do we require so expensive an experiment to address the social science question? That was not the original purpose of the experiment.

In short, services integration was too ad hoc for a focused contribution to social science knowledge and too broad and undirected for a definitive contribution to administration or professional practice. SIME-DIME was excellent economics research (its central study) but too long-term and too much guided by the needs of a rigorous experiment to yield a real policy result in real political time – and was almost destined to find flaws in proposed social innovation (whereas flaws in current programs are ignored).

In this company, *Project Redirection* is small and modest, even though in its own universe it is ambitious and impressive. It pulls together good ideas that have come out of many settings, demonstrations, and projects. It adds a new idea about mentoring from a local experiment. Then, without complex overarching social science or even relating any of this systematically to a literature of how to do professional practice, it assembles it into an intervention package that social workers and administrators would describe with such words as "case management," "coordination," "service brokerage," "accountability," "role modeling," and the like. The vehicles are apparently committed organizations and/or people concerned with an important community problem and accountable for results. Implementation and impact count, not practice theory or social science theory. There is evidence of reasonably successful implementation, good accountability, but only modest and selective impact on subjects. Intractable problems, tackled at the case level, do not disappear readily. This is useful, realistic, encouraging – but a very very modest result.

Yet Project Redirection and its record also offer raw material for several branches of social and behavioral science – as well as lessons for practitioners. This is also true of services integration – and a Florida group has taken up that challenge. SIME-DIME has made its social science contribution, but the policy take-offs are not yet visible.

None of this is an ideal pattern. None of it is wasted. None of it suggests that there is only one way for research and action to support one another. Nor have we factored into the equation the small, local demonstrations and service exponents, some with buttressing from systematic practice theory or social science.

The "action" in the social services, broadly considered, can involve clarifying, explicating, measuring, or diagnosing·a problem. It can focus on what to do. Or the emphasis can be on getting it done, implementing the response. Finally, there is the issue of trying to understand what occurred. Practitioners, officials, and scientists have different roles and relationships in each of these phases. There is no reason, therefore, to find one workable pattern for all projects or to be disappointed that none of our three cases (selected *before* we had made our assessments) tells an ideal story.

Our thinking draws as well on "natural experiments" in the form of cross-national comparative policy research in which we have had part (Kamerman and Kahn, 1976; Kamerman and Kahn, 1981; Kahn and Kamerman, 1983). Considering these experiences and the reported projects, we note that research can sometimes carry specific and direct implications for action if the research relates to outcomes of particular policies and practices that are the object of the inquiry and is so organized. Such research inevitably deals either with particular professional interventions (mentoring, case management, the intake interview), structures (co-location, the case conference), or policies (the level of income guarantee or tax rate and its impacts). These are in the domain of *professional knowledge:* operational principles, structures, eligibility rules, and the like. They belong to public administration, professions, semiprofessions, and occupations.

This research, even when directed by behavioral and social scientists, is not the same thing as basic research or theory testing in the respective disciplines, even though, if well conducted by qualified and interested personnel, it can provide relevant challenges and leads. For "action" is not merely applied social and behavioral knowledge. And research to develop and test action can be empirical, pragmatic, trial and error – and quite unrelated to behavioral and social science theory. Or it may be preoccupied with professional knowledge. "Knowledge," as developed by the sciences, often is merged with preferences and considerations of feasibility as it is translated by the professions into policy – and then guides or affects practice.

It is generally understood that medicine is not fully characterized as applied physiology, anatomy, biology, and chemistry. Nor is engineering merely applied physics. Social work, clinical psychology, and public administration go beyond applied social and behavioral science. Planning and policy analysis are multidisciplinary and both art and craft, as well as science.

It is these complex relationships, and particularly the tendency of applied fields to develop their own research into knowledge, methods, and principles that explain our inability to present a simple picture – and why these large projects proceed in diverse ways, ending by satisfying some constituents and objectives more than others.

Projects may be unidisciplinary or multidisciplinary, practice-dominated or social science–dominated.

Projects may be instances of co-equal collaboration or instances where one party structures, guides, and interprets – and the other serves.

Projects may seek information, knowledge, skill, or concentrate on task and results.

Projects may be reporting to behavioral and social science, to one of several professional constituencies, to client-consumers, to public officials, or to the public at large.

Projects may relate to a small, one-place, specific effort to accomplish something while learning – or to a multisite loosely or tightly coordinated effort with larger aspirations.

Nor is the pathway always a smooth one. We have observed in these and many other projects the following types of obstacles, among others: (1) practitioners are often of lower status than social scientists and their concerns are often overwhelmed by research and evaluation needs, to the point of loss of the project purpose; (2) the several participants often fail to communicate because of their different conceptual orientations, or meet on a level of oversimplified program structures and techniques that dilute the entire enterprise; (3) most of the major social and behavioral sciences are not unitary and the work in one place thus not readily added to what has gone before; (4) true scientific control is difficult to achieve and the price is often considerable; (5) funders, even benign funders, often have agendas that, however well meaning, may make competent, balanced analysis difficult.

Most applied research must be multidisciplinary and is affected by political and interest-group constraints, cost concerns, and publicly relevant time-horizons. One would not therefore propose it as the most rapid route to basic behavioral and social science knowledge – except in those limited instances where the scientific subject is quite specific to the applied interest: change, organizational structure, leadership, labor market behavior, family choices, and so forth. Although behavioral and social science theory is often lacking as a useful takeoff for some of the professional and practice knowledge on which the applied fields depend (Lindbloom and Cohen, 1979; Scott and Shore, 1979), it does on occasion make a major contribution to action. Also, behavioral and social scientists as researchers, educators, consultants, and methodologists can study or participate in studies of complex intervention that do not directly or immediately contribute social science theory – but that are useful to action. In the course of the participation the science may gain too, in the ways suggested; but to push each time for generalizability is to be caught in a trap (Szanton, 1981:159).

Action-research, in short, is not a uniform phenomenon and not always a good investment; yet its potential contributions are invaluable. Alert social scientists and professionals, expert with regard to social science findings, can often help locate important leads for dealing with practice and policy issues. Their disciplined research skills and stores of relevant ideas can contribute significantly to setting up programming and policy initiatives, particularly if they recognize that public action usually must be multidisciplinary, cost conscious, alert to political and interest group concerns, and guided by action time-horizons. Nor would they want to ignore relevant professional knowledge that is something other than applied social science. Nor can they ignore the complicated process by which results of action-research may – or may not – influence public policies.

They should continue to be willing at times, as their predecessors clearly have been, to serve as researchers, evaluators, consultants, and methodologists in projects involving complex interventions with no prospect of making social science contributions – but potentially useful in the world of action. On the other hand, the experience and the raw material nonetheless may offer theoretical leads and challenge, as seen in the reports from Project Redirection and services integration.

Action research is obviously not a simple domain, not a unitary phenomenon. Yet clarity as to circumstance and opportunity may yield continuing valuable possibilities.

References

Abt Associates. *Services integration* (three parts). Cambridge, Mass.: 1971.

Agranoff, R., and Pattakos, A. Dimensions of services integration. Rockville, Md.: Project Share Human Services Monograph, Series No. 13, April 1979.

Bradbury, K. L., and Downs, A. (Eds.). *Do housing allowances work?* Washington, D.C.: The Brookings Institution, 1981.

Branch, A., and Quint J., with Mandel, S., and Russell, S. S. *Project redirection: Interim report on project implementation.* New York: Manpower Demonstration Research Corporation, 1981.

Branch, A., Riccio, J. A., and Quint, J. *Building self-sufficiency in pregnant and parenting teens: Final implementation report of Project Redirection.* New York: Manpower Demonstration Research Corporation, 1984.

Burtless, G., and Haverman, R. Policy lessons from three labor market experiments (*IRP Discussion Papers, #746–84*). Madison, Wis.: Institute for Research on Poverty, 1984.

Gans, S. P., and Horton, Gerald T. *Integration of human services: The state and municipal levels.* New York: Praeger, 1975. Includes reprint of Vol. 1: *Integration of human services in HEW.* San Francisco: Marshall Kaplan, Gans, and Kahn, 1973.

Gardner, S. Roles for general purpose governments in services integration. Rockville, Md.: Project Share Human Services Monograph, Series No. 2, August 1976.

Hager, H., and Hansan, J. E. How the states put the programs together. *Public Welfare,* Summer, 1978, *36*(3), 43–47.

Hayes, C. D. (Ed.). *Making federal policy affecting children.* Washington, D.C.: National Academy of Sciences, 1981.

Horton, G. T., Carr, V. M. E., Corcoran, G. J. Illustrating services integration from categorical bases. Rockville, Md.: Project Share Human Services Monograph, Series No. 3, November 1976.

Human Ecology Institute. *Human service development programs in sixteen allied services (SITO) projects.* Wellesley, Mass., 1975.

Imershein, A. W., Chackerian, R., Martin, P., and Frumkin, M. Measuring organizational change in human services. *New England Journal of Human Services,* Fall 1983, *3*(4), 21–28.

Institute for Research on Poverty (IRP), University of Wisconsin. *Technical papers on the Rural Income Maintenance Experiment* (5 vols.) and *Summary report.* Washington, D.C.: Department of Health, Education and Welfare, 1976.

John, D. Managing the human services system: What have we learned from services integration? Rockville, Md.: Project Share Human Services Monograph, Series No. 4, August 1977.

Kahn, A. J. Service delivery at the neighborhood level: experience, theory, and fads. *Social Service Review,* March 1976.

Kahn, A. J. *Social policy and social services.* New York: Random House, 1979.

Kahn, A. J. Following the problem in policy research in the family and children's fields. *Acta Paedologica,* January 1984, *1*(1).

Kahn, A. J., and Kamerman, S. B. *Income transfers for families with children: An eight-country study.* Philadelphia: Temple University Press, 1983.

Kamerman, S. B. The new mixed economy of welfare: Public and private. *Social Work,* January–February 1983, *28*(1).

Kamerman, S. B., and Kahn, A. J. *Social services in the United States* (Chap. 7, The delivery of social services). Philadelphia: Temple University Press, 1976.

Kamerman, S. B., and Kahn, A. J. *Child care, family benefits and working parents: A study in comparative family policy analysis.* New York: Columbia University Press, 1981.

Kershaw, D., and Fair, J. *The New Jersey Income Maintenance Experiment.* Vol. 1: *Operations, survey and administration.* New York: Academic Press, 1976.

Levy, S. B., and Grinker, W. J. *Choices and life circumstances: An ethnographic study of Project Redirection teens.* New York: Manpower Demonstration Research Corporation, 1983.

Lindbloom, C. E., and Cohen, D. K. *Usable knowledge: Social science and social problem solving.* New Haven: Yale University Press, 1979.

Lynn, L. E., Jr., guest editor. Special issue on the HEW Mega-Proposal. *Policy Analysis,* Spring, 1975, *1*(2). Includes preface by Elliot L. Richardson.

Lynn, L. E., Jr. (Ed.). *Knowledge and policy: The uncertain connection.* Washington, D.C.: National Academy of Sciences, 1978.

Lynn, L. E. *The state and human services.* Cambridge, Mass.: MIT Press, 1983.

Maccoby, E. E., Kahn, A. J., and Everett, B. A. The role of psychological research in the formation of policies affecting children. *American Psychologist,* January 1983, *38*(1), 80–84.

National Academy of Public Administration. *Reorganization in Florida – How is services integration working?* Washington, D.C., 1977.

Polit, D. F., Kahn, J. R., Stevens, D. W. *Project Redirection impact analysis.* In press.

Polit, D. F., Tanner, M. B., and Kahn, J. R. *School, work, and family planning: Interim impacts in Project Redirection.* New York: Manpower Demonstration Research Corporation, 1983.

Polit, D., et al. *Needs and characteristics of pregnant and parenting teens: The baseline report for Project Redirection.* New York: Manpower Demonstration Research Corporation, 1982.

Project Share Human Services Bibliography Series. *Evaluation of Services Integration Demonstration Projects* (June 1976). *Multi-service centers: Co-location, and services integration* (December 1977). *Case Management in Delivery Systems* (March 1978). Washington, D.C.: Department of Health, Education and Welfare.

Rivlin, A. M. *Systematic thinking for social action.* Washington, D.C.: The Brookings Institution, 1971, chap. 5, quotation from p. 86.

Scott, R. A., and Shore, A. R. *Why sociology does not apply.* New York: Elsevier North-Holland, 1979.

SRI International. *Final report of the Seattle-Denver Income Maintenance Experiment.* Vol. 1: *Design and results.* Washington, D.C.: Government Printing Office, 1983.

Szanton, P. *Not well advised.* New York: Russell Sage Foundation, 1981.

Watts, H. W., and Reese, A. *The New Jersey Income Maintenance Experiment.* Vol. 2: *Labor-supply responses.* Vol. 3: *Expenditures, health, social behavior and the quality of the evidence.* New York: Academic Press, 1977.

Weiss, C. H. (Ed.). *Using social research in public policy making.* Lexington, Mass.: Lexington Books, 1977.

6   Family dynamics: strengthening families through action-research

Hamilton I. McCubbin, David H. Olson,
and Shirley L. Zimmerman

This chapter is devoted to the discussion of the family as a unit of study to complement child development research and to highlight issues of interaction between research and action. The well-being of children in society is greatly influenced by family dynamics. We approach well-being not as a static "end state" but as a constructive response of children to their interpersonal and social environments. This kind of response allows them to continue developing without major impairment of psychological, behavioral, and social functions.

The wellness problem that challenges us in the United States is the unnecessarily large amount of illness and dysfunction that threatens children's capacity to live productive lives, especially those from less advantaged groups. Measured in days of restricted activity, or in other ways, much of this disability can be prevented—but not mainly by attacking each index of illness or dysfunction as it emerges or surfaces in each individual or family. When wellness is viewed as enabling responses for children in their environments, the task for family researchers becomes one of investigating and understanding family and social environments. Both of these interpersonal environments have biotic and sociocultural facets that are likely to elicit health and wellness responses from most children, most of the time (Gulotta, 1984).

This chapter focuses on family action-research directed at these themes of promoting wellness and strengths in families. Specifically, we examine developments in family research that link to action in the areas of family impact analysis, treating family relationships, and family stress, coping, and strengths. Finally, in an effort to shed light on the collaborative element in family action-research, we examine three major investigations of stress in military families conducted during the "open," "expanding," and "closed" eras of "collaborative" research.

126

Family impact analysis at the interface of family policy and family strengths

Policymakers, administrators, and the general public have become increasingly aware of the importance of learning how policies, both public and private, affect families. Such awareness emanates from a long stream of activities dating from the hearings of the Senate Subcommittee on Children and Youth in 1973 and culminating in the White House Conference on Families in 1981, the first such conference in the United States. During the intervening period, the federal government funded several university-sponsored programs such as those at the University of Minnesota, George Washington University, and Duke University to train researchers to undertake analyses of the effects or impacts of government and other organizations' (i.e., corporations, social service agencies, etc.) policies and programs on families.

To ascertain the validity of the claim that social policies and programs of the 1960s and 1970s have been detrimental to family life, research in several areas of government activity, such as income maintenance, deinstitutionalization, compensatory preschool education, divorce reform, and some community-based interventions were reviewed for their family implications (Zimmerman, 1983). Although not necessarily undertaken with questions of family well-being in focus, such research provided important clues for arriving at conclusions concerning the impact of government policies on families and as such is considered here as a loose-knit form of action-research.

Income maintenance

In the areas of welfare and welfare reform, four experiments were undertaken over a ten-year period in four geographic areas of the country to assess the effects on family work patterns of a guaranteed minimum income in the form of a negative income tax on family work behaviors (Robins et al., 1980). These experiments are discussed by Kahn and Kamerman in Chapter 5.

The research findings, although inconclusive because of the relatively small sample sizes, differential attrition of families from the experiments, and imperfect measurements of marital dissolution, indicate mixed family incomes. At first glance they appear to have had negative consequences for families participating in the experiment. Family members reduced rather than increased or maintained their work effort, and marital dissolution rates increased rather than decreased. Such consequences were mitigated, however, by other effects. For example, although the income guarantees had the greatest effect on working wives and young people 16 to 21 years of age who reduced their work effort 22 percent and

20 percent, respectively, participants used their increased nonwork time to devote more time to the rearing and caring of their children, as well as to pursuing additional education, thereby improving their job prospects. Although marriages dissolved 18 to 63 percent more frequently among white families, 15 to 73 percent more frequently among black families, and 37 percent more frequently among Hispanic families supported at below the poverty level than in control groups, the overall marital dissolution rate was 30 percent lower. This finding is often overlooked or disregarded in discussions about experiments, although it serves to highlight the known relationship between income level and family stability (Morgan et al., 1974; Bishop, 1977). According to Robert Spiegelman, the economist who directed the income guarantee experiments, the experiments, although not actively encouraging people to divorce, gave them options for changing and improving their personal lives. Such changes were followed by self-reports of enhanced self-esteem and a reduction in alcohol consumption, outcomes that can hardly be considered detrimental to family life. While perhaps disappointing in terms of participant work effort, the findings suggest that the income guarantee experiments helped to facilitate positive family change and task performance.

Findings from a panel study on changes in the economic well-being of 5,000 families in the United States over a five-year period (1968–73) that could be attributed to public policies show that the best predictors of family welfare status are not welfare policies themselves, as is commonly supposed, but such variables as family life-cycle stage, family structure or composition, race, and employment rates. For example, transitions into welfare were found to occur primarily among families with young children recently headed by a woman; families with older children already headed by a woman who had not made the transition into welfare at an earlier point in the family's life cycle were no more likely than other families to make the transition later. Once they had made the change, however, they were not likely to reverse it until the children were grown or the women married, a finding that applied equally to both white and black families. Variables showing little or no relationship to changes in family economic well-being – that is, in their welfare status – were the employability of the family head as measured by attitudes, and by level of educational achievement and ability test scores. Disability, however, was related to welfare status change and, among those making the transition out of welfare, trusting and goal-related attitudes. Once families made the transition into welfare, their economic situation improved with age for all age groups. However, with each additional child, the level of support for whole families declined consistently, a finding that refutes the commonly held view that mothers in the Aid to Families with Dependent Children (AFDC) program have additional children to increase the size of their AFDC payments.

In general, the findings of the panel study indicate that changes in family structure and composition over the family life cycle are more important for changes in family economic well-being than employment rates, wage rates, education, attitudes, or urban/rural residence. By providing the economic resources needed during family life-cycle transitions that coincide with more disruptive changes in family structure, welfare policies appear to contribute to family task performance and economic functioning, not to hamper them.

The research findings also refute the view that AFDC, by providing single-parent families with an alternative source of financial support, has a destabilizing effect on existing marriages and decreases the likelihood of remarriage (Bradbury et al., 1977). Although demographic trends and changes in family composition and structure are correlated with an increase in more generous AFDC payments, the program appears to be consistent with prevailing social trends, such as the increased independence of women, improved living standards, and more liberal attitudes toward divorce, but does not cause them.

The effects of program changes from Old Age Assistance (OAA) to the Supplemental Security Income (SSI) program on the living arrangements of aged welfare recipients were examined in a panel study of changes in the economic well-being of American families undertaken by the Bureau of the Census (Tissue and McCoy, 1981). This study revealed that the economic well-being of most recipients improved after the change to SSI. Improvement in their economic well-being was not necessarily related to subsequent change in their living arrangements. However, their age, health, sex, and family status were all relevant. Specifically, being in the younger age range of the older population, male, a parent, functionally self-sufficient, and living in a combined household prior to SSI and the subsequent change in their financial situation were important determinants of changes in the living arrangements of participants in the study.

Such findings are supported by data on the effects of Social Security payments on the living arrangements of female beneficiaries, which show that the relationship is modified by family structure. For example, the proportion of women over 65 who either were never married or were divorced, separated, or widowed living with relatives decreased sharply between 1940 and 1970, from 58 to 29 percent (Kobrin, 1976). At the same time, older persons experienced a 38 percent increase in real income as a result of the maturation of the Social Security program and expansion of means-tested programs for older persons (Warlick, 1979). Also occurring at the same time, however, were important demographic changes showing marked increase in the ratio of older persons to adult children with whom they might live (Kobrin, 1976). Thus, any conclusions with regard to the effects of Social Security payments on the living arrangements of older persons must take into account the nature of their family structures and the alternative living arrangements such structures realistically can provide. When the family system has contracted and income potential from work has severely diminished, thereby threatening the economic stability of the older family unit, SSI and Social Security clearly seem to contribute to family equilibrium and task performance.

Deinstitutionalization of mentally ill and mentally retarded members

The same kind of conclusion cannot necessarily be drawn with respect to deinstitutionalization policies as they pertain to families with members who are mentally ill or mentally retarded. One of the first studies on this subject was conducted by Grad and Sainsbury (1968) in England to determine whether the trend toward community care created an additional burden for families of deinstitutionalized mentally ill members. As expected, family burden was greater among families participating in the community care than in the hospital care approach, not only because of the patient's presence in the home, but also because home visits were not incorporated in the community care approach as they were in the hospital care approach. These findings suggest that deinstitutionalization policies that do not include supportive services to families of mentally ill persons tend to exacerbate family disequilibrium and impair task performance. Such a conclusion is supported by other studies of family burden of families of former mental patients. Hoenig and Hamilton (1969) found that patient's age, marital status, severity of illness, and length of hospitalization affected the family burden. Families experienced greater subjective burden if the member was older, married, rated sicker, or was hospitalized for a longer time during the period covered by the study. Although most families were sympathetic toward the patient, over half were relieved when the member returned to the hospital, indicating that hospitalization of the patient provided respite for his or her family.

The Training in Community Living program, a project of the Mendota Mental Health Institute in Madison, Wisconsin (Test and Stein, 1977), addresses the question of family burden in families with deinstitutionalized mentally ill members. They found that there was no significant difference in the relative burden of experimental and control approaches on family members. Families of patients in the experimental group did not experience excessive burden or greater burden than those in the control group. However, at four months, experimental families reported a significant decrease in burden with no such decrease reported for families in the control group. The authors attribute these findings to the tremendous amount of supportive services that both patients and their families in the experimental group received. As Kreisman and Joy (1975) conclude, it appears that optimal conditions for posthospital adjustment vary with each patient and family. For some families the care of a mentally ill member may be so debilitating that the family is destroyed in the process. For other families such care may depend on community supports, whether such supports take the form of counseling, homemaker service, or day care for the patient.

In terms of families with mentally retarded members, the extent to which they are affected by policies of deinstitutionalization is suggested by a national survey showing that about 40 percent of all mentally retarded persons discharged from public institutions return to their natural families. To learn about their situation after discharge and the effects of discharge on their families, a mail-questionnaire survey was conducted with individuals who had been released from one of six institutions in New York State and who had been institutionalized for at least one year (Willer, Intagliata, and Wicks, 1981).

For many families the deinstitutionalization of the retarded member represented a time of crisis, for some because they were fearful that they would be unable to deal effectively with the behaviors of the retarded member and for others because they felt guilty about their original decision to institutionalize the member. For most families, particularly female-headed families, implicit in the return of the retarded member was the burden of the member's long-term care. Factors contributing to such feelings were the caretaker's inability to obtain even brief relief from the responsibility of such care, the financial costs implicit in such care, and the generally more limited financial resources of families to whose homes retarded members were most likely to return. Because they worked full time, about one-fourth of female heads of families refused to accept the return of the deinstitutionalized member, feeling that were they to do so, they would have to relinquish their jobs and change their life-style in ways they could not or would not accept. Most families to which a retarded member had returned cited a number of benefits, such as an enriched family life (72%), household assistance (60%), greater understanding of mental retardation (72%), and companionship (76%). For this latter group of families, deinstitutionalization policies apparently contributed to family morphogenesis and task performance.

Services to prevent out-of-home placement

Many approaches, including community-based services and programs, now try to prevent the out-of-home placement of vulnerable family members and thereby contain the costs of health care. One approach with severely mentally retarded children is a family subsidy averaging $245 per month to help families care for their retarded child at home. A telephone survey of a family subsidy program in Minnesota indicated that the program enabled families to perform their functions better in almost all areas measured: for purchasing items needed by the child (95%); attending to the child's needs (92%); purchasing respite care (71%); doing things they enjoyed outside the home (61%); doing things with other family members (59%); keeping up with household chores (26%); working outside the home (36%); doing things they enjoyed at home (29%) (Zimmerman, 1984a). Although half of the families stated that they anticipated having to place the child out of the home in the future, despite the subsidy, only two families stated they presently planned to do so. Future placement plans are affected by the mother's age and employment status, family size, and severity of the child's disability. If the mother was younger, employed, had few children, and the child was very severely disabled, the likelihood of the child's out-of-home placement was greater than if the mother was older, not employed outside the home, had several children, and the child was less severely disabled.

Adult day care is one approach used to prevent out-of-home placement of elderly and disabled members. This program provides a range of health and social services in nonresidential community-based facilities. Persons may attend for as little as once a week or as much as five days per week. For persons who otherwise would require nursing home placement and are Medicaid eligible, program costs may be met by Medicaid funds through the use of a Medicaid waiver. A telephone survey of a population of 82 family care-givers of elderly persons attending adult day-care programs in three contiguous counties in Minnesota revealed improved family task performance and functioning for this group (Zimmerman, 1984b). Although almost none of the families presently planned to place the older member out of the home, almost half of them anticipated doing so in the future, again primarily because of the severity of the older person's disability. With respect to these latter two social interventions, the family subsidy program and adult day care, the data indicate they indeed are supportive of family life.

Divorce and abortion policies

The view that the rise in divorce rates is attributable to no-fault divorce laws is refuted by data showing that such reforms are more likely to be the consequences of family decisions and behaviors rather than their causes. No-fault divorce is based on the principle of marital breakdown or failure rather than on the fault of one spouse as opposed to the innocence of the other (Wright and Stetson, 1978). To support the view that no-fault divorce laws are the cause of increased divorce rates, the data would have to show that postreform changes in divorce rates in reform states are significantly greater than rates in no-reform states. Instead, the data indicate that divorce rates during the period between 1960 and 1975 tended to climb in both reform and no-reform states. Although divorce rates increased substantially in states such as California when no-fault divorce reform was first introduced, part of the increase is attributable to the reduction in the waiting period between filing and decree from one year to six months, thus reflecting only a short-term increase in the divorce rates in these states. Indeed, in none of the twenty-five "experimental" divorce reform states was there a clear and enduring rise in divorce rates. Further, the strong relationship between mobility and divorce in states experiencing large increases in migration indicates increasing divorce rates are not so much the outcome of liberalized divorce laws as they are of demographic and other social changes affecting marriages. Thus, it would appear that divorce reform laws could well contribute to subsequent family equilibrium and task performance by alleviating some of the tensions and stresses commonly associated with the legal aspects of the divorce process.

Just as high divorce rates cannot be attributed to liberalized divorce laws, increased abortion rates cannot be attributed to liberalized abortion laws, which, since the mid-1960s and until more recently, have reflected a shift from a limited to a more widespread tolerance of abortion (Krannich, 1980).

Not only has legal abortion apparently contributed to a significant decline in high-risk teenage marriages that often produce unwanted babies, it also has been associated with a decline in out-of-wedlock births in some states. Findings from a series of research studies on teenage childbearing conducted under the auspices of the Center for Population Research show that children born to teenagers suffer intellectual deficits because of the economics and social circumstances of early childbearing and young parenthood (Baldwin and Cain, 1980). Such children are likely not only to spend at least part of their childhood in one-parent families but also to have children themselves while they are still adolescents, which suggests a generational effect that has long-term adverse consequences. Another study comparing a group of 220 children born to women twice denied abortion for the same pregnancy with a matched control group of 220 children born to women who had not requested abortion (Dytrych et al., 1975) indicates that the study group of initially unwanted children at age nine had (1) a higher incidence of illness and hospitalization despite having had the same biological start; (2) slightly poorer school grades and performance levels despite having the same level of intelligence; and (3) somewhat poorer peer relationships and thus a higher potential for maladaptation. Among these unwanted children, boys tended to be more vulnerable to problems than girls, showing a higher incidence of chronic disease and a greater degree of excitability and mobility. In such respects, laws criminalizing abortion practice would seem to threaten family life and well-being.

Although it has been predicted that the criminalization of abortion would lead to an increase in illness and disease among American women, not necessarily to the decreased incidence of abortion, it also has been predicted that abortion rates should stabilize by the mid-1980s. The basis for this prediction is current demographic data indicating the movement of baby-boom era adults into the post-reproductive years and more widespread use of fertility control measures (Krannich, 1980). Thus, although current abortion policies are not the cause of increased abortion rates, by being adaptive to actual family behaviors they apparently contribute to enhanced family task performance with respect to family procreation and formation.

Clearly family action research, involving family impact analysis and linking social policy to family functioning, has much to offer social and behavioral scientists, policymakers, and social program developers and evaluators. Social policies and programs designed to address a social or health problem may have adverse consequences for family life and therefore a negative impact upon developing children and adult members. Conversely, social policies and programs may have a powerful and strengthening impact upon families and their ability to make appropriate choices and to care for their members. However, in the field of large-scale policy analysis, the connection seems to be a loose-knit one, with many intervening variables between researcher and action agency. We now examine another arena of family action programs where the connections between research and action are potentially tight – that is, family therapy.

Treating family relationships: target for family action-research

Issues bridging research, theory, and practice in the field of marital and family therapy have been both aided and limited by the fact that the single scholar-therapist has adopted and utilized all three orientations. This has had the effect of inhibiting the specialist development of a field with sophisticated and well-integrated components of theory, research, and practice (Olson, 1976; Sprenkle, 1976). However, it is important to call attention to the notable advances that are currently being made in this field, and the potential in it for collaborative interactive action-research.

In his previous reviews in the area of family therapy, Olson (1970, 1980) noted that the exploration and refinement of existing ideas have characterized the two decades of research rather than the introduction of dramatically new theoretical approaches. Most recent family therapy literature has been devoted to: (1) the integration and refinement of previous models (i.e., Minuchin's 1974 synthesis of family development, family systems, and structural functionalism); (2) simplified descriptions of previous theoretical work (i.e., cookbooks or working guides of family therapy and textbooks of family therapy); or (3) extensions of existing theoretical frameworks to specific problems, such as chemical addiction (Steinglass, 1976; Stanton, 1979) and aging (Herr and Weakland, 1979).

Family action-research is evident in three major developments in marital and family therapy: (1) identification of critical dimensions of treating relationships; (2) testing the effectiveness of marital and family therapy; and (3) the advancement of family typologies and clinical assessment.

Isolating critical dimensions of relationships

Although it is useful to describe and evaluate various approaches to family therapy, a critical step is to begin integrating concepts and principles and to develop theoretical models. One recent attempt to develop an integrative model of the family was done by Olson, Russell, and Sprenkle (1979, 1980) in their Circumplex Model. In developing the Circumplex Model, three dimensions emerged from the conceptual clustering of concepts from six social science fields, including family therapy. The three dimensions were: cohesion, adaptability, and communication.

Evidence for the salience of these three dimensions is the fact that numerous theorists and therapists have independently selected concepts related to these dimensions as critical to their work (see Table 6.1). (See Fisher and Sprenkle [1978] and Sprenkle and Fisher [1980] for empirical evidence of the importance of these three dimensions.)

Family cohesion is defined as the emotional bonding that family members have toward one another (Olson et al., 1979). At the extreme high end of the cohesion dimension (enmeshed systems) there is an overidentification with the family that results in an extreme emotional, intellectual, and/or physical closeness. The low extreme of cohesion (disengaged systems) results in emotional,

Table 6.1. *Theoretical models of family systems utilizing concepts related to cohesion and adaptability and communication dimensions*

Cohesion	Adaptability	Communication	References
Affiliation	Interdependence		Benjamin (1974 and 1977)
Affective involvement	Behavior control problem-solving roles	Communication Affective responsiveness	Epstein, Bishop, and Levin (1978)
	Capacity to change power		French and Guidera (1974)
Affect dimension	Power dimension		Kantor and Lehr (1975)
Affection-hostility	Dominance-submission		Leary (1957) and Constantine (1977)
Closeness autonomy coalitions	Power negotiation	Affect	Lewis et al. (1976) and Beavers (1977)
Expressive role	Instrumental role		Parsons and Bales (1955)

intellectual, and/or physical isolation from the family. It is hypothesized that the central area of this continuum is most viable for family functioning because individuals are able to experience and balance being independent from, as well as connected to, their families.

Family adaptability is the second major dimension and is defined as the ability of a marital or family system to change its power structure, role relationships, and relationship rules in response to situational and developmental stress (Olson et al., 1979). As with cohesion, adaptability is a continuum where the central levels of adaptability are hypothesized as more conducive to marital and family functioning than the extremes. In family theory, adaptability was originally presented as homeostasis or the ability of a system to maintain equilibrium (Haley, 1964). More recently, writers have stressed the dual concepts of morphogenesis (system altering or change) and morphostasis (system maintaining or stability) and the family's need for a dynamic balance between these two (Speer, 1970; Wertheim, 1973, 1975). Families very low on adaptability (rigid systems) are unable to change even when it appears necessary. On the other hand, families with too much adaptability (chaotic systems) also have problems dealing with stress and problems. Thus, a balance of stability and change appears most functional to individual and family development (Olson et al., 1979).

By placing these two dimensions of cohesion and adaptability at right angles, Olson et al. (1979) have developed a Circumplex Model that delineates sixteen family types (see Figure 6.1). These authors have also developed a series of hypotheses with direct clinical utility derived from the model, several of which have already been tested empirically (Olson et al., 1980).

The theme of cohesion is highly developed in Minuchin's work (1974; Minuchin et al., 1975, 1978). He writes that the human experience of identity has two elements: a sense of belonging and a sense of separateness. A family's structure may range from the one extreme of the "enmeshed" family to the other extreme of the "disengaged" family. In the former, the quality of connectedness among members is characterized by "tight interlocking" and extraordinary resonance among members. The enmeshed family responds to any variation from the accustomed with excessive speed and intensity. In sharp contrast, individuals in disengaged families seem oblivious to the effects of their actions on each other. "Actions of its members do not lead to vivid repercussions . . . the overall impression is one of an atomistic field; family members have long moments in which they move as in isolated orbits, unrelated to each other" (Minuchin et al., 1967:354).

Minuchin also devotes considerable attention to family adaptation. He stresses the importance of the family's capacity to change in the face of external or internal pressures, for example, those related to developmental changes such as the

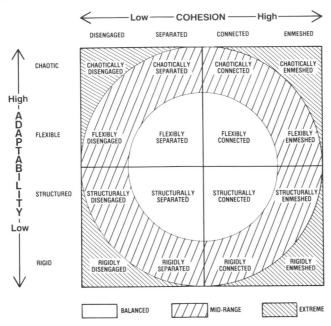

Figure 6.1. Circumplex Model: sixteen types of marital and family systems. (From Olson, Russell, and Sprenkle, 1979, 1980)

addition or loss of members or changes in life-cycle stages. Minuchin notes that many families in treatment are simply going through transitions and need help in adapting to them. ''The label of pathology would be reserved for families who, in the face of stress, increase the rigidity of their transactional patterns and boundaries, and avoid or resist any exploration of alternatives'' (Minuchin, 1974:60).

Family communication has been stressed by most family theorists from Ackerman to those associated with the ''Palo Alto'' communications group (Watzlawick, Beavin, and Jackson, 1967; Watzlawick, Weakland, and Fisch, 1974; Satir, 1972). Also, many practitioners have begun to isolate the specific components of effective marital and family communication (Miller, Corrales, and Wackman, 1975) and have created skill-development workshops to facilitate family communication (Miller, Nunnally, and Wackman, 1976; Guerney, 1977).

Family action-research has contributed to the emergence of a relative sense of consensus among family therapists about the salience of the cohesion, adaptability, and communication dimensions. How these dimensions are operationalized, hypothesized to relate to each other, and utilized in therapy are still areas requiring considerable investigation.

Effectiveness of strategies for treating relationships

During the last two decades of family action-research, the empirical outcome literature has improved in both quantity and quality. This progress is clearly documented by the several comprehensive reviews already available (e.g., Gurman, 1973, 1975; Beck, 1976; Jacobson and Martin, 1976; Wells, Dilkes, and Burckhardt, 1976; Gurman and Kniskern, 1978a, 1978b; Jacobson, 1978; Wells and Denzen, 1978; Jacobson and Margolin, 1979).

The trend in the family action-research appears to be toward specifying which mode of therapy is most effective for which group of families presenting which sorts of problems (Olson et al., 1980). This is a more effective approach to therapeutic outcome studies. As Frank (1979:312) has suggested: "Instead of continuing to pursue the relatively unrewarding enterprise of statistically comparing the effectiveness of different therapies, we should focus on particular forms of therapy that seem to work exceptionally well with a few patients and seek to define the characteristics of both the therapy and the patients that lead to this happy result."

An alternative to focusing on presenting symptoms is to focus on the type of family system. Olson et al. (1980) have emphasized the importance of system diagnosis prior to intervention. A given "symptom" may serve multiple functions in a relationship system. Therefore, the "system diagnosis" and presenting complaint may not uniformly co-vary. For instance, Killorin and Olson (1980) describe the course of therapy with four alcoholic families, each of whom operated at different levels of family cohesion and adaptability. There are other recent projects where the type of system is diagnosed prior to treatment, specific treatment programs are planned, and outcome is assessed for a narrowly defined treatment group (e.g., Alexander and Barton, 1976; Minuchin et al., 1978; Stanton et al., 1979; Steinglass, 1979a, 1979b).

Table 6.2 provides a summary of relationship-oriented treatment strategies that have yielded some degree of documented effectiveness. Unfortunately, we do not have sufficient space to provide a detailed review of the current literature on outcome research.

However, Table 6.3 may be used as a brief summary of improvement rates for four family-therapy approaches by "identified patient." Details of these studies can be obtained from Gurman and Kniskern's (1978b) relatively recent review. Overall, it appears that marital and family therapy improvement rates are superior to those reported for individual therapies.

The following implications for practice are supported by the empirically based family action-research and overlap with the recommendations Gurman and Kniskern (1978b) make for the training of marriage and family therapists:

Table 6.2. *Relationship-oriented treatment strategies yielding some degree of documented effectiveness by presenting problem*

Presenting problem	Behavioral exchange contracting	Conjoint couples group therapy	Behavioral family therapy	Conjoint interactional family therapy	Structural family therapy	Strategic family therapy	Zuk's triadic approach	Multiple family therapy	Drug therapy plus marital therapy	Family crisis intervention[c]
Alcoholism	x	x								
Drug abuse					x	x		x		
Juvenile status offense			x[a]	x[b]	x					
Adolescent psychopathology				x			x			
Childhood conduct problems			x							
School and work phobias								x		x
Psychosomatic symptoms						x				
Adult depression									x	
Marital distress	x									

[a]Limited primarily to outcome studies reported 1970–79.
[b]Though labeled behavioral, the Alexander group at Utah actually used a mix of behavioral and communication approaches in conjoint family sessions.
[c]Langsley et al.

Table 6.3. *Improvement rates in marital and family therapy*

	Number of studies	Number of patients	Improved	Outcome (%)	
				No change	Worse
Marital therapy					
Conjoint	8	261	70[a]	24	1
Conjoint group	15	397	66	30	4
Concurrent and collaborative	6	464	63	35	2
Individual	7	406	48	45	7
Total	36	1,528	61	35	4
Family therapy					
Child as identified patient	10	370	68	32	0
Adolescent as identified patient	9	217	75	25	0
Adult as identified patient	11	475	65	33	2
Mixed identified patient	8	467	81	17	2
Total	38	1,529	73	26	1

[a]Five percent unknown.
Source: Abstracted with permission from A. S. Gurman and D. P. Kniskern, "Research on marital and family therapy: Progress, perspective, and prospect," in *Handbook of Psychotherapy and Behavior Change,* by Garfield and Bergin (1978).

1. Conjoint marital therapy appears more useful than individual therapy for improving marital relationships.
2. Family therapy appears as effective as individual therapy for a wide range of presenting problems. However, for most presenting problems, it is not possible to specify the best type of family treatment.
3. No one "school" of marital or family therapy has been demonstrated to be effective with a wide range of presenting problems.
4. Therapist relationship skills are important regardless of the conceptual orientation or "school" of the family therapist.

Advancing the development of family typologies

The use of typologies of couples and families constitutes a major breakthrough for family action-research because they help to bridge the gap between research, theory, and practice (Olson, 1980). Typologies, whether developed empirically or intuitively (theoretically and clinically), offer numerous conceptual and methodological advantages over traditional variable analysis.

Conceptually, they bridge research and practice by focusing on actual couples and families, rather than on variables. Classifying a family system as a "rigidly enmeshed" type provides considerable information about the family, since the typology incorporates and summarizes a cluster of variables uniquely related to each type. Typologies enable a researcher or therapist to: (1) classify and describe couples and families on a number of variables; (2) summarize numerous characteristics of all the cases of a particular type; (3) establish criteria that determine whether a couple or family fits within a particular type; and (4) distinguish and describe differences between types.

Methodologically, typologies enable an investigator to: (1) pool statistical variance across a number of variables uniquely related to each type; (2) empirically discover more stable and meaningful relationships between variables and types; and (3) translate the findings directly to couples and families rather than to variables.

In the last few years, there has been increasing interest among family action-researchers in identifying types of marital and family systems. For example, Cuber and Haroff (1955) developed one of the first inductively derived typologies of marriages based on interviews with high-status couples. A typography of husbands' and wives' personality traits was derived from condensed interview reports with 200 couples (Ryder, 1970a, 1970b). Kantor and Lehr (1975) developed a typology of families based on the concepts of open, closed, and random systems. Constantine (1977) extended the four-player model into a more comprehensive and unified typology. A descriptive analysis of dysfunctional, mid-range, and healthy families was developed by Lewis et al. (1976), whereas Wertheim (1973) developed a typology based on three aspects of the morphogenesis-morphostatis dimension that described eight types of family systems related to the empirical types of families described by Reiss (1971). Most major typologies, however, have been developed intuitively and have suffered from one or more of the following problems: (1) Criteria for classifying are not clearly specified; (2) procedures for assigning couples to types are subjective and ambiguous with unknown reliability; and (3) types are not exhaustive or mutually exclusive (Miller and Olson, 1978).

The empirical approach to developing typologies of marital and family systems is becoming more popular because of recent developments in computer programs on cluster and small-space analyses. Some of the first attempts to develop "couples types" empirically were done by Goodrich, Ryder, and Rausch (1968) and Ryder (1970b), using profile analysis to describe newlywed couples. Shostrum and Kavanaugh (1971) used a self-report instrument to develop types of couples based on their scores on the dimensions of anger-love and strength-weakness, and Moos and Moos (1976) developed a typology of families based on their Family Environment Scale. Similarly, using the Ravich Interpersonal Game-Test, Ravich and Wyden (1974) described eight types of marital interaction patterns.

Olson and his colleagues have been working for the past five years developing two different approaches to couple and family typologies, one empirical and the other theoretical. The empirical approach has focused on typologies of couples and families based on their verbal interaction patterns (Miller and Olson, 1978), generated by the Inventory of Marital Conflicts (Olson and Ryder, 1970) and other related inventories. The theoretical typology is the Circumplex Model of marital and family systems developed by Olson et al. (1979).

Advancement in clinical and family system assessment

Although a variety of diagnostic tools have been developed that could be used by marital and family therapists (Cromwell and Fournier, 1976; Cromwell and Fournier, in progress), the statement made by Olson (1970:512) in the last decade review of the field still applies: "Most therapists seem to make their diagnostic evaluations in rather unsystematic and subjective ways using unspecified criterion that they have found helpful in their clinical practice." However, for the field to advance it is important to learn what types of therapeutic intervention work best with specific presenting symptoms or family systems. As Broderick (1976:xv) stated: "It is a simpleminded but often overlooked concept that couples are different and require differential diagnosis procedures leading to different treatment procedures."

There is a variety of reasons why most marital and family therapists do not currently use standardized diagnostic tools for their clinical assessment. First, most therapists have not clearly identified the conceptual dimensions they consider important for diagnostic assessment. Second, there is a lack of concern with systematic diagnosis because it has often had little relationship to the therapeutic approach used. Third, most marital and family assessment tools do not assess clinically relevant concepts, are not designed for use in clinical settings, and do not adequately capture the complexity of marital and family systems.

There are, however, some recent attempts to base the treatment program on the diagnostic assessment. These bridging projects are different because they can be accomplished only when the conceptual, clinical, and empirical domains are integrated. Five examples of projects where this integrated approach has been attempted are the McMaster Model of Therapy by Epstein and colleagues (Santa-Barbara et al., 1977; Epstein, Bishop, and Levin, 1978), the Circumplex Model by Olson and colleagues (Olson et al., 1979, 1980); the Timberlawn project by Lewis and colleagues (Lewis et al., 1976; Beavers, 1977); the Social Ecology project at the Veterans Administration Medical Center in Palo Alto (Fuhr, Moos, and Dishotsky, 1981); and the Family Stress, Coping and Health project by McCubbin and Patterson (1981; 1983a; 1983b). All five projects have developed clinical indicators for diagnosis, and research-based procedures for assessing couples and family systems and their properties. These assessment tools enable the investigators to do clinical diagnosis before treatment and postevaluation at the end of treatment.

There are also attempts to develop more clinically relevant and useful diagnostic tools for couples and families. In this regard, Cromwell and colleagues are continuing to describe the value of "systemic diagnosis" (Cromwell and Keeney, 1979), which integrates systems theory and a multilevel (individual, interpersonal, and total system), multitrait, and multimethod assessment. This comprehensive approach is very ambitious but reflects the type of systematic assessment that has been lacking in the field to date.

There are few therapeutic models that integrate the clinical assessment and the therapeutic approach. However, this type of integration could be accelerated if family therapists and family researchers worked together in a more collaborative manner. Numerous benefits could be accrued by both therapists and researchers if they formed a more cooperative relationship (Olson et al., 1980). A promising new direction that is consistent with the collaborative interactive model of action-research rather than the segregated scholar/clinician and therapy-researcher models is suggestive in the development of integrative models that bridge research and action. The theoretical and empirical typologies that have been described facilitate the bridging process and ultimately the mutual benefit of theory and practice in the family therapy field.

Family stress, support, coping, and strengths in family action-research

One of the major developments in family action-research involves the systematic study of stresses in families undergoing transitions. The central research questions for family transition investigations center on identifying the linkages and intervening factors between various kinds of stressors and various patterns of family adaptation.

Since the classic studies of Burgess (1926), Angell (1936), Cavan and Ranck (1938), and Koos (1946), and particularly Reuben Hill's (1949) research and theory-building efforts based observations on family responses to war-induced separation and reunion, we have witnessed a major shift in family stress research. The exciting new possibility exists of not only explaining and predicting dysfunctional family behavior in response to stress, but understanding how family members interact with and support each other, what strengths and capabilities families call upon to adjust and adapt, the specific roles and transactions the

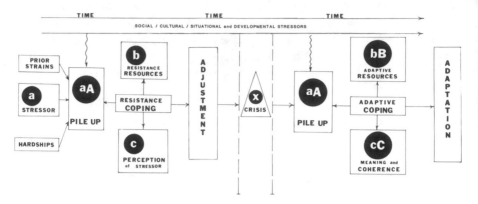

Figure 6.2. The FAAR Model.

community plays and enacts in family coping and adaptation, and suggesting ways to improve the resiliency in families. Concomitantly, we have witnessed the emergence of prevention-oriented family action studies designed to strengthen families, as well as to promote the physical and psychological well-being of their members.

Identifying critical family strengths and resources

A conceptual scheme that has been developed and refined to meet the dual requirements of action-research is the Family Adjustment and Adaptation Response Model (FAAR). Based on Hill's (1949) ABCX Model of stress, and McCubbin and Patterson's (1983a, 1983b) modifications, this model provides the kind of framework that has been found useful in the family field.

Figure 6.2 outlines the FAAR Model and the critical components of family stress research. Four of these factors that affect a family's adjustment to stressors and adaptation to crises have been elaborated in current research: (1) community resources and social support for families; (2) family coping and adaptation; (3) family appraisal; and (4) resistance strengths and adaptive strengths in families.

Social support as a mediator of family stress

Although social support will be discussed in Chapter 7 by Zigler and Weiss, it deserves brief mention here as an integral part of the conceptual framework being discussed. Social support has been analyzed in various dimensions: financial, emotional, informational, affectional, and service behavioral (Troll, 1971; Granovetter, 1973; Cobb, 1976; Lowenthal and Robinson, 1976; Lee, 1979). The various support actions occur in *neighborhoods* (Litwak and Szelenyi, 1969;

Patterson, 1971; Zunin, 1974), *family kinship networks* (Caplan, 1976; Lopata, 1978; Lin et al., 1979), between *generations* (Hill, 1970; Troll, 1971; Sussman, 1976), and through the formation of *mutual self-help* groups (Katz, 1970; Lieberman et al., 1979; McCubbin, 1979).

Research on the mediating influence of social support for specific stressor events has emphasized the role of social support in protecting against the effects of stressors and thereby contributing to a family's invulnerability. Research has also emphasized the importance of social support in promoting recovery from stress or crisis experienced in the family as a result of life changes, thereby contributing to the family's adaptative power. Social support has been demonstrated to provide a protective factor against complications of pregnancy and childbirth (Nuckolls, Cassel, and Kaplan, 1972) and in promoting medical compliance (Baekland and Lundwall, 1975). Investigations have indicated that social support makes individuals and family units less vulnerable to crisis when they experience stressors such as job terminations or difficult work environments (Gore, 1978), illnesses due to asthma (deAraujo et al, 1973) or leukemia (Kaplan et al., 1973) and natural disasters such as floods (Erikson, 1976) or tornadoes (Drabeck et al., 1975). The role of social support in promoting the family's recovery from crisis has been indicated in the case of psychiatric illnesses (Caplan, 1976); death (Parkes, 1972); divorce (Colletta, 1979); and multiproblem families (Burns and Freedman, 1976).

Family coping and adaptation

The picture of family adaptation to change depicts the family as a reactor to stress and as a manager of resources within the family system. The active processes of family adaptation involving coping strategies within the family as well as in transactions with the community have received limited attention in both research and theory building (McCubbin, 1979).

However, there is a mounting belief among researchers and family clinical workers that understanding how families cope with stress is as important as understanding the stressful life changes and transitions themselves (Coelho, Hamburg, and Adams, 1974; Moos, 1977).

Traditionally, family stress and the demand for adaptation has been viewed as a deleterious situation to be contrasted with the smooth operation of the family unit. Accordingly, the traditional approach to the study of family stress has been to document the numerous psychological, interpersonal, and social abberations in the family's response to stressors and related hardships. Most investigations appear to be shifting away from this emphasis on dysfunctions to an interest in accounting for why some families are better able to endure and cope with hardships over the life span.

Coping research as part of family action-research has drawn from cognitive psychological theories (Hann, 1977), as well as from sociological theories (Mechanic, 1974; Antonovsky, 1979; Pearlin and Schooler, 1978). The focus on cognitive coping strategies emphasizes how the individual family member defines the situation, which, in turn, determines coping behavior. Sociological theories of coping have emphasized stressful conditions in the social environment.

Four basic hypotheses have been suggested in the family-oriented coping studies conducted in the 1970s. Coping behaviors will: (1) decrease the presence of vulnerability factors (e.g., emotional instability of a family member is a vulnerability factor that may need attention in the face of stressors) (Pearlin and Schooler, 1978; Boss, McCubbin, and Lester, 1979); (2) strengthen or maintain those family resources (e.g., family cohesiveness, organization, adaptability, which serve to protect the family from harm or disruption) (Adams, 1975); (3) reduce or eliminate stressor events and their specific hardships; and (4) involve the process of actively influencing the environment by doing something to change the social circumstances (McCubbin et al., 1976; Pearlin and Schooler, 1978).

These investigations have revealed that the family strategy of coping is not created in a single instant but is progressively modified over time. Because the family is a system, coping behavior involves the management of various dimensions of family life simultaneously (McCubbin et al., 1980): (1) maintaining satisfactory internal conditions for communication and family organization; (2) promoting member independence and self-esteem; (3) maintenance of family bonds of coherence and unity; (4) maintenance and development of social supports in transactions with the community; and (5) maintenance of some efforts to control the impact of the stressor and the amount of change in the family unit. Coping then becomes a process of achieving a balance in the family system that facilitates organization and unity and promotes individual growth and development.

Identification and promotion of family strengths

The emphasis on coping leads to a line of research and action to identify and build upon family strengths. This has roots in earlier research but has recently experienced a new interest. Earlier work includes Pollak's (1953) identification of the following family strengths as keys to family adaptation: altruism (giving to others), a balance of independence, positive outlook, flexibility, compromise, the ability to foster growth of members and supportive relationships.

Another early study, by Otto (1963), called attention to the importance of: (1) concern for family unity, loyalty, and interfamily cooperation; (2) utilizing consciously fostered ways to develop strong emotional ties; (3) mutual respect for individual members; (4) flexibility in performing family roles; (5) ability to grow through children; (6) effective communication; (7) sensitive listening; (8) meeting spiritual needs of the family; (9) the ability to maintain relationships outside the family; (10) the ability to seek help when appropriate; (11) love and understanding; (12) spirituality commitment; and (13) active participation in the community.

More recently, Stinnet and his associates at the University of Nebraska have made substantial contributions to this topic (Stinnet and Saur, 1977; and Stinnet, 1981), identifying the following as salient family strengths: (1) the ability to deal with crisis in a positive manner; (2) spending time together; (3) love; (4) appreciation and commitment; (5) respect for individuality; (6) good communication patterns; and (7) a high degree of religious orientation.

Through a survey of family professionals in the field of family counseling and family life education, Dolores Curran (1983) identified what she refers to as "Traits of a Healthy Family." Specifically, Curran identified fourteen traits: (1) The healthy family communicates and listens; (2) members of the healthy family affirm and support one another; (3) the healthy family teaches respect for others; (4) the healthy family develops a sense of trust; (5) the healthy family has a sense of play and humor; (6) the healthy family has a balance of interaction among members; (7) the healthy family teaches a sense of right and wrong; (8) the healthy family has a strong sense of family in which rituals and traditions abound; (9) the healthy family has a shared religious core; (10) members of the healthy family respect the privacy of one another; (11) the healthy family values service to others; (12) the healthy family fosters table time and conversation; (13) the healthy family shares leisure time; and (14) the healthy family admits to and seeks help with problems.

At the University of Minnesota, as part of the program of studies of healthy families, a number of projects are relevant to our understanding of how families cope with stress. Perhaps the most relevant (outside the military-family studies, which will be described below) is the national survey of 1,000 families (Olson et al., 1983). This survey takes a life-cycle perspective and contributes to our understanding of how family strengths may contribute to balancing stresses experienced over the life cycle. Many of the variables identified in earlier research were examined, and evidence was produced to indicate how families with different structures and at different stages of the family life cycle combine them differently in attempting to achieve a family balance. The stresses, for example, of families with young children are different from those of families with adolescent children or in the "empty nest" and retirement stages. The family strengths that were reported to balance these stresses included a core of strengths common to many stages and types of families – for example, the ability to resolve conflicts, to communicate with one another, to generate friendship networks and achieve a degree of marital satisfaction. In the stage of rearing young children, issues of financial management and resolution of personality differences became salient, and in later stages (perhaps partly attributable to cohort differences) religious and spiritual involvements were found to be relevant. Health practices and the availability of personal and community support resources increased in salience in the later stages.

Aside from their contributions to theory building, these studies have fed into the developing action field of family enrichment, and into action-research programs such as the military-family studies.

The development of the marital enrichment movement has been reviewed by L'Abate (1974), Mace and Mace (1976), and Otto (1976). Most marital and family therapists have been so preoccupied with treating problematic relationships that they have neglected to develop or use more preventative approaches. Although a general goal of enrichment programs has been prevention through the attempt to improve the quality of the marital and family relationship, there have been two basically different types of enrichment programs.

Although both types of enrichment approaches have primarily focused on couples rather than families, one approach has focused on structured communication skill–building programs, whereas the other approach (often called "marriage encounter") has been composed of more loosely focused programs. Although marriage encounter programs were developed in the last two decades, they have gained increasing acceptance as churches have begun sponsorship. The Catholic Church developed one of the earliest versions (Bosco, 1972; Koch and Koch, 1976), and now most church denominations have developed some type of marriage encounter program. David and Vera Mace (1976) have been leading advocates of marriage enrichment. They have developed an Association for Couples for Marital Enrichment (ACME), which offers weekend retreats and other programs.

Communication skill–building programs have been more systematically developed and researched than marriage encounter programs and represent a significant advance in the field. Miller and associates (1976) have developed a Couples Communication Program (CCP) and recently completed a program for families entitled "Understanding Us." Guerney (1977) and colleagues have developed a Conjugal Relationship Enhancement (CRE) program (Rappaport, 1976) and a program for Parent-Adolescent Relationship Development (PARD). L'Abate (1974, 1977) and associates have developed and evaluated a variety of programs for marital and family enrichment.

In a recent review of marital enrichment programs, Gurman and Kniskern (1977) concluded that one must be cautious about the overly zealous claims about the impact of these programs – especially the marriage encounter programs. They reviewed twenty-nine studies of marital and premarital enrichment programs and found that only six had an untreated control group. Although these studies generally demonstrated positive change, the results should be tempered by the serious methodological limitations.

Another promising preventative approach is the development of premarital programs and tools for preparing couples for marriage. There is growing evidence that traditional lecture programs for premarital couples most often offered by churches are not very effective (Druckman et al., 1979; Norem et al., 1980). A recent Canadian study by Bader and associates (Microys and Bader, 1977) demonstrated that experiential programs are helpful to premarital couples. Another recent study (Druckman et al., 1979) found that a structured premarital instrument called PREPARE was more useful than traditional education programs.

The military-family studies: vicissitudes of action research

Many of the issues in family action-research can be identified by examining three family action projects that had a common theme and that were conducted over a period of time. By examining family research conducted in collaboration with the Department of the Army and the Department of the Navy, we can shed light on the dynamic dialogue between social scientists and these action branches of the Department of Defense. The three major projects were conducted in three time periods, in each of which the ethos was different. We characterize them as the "open," "developing," and "closed/control" eras of family action-research.

In 1972 the Departments of the Navy and Army began an "open" era of family research by creating the Family Studies Branch of the Center for Prisoners of War Studies as an integral part of the Navy Medical Neuropsychiatric Research Institute located in San Diego, California. This new unit was challenged to conduct longitudinal studies of families faced with the unprecedented trauma of having a husband/father either missing in action or a prisoner of war, a condition created by the U.S. armed conflict in Vietnam. The research team consisted of both uniformed (in the military) and civilian social scientists brought together to initiate a longitudinal study of these families and to formulate support measures for family action studies, based upon the newly developed theoretical models. This research effort, particularly the development of theories and family level measures, was incorporated into the family research investigations conducted at the University of Minnesota, Family Stress, Coping, and Health project.

The expansion of family research in what we have called the "developing era" began with the return of American prisoners of war in 1973 and the initiation of longitudinal studies of these men and their families. In 1976, the family studies branch broadened its mission to include the study of families faced with other

Table 6.4. *Family action-research project I in the "open" era of collaborative research*

Families of prisoners of war and missing in action

Project characteristics	Short- and long-term "action" outcomes
Topic: Effects of war-induced separations on the families of soldiers, sailors, and airmen	Creation of the Military Family Study Center in the U.S. armed forces[a]
	Legitimization of research on the linkage between family functioning and military policies[b]
Collaborators: Family Studies Branch of Navy Medical Neuropsychiatric Research Institute and Departments of the Army and Navy	Development of recommendations to reduce the stress in military families, based on family action-research[c]
	Development or expansion of psychology and social work services for military families[d]
	Development of long-range federal legislation to support military families faced with prolonged war-induced stressors[e]
	Development of recommendations and programs to support military families during the separation and following the return of American prisoners of war, and the end of armed conflict in Southeast Asia[f]
	The publication of research findings in scholarly and refereed professional publications[g]
	Open exchange of nonclassified information with the scientific community without constraints or administrative controls, and with supportive leadership (military and civilian) committed to academic freedom[h]
Research continued at the University of Minnesota, Family Stress, Coping and Health project but based on family data and observations from this project	Development and testing of family research instruments to measure and assess family stress and functioning[i]
	Development of the Double ABCX and Adjustment and Adaptation Response (FAAR) from frameworks to guide future research on families under stress[j]
	Development, refinement, and testing of family research instruments to assess family stress, family resources, family social supports, family coping, and family adaptation[k]
Collaborator: research staff of Purdue University drawing from data and observations from this project	Development of recommendations to guide the family stress management and return of Americans held hostage in Iran[l]

[a]Hunter and Plag, 1973; [b]McCubbin and Marsden, 1978; [c]McCubbin et al., 1974; [d]McCubbin and Dahl, 1974a; [e]Powers, 1974; [f]McCubbin and Dahl, 1974b; [g]McCubbin, Dahl, and Hunter, 1976; [h]Hunter, McEvoy, and Whitworth, 1982; [i]McCubbin, Patterson, and Wilson, 1972; [j]McCubbin and Patterson, 1983a, and McCubbin and Patterson, 1983b; [k]McCubbin and Patterson, 1982; [l]Figley and McCubbin, 1983.

stressors. The Bureau of Medicine and Surgery and its San Diego–based laboratory, now renamed the Naval Health Research Center, encouraged the advancement of family action-research by funding new research on families coping with routine (nine month) separations. The investigators were encouraged to advance family-based theories and hypotheses that emerged out of the Prisoner of War studies. Eighty-two families of naval aviators and their crews were studied, prospectively, before, during, and following the navymen's separation on a tour to the Philippines and the Indian Ocean. Additionally, the family scientists studied the navymen at sea to determine their "long distance" support of families and the management of crises. The Navy was interested in advancing its understanding of what strengths and supports families have and use to manage the hardships of family separation. This information was intended to be helpful to those professionals responsible for counseling families and to policymakers committed to supporting and strengthening families in the Navy. This prospective investigation was the first of its type in the history of military family research.

The third investigation was conducted in collaboration with the Department of the Army and the Army Research Institute (ARI) in Alexandria, Virginia, but in its course there was a shift in ethos toward more closed and controlling forms of relating; hence our label the "closed control era." At the invitation of the Deputy Chief of Staff for Personnel (DCSPER) the research team of the Family Stress, Coping, and Health project at the University of Minnesota entered into a collaborative venture to study the strengths and supports of families relocated to West Germany as part of their "normal" military tour of duty. The Department of the Army had already demonstrated its commitment to families as reflected in its three major symposia on army families. The Army leadership was interested in obtaining current information about what hardships families faced, what families wanted and needed, and what strengths they had to cope with stressful situations. The unique aspect of this study was its emphasis on family strengths and competencies, rather than family problems and vulnerabilities.

The resulting study involving 1,036 families of officer and enlisted personnel in West Germany, located in three types of Army-German communities, emerged after a year of negotiation and collaboration with the research and administrative staff of the Army Research Institute, and the operational research laboratory and staff in U.S. Army Europe. This too was a landmark investigation in that the large-scale survey involved both military member and spouse. Thus, the study was viewed as a "test" of the feasibility of involving spouses in important surveys.

The Army Research Institute, in contrast to the Naval Health Research Center, did not have a record of family-oriented research, was hesitant to enter into this collaboration, reluctant to move the study forward, and absolute in its demand for total control of scientific information. This challenging situation was exac-

Table 6.5. *Family action-research project II in the "expansive" era of collaborative research*

Families' management of prolonged Navy separations	
Project characteristics	Short- and long-term "action" outcomes
Topics: Family preparation for and coping with Navy mission involving separation and family reunions	Expansion of the research activities of the Family Studies Branch of the Naval Health Research Center (formerly Navy Neuropsychiatric Research Institute) to include family coping with "normal" military-family stressors and strains[a]
Collaborators: Family Studies Branch and Department of the Navy	
	Introduction of individual, family system, and community-level measures in family research[b]
	Introduction of a prospective panel research design: families before, during, and following a stressor
Research continued at the University of Minnesota, Family Stress, Coping, and Health Project	Refinement in measurement of family strengths, coping, and social support[c]
	Identification of critical factors in family adaptation to Navy missions involving long-term separations at sea[d]
	Development of general policies and guidelines for family counseling and support programs in the Army and Navy[e]
	Continued application of family stress frameworks to other family stressors and strains in health care settings[f]
	Development of research instruments for future application to both health and military settings[g]

[a] McCubbin, 1979; [b] Patterson and McCubbin, 1983; [c] Boss, McCubbin, and Lester, 1979; [d] McCubbin and Patterson, 1982; [e] McCubbin and Patterson, 1982; [f] Patterson and McCubbin, 1983; [g] McCubbin and Patterson, 1982, and McCubbin, Patterson, and Glynn, 1982.

erbated by the Army Research Institute's prior negative experiences with social science research on ethnic minorities and the release of allegedly damaging information that the institute regarded as unwarranted. Furthermore, although the uniformed (military) leadership pushed the project forward and acknowledged its potential value to families, the civilian leadership in the Army Research Institute, represented by doctorally trained civil service personnel, viewed this collaborative venture as an intrusion in their territory and a threat to the status quo.

The directive from the Deputy Chief of Staff for Personnel to the Army Re-

Table 6.6. *Family action-research project III in the "closed and controlling" era of collaborative research*

Family strengths and supports in adaptation to overseas relocations

Project characteristic	Short- and long-term "action" outcomes
Topic: Family strengths and community supports in family adaptation to overseas assignments	Application of family research Experience of the Family Stress, Coping, and Health project, to the study of strengths, coping, and supports, in army families relocated to West Germany[a]
Project initiated and directed by the Army Deputy Chief of Staff for Personnel	Introduction of research design and data collection procedures to include spouses as well as military member[b]
Collaboration between the Department of the Army through the Army Research Institute, and the Family Stress, Coping, and Health Project, University of Minnesota	Application of family stress framework developed out of projects I and II[c]
	Development of recommendations and policy considerations based on data[d]
	Legal constraints placed on data analysis
	Legal constraints placed on access to data
	Legal constraints placed on university rights to research data and to publish
Research continued at the University of Minnesota, Family Stress, Coping, and Health project	Isolation of critical factors associated with family satisfaction, family distress, family wellness, and family adaptation[e]
	Isolation of critical factors associated with black family adaptation[f]
	Isolation of family life-cycle factors associated with enlisted military family adaptation to foreign military assignments[g]
	Isolation of family and military member factors associated with plans for extension of duty in West Germany[h]
	Refinements in family stress and coping framework based on causal analyses[i]

[a]McCubbin, Patterson, and Lavee, 1983; [b]McCubbin, Patterson, and Lavee, 1983; [c]McCubbin, Patterson, and Lavee, 1983; [d]McCubbin, Patterson, and Lavee, 1983; [e]Patterson, McCubbin, and Lavee, 1984; [f]McCubbin, Patterson, and Lavee, 1984; [g]McCubbin, Patterson, and Lavee, 1983; [h]McCubbin, Patterson, and Lavee, 1984; [i]Lavee, McCubbin, and Patterson, 1985.

search Institute "to provide the University of Minnesota the support it needs to execute the project" was viewed as an administrative problem to the Army Research Institute. This explosive situation was exacerbated by ongoing but suppressed conflict between the Office of the Deputy Chief of Staff for Personnel

(ODCSPER) and the Army Research Institute over who was "really in control" and whether the generals had authority to direct that such a project be executed, or even whether the Army Research Institute was under the DCSPER's command. To add fuel to the fire, the Alexandria (home) office of the Army Research Institute was in conflict with the Europe-based laboratory and its civilian leadership. The Europe laboratory was being reduced in staff and mission, which was in direct opposition to the desires of the sociologist in charge of the Europe operation. In an effort to force the matter, the civil service leadership within the Army Research Institute took it upon themselves to undermine the new family action-research effort, discredit the collaboration, with the hope that the project would lose its momentum and value.

It took another directive and intervention of the Office of the Deputy Chief of Staff for Personnel to revive the research project and to move it forward. Through a set of mandates and directives, the project was launched, but not without continued conflicts between the Army Research Institute and the research group at the University of Minnesota. Unfortunately, in the context of a developing and positive cooperation between the two research teams – U.S. Army Europe and the university, who saw the value of the family action study – the senior civilian scientists in the Army Research Institute asserted their power and authority. Their actions were unique and provocative. The research team from the University of Minnesota was confronted with legal and political confrontations unprecedented in the annals of collaborative family research. Specifically, the Army Research Institute implemented a set of strategies, policies, and demands, including the threat of using military police to curtail the activities of the social scientists, the systematic manipulation of scientific data so as to eliminate the statistical confirmation of observed differences recorded by the social scientists, and the exercise of legal and military controls in the impounding of copyrighted (University of Minnesota) research instruments. Their legalistic and intimidating efforts were designed to (1) remove any official Army Research Institute affiliation with the research project; (2) regain total control of the research data by failing to execute the data analysis in time to complete the project and at the same time not permitting the University of Minnesota appropriate extensions; (3) undermine the collaborative agreements between the Army and the University of Minnesota by prematurely terminating the contract without due cause; (4) discredit the research effort by placing the blame for the excessive delays on the University of Minnesota; (5) ensure that the Army Research Institute would exercise total control of the management of publications and reports by inserting legal contractual stipulations after the project was initiated.

However disturbing this situation may have been, the project was completed by the research staff at the University of Minnesota and with relatively positive results, which included the (1) identification of critical family strengths and personal resources associated with family adaptation to overseas assignments; (2) identification of critical black family strengths and community supports associated with black enlisted family adaptation; (3) identification of family strengths and community supports associated with families at different stages of the family life cycle; (4) identification of specific policies and programs that deserve special consideration in the Army's efforts and specifically the Army Chaplain's mission to improve upon family supports and community programs; (5) the testing of important concepts and research instruments that were developed at the University of Minnesota and that could be used in future programs and research in both the Army and other settings; and (6) advancement in the testing and development of family stress theory, which had its origin in the first project (I) conducted in 1972 (see also McCubbin and Patterson, 1981; McCubbin et al., 1980; Patterson and McCubbin, 1983).

The relatively positive outcomes should not distract from the Army Research Institute's disquieting display of power and legalistic controls. When viewed in a broader context of governmental strategies and policies regarding university-based research and scientific research in collaboration with the government and particularly the Department of Defense (DOD), the matter takes on profound importance as a threat to the principle of academic freedom and family action-research.

Floyd Abrams (1983), a legal specialist in constitutional issues, reported that the Reagan administration was at odds with the concept that widespread dissemination of information from diverse sources furthers the public interest. "The administration has consistently sought to limit the scope of the Freedom of Information Act (F.O.I.A.) and flooded the Universities with a torrent of threats related to their rights to publish and discuss unclassified information – usually of a scientific or technological nature or on campuses" (pp. 22–23). Unfortunately, these efforts to control information have been noticed by those most directly affected, in this example by the University of Minnesota, but by few others. Furthermore, wrote the *New York Times* analyst, "this is an Administration that seems obsessed with the risks of information, fearful of both its unpredictability and its potential for leading the public to the wrong conclusions." Both the administration and the operational components of the U.S. government, the Army Research Institute in this case, appear "to treat information as if it were a potentially disabling disease which must be controlled, quarantined, and ultimately controlled." Abrams (1983) concluded that "clearly, changes in the law to assure that far more information will be kept from entering the public domain, are only one aspect of the Administration's new era of information management and secrecy."

A far less known plan has pitted the administration against much of the country's university communities. The problem has been with data and information, not classified at all. Obviously, the U.S. government's activities have not been limited to threats. In 1982, the Defense Department prevented the publication of about one hundred unclassified scientific papers at an international symposium on optical engineering (Abrams, 1983). The American Association of University Professors (AAUP) challenged the Department of Defense. In a letter to Secretary of Defense Caspar Weinberger, AAUP President Victor S. Stone expressed concern about DOD efforts to restrain the dissemination of unclassified knowledge and the restriction of academic freedom. The Army Research Institute actions (including legal threats, data manipulation to mask or distort findings, military police–supported impounding of research instruments, systematic delays in data analysis to undermine the fulfillment of contracts, and premature termination of contracts) to establish total and unequivocal control of jointly (with the University of Minnesota) sponsored and supported research reflect the extremes to which the Department of Defense is willing to go to control information. Such efforts are directed at universities that have historically received the special First Amendment protection of academic freedom to assure the free exchange of ideas. It is reasonable to argue that although it seems most unlikely that disclosing unclassified research material can, consistent with the First Amendment principles, be made illegal, the intimidating process of legal threat, financial sanctions (and the threat of military force) against universities cannot be ignored and is likely to disrupt the advancements in family action-research.

Summary and conclusions

The past two decades of family action-research have been fruitful. Through collaborative research between social and behavioral scientists and government agencies, service agencies, and corporations, we have all benefited. Scientists have been able to advance the development of theories particularly in the areas of family impact analysis, treating relationships, and family stress, coping, and strengths. Research methods have evolved and been tested through these collaborative investigations. The collaborating agencies have gained meaningful information about areas in which their programs could be enhanced, new targets for intervention – prevention and treatment – and what new and relevant programs and policies can and should be developed to better meet the needs of families.

Five challenges have emerged in the interaction between action agents such as family life educators, clinicians, and policymakers on the one hand and family scholars on the other. One of the ways in which family research has flourished through its collaborative efforts with educators, therapists, corporations, and governments has been through the formulation of five major research challenges that continue to present themselves as shaping future directions for family action-research:

Challenge 1: To enhance the development of children and families by identifying the critical aspects of family life that promote the well-being of family members and the family unit.

Challenge 2: To enhance the well-being of children and other family members by recognizing variations by stages of individual and family development.

Challenge 3: To develop family typologies that are effective in representing patterns of interaction and functioning of families under various conditions.

Challenge 4: To identify the relevance and impact of social policies and programs emanating from agencies, businesses, corporations, and the state and federal governments on family capacity to cope with stresses and transitions.

Challenge 5: To develop effective family support programs to meet the needs of children and families.

All of these challenges have stimulated constructive action responses and new conceptual and methodological development, as seen, for example, in the military-family studies.

However, the climate for government-sponsored family action-research has changed for the worse over the years. There is reason to be concerned about the "freedom of information" that will flow from collaborative studies with government agencies in the near future. As the government sets tighter and tighter controls through its contractual arrangements with universities and other research agencies, there is reason to believe that social science research will be hampered. Even though government contracts may include provisions to encourage and "allow" publications, these stipulations include the added requirements that all manuscripts and presentations be "cleared" by designated government agencies in advance and that the government has the right to require modifications before such a clearance is authorized. Government agencies also have the right to stop publication of results. Universities, committed to the principles surrounding the Freedom of Information Act, have been reluctant to embrace such contracts, and some universities prohibit contracts with these stipulations.

Family action-research has flourished in the past and this is likely to continue, even in the face of such restrictions. There are scientists, universities, and private research corporations who are not encumbered by the current policies and practices that challenge academic freedom. Families have themselves pressured the government and corporations to move ahead with such research because they believe that family research data are needed to guide government and corporate policies, programs, and services. In the face of this pressure, there is hope that family action-research will survive and even thrive.

References

Abrams, F. The new effort to control information. *The New York Times,* September 25, 1983, pp. 22–28, 72–73.

Adams, B. *The family: A sociological interpretation* (2nd ed.). Chicago: Rand McNally, 1975.

Alexander, J., and Barton, C. Behavioral systems therapy with delinquent families. In D. Olson (Ed.), *Treating relationships.* Lake Mills, Iowa: Graphic Publishing Company, 1976, pp. 167–88.

Angell, R. The family encounters the Depression. New York: Scribner, 1936.

Antonovsky, A. *Health stress and coping.* San Francisco: Jossey-Bass, 1979.

Baekland, F., and Lundwall, L. Dropping out of treatment: A critical review. *Psychological Bulletin,* September 1975, *82,* 738–83.

Baldwin, W., and Cain, V. The children of teenage parents. *Family Planning Perspectives,* 1980, *21,* 34–43.

Beavers, W. *Psychotherapy and growth: A family systems perspective.* New York: Brunner/Mazel, 1977.

Beck, D. Research findings on the outcomes of marital counseling. In D. Olson (Ed.), *Treating relationships.* Lake Mills, Iowa: Graphic Publishing Company, 1976, pp. 433–73.

Benjamin, L. Structural analysis of social behavior. *Psychology Review,* 1974, *81,* 392–425.

Benjamin, L. Structural analysis of a family in therapy. *Journal of Counseling and Clinical Psychology,* 1977, *45,* 391–406.

Bishop, J. *Jobs, cash transfers, and marital instability: A review of the evidence.* Madison, Wis.: Institute for Research on Poverty, 1977.

Bosco, A. *Marriage encounter: The re-discovery of love.* St. Meinrad, Ind.: Abbey Press, 1972.

Boss, P., McCubbin, H., and Lester, G. The corporate executive wife's coping patterns in response to routine husband-father absence. *Family Process,* March 1979, *18,* 79–86.

Bradbury, K., et al. *The effects of welfare reform alternatives on the family.* Madison, Wis.: Institute for Research on Poverty, 1977.

Broderick, C. Forward. In D. Olson (Ed.), *Treating relationships.* Lake Mills, Iowa: Graphic Publishing Company, 1976, pp. xv–xvii.

Burgess, E. The family as a unity of interacting personalities. *The Family,* 1926, *7,* 3–9.

Burns, K., and Freedman, S. In support of families under stress: A community based approach. *The Family Coordinator,* January 1976, *25,* 41–46.

Caplan, G. *American handbook of psychiatry* (Vol. 2). New York: Basic Books, 1974.

Caplan, G. The family as a support system. In G. Caplan and M. Killilea (Eds.), *Support systems and mutual help.* New York: Grune & Stratton, 1976, pp. 19–36.

Cavan, R., and Ranck, K. *The family and the Depression.* Chicago: University of Chicago Press, 1938.

Cobb, S. Social support as a moderator of life stress. *Psychosomatic Medicine,* September-October 1976, *38,* 300–314.

Coelho, G., Hamburg, D., and Adams, J. *Coping and adaptation.* New York: Basic Books, 1974.

Constantine, L. A verified system theory of human process. Paper presented at Department of Family Social Science, University of Minnesota, 1977.

Colletta, N. Support systems after divorce: Incidence and impact. *Journal of Marriage and the Family,* November 1979, *41,* 837–46.

Cromwell, R., and Fournier, D. Diagnosing and evaluation in marital and family counseling. In D. Olson (Ed.), *Treating relationships.* Lake Mills, Iowa: Graphic Publishing Company, 1976, pp. 499–516.

Cromwell, R., and Fournier, D. *Diagnosing relationships: Clinical assessment for marriage and family therapists.* San Francisco: Jossey-Bass, in progress.

Cromwell, R., and Keeney, B. Diagnosing marital and family systems: A training model. *Family Coordinator,* 1979, *28,* 101–8.

Cuber, J., and Haroff, P. *The significant Americans: A study of sexual behavior among the affluent.* New York: Appleton-Century-Crofts, 1955.

Curran, D. *Traits of a healthy family.* Minneapolis: Winston, 1983.

deAraujo, G., Van Arsdel, P.P., Holmes, T., and Dudley, D. L. Life change, coping ability and chronic intrinsic asthma. *Journal of Psychosomatic Research,* December 1973, *17,* 359–63.

Drabeck, T., Key, W., Erickson, P., and Crowe, J. The impact of disaster on kin relationships. *The Journal of Marriage and Family,* August 1975, *37,* 481–94.

Druckman, J., Fournier, D., Robinson, B., and Olson, D. Effectiveness of five types of pre-marital preparation programs. Final Report for Education for Marriage Conference, Grand Rapids, Michigan, 1979.

Dytrych, Z., Matejcek, Z., Schuller, V., David, H., and Friedman, H. Children born to women denied abortion. *Family Planning Perspectives,* 1975, 7(4), 165–71.

Epstein, N., Bishop, D., and Levin, S. The McMaster model of family functioning. *Journal of Marriage and Family Counseling,* 1978, *40,* 19–31.

Erikson, K. *Everything in its path: Destruction of the community in the Buffalo Creek flood.* New York: Simon & Schuster, 1976.

Figley, C. R., and McCubbin, H. I. *Stress and the family.* Vol. 2: *Coping with catastrophe.* New York: Brunner/Mazel, 1983.

Fisher, B., and Sprenkle, D. Therapists' perceptions of healthy family functions. *International Journal of Family Counseling,* 1978, *6,* 9–18.

Frank, J. The present status of outcome studies. *Journal of Counseling and Clinical Psychology,* 1979, *47,* 310–16.

French, A. P., and Guidera, B. J. The family as a system in four dimensions: A theoretical model. Paper presented at American Academy of Child Psychiatry, San Francisco, 1974.

Fuhr, R., Moos, R., and Dishotsky, N. The use of family assessment and feed-back in on-going family therapy. *American Journal of Family Therapy,* 1981, *9,* 24–36.

Goodrich, D., Ryder, R., and Rausch, H. Patterns of newlywed marriage. *Journal of Marriage and the Family,* 1968, *30,* 383–89.

Gore, S. The effect of social support in moderating the health consequences of unemployment. *Journal of Health and Social Behavior,* June 1978, *19,* 157–65.

Grad, J., and Sainsbury, P. The effects that patients have on their families in a community care and control psychiatric service—a two year follow-up. *British Journal of Psychiatry,* 1968, *114,* 265–78.

Granovetter, M. The strength of weak ties. *American Journal of Sociology,* May 1973, *78,* 1360–80.

Guerin, P., Jr. *Family therapy: Theory and practice.* New York: Gardner Press, 1976.

Guerney, B. *Relationship enhancement.* San Francisco: Jossey-Bass, 1977.

Gulotta, T. Prevention's parable revisited. Paper presented at the National Council on Family Relations Pre-Conference Workshop, San Francisco, California, 1984.

Gurman, A. The effects and effectiveness of marital therapy: A review of outcome research. *Family Process,* 1973, *12,* 145–70.

Gurman, A. The effects and effectiveness of marital therapy. In A. Gurman and D. Rice (Eds.), *Couples in conflict.* New York: Jason-Aronson, 1975, pp. 383–406.

Gurman, A. Contemporary marital therapies: A critique and comparative analysis of psychoanalytic behavioral and systems theory approaches. In J. Paolino, Jr., and B. McCrady (Eds.), *Marriage and marital therapy.* New York: Brunner/Mazel, 1978, pp. 445–566.

Gurman, A., and Kniskern, D. Enriching research on marital enrichment programs. *Journal of Marriage and Family Counseling,* 1977, *3,* 3–11.

Gurman, A., and Kniskern, D. Deterioration in marital and family therapy: Empirical clinical and conceptual issues. *Family Process,* 1978(a), *17,* 3–20.

Gurman, A., and Kniskern, D. Research on marital and family therapy: Progress, perspective, and prospect. In S. Garfield and A. Bergin (Eds.), *Handbook of psychotherapy and behavior change.* New York: Wiley, 1978(b), pp. 817–901.

Haley, J. Research on family patterns: An instrument measurement. *Family Process,* 1964, *3,* 41–65.

Hann, N. *Coping and defending: Processes of self-environment organization.* New York: Academic Press, 1977.

Herr, J., and Weakland, J. *Counseling elders and their families.* New York: Springer-Verlag, 1979.

Hill, R. *Families under stress.* New York: Harper & Row, 1949.

Hill, R. Generic features of families under stress. *Social Casework,* February-March 1958, *49,* 139–50.

Hill, R. *Family development in three generations.* Cambridge, Mass.: Schenkman, 1970.

Hoenig, J., and Hamilton, M. *The desegregation of the mentally ill.* Boston: Routledge & Kegan Paul, 1969.

Hunter, E., McEvoy, P., and Whitworth, S. Annotated bibliography. In E. Hunter, *Families under the flag.* New York: Praeger, 1982.

Hunter, E., and Plag, J. An assessment of the needs of POW/MIA wives residing in the San Diego metropolitan area: A proposal for the establishment of family services (Report No. 73–39). San Diego, California, Navy Medical Neuropsychiatric Research Unit, 1973.

Jacobson, N. S. Specific and non-specific factors in the effectiveness of a behavioral approach to marital discord. *Journal of Consulting and Clinical Psychology,* 1978, *46,* 442–52.

Jacobson, N., and Margolin, G. *Marital therapy: Strategies based on social learning and behavior exchange principles.* New York: Brunner/Mazel, 1979.

Jacobson, N., and Martin, B. Behavioral marriage therapy: Current status. *Psychological Bulletin,* 1976, *83,* 540–56.

Kantor, D., and Lehr, W. *Inside the family.* San Francisco: Jossey-Bass, 1975.

Kaplan, D., Smith, A., Grobstein, R., and Fischman, R. Family mediation of stress. *Social Work,* July 1973, *18,* 60–69.

Katz, A. Self help organizations and volunteer participation in social welfare. *Social Work,* January 1970, *15,* 51–60.

Killorin, E., and Olson, D. Clinical application of the Circumplex Model to chemically dependent families. Unpublished manuscript, Family Social Science. St. Paul, University of Minnesota, 1980.

Kobrin, F. The fall of household size and rise of the primary individual in the United States. *Demography,* 1976, *13,* 136.

Koch, J., and Koch, L. The urgent drive to make good marriages better. *Psychology Today,* 1976, *10,* 33–35.

Koos, E. *Families in trouble.* New York: Kings Crown Press, 1946.

Krannich, R. Abortion in the United States: Past, present and future trends. *Family Relations,* 1980, *29,* 365–74.

Kreisman, D., and Joy, Y. The family as reactor to the mental illness of a relative. In M. Guttentag and E. Struening (Eds.), *Handbook of evaluation research* (Vol. 2). Beverly Hills, Calif.: Sage, 1975.

L'Abate, L. Family enrichment programs. *Journal of Family Counseling,* 1974, *2,* 32–44.

L'Abate, L. *Enrichment: Structured intervention with couples, families, and groups.* Washington, D.C.: University Press of America, 1977.

Lavee, Y., McCubbin, H., and Patterson, J. The Double ABCX model of family stress and adaptation: An empirical test by analysis of structural equations with latent variable. *Journal of Marriage and the Family,* 1985, *47*(4).

Leary, T. *Interpersonal diagnosis or personality.* New York: Ronald, 1957.

Lee, G. Effects of social networks on the family. In W. Burr, R. Hill; R. Nye, and I. Reiss (Eds.), *Contemporary theories about the family* (Vol. 1). New York: Free Press, 1979, pp. 27–56.

Lewis, J., Beavers, W., Gussett, J., and Philips, V. *No single thread: Psychological health in family systems.* New York: Brunner/Mazel, 1976.

Lieberman, M., Borman, L., and associates. *Self-help groups for coping with crisis.* San Francisco: Jossey-Bass, 1979.

Lin, N., Ensel, W., Simeone, R., and Kuo, W. Social support, stressful life events and illness: A model and an empirical test. *Journal of Health and Social Behavior,* June 1979, *20,* 108–19.

Litwak, E., and Szelenyi, I. Primary group structures and their functions: Kin, neighbors, and friends. *American Sociological Review,* August 1969, *34,* 465–81.

Lopata, H. Contributions of extended families to the support systems of metropolitan area widows: Limitations of modified kin network. *Journal of Marriage and the Family,* May 1978, *40,* 355–66.

Lowenthal, M., and Robinson, B. Social networks and isolation. In R. Binstock and E. Shanas (Eds.), *Handbook of Aging and the Social Sciences.* New York: Van Nostrand Reinhold, 1976.

McCubbin, H. Integrating coping behavior in family stress theory. *Journal of Marriage and the Family,* August 1979, *41,* 237–44.

McCubbin, H., Boss, P., Wilson, L., and Lester, G. Developing family invulnerability to stress: Coping strategies wives employ in managing separation. In Jan Trost (Ed.), *Proceedings: World Congress of Sociology.* Beverly Hills, Calif.: Sage, 1980.

McCubbin, H., and Dahl, B. Social and mental health services to families of returned prisoners of war. Paper presented at American Psychiatric Association Meeting, Detroit, Michigan, May 1974(a).

McCubbin, H., and Dahl, B. An overview of the initial stages of longitudinal study of families of servicemen missing in action and returned prisoners of war. Paper presented at Prisoner of War Research Conference, Naval Health Research Center, San Diego, California, April, 1974(b).

McCubbin, H., Dahl, B., and Hunter, E. Research on the military family: A review. In H. McCubbin, B. Dahl, and E. Hunter (Eds.), *Families in the military system.* Beverly Hills, Calif.: Sage, 1976, pp. 291–319.

McCubbin, H., Dahl, B., Lester, G., Benson, D., and Robertson, M. Coping repertoires of families adapting to prolonged war-induced separations. *Journal of Marriage and the Family,* August 1976, *38,* 461–71.

McCubbin, H., Dahl, B., Metres, P., Jr., Hunter, E., and Plag, J. (Eds.). *Family separation and reunion: Families of prisoners of war and servicemen missing in action.* Washington, D.C.: Superintendent of Documents, Government Printing Office, 1974.

McCubbin, H., Joy, C., Cauble, A., Comeau, J., Patterson, J., and Needle, R. Family stress, coping and social support: A decade in review. *Journal of Marriage and the Family,* November, 1980, *42,* 855–71.

McCubbin, H., and Marsden, M. The military family and the changing military profession. In F. Margiotta (Ed.), *The changing world of the American military.* Boulder, Colo.: Westview Press, 1978, pp. 207–21.

McCubbin, H., and Patterson, J. Broadening the scope of family strengths: An emphasis on family coping and social support. In N. Stinnet, J. DeFrain, K. King, P. Knaub, and G. Rowe (Eds.), *Family strengths.* Vol. 3: *Roots of well-being.* Lincoln: University of Nebraska Press, 1981.

McCubbin, H., and Patterson, J. Family adaptation to crises. In H. McCubbin, A. Cauble, and J. Patterson (Eds.), *Family stress, coping and social support.* Springfield, Ill.: Thomas, 1982.

McCubbin, H., and Patterson, J. The family stress process: The Double ABCX model of adjustment and adaptation. In H. McCubbin, M. Sussman, and J. Patterson (Eds.), *Social stress and the family: Advances and developments in family stress theory and research.* New York: Haworth Press, 1983(a), pp. 7–37.

McCubbin, H., and Patterson, J. Family stress and adaptation to crises: A Double ABCX model of family behavior. In D. Olson and B. Miller (Eds.), *Family studies review yearbook* (Vol. 1). Beverly Hills, Calif.: Sage, 1983(b), pp. 87–106.

McCubbin, H., Patterson, J., and Glynn, T. *Social support index.* St. Paul: University of Minnesota, Family Social Science, 1982.

McCubbin, H., Patterson, J., and Lavee, Y. *One thousand Army families: Strengths, coping and supports.* St. Paul: University of Minnesota, Family Social Science, 1983.

McCubbin, H., Patterson, J., and Lavee, Y. Strengths in enlisted soldiers and their families: A life cycle perspective. Paper presented at the Family Strength Symposium, Lincoln, Nebraska, 1984.

McCubbin, H., Patterson, J., and Wilson, L. Family inventory of life events and changes (FILE) Form A. St. Paul: University of Minnesota, Family Social Science, 1972.

Mace, D., and Mace, V. Marriage enrichment: A preventive group approach in couples. In D. Olson (Ed.), *Treating relationships.* Lake Mills, Iowa: Graphic Publishing Company, 1976.

Mechanic, D. Social structure and personal adaptation: Some neglected dimensions. In G. Coelho, D. Hamburg, and J. Adams (Eds.), *Coping and adaptation.* New York: Basic Books, 1974, pp. 32–44.

Microys, G., and Bader, E. Do pre-marriage programs really help? Unpublished manuscript, University of Toronto, 1977.

Miller, B., and Olson, D. Typology of marital interaction and contextual characteristics: Cluster analysis of the IMC. Unpublished manuscript, Family Social Science. St. Paul, University of Minnesota, 1978.

Miller, S., Corrales, R., and Wackman, D. Recent progress in understanding and facilitating marital communication. *The Family Coordinator,* 1975, *24,* 143–52.

Miller, S., Nunnally, W., and Wackman, D. Minnesota couples communication program (MCCP): Premarital and marital groups. In D. Olson (Ed.), *Treating relationships.* Lake Mills, Iowa: Graphic Publishing Company, 1976.

Minneapolis Star. Statement citing procedure's benefits reported suppressed. July 1981, *13,* 1A.

Minuchin, S. *Families and family therapy.* Cambridge, Mass.: Harvard University Press, 1974.

Minuchin, S., Baker, L., Rosman, B., Liebman, R., Milman, L., and Todd, T. A conceptual model of psychosomatic illness in children. *Archives of General Psychiatry,* 1975, *32,* 1031–38.

Minuchin, S., Montalvo, B., Guerney, B., Jr., Rosman, B., and Schumer, F. *Families of the slums: An exploration of their structure and treatment.* New York: Basic Books, 1967.

Minuchin, S., Rosman, B., and Baker, L. *Psychosomatic families: Anorexia nervosa in context.* Cambridge, Mass.: Harvard University Press, 1978.

Moos, R. *Coping with physical illness.* New York: Plenum, 1977.

Moos, R., and Moos, B. Typology of family social environments. *Family Process,* 1976, *15,* 357–71.

Morgan, J., Dickinson, K., Dickinson, J., Benus, J., and Duncan, G. *Five thousand American families: Patterns of economic progress.* Ann Arbor: Institute for Social Research, University of Michigan, 1974.

Norem, R. H., Schaefer, M., Springer, J., and Olson, D. H. Effective premarital education: Outcome study and follow-up evaluation. Unpublished manuscript, St. Paul, University of Minnesota, Family Social Science, 1980.

Nuckolls, K., Cassel, J., and Kaplan, B. Psychosocial assets, life crisis and the prognosis of pregnancy. *American Journal of Epidemiology,* May 1972, *95,* 431–41.

Olson, D. Effective premarital education: Outcome study and follow-up evaluation. Unpublished manuscript, St. Paul, University of Minnesota, 1980.

Olson, D. (Ed.). Marital and family therapy: Integrative review and critique. *Journal of Marriage and the Family,* 1970, *32,* 501–38.

Olson, D. (Ed.). *Treating relationships.* Lake Mills, Iowa: Graphic Publishing Company, 1976.

Olson, D., McCubbin, H., Barnes, H., Carsen, A., Muxen, M., and Wilson, M. *Families: What makes them work.* Beverly Hills, Calif.: Sage, 1983.

Olson, D., Russell, C., and Sprenkle, D. Circumplex model of marital and family systems. II: Empirical studies and clinical intervention. In J. Vincent (Ed.), *Advances in family intervention, assessment and theory* (Vol. 1). Greenwich, Conn.: JAI Press, 1980, pp. 129–76.

Olson, D., and Ryder, R. Inventory of marital conflicts: An experimental interaction procedure. *Journal of Marriage and the Family,* 1970, *32,* 433–88.

Olson, D., Sprenkle, D., and Russell, C. Circumplex model of marital and family systems: I. Cohesion and adaptability dimensions, family types, and clinical applications. *Family Process,* 1979, *18,* 2–28.

Otto, H. Criteria for assessing family strength. *Family Process,* 1963, *2*(2), 329–37.

Otto, H. *Marriage and family enrichment: New perspectives and programs.* Nashville: Abingdon, 1976.

Parkes, C. *Bereavement: Studies of grief in adult life.* New York: International Universities Press, 1972.

Parsons, T., and Bales, R. F. *Family socialization and interaction process.* New York: Free Press, 1955.

Patterson, S. E. Twenty older natural helpers: Their characteristics and patterns of helping. *Public Welfare,* Fall 1971, *29,* 400–403.

Patterson, J., and McCubbin, H. The impact of family life events and changes on the health of a chronically ill child. *Family Relations,* April 1983, *32,* 255–64.

Patterson, J., McCubbin, H., and Lavee, Y. Family adaptation to stress: A canonical analysis. Paper presented at the National Council on Family Relations Annual Meeting, San Francisco, California, October 1984.

Pearlin, L., and Schooler, C. The structure of coping. *Journal of Health and Social Behavior,* March 1978, *19,* 2–21.

Pollak, O. Design of a model of healthy family relationships as a basis for evaluative research. *Social Services Review,* 1953, *31,* 369–76.

Powers, I. National League of Families and the development of family services. In H. McCubbin, B. Dahl, P. Metres, Jr., E. Hunter, and J. Plag (Eds.), *Family separation and reunion.* Washington, D.C.: Government Printing Office, 1974, pp. 1–10.

Rappaport, A. F. Conjugal relationship enhancement program. In D. Olson (Ed.), *Treating relationships.* Lake Mills, Iowa: Graphic Publishing Company, 1976.

Ravich, R., and Wyden, B. *Predictable pairing.* New York: Wyden Publishing, 1974.

Reiss, D. Varieties of consensual experience: I. A theory for relating family interaction to individual thinking. *Family Process,* 1971, *10,* 1–27.

Robins, P., Spiegelman, R., Weiner, S., and Bell, J. (Eds.). *A guaranteed annual income: Evidence from a social experiment.* New York: Academic Press, 1980.

Ryder, R. A topography of early marriage. *Family Process,* 1970(a), *9,* 385–402.

Ryder, R. Dimensions of early marriage. *Family Process,* 1970(b), *9,* 51–68.

Santa-Barbara, J., Woodward, C. A., Levin, S., Streiner, D., Goodman, J. T., and Epstein, N. B. Interrelationships among outcomes measures in the McMaster family therapy outcome study. *Goal Attainment Review,* 1977, *3,* 47–58.

Satir, V. *Peoplemaking.* Palo Alto, Calif.: Science and Behavior Books, 1972.

Schweinhart, L., and Weikart, D. *Young children grow up: The effects of the Perry Pre-school*

Program on youths through age 15. Monograph #7. Ypsilanti, Mich.: High/Scope Educational Research Foundation, 1980.

Shostrum, E., and Kavanaugh, J. *Between man and woman.* Los Angeles: Nash Publishing, 1971.

Speer, D. Family systems: Morphostatis and morphogenesis, or is homeostasis enough? *Family Process,* 1970, *9,* 254–78.

Sprenkle, D. The need for integration among theory, research and practice in the family field. *The Family Coordinator,* 1976, *24,* 261–63.

Sprenkle, D., and Fisher, B. Goals of family therapy: An empirical assessment. *Journal of Marriage and Family Therapy,* 1980, *6*(12), 132–36.

Stanton, M. Family treatment approaches to drug abuse problems: A review. *Family Process,* 1979, *18,* 251–80.

Stanton, M., Todd, T., Steier, F., VanDeusen, J., Marder, L., Rosoff, R., Seaman, S., and Skibinski, I. Family characteristics and family therapy of heroin addicts: Final report 1974–1978. Report prepared for the Psychosocial Branch, Division of Research, National Institute on Drug Abuse, Department of HEW. Washington, D.C.: Government Printing Office, 1979.

Steinglass, P. Experimenting with family treatment approaches to alcoholism 1950–1975: A review. *Family Process,* 1976, *15,* 97–123.

Steinglass, P. The alcoholic family in the interaction laboratory. *Journal of Nervous and Mental Disease,* 1979(a), *167,* 428–36.

Steinglass, P. An experimental treatment program for alcoholic couples. *Journal of Studies on Alcohol,* 1979(b), *40,* 159–82.

Stinnett, N. In search of strong families. In N. Stinnett, B. Chesser, and J. DeFrain (Eds.), *Building family strengths: Blueprints for action.* Lincoln: University of Nebraska Press, 1981.

Stinnett, N., and Saur, K. Relationship characteristics of strong families. *Family Perspectives,* 1977, *11*(4), 3–11.

Streiner, J., Goodman, T., and Epstein, N. Interrelationships among outcome measures in the McMaster family therapy outcome study. *Goal Attainment Review,* 1977, *3,* 47–58.

Sussman, M. The family life of older people. In R. Binstock and E. Shanas (Eds.), *Handbook on aging and the social sciences.* New York: Van Nostrand Reinhold, 1976, pp. 218–43.

Test, M., and Stein, L. A community approach to the chronically disabled patient. *Social Policy,* 1977, *8*(9), 8–16.

Tissue, T., and McCoy, J. Income and living arrangements among poor aged singles. *Social Security Bulletin,* 1981, *44,* 3–13.

Troll, L. The family of later life: A decade review. *Journal of Marriage and the Family,* May 1971, *33,* 263–90.

Warlick, J. The relationship of the Supplemental Security Income program and living arrangements of low income elderly. Presented at the National Conference on Social Welfare, Philadelphia, Pennsylvania, May 1979.

Watzlawick, P., Beavin, J., and Jackson, D. *Pragmatics of human communication.* New York: Norton, 1967.

Watzlawick, P., and Weakland, J. (Eds.). *The interactional view.* New York: Norton, 1977.

Watzlawick, P., Weakland, J., and Fisch, R. *Change: Principles of problem formation and problem resolution.* New York: Norton, 1974.

Wells, R., and Denzen, A. The results of family therapy revisited: The non-behavioral methods. *Family Process,* 1978, *17,* 251–74.

Wells, R. A., Dilkes, T., and Burckhardt, T. The results of family therapy: A critical review of the literature. In D. Olson (Ed.), *Treating relationships.* Lake Mills, Iowa: Graphic Publishing Company, 1976, pp. 499–516.

Wertheim, E. Family unit therapy and the science and typology of family systems. *Family Process,* 1973, *12,* 361–76.

Wertheim, E. The science typology of family systems. II. Further theoretical and practical considerations. *Family Process,* 1975, *14,* 285–308.

Willer, B., Intagliata, J., and Wicks, N. The return of retarded adults to natural families: Issues and results. In R. Bruininks, C. Meyers, B. Sigford, and K. Lakin (Eds.), *Deinstitutionalization and community adjustment of mentally retarded people.* Washington, D.C.: American Association of Mental Deficiency, 1981.

Wright, G., Jr., and Stetson, D. The impact of no-fault divorce law reform on divorce in American states. *Journal of Marriage and the Family,* 1978, *40,* 575–84.

Zimmerman, S. Families and government as interacting systems: outputs, inputs and outcomes. In E. Seidman (Ed.), *Handbook of social intervention.* Beverly Hills, Calif.: Sage, 1983.

Zimmerman, S. The mental retardation family subsidy program: Its effects on families with a mentally handicapped child. *Family Relations,* 1984(a), *33*(1), 105–18.

Zimmerman, S. *Adult Day Care: Its effects on families of an elderly disabled member.* St. Paul: University of Minnesota, Family Social Science 1984(b).

Zunin, L. A program for the Vietnam widow: Operation second life. In H. McCubbin, B. Dahl, P. Metres, Jr., E. Hunter, and J. Plag (Eds.), *Family separation and reunion.* Washington, D.C.: Government Printing Office, 1974, pp. 218–24.

7 Family support systems: an ecological approach to child development

Edward Zigler and Heather Weiss

Introduction

The past twenty years have been a period of tremendous change for American families as a result of now familiar shifts in employment patterns, family composition, and the age structure of the population. These changes pose major challenges for those who design programs that attempt to support families in their child-rearing and human development capacities. Many of those who have analyzed policy and programmatic initiatives for young, and particularly for poor, children and families, write off the last twenty years as a time of naive optimism with respect to what newly designed services could do to eliminate poverty, promote equal opportunity, and enhance human health and development (Steiner, 1981). In the midst of such disillusionment, it is easy to throw the baby out with the bathwater and forget that it was also a period of experimentation that left a substantial legacy of hard-won knowledge about how to design, implement, and evaluate interventions for children and families. Head Start, and the many initiatives it spawned, first focused attention on young children and then began a cycle of programmatic experimentation, feedback, and revision that continues through today (Zigler, 1979a). As a result of this cycle, and of recent research interest in how the child's environment affects his or her growth and well-being, the conventional wisdom about how to promote early child and family development is shifting from a child-centered to a more ecological approach, one that emphasizes the importance of interrelationships between the child, the family, and the social support available for them (Bronfenbrenner, 1979; Weiss, 1983a; Zigler and Berman, 1983). This approach is currently embodied in many diverse programs that attempt to increase the social support available for young families (Zigler, Weiss, and Kagan, 1983).

In this chapter we will examine selected action-research initiatives, primarily in the early childhood area, to trace the recent history and implications of this more family support–oriented approach to promoting the development of young children and families. We are particularly interested in what these initiatives

166

have to tell about the nature of social support for young families, about the development of effective programs, and about action-research strategies per se. Because we argue that the time is especially ripe for a productive new round of action-research on family support programs, throughout the paper we will also draw out the implications of these past research experiences for such future research.

Action-research has been variously defined, but at its heart, ideally it reflects a mutually beneficial and collaborative partnership between researchers and practitioners to attain two interwoven goals: solutions to social problems and contributions to social scientific knowledge (Rapoport, 1985). We think that it is an auspicious time for action-research on family support because practitioners and researchers each have a substantial amount to bring to and gain from such partnerships. Family support programs provide social support as it is defined by social support researchers; to wit, they provide emotional, informational and instrumental assistance to young families. In the more interpersonal terms that Cobb uses to characterize social support, these programs can convey to participants that they are "cared for and loved," "esteemed and valued," and "part of a network of communication and mutual obligation" (Cobb, 1976:300). It will be clear as the chapter proceeds that through practice, much has been learned about how to build and evaluate family support programs to accomplish a variety of ends for both children and adults. But much remains to be done to document their effectiveness, to understand the changes in family processes that underlie them, and to determine what types of interventions work for different kinds of families. In fact, at this juncture, the development of programs that provide social support to families has far outstripped the capacity to evaluate them and to understand how and why they work. Further, there have been few attempts to conceptualize and measure the social support provided by these programs, whether one thinks of increased social support as a mediator of child or parent outcomes or as an end in itself. In the words of a recent National Academy of Sciences panel convened to address issues in the evaluation of early childhood intervention programs: "There is an overarching need to test the basic assumptions of these programs: that the most effective way to create and sustain benefits for the child is to improve his or her family and community environment" (Light and Travers, 1982:23).

Similarly, although child and family researchers have steadily accumulated evidence about the significance of naturally occurring social support for individual and family functioning and development, no consensus has emerged on such central issues as what social support is or how to measure it. As one overview of research on social support recently put it, the area "is still in a state of chrysalis" (Gottlieb, 1983). Nonetheless, the accumulating body of research about the relationship between stress, support, and human well-being, as well as the research results from recent programs that attempt to provide social support for families to be reviewed subsequently, indicate that this is a very fruitful area of inquiry (Cobb, 1976; Hamburg and Killilae, 1979; Mitchell and Trickett, 1980). From the point of view of researchers with a theoretical interest in social support, the bulk of the research on the relationships between stress, support, and various health and developmental outcomes has been correlational; carefully done investigations of social support interventions offer the possibility of exploring causal relationships. Social support researchers frequently note that their work has implications for preventive interventions; action-research partnerships with practitioners who provide support to young families would be a useful arena in which to lay out and test these implications. In sum, given the current state of knowledge about the provision and consequences of social support for young families, researcher and practitioner alike could benefit from action-research efforts to "do more than the available knowledge permits, by expanding it while putting it to use" (Swartz, 1981).

In the pages that follow, we first trace the evolution of more ecological and social support–oriented approaches to child and family development with particular emphasis on the Head Start program. We then turn to describe the growing convergence of child development research, social network and social support research and program practice on questions about the relationships between social support and child and family development. This is followed by a selective examination of the evidence on the effectiveness of early childhood interventions; it is selective in that we focus our examination on the lessons past evaluations hold for future assessments of family support interventions. This will be followed by a discussion of three action-research collaborations aimed at enhancing social support for families to promote child and family health and development; these are the Yale Child Welfare Research Program, the Brookline Early Education Project (BEEP), and the Head Start Child and Family Resource Program (CFRP). These three particular cases were chosen for several reasons. They illustrate the increasing recognition of the importance of family social support activities as part of early childhood programs. Each one has also contributed to the understanding of what social support is and of how to provide it for young families. Further, these three programs suggest some of the types of child and family outcomes that other social support programs might also be expected to influence. This is particularly important because the bulk of the evaluations of early childhood interventions have limited themselves to gains in the child's IQ as their primary outcome measure; the programs that will be reviewed here have examined some of the program's effects on parents and, in one case, on the parent-child system. The chapter ends with a brief discussion of some of the questions and action-research strategies that might usefully be pursued in a new round of research on family support systems for young families.

Head Start: program evolution and the development of a family support approach

Head Start, the national program designed to provide compensatory education and health and social services to disadvantaged children, was born in the political cauldron of the 1960s War on Poverty. A new era of action-research for children began at this time, as child development experts entered the political arena to advise on the need for and design of programs for young disadvantaged children. Part of the impetus for Head Start came from contemporary ideas about the importance and malleability of environmental influences on child development. Additional impetus was provided by the then emerging belief that early childhood was a critical developmental period and by evidence of the effectiveness of a few early intervention programs designed to stimulate the development of poor children (see Zigler and Valentine, 1979, for a comprehensive history of Head Start). Child development experts brought their knowledge into a politically charged arena where policymakers, imbued with the long-standing American belief in education, were intent on finding ways to promote equal opportunity and eradicate poverty. From the outset, this committee of child development experts grappled with one of the perennial tensions inherent in the relationship between research and action: that between researchers aware of the limitations of available knowledge and policymakers demanding evidence and assistance to mount and design a major new policy initiative. Accounts of committee deliberations indicate that many members preferred to start with a small pilot project and accumulate the experience and evidence on which to base a larger program, but the group recognized the "political constraints" of the situation and struggled to design a large-scale national intervention (Zigler and Anderson, 1979).

This committee operated under tight deadlines and they "soon realized that [the group] did not have the time, the knowledge, or the human resources with which to create the ideal program" (Zigler and Anderson, 1979:14). Therefore they designed a flexible program to provide both educational enrichment and comprehensive health and social services to poor children aged 3 to 5 and their families. From the outset, the intention was to provide for community input and to allow the individual programs to be molded to meet the needs of local populations, whether bilingual, handicapped, or whatever. Therefore there are substantial variations among individual Head Start programs. Although this flexibility and variation have made the overall program harder to evaluate, it did, as the senior author has noted elsewhere, perhaps better equip the programs for their subsequent Darwinian struggle for survival in that each one could gather strength by adapting to local needs and political realities (Zigler and Anderson, 1979).

In retrospect, some of the committee participants look back on Head Start's initial period and suggest that the program was oversold, that no brief program could hope to achieve the kinds of changes, including dramatic gains in children's IQ, that some had suggested Head Start could (Caldwell, 1974; Zigler and Berman, 1983). Insofar as it takes a great deal of effort, optimism and momentum to mount a major national policy initiative, it is perhaps inevitable that the benefits will sometimes be overstated. However, as the senior author has written elsewhere, "Although optimism is a great promoter of action, danger lies in the inevitable counterreaction of pessimism" when expectations are set unrealistically high (Zigler and Berman, 1983:898). We will never know if the original Head Start summer program could have been started and subsequently expanded to a full-year program with less optimism and lower expectations of benefits for children. Nor will we know if there would have been a national Head Start program at all if the path of small pilot projects that some members of the initial expert planning committee recommended had been followed. But given the timing and the declining fortunes of the War on Poverty programs in general by the late 1960s, it is at least questionable. As Zigler has argued elsewhere, Head Start represented a "calculated risk" for the original planning committee, and as such it raises still current larger questions about the relationship between research and action and about the basis on which social policy decisions to allocate scarce public dollars are made (Zigler, 1979a). This tension between sufficient research evidence and the effort to design action programs was partly resolved by the commitment to a continuous cycle of experimentation, evaluation, and feedback for program improvement that has been built into Head Start. This cycle created some difficult moments when initial program evaluation results were negative, but it has helped to compensate for imperfect initial knowledge and has led to an increasingly strong Head Start program (Collins, 1984).

In her review of Head Start's program development through 1978, Valentine (1979) describes how through ongoing research and development activities, Head Start has experimented with a variety of ways to provide services to poor children and increasingly to their families. These experimental programs have focused on: greater involvement of families through parental participation in both center and home-based services; the provision of more comprehensive health, developmental, and social services and service coordination; ensuring the child's continuing development after his or her participation in Head Start; and provisions for special populations, including migrant and handicapped children.

In many of its experimental programs, Head Start has also moved toward the development and refinement of intervention models especially designed to emphasize and support the parents' and family's role in child development. This shift is evident in Home Start and in the Child and Family Resource Program. The Home Start program operated at sixteen sites between 1972 and 1975 and provided Head Start services through home visits. It was particularly aimed at encouraging parents to work with their children at home in order to foster the child's development. The evaluation of the program indicated it was as successful as the regular center-based program in promoting child development (Love et al., 1976) and that many parents felt that they, as well as their children, had benefited in major ways from their experience with the program (Grogan et al., 1976). As a result, six Head Start training centers were established to encourage the incorporation of home-based services into the regular Head Start program; by 1978 about 20 percent of the centers had a home visit component (Valentine, 1979). The Child and Family Resource Program, to be described in detail in the case-study section, built on individualized family development plans to provide comprehensive services to families from the prenatal period through age 8. The program was firmly grounded in the idea that the way to help the child is through the family (Nauta and Travers, 1982). In addition to regular home visits, the program made a major effort to link families into local social and health services and to provide center-based activities for parents and children. The program's family assessment and service coordination strategies have been disseminated through regional and federal training and technical assistance efforts.

Although the regular center-based Head Start program has often been viewed as a program for children, it has been particularly significant and influential because of the way it has perceived parents and defined their role for both child and program development. Definitions of what parent involvement has meant within the program have varied to some extent with the social and political climate of the times (see Valentine and Stark, 1979, for a cogent discussion of the history of parent involvement). But from the outset, whether it meant collective parental decision making, involvement as a means to larger social change, or individual participation as a program volunteer or participant in parent education, the relationship between Head Start parents and professionals was to be different from that in previous programs for the poor; parents were "no longer seen as passive recipients of services dispensed by professionals" (Zigler and Anderson, 1979:16).

Services for young children and families can be viewed as varying along a continuum with respect to sources of support and the relationship between the parents and those who work with them. This continuum ranges from a unilateral relationship between the parent and a professional source of assistance (wherein the parent is viewed as the passive recipient of professional expertise) through bilateral relationships between parents and professionals (wherein the parent is seen as a partner with his or her own expertise about the child) to more multilateral arrangements whereby information and support comes from professionals, peers, and other sources of informal support (wherein the parent is both the recipient and provider of support to others through peer support and informal helping arrangements). Head Start reflects the movement toward bilateral and multilateral relationships; it, along with many other early childhood and infant interventions, has attempted to incorporate a service philosophy whereby professionals do things not *to* but *with* parents (Weiss, 1983b). In this sense, Head Start was one of the first programs to head down the long road toward nondeficit models of service delivery.

Twenty years ago, Head Start's birth initiated a major round of program development and research aimed at enhancing the life chances of poor children. During the ensuing period, the conventional wisdom about how to do this has gradually changed. The role of the parent in child development has been reinforced and there is growing recognition that parents and children are embedded in larger systems that influence their well-being. The concept of nondeficit programs that build on family strengths, not weaknesses, has also begun to permeate the ideology and practice of service delivery. Given the previously stated definition of social support, many Head Start programs, and some of the other early childhood programs with parent components that began in the 1960s, have evolved to the point where they would qualify as family support programs.

Now, when federal support for social service programs is declining, it is even more critical to work to ensure that the quality of Head Start services is not eroded and that the program continues to evolve to meet the changing needs of children and families (Zigler and Lang, 1983). Results from the cycle of experimentation and evaluation that point to the components of effective programs suggest that there are both direct and indirect threats to the quality of the program that may jeopardize its current effectiveness. Some of the direct threats include cutbacks in staff development and training, decreases in staff that raise the staff-child ratio, and the failure to provide salaries and benefits to attract and retain qualified staff. Experience with Head Start and other early education programs has made it clear that staff quality and the attendant support to maintain it are among the main determinants of a successful program. Indirect threats include cutbacks in programs providing services to Head Start children, including Aid to Families with Dependent Children (AFDC), surplus food distribution programs, and Comprehensive Employment and Training Act (CETA) training programs for staff. We have learned that successful parenting requires a variety of formal and informal support from the community, and this is also the case for successful programs. Given these threats and the knowledge about the design and targeting of programs that has accrued since Head Start began, two points are clear with respect to the future development of the program. First, the program should not be diluted by expansion to serve more children, because it is unlikely that quality services could be provided (Zigler and Valentine, 1979). Second, it is time to reconsider the changing needs of children and families and to examine the implications for program services and eligibility. As Zigler and Lang (1983) have argued:

The standard Head Start program should no longer be viewed as a panacea required by every child whose family income falls below some arbitrary level. Low-income families, like more affluent ones, face a number of stresses and have a variety of needs. Some children do need early intervention of the Head Start type, and for these children the program must be preserved in its best form. Other children need alternative types of services that the founders of Head Start did not even envision when it began. [p.5]

The seeds of some of these alternatives are contained in past Head Start experimental programs and in contemporary family support programs to be described subsequently.

The importance of social support for parents and families: the convergence of research, program evaluation, and practice

This shift toward parental involvement and the reinforcement of the parent-child relationship was given thrust by two secondary analyses of the evaluation results from a variety of non-Head Start early childhood intervention programs for disadvantaged children. In two mid-1970s assessments of the effectiveness of such programs, Bronfenbrenner (1979) and Goodson and Hess (1975) compared data on twenty-three and twenty-nine programs respectively. Addressing the question of whether working not only with children but with parents made a difference in program impact, each came to the tentative conclusion that a parent component does result in a more successful intervention, where success was defined as the maintenance of the child's IQ test gains after program termination. Both reviewers underscored the tentative nature of the conclusion, warning that the available data were not designed to address this question.

Bronfenbrenner went on to offer a set of hypotheses about why working with parents might result in longer-lasting gains for children and to recommend a parent-child- rather than an exclusively child-focused approach to early childhood programs. He argued that programs that stress reciprocal mother-child interaction around a joint task or activity early in the child's life reinforce the mother-child system. Intervention in this system affirms the parental role in development and as such, it can "maximize the possibility that gains made by the child will be maintained" because the system develops its own momentum (Bronfenbrenner, 1974:291–92). Bronfenbrenner's analysis had a sizable impact on early childhood programming and is frequently cited to justify more parent and child-oriented programs (Powell, 1982).

Two research strands have also recently come together to underline the health and developmental consequences of the provision of social support for parents and children: Bronfenbrenner's emerging theories about the ecology of human development (1979) and concurrent research on social networks and social support (Cochran and Brassard, 1979; Gottlieb, 1981a). Within child development, Bronfenbrenner's (1979) advocacy of the study of development in context, and his formulation of context in terms of a set of interacting concentric systems or ecological levels, has provided some of the conceptual purchase necessary to examine how various forms of support can directly and indirectly influence family functioning and child development. Citing Wolfle's (1959) work on receptivity to new scientific ideas, Rapoport (1985) suggests the importance of a new generation "who have the new idea in their bones" to the development of scientific innovations. Bronfenbrenner's theories about the ecology of human development have inspired a set of younger researchers who are now testing and refining ideas about how support affects different aspects of parent-child interaction and development (Crockenberg, 1981; Dunst, 1982; Olds, 1982; Belsky, 1984).

During the 1970s, questions about the structure and composition of social networks and the functions of social support were widely addressed among social and health researchers with promising results for those interested in the design of individual and family support interventions. As Cobb (1976) noted in an early review on the topic, it is not news that supportive interactions are important. "What is new," he suggested, "is the assembling of hard evidence that adequate social support can protect people in crisis from a wide variety of pathological states: from low birth weight to death, from arthritis through tuberculosis to depression, alcoholism and other psychiatric illness" (p. 310). Health and mental health researchers as well as family sociologists and child development researchers have focused attention on social support as a moderator of life stress (Haggerty, 1980; Mitchell and Trickett, 1980; McCubbin and Figley, 1983) and examined support as a coping resource (Hamburg and Killilae, 1979). Others have specifically examined the mediating effects of social support on different aspects of parenting attitudes and parent-child interaction (Cochran and Brassard, 1979; Crockenberg, 1981; Crnic et al., 1983). In a longitudinal study of the development of a group of Hawaiian children considered vulnerable because of a series of socioeconomic, biological, and family factors, Werner and Smith (1982) found that the presence of an informal multigenerational network of kin to provide support to the family in its child-rearing was one of the variables that distinguished the children who grew into competent adults from those who did not. At this early stage in the understanding of the distribution, sources, processes, and effects of social support, these various research studies have contributed empirical evidence for the working hypothesis that it plays a crucial role in family coping, well-being, and child development.

Recognition of the importance of providing social support for young families has also been spurred by evolving practice knowledge in the fields of early childhood and infant intervention. This evolution may be partly a function of the fact that because of home visits and peer support groups, even unilateral early childhood programs were sometimes on the parents' turf. For example, task-oriented home visitors, intent on demonstrating ways the mother could interact with her child, probably provided a variety of support and information services as they sat and chatted at the kitchen table. As early childhood programs moved from didactic efforts toward more bilateral and multilateral partnership models, it was increasingly recognized that much of what such programs did informally (answering mothers' questions, praising parenting skills, referring parents to other community services) constituted social support and was, in fact, a very important part of the overall service. Although it has largely gone unmeasured, such support, some program evaluators have argued, helps to explain the appeal and effectiveness of family support–based intervention programs (Weiss, 1979; Bromwich, 1981; Seitz, Rosenbaum, and Apfel, in press).

Over the last ten years there has also been a proliferation of new, often local grass-roots but occasionally state or federal programs, overtly aimed at providing social support to young families through such mechanisms as home visits, parent groups, drop-in centers, and information and referral services. These programs are not limited to early childhood interventions for poor children; they include efforts to promote prenatal and infant health and development, to prevent child abuse and neglect, to enhance the development of handicapped children, and to support and educate parents (for a guide to these programs, see Zigler et al., 1983). Insofar as these programs share many common characteristics, including a commitment to strengthening families, we, along with others, have suggested that they constitute a growing, if infant, family support movement (Weiss, 1983c; Zigler, 1983; Weissbourd, 1983). These multilateral family support programs exemplify an emerging new paradigm for the human services, one undergirded by "the principle, stated in a general form that reveals its dialectic nature . . . that the need is to create formal support systems that generate and strengthen informal support systems, that in turn reduce the need for the formal system" (Bronfenbrenner and Weiss, 1983:405). However, as we noted in this chapter's introduction, when one turns to examine the evidence for the effectiveness of this evolving approach to providing support for children and families, it is clear that program development and social support theory and research are substantially ahead of the evaluation of these family-oriented programs.

As will be clear from the following review of evaluation research on Head Start and other early childhood interventions, this lack of knowledge about the effectiveness of family support approaches to enhancing child and family development is in good part a result of the fact that as programs broadened their focus to work with parents and families, measures of program effects remained narrowly focused on changes in the child's IQ (Weiss, 1983a; Zigler and Berman, 1983). There are very promising exceptions, which will be reported below and in the ensuing case studies, but for the most part, the change in the conventional wisdom about how to promote child development has not been buttressed by a substantial amount of evidence in favor of the new approach. Therefore we have designed our review of past evaluations of early childhood interventions in order to raise questions and methodological considerations for future designers and evaluators of family support programs.

The evaluation of early childhood interventions: considerations for future evaluations of family support programs for young children and their families

We have organized our review of what has been learned through research on early childhood interventions to address three questions: (1) What is the best age to intervene in order to promote the child and family development? (2) What is known about the effects of various kinds of interventions on children and parents? (3) What lessons about evaluation designs and procedures have been learned to guide future evaluations of programs?

Considerations for the timing of interventions

The decision to provide Head Start for 3- to 5-year-olds was heavily influenced by Bloom's (1964) idea that there are critical periods during which to intervene in order to have the maximum effect on the development of the child's intelligence. Based on his argument that much of intelligence developed early and that interventions should occur during periods of rapid growth, the conventional wisdom became the earlier the intervention, the better. However, as the senior author has argued elsewhere, "The problem with Bloom's hypothesis is that it limits the potential effects of intervention to a single period of time, whereas intervention might be effective at any time a trait is subject to considerable environmental influence" (Zigler and Berman, 1983:897). Assessing the data on the timing issue, Ramey, Bryant, and Suarez (1983) concluded that significant gains were made in the child's cognitive development whether programs began in infancy, early childhood, or kindergarten. Hence the critical-period theory of intervention should be laid to rest with the epitaph: "The Head Start year in the child's life is important; the first five years are important. So are the next five, and the five after that" (Zigler, 1979b:507).

We would argue instead that supportive interventions should be continuous. Using the metaphor of a secure family to guide ideas about the timing and nature of such interventions, Seitz (1981) notes that parents do not limit their attention to critical periods; they have a continuous commitment and shape their behavior in accord with the demands of particular developmental stages. This suggests that age-appropriate interventions should dovetail and provide continuous support throughout the child-rearing years (Zigler and Berman, 1983).

When considering the timing, continuity, and content of interventions, recent research suggests that it is important to consider not only the child's but the family's stage and particular circumstances. Work being done on family stress, support, and coping indicates that support may play a major role in how successfully families negotiate various transitions across the life cycle (McCubbin and Figley, 1983; Miller and Myers-Walls, 1983). In the case of normative transitions such as that into early parenthood, for example, there is accumulating evidence that certain types of support have positive effects on aspects of maternal-child attachment and interaction. In a recent study of maternal stress, social support, and coping around the transition to parenthood, Crnic and Greenberg (in press) found that supportive relationships were especially important during the transition period when mothers are adjusting to new roles and responsibilities. In the case of nonnormative transitions such as divorce, Hetherington (1981) has found that the amount of support available to divorced mothers has significant effects on their parenting behavior. Colletta (1979) has also found relationships between the child-rearing practices of divorced mothers and aspects of social support. These various transitions can have indirect as well as direct effects on children through their effects on family processes and parental child-rearing capacities (Bronfenbrenner, 1984). As we learn more about the relationships between support, stress, and coping during such child and family transitions as school entry, maternal reentry into the labor force, and the onset of adolescence, it may be possible to better tailor dovetailed supportive interventions to evolving family needs and circumstances.

The promise of broader measures of program impact: present and future directions

Turning to research that addresses the question of what has been learned about the effects of Head Start and other early childhood programs, several points are immediately obvious. As mentioned above, even in programs that work with parents and provide comprehensive services to families, the concern until fairly recently has been with the effects of the intervention on the child, and, more specifically, with changes in the child's cognitive development (Zigler and Trickett, 1978; Ramey et al., 1983; White, 1984). This is abundantly clear from a recent meta-analysis of programs for disadvantaged and handicapped children. Citing the prevalence of IQ as the primary outcome in the more than two hundred studies he examined, White (1984) suggests that his meta-analysis underscores the need for broader child and family outcome measures. Therefore, in this review we will emphasize studies that have used alternative outcomes and will suggest ways in which new measures of the program's impacts beyond the child might be developed.

Head Start and a number of other early interventions have been able to demonstrate that in comparison with controls, program children show IQ gains immediately after the program (Datta, 1979; White, 1984). However, the longer-term maintenance of effects on children and their translation into school performance have been a central issue among analysts of such early childhood interventions (Bronfenbrenner, 1974; Lazar and Darlington, 1982). In an effort to resolve this issue and to stem the rising tide of negative views about early childhood programs for the disadvantaged, a group of programs for poor children that had begun shortly before and after Head Start, followed up their participants and control children to see if the differences between them immediately after the intervention had persisted. The analyses conducted by this Consortium for Longitudinal Studies showed that program children outscored controls on IQ measures for up to three years after the intervention. More importantly, their work demonstrated that the intervention experience translated into "real world" gains in that program children were significantly less likely to be assigned to special education classes or retained in grade (Lazar and Darlington, 1982). One of the Consortium's programs, the Perry Preschool Program, has continued its follow-up study with dramatic results. Compared to the controls, project participants were more likely to be employed or in training and less likely to be teenage parents, to have been arrested or to have dropped out of high school (Berrueta-Clement et al., 1984). Participants also did better than controls in a test of functional competence.

The Perry Preschool Program's results as well as those from the Consortium for Longitudinal Studies, the Yale Child Welfare Research Program, and the Brookline Early Education Project provide important evidence about the long-term benefits of early interventions, particularly those that involve support and education for families. These studies also illustrate the payoffs of investment in longitudinal research, a type that it is notoriously difficult to get funded. They also highlight the importance of going beyond IQ as the exclusive outcome measure by which to judge the effectiveness of comprehensive early childhood interventions. Zigler (1970) has long argued for the use of measures of the child's social competence in assessing the effects of early intervention programs on children, arguing that social competence may be a better indicator of eventual "real life" performance after school completion. Zigler and Trickett (1978) propose that social competence has four dimensions: measures of the child's physical health, formal cognition, achievement, and motivational and emotional status. These studies also suggest the utility of employing follow-up measures that reflect the individual's capacity to perform as an independent and productive member of society. Such outcomes, particularly where they are accompanied by cost-effectiveness data, are of considerable interest to both taxpayers and decision makers because they demonstrate the economic and societal benefits possible from preventive interventions. (See Weikert, 1982 and Seitz et al., in press, for examples of reports that couple socially relevant outcomes with cost-effectiveness data.)

Now that the field has begun to accrue policy-relevant data across studies demonstrating the effectiveness of early childhood programs on children through to adulthood, it is an appropriate time to move to the next phase – one in which research focuses on the broader effects of these programs on parents, families, and communities. Families, no longer just children, are the appropriate unit for the analysis of the effects of intensive family support programs. Broadening the outcomes measured for comprehensive early interventions would contribute to a better understanding of the parent and family processes underlying these programs and would allow comparisons of the *range of effects* of different programs. We suggest that where appropriate to the program, efforts be made to assess effects on: parents, parent-child interaction, marriage and family dynamics, the family and its relations with sources of formal and informal support, and the community per se (Weiss and Jacobs, 1984). (See Light and Travers, 1982, for a similar argument about the need to develop individual and family measures to assess programs that work to change the child's social milieu.)

A number of programs that work with parents and children during the prenatal and infant-toddler periods have begun to experiment productively with such differentiated measures in the past five years. Some of the types of measures that have been employed include parenting attitudes and aspects of parent development and coping (Wandersman, Wandersman, and Kahn, 1980; Dawson, Robinson, and Johnson, 1982; Nauta and Travers, 1982; Olds et al., 1983; and Slaughter, 1983); parent status with respect to employment, welfare dependence, education and participation in the community (Siegel et al., 1980; Dawson et al., 1982; Trickett et al., 1982; and Slaughter, 1983); family processes such as marital interaction (Wandersman et al., 1980; Cowan and Cowan, in press) and the use of informal and formal community resources that provide services to children and families (Dawson et al., 1982; Olds et al., 1983). At this juncture we know that certain programs, including those providing a range of services to both children and families, can produce significant "real world" gains for children. There is less evidence to understand how these programs bring about their effects. The use of more differentiated measures and research designs should help researchers to build and test causal models of how these programs work. Is it, as Bronfenbrenner (1974) hypothesizes, because the parent-child system is reinforced with positive consequences for the amount and type of parent-child interaction? Or is it, as Zigler and Berman (1983) have suggested, that these programs have positive effects on parents and their sense of control over the child's future that are translated into effects on children, "both directly through the educational process and indirectly through their parents' increased happiness, self-esteem, or sense of control over what life holds in store" (p. 899)? Systematic evidence about which programs promote adult as well as child development is also needed. As we have argued elsewhere, if some programs benefit not only the child but the family and the community as well, they may be preferable to those that benefit only the child (Weiss, 1983a; Zigler and Berman, 1983). It is because of the complexity of the theoretical and design issues involved in these broader assessments that we suggest that action-research, with its commitment to both program improvement and theory development, and not straight program evaluation, is necessary for the next phase of family support program evaluation and development.

It is particularly important not to overlook the impact of family support programs on their communities. First, there is suggestive evidence from a few Head Start evaluations that such interventions can have an impact at the community level. This program, with its emphasis on parent involvement, has influenced parental participation in other community organizations (Adams, 1976), and the presence of a Head Start center in a community has been shown to influence positively the delivery of other social services to low-income families (Kirschner Associates, 1970). One of the most frequently cited benefits of Head Start and other early interventions with parent components is the opportunity the programs afford for contact with other parents and adults (Weiss, 1979; Zigler and Berman, 1983). The popularity of the Head Start program with parents is in itself a measure of success and, as anyone familiar with the recent history of the program knows, this has translated into community advocacy efforts to ensure Head Start's survival in the face of broad cutbacks in other services for children and families.

Second, there is accumulating evidence about the negative consequences of the lack of informal and formal social support for families within the community, particularly with respect to child maltreatment. Garbarino and Sherman (1980), for example, compared two neighborhoods, one at high risk and one at low risk for child abuse. They found that parents in the high-risk neighborhood, although socioeconomically similar to those in the low-risk one, had less positive evaluations of their neighborhood for child-rearing and a general pattern of "social impoverishment." This social impoverishment was a result of fewer social relationships and helping exchanges with others and of perceptions that neighbors would not be forthcoming with support if it were needed. This is reminiscent of Giovannoni and Billingsley's (1970) earlier work on child neglect, which indicated that it was less likely when families had support from strong kinship networks. One of the most promising elements of family support programs may lie in their potential to strengthen the local social infrastructure, both by means of strengthening informal supportive relationships among families and by the provision of more formal support services (Weiss, 1983a).

Encouraging the use of more diverse outcome measures for family support programs involves some important trade-offs, as Halpern (1984) has suggested in a recent assessment of the effectiveness of home-based early interventions. He notes that there are few valid and reliable measures in these broader areas and that, therefore, program directors have tended to create their own. As a result, "it is difficult to have confidence in or interpret such reports" (p. 38) or to combine the results of different studies to find overall trends for future program development or policy purposes. Programs and researchers appear to be in a Catch-22 situation: They can decide not to move beyond the limited number of standardized (usually child) measures because there are no validated broader ones, or they can use measures of unknown psychometric properties and run the risk of "no gains" due to measurement problems.

We suggest, and Halpern implies, that what is needed is some mechanism to encourage researchers and programs to field-test, improve, and establish the psychometric properties of selected measures in order to build a collection that can be used to assess complex early interventions that work with more than just the child (see Weiss and Jacobs for a collection of essays, now in manuscript, about measures beyond the child level that could be used to evaluate family support programs). We recognize that this is a formidable task perhaps best accomplished by a small study group or a consortium of action-researchers who are evaluating family support programs.

One of the biggest issues facing such a group will be that of how to create parenting and family functioning measures that respect cultural differences and allow for a range of parenting styles. Examining this issue in the context of its implications for parent education, Laosa (1983) argues that on the basis of his research with Hispanic families, it is evident that cultural groups differ in their patterns of family interaction and in their conceptions of appropriate child behavior and development. He calls into question theories and measures of competent parenting that are not grounded in the norms of the particular culture. Similarly, Gottlieb (1981b) warns social support researchers to be mindful of the fact that definitions and perceptions of social support are subject to cultural norms. The complexity of these cultural and psychometric issues would argue for a multidisciplinary working group of action-researchers from anthropology, child development, and family sociology, and practitioners from family-oriented interventions, to develop and test parent and family measures.

Turning to the question of what types of programs or combinations of program components are most effective in promoting the health and development of young children and families, several points are clear. First, there is an emerging consensus among early childhood educators, partly as a result of studies comparing various curriculums, that it may be the quality of the implementation (including staff training and supervision, parent involvement, and administrative leadership) as much as the curriculum per se that contributes to the success of these programs (Ramey et al., 1983; Berrueta-Clement et al., 1984). The importance of such implementation issues as training and supervision is also a dominant theme in the accumulating body of practice knowledge written by program directors. (See Bromwich, 1981, and Provence and Naylor, 1983, for example). Second, it is clear that there is a need for research to provide a more differentiated sense of effectiveness – to address not only questions about what works but for whom, how, and why? For example, do certain types of programs work better for some types of families than for others? What are the key characteristics of children and families (marital status, social isolation, parental learning style, sociocultural group) that determine this? At present there is only sketchy evidence on these questions (see Olds et al., 1983, for an evaluation research design that allows one to unravel relationships between family type and program intensity). In her comparison of a home-visit versus a mother's-discussion-group model of early intervention with low-income black mothers, for example, Slaughter (1983) argues that the discussion group is a more culturally consonant intervention for these women. Ramey et al. (1983) suggest that the high attrition rate of programs that require substantial participation by low-income mothers may be an indication that this is not an acceptable intervention mode. In any case, more differentiated research about the appeal and effects of different types of programs for different population groups is a high priority.

Designing useful evaluations: lessons and future directions

The experience with the evaluation of Head Start and other early interventions raises a number of questions about the evaluation designs and methods to be used in the next round of action-research on family support programs. From the outset of Head Start's research and evaluation efforts through to the present, there has been a great deal of debate about whether or not one can or should employ strict experimental design standards to the evaluation of early intervention programs (C. Weiss, 1981; Cronbach and Associates, 1980). As Head Start's first director of research and evaluation described the early debates about how to evaluate the program, there was constant tension between the desire to apply the "techniques of small-scale, controlled laboratory research and the more realistic pressure to apply flexible strategies for the collection and analysis of a mass of data being gathered from the field" (Gordon, 1979:399). In the interim, the debate about whether or not to employ the experimental paradigm to program evaluation has gotten considerably more sophisticated and both sides are realistic with respect to the difficulties of conducting research in field settings. Ramey et al. (1983) argue, based on their own and others' careful application of the experimental paradigm to early intervention evaluations, that experimentally adequate research designs can be fielded despite such perennial problems as sample attention, difficulties with the long-term follow-up of the participants and the control group, and ethical dilemmas involved in assignment to treatment and control groups. In an excellent review of lessons from a variety of evaluations of social programs conducted during the 1970s, Bryk (1978), however, suggests that there have been many subtle problems in the actual implementation of experimental and quasi-experimental research designs that threaten the validity and generalizability of their results.

Whatever one's position on this issue, it is increasingly clear that if evaluations are to be useful for program development and policy purposes, they should be designed not only to address whether or not the program "worked," but also *how* and *why* it did or did not (Cronbach and Associates, 1980; Tornatzky and Johnson, 1982). As one of the foremost analysts of the research and policy process recently argued, "Evaluations that look at a broad range of questions – questions of program process and intermediate outputs as well as outcomes – have a better chance of being relevant and above all, when they help people understand why expected improvements do or do not occur, they help the policy community learn how to deal more wisely with social problems" (C. Weiss, 1981:398).

Hence, there has been increasing emphasis on the study of the process of program implementation using such qualitative techniques as intensive interviewing, ethnographies, and case studies. As a result of this interest in qualitative methods, considerable attention has been paid to developing systematic qualitative research strategies that can be used alone or in conjunction with quantitative evaluation methods (Louis, 1982).

The development of evaluation designs that include both qualitative process as well as quantitative outcome components is important for four reasons. First, process data can help programs assess the unanticipated consequences of their interventions on families. Ten years ago, in their review of early childhood interventions, Goodson and Hess (1975) suggested: "It might be worthwhile to study whether a family's participation brought consequences which are not reflected in the test scores or whether it altered parent behavior of kinds not built into the program approach . . . and to ask what are the unintended consequences of family intervention? Have there been problems associated with a family's involvement?" (p. 234). Second, qualitative descriptions of program processes that document how the program worked are essential if we are to capture the practice knowledge so helpful to others interested in replicating the program. Third, process data help to determine whether the program was implemented as designed. Finally, such data can help to explain the pattern of program outcomes (R. Weiss and Rein, 1972).

Implementation issues are also getting increased attention from evaluators because of the recognition of site-to-site variations in multisite programs such as Head Start. The assumption that all such programs were the same has given way to the recognition of program and site interactions. Further, some evaluators now argue that implementation, as it is affected by local factors, and the mutual adaptation that takes place between program and site, are among the most important keys to understanding a program's success or failure (McLaughlin, 1980). In their recommendations to future early childhood program evaluations, the National Academy of Sciences panel concluded that the study of how programs adapt to their settings is important because it sheds light on the potential generalizability of a program and on the local circumstances that appear to enhance the chances that an innovation will succeed (Light and Travers, 1982).

In addition to site variation, evaluators have also been challenged by variation in the services given to clients within a particular program. Family-oriented interventions have become increasingly sensitive to meeting the needs of individual families, with the result that each one gets a different "treatment" (Hewett and DeLoria, 1982). This is especially the case in programs designed to provide social support (Light and Travers, 1982). Although there have been discussions of the problems this poses for experimental design with its assumptions about standardized treatments, evaluators have just begun to grapple with the problem. Individualized programs are here to stay, so this is an area where action-research involving creative methodologists could make a substantial contribution.

The various evaluations of Head Start and other early interventions, on balance, have pointed up the importance of program evaluation designed in accord with Campbell's idea of "the experimenting society" (Campbell, 1971): "The experimenting society will [be] one which will rigorously try out proposed solutions to recurrent problems, which will make hard-headed and multidimensional evaluations of the outcomes, and which will move on to try other alternatives when evaluation shows one reform to have been ineffective or harmful. We do not have such a society today" (p. 1). We believe that sustained action-research, not "quick and dirty" program evaluation, is key in an experimenting society attempting to develop ways to support today's changing families. Action-research to assess the effectiveness of interventions for young families should have the following characteristics. First, it would be divorced from any contributions to regular administrative decision making, particularly with respect to short-term decisions about program survival (Campbell, 1983). As Slaughter noted about her evaluation of two types of early childhood interventions, "the purpose of the research is not to justify the permanency of the programs; rather it is to point to better ways of continuing to serve children and parents" (1983:91). Second, it would be multidimensional with respect to outcomes. As we argued previously, it is imperative that we conduct research to assess the effects of these programs on a variety of child as well as parent and family outcomes. These outcomes should include health as well as social and psychological measures (see Walker and Richmond, 1984, for a good discussion of child health measures). Third, action-research in this area would focus on program process and implementation issues as well as outcomes, not least because of the insights this could provide for the understanding of the developmental processes these programs set in motion.

Finally, past experience with program evaluation has taught us about some of the characteristics researchers and practitioners need for successful action-research partnerships. The characteristics Kelly, Munoz, and Snowden (1979) suggest are important for successful research in community settings also apply for both researchers and practitioners in an action-research partnership. They include the capacity to handle the unpredictable political and social forces one encounters in any field setting, the commitment of the necessary time and energy, flexibility, and a personal commitment to action-research as a process that benefits both science and practice. The above authors also point to the need for social support and professional reinforcement for action-researchers; in our conclusion we will suggest some of the types of training support and resources we believe are necessary if action-research is to attain professional credibility. Program directors who participate in action-research efforts should be "experimental," not "trapped," administrators (Campbell, 1972). The latter, Campbell argues, "have so committed themselves in advance to the efficacy of the reform that they cannot afford honest evaluation," whereas the former "have justified the reform on the basis of the importance of the problem, not the certainty of the answer" (p. 220).

We turn now to examine collaborations between action-researchers and practitioners designed to assess the effectiveness of three intensive family support programs. In the case of the Yale Child Welfare Research Program, child development researchers worked with the program's developers separately and jointly to assess the longitudinal effectiveness of the intervention. The evaluation of the Brookline Early Education Project involved a long-term multidisciplinary collaboration between child development researchers, early childhood educators, pediatricians, research methodologists, and program staff to assess the longitudinal effects of the program. The multisite Child and Family Resource Program was evaluated by an external research group under contract with the federal government; this evaluation required collaboration among a diverse research staff of child development specialists, field-based ethnographers, and program staff.

Case studies of action-research efforts to evaluate family support programs: the Yale Child Welfare Research Program

This research and demonstration project was funded by a grant from the United States Children's Bureau and operated between 1967 and 1972. The program formed a partnership with low-income parents, from the time the child was born until he or she reached 30 months, to provide a multidisciplinary and comprehensive set of medical, educational, social, and psychological services to promote both child and adult development. It was based on the theoretical assumption that because such parents face a great deal of environmental and personal stress, and have few of the supports necessary for adequate coping and adaptation, "better parenting may be possible mainly as an indirect result of helping the adult to reduce his own psychological neediness and stress" (Provence and Naylor, 1983). The theoretical base for the intervention was interdisciplinary, drawing on knowledge from clinical pediatrics, psychiatry, psychoanalysis, developmental psychology, social work, and early childhood education. The program was a family support intervention not unlike more recent ones designed to support family functioning in high-risk families with a comprehensive variety of services for both children and adults (Seitz et al., in press).

From the outset, it was also part of a service-centered investigation of a clinical-development approach aimed at making contributions to practice, research, and theory development. "In its study aspect," its founders write, "the program was developed as a type of action research in which the investigator not only observes but acts within the field of observation and is part of the process of being studied" (Provence and Naylor, 1983:6). Outstanding features of this effort include two books detailing how the program operated in order to work with parents and providing case studies of program interventions with a range of kinds of families. These books make a substantial contribution to evolving knowledge about successful implementation of effective family support programs (Provence, Naylor, and Patterson, 1977; Provence and Naylor, 1983).

In this program, an interdisciplinary team, coordinated through regular case conferences, delivered a flexible and individualized set of services to eighteen children from seventeen low-income families who had healthy firstborn infants. The program began shortly after birth and terminated at 30 months; it attempted to promote the development of the whole child rather than simply the child's cognitive development. The services included four components: home visits, pediatric care, day care and/or a toddler school, and seven to nine regularly scheduled developmental exams at which the parent was present as an observer.

The home visits were conducted by social workers, psychologists, and a nurse on the staff; they were a main link with the program. The goal of the visits, which took place approximately twice a month, was to develop a relationship with the parents in order to provide emotional and psychological support, child-care advice, therapeutic counseling, and help in obtaining services from local social service agencies (Provence and Naylor, 1983). The home visitors were sympathetic listeners and responded to the needs each family expressed; they attempted to respond to parents' questions rather than give unsolicited advice. Every family received regular pediatric care, including sick-child care and regularly scheduled well-child examinations. Pediatricians made the first service contact with the families, often during the mother's postdelivery hospital stay. The emphasis of pediatric care was on psychological support and prevention of illness and on helping parents to use medical care confidently and effectively. It is significant that well-baby exams were scheduled to allow a full hour of interchange between the mother and the doctor. Developmental exams were also administered regularly, and were set up so that parents could attend in order to learn about the child in the context of the exam and to receive feedback about his development. All but one child received regular day care or participated in a twice-weekly toddler school. The day care was individualized through the assignment of a primary care-giver for each child and the provision of appropriate developmental opportunities. Day-care staff and parents communicated regularly so that there could be continuity in child-care practices and agreement on how to handle problems.

Based on their experience and analysis of the program, its founders have suggested some of the program processes and characteristics that contributed to its subsequently demonstrated success and its appeal to participating families (Provence and Naylor, 1983). Many of these factors are similar to those indicated as important in studies of other successful family support interventions (Weiss, 1979). These include a program that can flexibly respond to the needs of individual families as they change over time, and the presence of a person, in this instance the social worker, who is "the parents' person" to respond to their personal and parental needs. Other elements that were identified as key in serving families included the availability of a center, Children's House, where parents could go and meet with staff for informal exchanges of information, and regular home visits that enabled staff to maintain relationships with the parents as well as with the children. Access to medical care when needed was a primary factor explaining parents' attachment to the program. Finally, in a world where most relationships with professionals are very time-pressed, this program consistently arranged it so that parents would have plenty of time and opportunities to exchange information with everyone on the staff.

Critics of family support programs have argued that they may foster an unhealthy dependence on professional expertise (Lasch, 1978; Weiss, 1979; Zigler and Berman, 1983). This is a criticism that should be taken seriously as one examines program goals, practice, and evaluation results. In the case of the Yale Child Welfare Research Program, the goal was to support parents, not to take over their parenting responsibilities. Parents described the program as "friendly," a term that suggests that, at a minimum, they did not find it to be overwhelming. This is a term that frequently appears in reports of parents' perceptions of comprehensive family support interventions (Grogan et al., 1976; Weiss, 1979). With respect to program practice, Provence and Naylor advise: "One must distinguish in one's work, for example, between outreach and intrusiveness, between guiding parents and lecturing them, between providing them with tangible supports they appear to need and enabling them to get these for themselves, between imposing, even in a benevolent fashion, one's own goals for them and helping them to define and consider their goals for themselves'' (p. 161). Their analysis of the process of delivering support services makes it clear that they felt their success was dependent on a competent, interdisciplinary staff who received constant and substantial supervision and support for the work they did with the families. The program's evaluation results indicate that parents were helped to attain more control over their own lives and that they went on to advocate for their children by means of such things as initiating contacts with the child's teachers. Intensive examinations of the Yale program as well as other such interventions indicates that the attitudes and assumptions that inhere in how programs are delivered to parents are as important as the services themselves (Weiss, 1979).

The effects of the Yale Child Welfare Research Program on both children and parents was assessed at three points: at the end of the intervention (Rescorla, Provence, and Naylor, 1982), and five (Trickett et al., 1982) and ten (Seitz et al., in press) years later. These studies suggest that the program's major contribution was its long-term impact on family patterns – specifically in terms of limitations on family size, improvements in residence, educational advancement, economic self-sufficiency, and quality of life (Rescorla et al., 1982). Many of these changes occurred after the intervention ended; Seitz et al. (in press) indicates that this may reflect a sleeper effect detectable only through longitudinal assessment. The program evaluators hypothesize that the main mediating factors of such family support interventions may be interpersonal and motivational ones; social support contributes to the development of self-esteem and enlarges parents' personal aspirations, which in turn has positive consequences for adult development, family functioning, and the quality of the parent-child relationship. Seitz et al. (in press) suggests that the intervention first affected the mothers' decisions to limit family size (participants waited a median of nine years before having another child) and that this in turn enabled them to further their education and/or seek employment to become self-supporting.

A ten-year follow-up by Seitz et al. (in press) indicated that there were important differences between the program and control children with respect to their school adjustment and performance. While there were no differences on IQ measures, program children had better school attendance records and scored better on a combined index of current school adjustment. The program appears to have had a major impact on program boys in that they were noted less negatively by their teachers and they were less likely to have received remedial or supplemental services from the school. Finally, mothers who participated in the program were more likely to initiate contacts with the child's teachers.

Although these results should be interpreted cautiously because of the small sample size and nonrandom assignment of treatment and controls, they nonetheless suggest the value of employing broader outcome measures to assess program effectiveness and in order to begin to understand the causal mechanisms which underlie family support interventions. Additional action-research on family support programs is needed to determine if they achieve similar changes in the life performance of both children and adults; if they can, they deserve the attention of policymakers intent on providing cost-effective services to strengthen families and promote child development. Finally the experience with the program has led its founders to suggest revisions in some of the psychoanalytic theory on which the intervention was based; specifically, Provence and Naylor (1983) argue that future research should examine how mothers can be supported by others in the process of promoting the parent-infant attachment necessary for child development.

The Brookline Early Education Project (BEEP)

In 1972, the public schools of Brookline, Massachusetts, initiated a long-term foundation-funded research and demonstration effort aimed at enhancing child development through an alliance with parents from the newborn period through to school entry. Influenced by the emerging literature suggesting the developmental importance of the early years and convinced that the school system should reallocate some of its energies accordingly, the school superintendent worked with a group of educators and child development researchers to design a comprehensive program to support and educate children and families during the preschool years. The school system brought in a team of pediatricians from Boston's Children's Hospital as active collaborators in both diagnostic assessment and interdisciplinary research. The project represents a field trial of a family-oriented early education model in which a school system takes responsibility for coordinating health and educational services for children and families during the first six years of life in order to promote the development of later school competence. Through its diagnostic monitoring, BEEP also hoped to detect health or developmental problems at an early stage in order to alert parents to the need for services to prevent more serious later difficulties.

BEEP was premised on the assumption that parents play the most crucial role in a child's development; therefore, the project could contribute to the development of school competence "only through a long-term interactive relationship with the family" (Weiss, 1979). Its underlying educational philosophy was to provide support and education so that the child could exercise his natural talent and the parents could be more informed in their roles as teacher and advocate for the child. Active parent involvement was reinforced consistently throughout the project by such means as home visits, parent attendance and feedback at diagnostic exams, and parents' and teachers' observations of the child in play groups. The project aimed to create a working relationship among the family, the school system, and the medical profession to ensure the best possible beginning for the child.

As an action-research project, BEEP brought together an interdisciplinary team of pediatricians, developmental psychologists, early childhood educators, research methodologists, and a nurse and social worker to design and provide the program and to conduct research on its effectiveness. In addition to program evaluation, research activities were designed to contribute more widely to an understanding of such areas as early screening and detection (Pierson and Levine, 1981) and the parents' perceptions of the costs and benefits of program participation (Weiss, 1979), and to knowledge about how such interventions affect subsequent relationships between parents and teachers (Hauser-Cram, 1983). Efforts to get beyond reliance on IQ and to assess the project's impact on school competence also generated several new measures, including a criterion-referenced teacher-rating scale, the Kindergarten Performance Profile (Walker and Swartz, 1981), a Pediatric Examination of Educational Readiness (Palfrey, 1981), and a naturalistic classroom observation instrument, the Executive Skill Profile (Bronson, 1981).

BEEP is rare among early interventions in that it provided an array of services to anyone who had a baby in 1973 or 1974, not simply to low-income members of the community, although extensive steps were taken to recruit a varied sample. The services provided to the 285 participating families were of three basic kinds: a diagnostic program to detect health or developmental problems, parent education and support programs, and direct educational services for children. These services were provided through home visits, parent groups and workshops, regular developmental and pediatric exams, a parent resource center, a toy- and book-lending library, play groups, and a prekindergarten program. After enrollment, families were randomly assigned to one of three treatment groups distinguished from each other by different amounts and, to a lesser degree, kinds of program services, so that the evaluators could examine relationships between program effects and service intensity for different groups of families. The evaluation design also included a process study intended to examine program implementation and mothers' perceptions of the intervention (Weiss et al., 1976). This process study, based primarily on qualitative analysis of intensive interviews with a sample of participating mothers, revealed some of the program practices that contributed to the success of the intervention, examined some of the unanticipated consequences of program participation, and highlighted some of the important qualities of the social support that BEEP provided (Weiss, 1979). Each of these will be briefly examined below.

Analyses of the mothers' descriptions of their interactions with project staff indicated that the process of how support and information were provided was as important as the services themselves. BEEP staff were felt to have a very successful style of presenting information and relating to parents; this style contributed a great deal to the mothers' predominantly positive views about their experiences with BEEP professionals. The mothers' views indicate that BEEP's style of interaction, as embodied in home visits, diagnostic exams, and center-based activities, had six facets: openness and accessibility; plenty of positive statements about parent behaviors; a nonjudgmental quality; the exploration of alternatives rather than the provision of advice or child-rearing directives; two-way communication and feedback; and an "unpressured" and noncoercive quality. In characterizing their relationships with their home visitors, the majority of the sample mothers described them as friends. This implies a more equitable and less detached relationship than that which often prevails between parents and so-called experts or professionals. This more equitable or bilateral relationship was built on the BEEP style described above, one that reinforced the mother's role as the expert on her child's development and that gave her some latitude in areas such as the determination of the agenda of issues to be covered in home visits. Analysts of child and family services have called for "nondeficit approaches" that build on family strengths and empower parents (Bronfenbrenner and Weiss, 1983); analysis of the implementation of programs such as BEEP are very instructive with respect to the processes underlying nondeficit approaches to the provision of support for families. Such programs are in the forefront of redefining relationships between parents and professionals.

The intensive interviews with the mothers indicated that there were five elements of BEEP's parent education and support efforts that were central to them, some of which had negative as well as positive effects. The five central aspects of parent education and support were: the provision of carefully timed and non-jargony information about child development; the reassurance that was provided by regular monitoring of the child's health and development; the reinforcement inherent in attention to and praise for their parenting; the opportunity to ventilate about frustrations of parenting to a sympathetic ear; and the formal and informal access to other parents with the peer support that this afforded. These supports could also be sources of stress in some instances, as the following examples illustrate. The diagnostic and developmental tests heightened the anxiety of some mothers with respect to their children's performance. Despite the project's efforts not to suggest or impose a particular child-rearing ideology, some mothers also felt caught between their own and what they perceived to be BEEP's way of handling child-rearing issues. In some cases, mothers reported that BEEP provided them with comprehensive knowledge about what they could do to encourage their children's development, and in doing so, pointed up their inadequacies. As one young, single, depressed, and very poor mother of three children under 4 years old caught in a struggle for daily survival put it, "They have shown me what I should do, and I feel bad because I can't." Finally, insofar as the home visitors were viewed as friends and the mothers had come to count on and enjoy their visits, it was hard for some to adjust to their termination when the more child-centered phase of the project began.

The mothers' perceptions of their experiences with BEEP point up several qualities of the provision of social support in the context of an early childhood intervention that deserve further attention in future action-research on family support. Participants valued the latitude they had in determining how involved they would get in the project beyond their participation in home visits, exams, and later child-focused activities; one mother reflected the views of many others when she said: "I'd say overall that BEEP was a support in the background, a resource that was available to be drawn upon when I needed it" (Weiss, 1979:152). The knowledge that support is available, even if one never utilizes it, may be a source of support unto itself; for many parents, BEEP constituted a kind of insurance policy or reserve source of support against potential future needs (Weiss, 1979). The data also suggest that basic support for parenting may involve the acknowledgment of the need for and provision of opportunities for mothers to get time away from their children.

One of the most powerful aspects of such comprehensive family support programs may indeed be the acknowledgment of adult needs in a context designed to support parenting and families. These include adult attachment needs, met through formal and informal contact with other parents. There is mounting evidence that peers in similar circumstances serve a powerful supportive role first by sharing that they have similar concerns and problems and then by sharing solutions. The leitmotiv running through the BEEP mothers' comments about the benefits of contact with other mothers is summed up by the short and emphatic phrase "You too? Me too!" – a phrase suggesting common recognition and normalization of a problem previously felt to be theirs alone (Weiss, 1979). Program provision of opportunities for formal and informal peer contact, or multilateral support interventions, may militate against any tendency for such programs to create dependence on professional expertise and may create bonds and sources of support that outlive the period of program participation. Finally, peer support provides opportunities for reciprocity, for parents to give as well as receive support; this may in turn enhance parental self-esteem. The role of reciprocity in the maintenance of family support systems remains to be explored, but the BEEP process study data suggest that structuring programs so that parents have opportunities to give as well as receive support may be important both for parent development and for the creation of nondeficit, empowerment models of social support interventions (Weiss, 1979).

The longitudinal effects of BEEP participation on children's school behavior has been examined at two points, during kindergarten and second grade, primarily by means of a classroom observation protocol and a teacher-rating scale. These instruments were developed within the context of the project to assess school competence because of the dearth of adequate existing measures. They allowed BEEP to avoid exclusive reliance on tests or on normative rating schemes that compare children to peers instead of to specific criteria (Pierson et al., 1983). Given the project's principal goal of reducing the proportion of children falling below certain minimum criteria of competence, the odds that program children would fall below minimum competence were compared with those for the control groups (see Pierson et al., 1983, for a discussion of odds ratios and the use of logistic regression procedures).

During kindergarten, the observation results showed significant differences favoring BEEP children, especially in the areas of social skill and use of time (Pierson et al., 1983). The teacher ratings showed two overall kindergarten effects: one favoring BEEP children in reading readiness in the fall, and one favoring the control group with respect to work skills in the spring (Pierson et al., 1983). Analyses of the relationships between the ratings and indicators of program participation and family background suggest that the program was especially important for subgroups often considered at risk for school problems (for example, those children with less-well-educated fathers). There were no differences between BEEP and control children on traditional measures of IQ at kindergarten entry; this illustrates the utility of classroom measures to assess the impact of such interventions (Bronson, Pierson, and Tivnan, 1984).

At second grade, children's classroom learning behaviors were observed again and teachers were asked to report on the child's reading level (Pierson, Walker, and Tivnan, 1984). The results continued to favor BEEP participants, regardless of family background characteristics. When both background factors and level of program participation were considered, the results showed that for children whose parents were not as well educated, a more intense level of the program was necessary. A study of parent-teacher interactions during second grade also indicated that BEEP had an effect on parents; BEEP parents were more likely to initiate contacts with the teacher concerning the child's progress in school (Hauser-Cram, 1983; Pierson et al., 1983). This parental result, as well as the effects on the children's school performance, is reminiscent of those of Seitz et al. (in press) with respect to the benefits of participation in the Yale Child Welfare Research Program.

Although BEEP did not collect data about the effects of the project on parenting attitudes, sense of competence, or parent-child interaction, the process study suggests that the program's emphasis on parent education and support activities may well have had a positive impact in these areas that subsequently contributed to enhanced child performance. In fact, the program's evaluators argue that parent education and support should be given foremost attention in any replications of the program (Pierson et al., 1983). The pattern of evaluation results suggests that more intensive outreach and service provision may be necessary for families with more limited educational backgrounds, whereas children from more highly educated families may benefit from less intensive efforts (Pierson et al., 1984). Along with the results from the longitudinal follow-up of the Yale Child Welfare Research Program, the BEEP data contribute further evidence of the lasting impact of a comprehensive and individualized package of child and family support services on subsequent child and parent development.

The Child and Family Resource Program

The CFRP program began in 1973 as a multisite Head Start demonstration program sponsored by the Administration for Children, Youth and Families (ACYF). In order to explore the effectiveness of family-oriented approaches to child development, the program was designed to promote the growth of low-income children through a set of family-oriented services beginning in the prenatal period and continuing through age 8. The program was also an outgrowth of recommendations emitting from the 1970 White House Conference on Children. These recommendations called for less fragmentation in services to children and for a redirection of services to the family unit by means of multiservice neighborhood centers (Travers, Nauta, and Irwin, 1982). The CFRP demonstration built on these recommendations and on the theory that child development programs needed to work closely with families to build a supportive environment for the child.

There were four cornerstones to the CFRP approach: an emphasis on services to the family and on support and education for parents; stress on developmental continuity through continuous service provision beginning prenatally and continuing through Head Start; an effort to provide and coordinate comprehensive social services through direct service provision and referrals to strengthen the family as the context for development; and the attempt to individualize CFRP services through needs assessment and goal setting in order to address each family's needs and strengths. CFRP had an infant-toddler component from birth to 3, Head Start for 3- to 5-year-old children while parents continued to receive CFRP services, and a preschool linkage component to ease the child's transition to school. Within this framework, ACYF urged programs to adapt their services in accord with local needs and resources, and as a result, evaluators found that there was a great deal of variation among the sites. They concluded the program "was invented eleven times" (Travers et al., 1982).

There have been two major evaluations of CFRP, one conducted by the Government Accounting Office (Comptroller General, 1979) and one by Abt Associates, a research firm under contract with ACYF to evaluate the infant-toddler component of the intervention. After conducting intensive site visits to CFRP programs, the GAO concluded that CFRP was exemplary in its efforts to provide and to coordinate community services for low-income families with young children. They recommended it for consideration by Congress as an exceptionally promising model to promote the well-being of low-income children and families. Abt Associates conducted a longitudinal and multifaceted evaluation of the program between 1977 and 1982. Their evaluation research design included a program study with site visits and interviews with staff at each program, an impact study of five sites to assess the program's effect on parents and on children at age 3, a process/treatment substudy to assess relationships between such factors as the amount of participation and measures of effectiveness, and a six-month ethnographic study of program implementation at the five sites selected for impact assessment. The Abt studies point to both positive and negative lessons for future efforts to develop family support services to enhance child and parent development; therefore we draw heavily from them here. Their work is especially noteworthy because it shows how a carefully done ethnographic study describing program implementation processes can help to explain the pattern of program outcomes.

The program and ethnographic studies documented the similarities and differences in the implementation of the program across the CFRP sites (Travers, Nauta, and Irwin, 1981). Some of the major variations between sites were in the areas of staff recruitment, training and supervision, and the frequency and content of center-based activities for children and families, and in the existence and nature of the relationship with the local Head Start program. There was also considerable variation both within and across sites in the frequency, content, and quality of home visits. The eleven programs were similar in their successful achievement of two of CFRP's major goals: the individualization of services, and the establishment of a network of community social services to ensure that families received needed services and to reduce service fragmentation. The program study part of the evaluation showed that this network was more extensive than that normally developed by Head Start programs.

The successful individualization of services was accomplished through formal needs assessment and goal-setting procedures at some sites and through the informal assessment efforts of family workers (home visitors) at others. The evaluators found that service coordination was often achieved by "a system of 'interlocking directorates' " in which CFRP staff sat on the boards of other child and family serving agencies and their staffs sat on the CFRP board (Travers et al., 1982:31). Some programs, such as the Nebraska Panhandle one, actively coordinated case-management activities with other agencies. This particular program is also an example of a CFRP program that had a broader impact on the whole community through its efforts to acquaint everyone with local resources available for families and to create needed new services such as a well-baby clinic (Zigler et al., 1983).

The Abt studies, particularly the ethnographic research, also indicated some areas where there were problems and tensions in the programs' implementation. One problem involved the failure to provide sustained training and supervision to the paraprofessionals who served as the main service providers. Drawing from the earlier evaluation of the Home Start program, the Abt evaluation team argue that paraprofessionals can provide effective developmental services, but only with intensive and continuous training and supervision. Other problems had to do in part with resource constraints. They included wide variations in the frequency and quality of home visits and center-based services. In their efforts to serve every eligible family, some programs had to dilute services. Finally, getting families to participate in the program was a problem at many sites, particularly with respect to working and student mothers.

The Abt team also suggest that there were important dilemmas or tensions inherent in the design of CFRP. A central one concerned the tension between the program's social service and child development goals; on balance, the ethnographic studies indicate more time was spent on helping mothers deal with pressing personal, economic, and housing problems than on child development–related activities. Working mothers presented another dilemma for the program, that involved in the trade-off between encouraging work or training to achieve financial independence on the one hand and the difficulties involved in trying to provide services to tired and extremely time-pressured working mothers on the other. Another dilemma centered around the issue of whether to risk the dilution of the impact of the program by the provision of services for everyone eligible for it or to concentrate program services selectively on fewer families. Finally, the CFRP program illustrates the dilemma inherent in efforts to achieve common child development and family goals while at the same time allowing enough flexibility so that the program could be tailored to both local and individual family needs. Some balance between adherence to a set of common program goals and practices and flexibility had to be worked out in three sets of relationships within the CFRP demonstration: that between the federal government and the local sites, that between local supervisors and family workers actually assessing and providing services to families, and that between the workers and the varied families they served. As the impact and ethnographic data show, the CFRP experience testifies that it is not easy to strike the necessary balance at any level.

The effects of the CFRP program were assessed on five sets of outcomes: child development and achievement; parent-child interaction and teaching skills; maternal and child health; family coping and functioning; and family circumstances. These outcome areas were chosen in accord with the theoretical model inherent in the CFRP approach: The provision of support services, including information on child development and the parents' role in it, would lead to enhanced family functioning and parent-child interaction, and ultimately, to improvements in the child's health and development. The results of three-year evaluation (Nauta and Travers, 1982; Travers et al., 1982) indicate that CFRP was effective in increasing access to and use of sources by clients and that it had a positive effect on family circumstances in that there was a substantial increase in the proportion of CFRP mothers who were employed or in training. The program had only a modest effect on the use of health care, perhaps because this was a high-priority area for both program and control families (Nauta and Travers, 1982). The program increased mothers' feelings of efficacy and sense of control over events in their lives and expanded their awareness of their role as educators. There is also some evidence, from a two-site observational study of families who participated heavily in the program, that CFRP had a positive effect on parent-child interaction.

However, the examinations of the effects of the program on children's social and cognitive development that were conducted after approximately eighteen months and three years of program participation showed no significant differences between program and control children. The Abt evaluators suggest that the lack of child effects is explained by some of the problems, pointed up in their ethnographic study, that resulted in an insufficiently intense child development intervention. These included the tension between social service and child development activities in highly stressed families, the low participation rates of many families, and the sometimes laissez-faire supervision of family workers. Alternatively, at least in the case of the subset of families who participated heavily in the program and who showed the greatest changes in child-rearing attitudes and practices, a sleeper effect could be operating. These children might well look different from the controls subsequently in school-performance measures. This would be consonant with results of previously described interventions, but it will remain an unknown because the CFRP evaluation does not have a longitudinal follow-up component.

The CFRP case illustrates the benefits of including an ethnographic or qualitative component in program evaluations. In this instance, the ethnographic data provided information useful in interpreting results, but, equally important, it pointed to some of the problems and tensions likely to occur in the implementation of such programs with low-income families. The results from the process/treatment substudy suggesting that the intensity and duration of participation are related to program effectiveness, coupled with ethnographic data indicating that some programs had low rates of service provision and participation, bespeak the importance of future studies that examine the determinants of participation, particularly among low-income families. Such studies should also point to strategies that promote participation for use by future programs. The CFRP and BEEP evaluations suggest the working hypothesis that intense programs with high participation may be necessary to affect the development of less-well-educated and low-income families. The results from CFRP as well as from BEEP and the Yale Child Welfare Research Program together suggest that the benefits of these intensive family support programs for children may lie both in immediate improvement in the quality of their lives and ultimately in longer-term impacts on their school and life performance.

Conclusions

At the outset, we argued that it is an auspicious time for a new round of action-research on family programs because both practitioners and researchers have much to bring to and gain from partnerships aimed at assessing this promising approach to child and adult development. As the review of past early childhood interventions and the case studies indicate, previous action-research efforts have begun to demonstrate the effectiveness of family support interventions for both children and adults in part because evaluators have moved from exclusive reliance on IQ to other types of measures. In the process, they have helped to revise understanding of the role that intelligence plays in human adaptation. Researchers have also begun to trace out the ways in which social support mediates various child and family health and developmental outcomes. In future rounds of action-research on family support, attention should broaden from consideration of the family's role in child development to include the examination of the relationships between the family and the external institutions with which it increasingly shares its responsibility for child nurturance, including child-care purveyors and schools.

Researchers and practitioners now have enough questions in common about the sources and consequences of social support to be able to design mutually beneficial and productive partnerships to further both knowledge and practice. Some of the questions currently at the intersection of research and practice include the following: What is the relative importance of internal (to the family) versus external support for parenting (Belsky, 1984; Crnic and Greenberg, in press), and what are the implications of this for the design of family support programs – for example: Should programs be designed to support and reinforce the father's role in the family because this would significantly enhance the support available for mothers? Should support programs for teenage mothers include a component for grandmothers and/or fathers, the two most often mentioned sources of support these mothers report they have (Colletta, 1981; Crockenberg, in press)? How important are reciprocity and exchange to social support processes and programs? (Are programs in which parents have to give as well as receive information and support better at building parental self-esteem and competence, and in promoting informal support networks [Weiss, 1979]?) What is the relationship between family functioning and social support? As Bronfenbrenner (1984) has suggested, future "research designs must take into account the possibility that causal processes may be operating in the reverse direction, with supportive social networks or participation in a family support program being a creation rather than a condition of constructive family functioning" (p. 43). What are the relationships between levels and sources of stress and support, and different measures of child and family development? Are there some families who are so stressed economically, emotionally, and otherwise that they do not benefit from available informal social support (Crockenberg, in press) or from formal support interventions? Is it necessary to achieve a certain threshold whereby basic needs for food, clothing, and shelter are met before families can benefit from social support interventions? Finally, under what familial conditions does support become a source of stress? Belle (1982) has pointed out, for example, that poor single mothers' efforts to maintain a supportive social network are often a significant source of stress.

The above questions as well as the nature and complexity of the issues involved in assessing family support programs are such that long-term and intensive action-research partnerships, rather than quick-and-dirty evaluation efforts, are essential. The next round of action-research should go beyond the question of whether or not a program "works" to ask what works, for whom, how, when, and why. These more differentiated questions require attention to the development of a broad set of outcome measures, collection of process and implementation data, and longitudinal research designs.

In addition to a legacy of knowledge about how to design and evaluate social action programs, Head Start – and the cycle of research and demonstration programs that it spawned – has increased the training and opportunities open to social scientists interested in action-research. These programs pointed up the tensions at the intersection of research, policy, and practice and called attention to the need for broader training in social policy and action-research for students of child development. As a result, during the 1970s a number of ongoing training programs and internships, such as the Bush Programs in Child Development and Social Policy and the Congressional Science Fellowships, were initiated to train interested professionals in the design of policy-relevant research, in the conduct of research in politically charged environments, and in the translation of research into a form relevant for policymakers. To reinforce the importance of action-research and provide an avenue for publication of the results of such work, the *Journal of Applied Developmental Psychology* was begun in 1980 (Zigler, 1980). These training and publication provisions may serve as powerful incentives for researchers to enter action-research partnerships. However, if there is to be a major new round of action-research on family support programs, we argue that the federal government also needs to get into the action.

Zigler and Muenchow (in press) have recently proposed that children be given a room of their own within the federal executive branch through a revivification of the Children's Bureau. One of the functions of the reorganized Bureau would be to initiate research and demonstration activities to discover and test promising intervention strategies; hence the Bureau could begin a coordinated effort to test the effectiveness of carefully selected family support programs. At the present time much of the information about effective family support programs is scattered in program reports and journal articles; distillation and dissemination would therefore be other key functions of such a bureau.

References

Adams, D. *Parent involvement: Parent development*. Oakland, Calif.: Center for the Study of Parent Involvement, 1976.

Belle, D. Social ties and social support. In D. Belle (Ed.), *Lives in stress: Women and depression*. Beverly Hills: Sage, 1982.

Belsky, J. The determinants of parenting: A process model. *Child Development, 1984, 55,* 83–96.

Berrueta-Clement, J., Schweinhard, L., Barnett, W., Epstein, A., and Weikert, D. *Changed lives: The effects of the Perry Preschool Program on youths through age 19*. Monographs of the High/Scope Educational Research Foundation, No. 8. Ypsilanti, Mich.: High/Scope Press, 1984.

Bloom, B. *Stability and change in human characteristics*. New York: Wiley, 1964.

Bromwich, R. *Working with parents and infants*. Baltimore: University Park Press, 1981.

Bronfenbrenner, U. Is early education effective? *Columbia Teachers College Record, 1974, 76(2),* 279–303.

Bronfenbrenner, U. *The ecology of human development: Experiments by nature and design*. Cambridge, Mass.: Harvard University Press, 1979.

Bronfenbrenner, U. The ecology of the family as a context for human development: Research perspectives. Paper prepared for the Human Learning and Behavior Branch of the National Institute of Child Health and Development, Cornell University, Ithaca, New York, 1984.

Bronfenbrenner, U., and Weiss, H. Beyond policies without people: An ecological perspective on child and family policy. In E. Zigler, S. Kagan, and E. Klugman (Eds.), *Children, families and government: Perspectives on American social policy*. Cambridge, Mass.: Harvard University Press, 1983.

Bronson, M. Naturalistic observation as a method of assessing problems at entry to school. Paper presented at the biennial meeting of the Society for Research in Child Development, Boston, Massachusetts, 1981.

Bronson, M., Pierson, D., and Tivnan, T. The effects of early education on children's competence in elementary school. *Evaluation Review, 1984, 8,* 615–29.

Bryk, A. Evaluating program impact: A time to cast away stones, a time to gather stones together. *New Directions for Program Evaluation, 1978, 1,* 31–58.

Caldwell, B. A decade of early intervention programs: What we have learned. *American Journal of Orthopsychiatry, 1974, 44,* 491–96.

Campbell, D. Reforms as experiments. *American Psychologist, 1969, 24,* 409–29.

Campbell, D. Methods for the experimenting society. Preliminary draft of paper delivered to the Eastern Psychological Association, April 17, 1971, and to the American Psychological Association, September 5, 1971.

Campbell, D. Reforms as experiments. In C. Weiss (Ed.), *Evaluating action programs: Readings in social action and education.* Boston: Allyn & Bacon, 1972.

Campbell, D. The threats to validity added when applied social science research is packaged as "program evaluation in the service of administrative decision-making." Paper presented at a conference on family support programs, Yale Bush Center in Child Development and Social Policy, New Haven, Connecticut, May 1983.

Cobb, S. Social support as a moderator of life stress. *Psychosomatic Medicine,* 1976, *38,* 300–314.

Cochran, M., and Brassard, J. Child development and personal social networks. *Child Development,* 1979, *50*(3), 601–16.

Colletta, N. Support systems after divorce: Incidence and impact. *Journal of Marriage and the Family,* 1979, *41*(4), 837–46.

Colletta, N. Social support and the risk of maternal rejection by adolescent mothers. *Journal of Psychology,* 1981, *109,* 191–97.

Collins, R. Head Start: A review of research with implications for practice in early childhood education. Paper presented at the American Educational Research Association, New Orleans, Louisiana, April 1984.

Comptroller General of the United States. Report to the Congress: Early childhood and family development programs improve the quality of life of low-income families. Washington, D.C.: Government Accounting Office, 1979.

Cowan, C., and Cowan, P. A preventive intervention for couples becoming parents. In Z. Boukydis (Ed.), *Research on support for parents in the postnatal period.* Norwood, N.J.: Ablex, in press.

Crnic, K., and Greenberg, M. Maternal stress, social support, and coping: Influences on the early mother-infant relationship. In Z. Boukydis (Ed.), *Research on support for parents and infants in the postnatal period.* Norwood, N.J.: Ablex, in press.

Crnic, K., Greenburg, M., Ragozin, A., Robinson, N., and Basham, R. Effects of stress and social support on mothers and premature and full-term infants. *Child Development,* 1983, *54,* 209–17.

Crockenberg, S. Infant irritability, mother responsiveness, and social support influences on the security of infant-mother attachment. *Child Development,* 1981, *52,* 857–65.

Crockenberg, S. Support for adolescent mothers during the postnatal period: Theory and research. In Z. Boukydis (Ed.), *Research on support for parents and infants in the postnatal period.* Norwood, N.J.: Ablex, in press.

Cronbach, L., and Associates. *Toward reform of program evaluation: Aims, methods and institutional arrangements.* San Francisco: Jossey-Bass, 1980.

Datta, L. Another spring and other hopes: Some findings from national evaluations of Project Head Start. In E. Zigler and J. Valentine (Eds.), *Project Head Start: A legacy of the War on Poverty.* New York: Free Press, 1979.

Dawson, P., Robinson, J., and Johnson, C. Informal social support as an intervention. *Zero to Three,* 1982, *3*(2), 1–5.

Dunst, C. Early intervention, social support, and institutional avoidance. Paper presented at the annual meeting of the Southeastern American Association on Mental Deficiency, Louisville, Kentucky, 1982.

Garbarino, J., and Sherman, D. High-risk neighborhoods and high-risk families: The human ecology of child maltreatment. *Child Development,* 1980, *51,* 188–98.

Giovannoni, J., and Billingsley, A. Child neglect among the poor: A study of parental adequacy in families of three ethnic groups. *Child Welfare,* 1970, *49,* 196–204.

Goodson, B., and Hess, R. *Parents as teachers of young children: An evaluative review of some contemporary concepts and programs.* Stanford, Calif.: Stanford University, 1979.

Gordon, E. Evaluation during the early years of Head Start. In E. Zigler and J. Valentine (Eds.), *Project Head Start: A legacy of the War on Poverty.* New York: Free Press, 1979.

Gottlieb, B. Social networks and social support in community mental health. In B. Gottlieb (Ed.), *Social networks and social support.* Beverly Hills, Calif.: Sage, 1981(a).

Gottlieb, B. Preventive interventions involving social networks and social support. In B. Gottlieb (Ed.), *Social networks and social support.* Beverly Hills, Calif.: Sage, 1981(b).

Gottlieb, B. Social support as a focus for integrative research in psychology. *American Psychologist,* 1983, *38*(3), 278–87.

Grogran, M., Hewett, K., Nauta, M., Rubin, A., and Stein, M. *The homesbook: What home-based programs can do with children and families.* Cambridge, Mass.: Abt Associates, 1976.

Haggerty, R. Life stress, illness and social supports. *Developmental Medicine and Child Neurology,* 1980, *22,* 391–400.

Halpern, R. Lack of effects for home-based early interventions? Some possible explanations. *American Journal of Orthopsychiatry,* 1984, *54*(1), 33–42.

Hamburg, B., and Killilae, M. Relation of social support, stress, illness and use of health services. In *Healthy people: The Surgeon General's report on health promotion and disease prevention.* Background papers. Report to the Surgeon General by the Institute of Medicine, National Academy of Sciences (DHEW Pub. No. 79-55071A), 1979.

Hauser-Cram, P. A question of balance: Relationships between parents and teachers. Doctoral dissertation, Harvard Graduate School of Education, 1983.

Hetherington, E. Children of divorce. In R. Henderson (Ed.), *Parent-child interaction.* New York: Academic Press, 1981.

Hewett, K. (assisted by D. DeLoria). Comprehensive family service programs: Special features and associated measurement problems. In R. Light and J. Travers (Eds.), *Learning from experience: Evaluating early childhood demonstration programs.* Washington, D.C.: National Academy Press, 1982.

Kelly, J., Munoz, R., and Snowden, L. Characteristics of community research projects and the implementation process. In R. Munoz, L. Snowden, and J. Kelly (Eds.), *Social and psychological research in community settings.* San Francisco: Jossey-Bass, 1979.

Kirschner Associates. *A national survey of the impact of Head Start Centers on community institutions.* Albuquerque, New Mexico, 1970.

Laosa, L. Parent education, cultural pluralism and public policy: The uncertain connection. Unpublished paper. Educational Testing Service, Princeton, New Jersey, 1983.

Lasch, C. *Haven in a heartless world.* New York: Basic Books, 1977.

Lazar, I., and Darlington, R. Lasting effects of early education: A report from the Consortium for longitudinal studies. *Monographs of the Society for Research in Child Development,* 1982, *47,* 2–3 (Serial No. 195).

Light, R., and Travers, J. *Learning from experience: Evaluating early childhood demonstration programs.* Washington, D.C.: National Academy Press, 1982.

Louis, K. Multisite/multimethod studies. *American Behavioral Scientist,* 1982, *25*(1).

Love, J., Nauta, M., Coelen, C., Hewitt, K., and Ruopp, R. *National Home Start evaluation: Final report, findings and implications.* Cambridge, Mass.: Abt Associates, 1976.

McCubbin, H., and Figley, C. (Eds.). *Stress and the family.* New York: Brunner/Mazel, 1983.

McLaughlin, M. Evaluation and alchemy. In J. Pincus (Ed.), *Educational evaluation in the public policy setting.* Santa Monica, Calif.: RAND, 1980.

Miller, B., and Myers-Walls, J. Parenthood: Stresses and coping strategies. In H. McCubbin and C. Figley (Eds.), *Stress and the family.* New York: Brunner/Mazel, 1983.

Mitchell, R., and Trickett, E. Task force report: Social networks as mediators of social support. *Community Mental Health Journal,* 1980, *16*(1), 27–44.

Nauta, M., and Travers, J. *The effects of a social program: Executive summary of CFRP's infant-toddler component.* Cambridge, Mass.: Abt Associates, 1982.

Olds, D. The prenatal/early infancy project: An ecological approach to prevention of developmental disabilities. In J. Belsky (Ed.), *In the beginning: Readings on infancy.* New York: Columbia University Press, 1982.

Olds, D., Henderson, C., Birmingham, M., and Chamberlain, R. Final report: Prenatal/early infancy project. Prepared for the Maternal and Child Health and Crippled Children's Services Research Grants Program, Elmira, New York, 1983.

Palfrey, J. Pediatric assessment of the health and development of children entering kindergarten. Paper presented at the biennial meeting of the Society for Research in Child Development, Boston, Massachusetts, 1981.

Pierson, D., and Levine, M. The integration of multiple perspectives in the assessment of children's educational problems. Paper presented at the biennial meeting of the Society for Research in Child Development, Boston, Massachusetts, 1981.

Pierson, D., Bronson, M., Dromey, E., Swartz, J., Tivnan, T., and Walker, D. The impact of early education: Measured by classroom observations and teacher ratings of children in kindergarten. *Evaluation Review,* 1983, 7(2), 191–216.

Pierson, D., Walker, D., and Tivnan, T. A school-based program from infancy to kindergarten for children and their parents. *The Personnel and Guidance Journal,* 1984, 62(8), 448–55.

Powell, D. From child to parent: Changing conceptions of early childhood intervention. In W. M. Bridgeland and E. A. Duane (Eds.), *The annals of the American Academy of Political and Social Science* (Vol. 461). Beverly Hills, Calif.: Sage, 1982, pp. 135–44.

Provence, S., and Naylor, A. *Working with disadvantaged parents and their children.* New Haven, Conn.: Yale University Press, 1983.

Provence, S., Naylor, A., and Patterson, J. *The challenge of daycare.* New Haven, Conn.: Yale University Press, 1977.

Ramey, C., Bryant, D., and Suarez, T. Preschool compensatory education and the modifiability of intelligence: A critical review. In D. Detterman (Ed.), *Current topics in human intelligence.* Norwood, N.J.: Ablex, 1983.

Rapoport, R. Research and action. In R. Rapoport (Ed.), *Children, youth, and families: The action-research relationship.* Cambridge University Press, 1985.

Rein, M. *From policy to practice.* New York: Macmillan, 1983.

Rescorla, L., Provence, S., and Naylor, A. The Yale Child Welfare Research Program: Description and results. In E. Zigler and E. Gordon (Eds.), *Daycare: Scientific and social policy issues.* Boston: Auburn House, 1982.

Seitz, V. Preschool intervention: Strategies for the 1980s. Paper presented at the meeting of the American Association for the Advancement of Science, Toronto, January 1981.

Seitz, V., Rosenbaum, L., and Apfel, N. Effects of family support intervention: A ten-year follow-up. *Child Development,* in press.

Siegel, E., Bauman, K., Schaefer, E., Saunders, M., and Ingram, D. Hospital and home support during infancy: Impact on maternal attachment, child abuse and neglect, and health care utilization. *Pediatrics,* 1980, 66(2), 183–90.

Slaughter, D. Early intervention and its effects on maternal and child development. *Monographs of the Society for Research in Child Development,* 1983, 48, 4 (Serial No. 202).

Steiner, G. *The futility of family policy.* Washington, D.C.: The Brookings Institution, 1981.

Swartz, P. Throwing science at problems. Paper prepared for the William T. Grant Foundation Conference on Action Research, New York, June 1981.

Tornatzky, L., and Johnson, E. Research on implementation: Implications for evaluation practice and evaluation policy. *Evaluation and Program Planning,* 1982, 5, 193–98.

Travers, J., Nauta, M., and Irwin, N. *The culture of a social program: An ethnographic study of CFRP – summary volume.* Cambridge, Mass.: Abt Associates, 1981.

Travers, J., Nauta, M., and Irwin, N. *The effects of a social program: Final report of the CFRP's infant-toddler component.* Cambridge, Mass.: Abt Associates, 1982.

Trickett, P., Apfel, N., Rosenbaum, L., and Zigler, E. A five-year follow-up of participants in the Yale Child Welfare Research Program. In E. Zigler and E. Gordon (Eds.), *Day care: Scientific and social policy issues.* Boston: Auburn House, 1982.

Valentine, J. Program development for Head Start: A multifaceted approach to meeting the needs of families and children. In E. Zigler and J. Valentine (Eds.), *Project Head Start: Legacy of the War on Poverty.* New York: Free Press, 1979.

Valentine, J., and Stark, E. The social context of parent involvement in Head Start. In E. Zigler and J. Valentine (Eds.), *Project Head Start: A legacy of the War on Poverty.* New York: Free Press, 1979.

Walker, D., and Richmond, J. *Monitoring child health.* Cambridge, Mass.: Harvard University Press, 1984.

Walker, D., and Swartz, J. Teachers' assessments of problems in kindergarten children. Paper presented at the biennial meeting of the Society for Research in Child Development, Boston, Massachusetts, 1981.

Wandersman, L., Wandersman, A., and Kahn, S. Social support in the transition to parenthood. *Journal of Community Psychology,* 1980, *8,* 332–42.

Weikert, D. The cost-effectiveness of high quality early childhood programs. A report prepared for the Southern Legislator's Conference (December). Ypsilanti, Mich.: High/Scope Educational Research Foundation, 1982.

Weiss, C. Doing science or doing policy? *Evaluation and Program Planning,* 1981, *4*(3 and 4), 397–402.

Weiss, H. Parent support and education: An analysis of the Brookline Early Education Project. Doctoral dissertation, Harvard Graduate School of Education, Cambridge, Massachusetts, 1979.

Weiss, H. Strengthening families and rebuilding the social infrastructure: A review of family support and education programs. State-of-the-art paper prepared for the Charles Stewart Mott Foundation, 1983(a).

Weiss, H. The state-of-the-art of family-oriented support programs: Early childhood intervention. Paper presented at a conference on Family Support Programs, Yale Bush Center in Child Development and Social Policy, New Haven, Connecticut, May 1983(b).

Weiss, H. Introduction. In E. Zigler, H. Weiss, and S. Kagan (Eds.), *Programs to strengthen families.* New Haven, Conn.: Bush Center in Child Development and Social Policy, 1983(c).

Weiss, H., and Jacobs, F. The effectiveness and evaluation of family support and education programs. A final report to the Charles Stewart Mott Foundation by the Harvard Family Research Project, Cambridge, Massachusetts, 1984.

Weiss, H. and Jacobs, F. (Eds.). *Evaluating family programs.* Unpublished manuscript. Harvard University Graduate School of Education, Cambridge, Massachusetts.

Weiss, H., Bryk, A., Malson, M., and Yurchak, M. Process studies to date-data collection and analysis. Unpublished paper. Brookline Early Education Project, 1976.

Weiss, R., and Rein, M. The evaluation of broad-aim programs: Experimental design, its difficulties and an alternative. *Administrative Science Quarterly,* 1970, *51*(1), 97–109.

Weissbourd, B. The family support movement: Greater than the sum of its parts. Paper presented at a conference on Family Support Programs, Yale Bush Center in Child Development and Social Policy, New Haven, Connecticut, May 1983.

Werner, E., and Smith, R. *Vulnerable but invincible: A longitudinal study of resilient children and youth.* New York: McGraw-Hill, 1982.

White, K. The different and legitimate roles of advocacy and science. Paper delivered at the CEC/DEC conference. Greeley, Colorado, February 1984.

Wolfle, D. *Science and public policy.* Nebraska: University of Nebraska Press, 1959.

Zigler, E. The environmental mystique: Training the intellect versus development of the child. *Childhood Education*, 1970, *46*, 402–12.

Zigler, E. Head Start: Not a program but an evolving concept. In E. Zigler and J. Valentine (Eds.), *Project Head Start: A legacy of the War on Poverty*. New York: Free Press, 1979(a).

Zigler, E. Project Head Start: Success or failure? In E. Zigler and J. Valentine (Eds.), *Project Head Start: A legacy of the War on Poverty*. New York: Free Press, 1979(b).

Zigler, E. Welcoming a new journal. *Journal of Applied Developmental Psychology*, 1980, *1*, 1–6.

Zigler, E. Family support programs: The state of the art. Opening remarks presented at a conference on Family Support Programs, New Haven, Conn.: Bush Center in Child Development and Social Policy, 1983.

Zigler, E., and Anderson, K. An idea whose time had come: The intellectual and political climate. In E. Zigler and J. Valentine (Eds.), *Project Head Start: A legacy of the War on Poverty*. New York: Free Press, 1979.

Zigler, E., and Berman, W. Discerning the future of early childhood intervention. *American Psychologist*, 1983, *38*(8), 894–906.

Zigler, E., and Lang, M. Head Start: Looking toward the future. *Young Children*, 1983, *37*(6), 3–6.

Zigler, E., and Muenchow, S. A room of their own: A proposal to renovate the Children's Bureau. *American Psychologist*, in press.

Zigler, E., and Trickett, P. IQ, social competence, and evaluation of early childhood intervention programs. *American Psychologist*, 1978, *33*(9), 789–98.

Zigler, E., and Valentine, J. (Eds.). *Project Head Start: A legacy of the War on Poverty*. New York: Free Press, 1979.

Zigler, E., Weiss, H., and Kagan, S. *Programs to strengthen families*. New Haven, Conn.: Bush Center in Child Development and Social Policy, 1983.

8   Child health: research in action

I. Barry Pless and Robert J. Haggerty

It should come as no surprise that the field of child health has been the scene of many excellent examples of action-research, particularly over the past two or three decades. The emotive nature of children's problems prompts investigators to seek solutions, and when promising results are found there is strong pressure to have them implemented promptly and widely. Unfortunately, what is eventually put in place is often quite different from what would be desired under ideal circumstances. Hence this imperfect model in turn often prompts further research and more action programs.

In this chapter several situations to which the term "action-research" may be applied are described using examples from several different aspects of child health. Each of the examples has in common the fact that a health problem has been recognized as a result of research and that the solutions proposed (and implemented in varying degrees) have been examined using research principles applied at a "micro" or community level. Most, in turn, have led to policy recommendations regulating their application on a wider scale. There are other examples of action-research having started in innovative action programs, with research following, but in general the process has more often followed the model described.

Porter (1985) has identified five successful innovations in child health services and has outlined the criteria for their success. Research has been less of a factor in the replication and dissemination of these models than salesmanship. Proof by research alone of effectiveness is usually not enough to spawn the replications so essential to the survival of good programs.

The examples chosen here include the following:

The authors wish to express their deep appreciation to Mary Flanagan, MSW, ACSW, Inta Zvagulis, BA, and Shirley Phipps for their invaluable assistance in the preparation of this chapter. IBP acknowledges the support of the National Health Research and Development Program (Ottawa) and the William T. Grant Foundation.

1. The development of neighborhood health centers to provide primary health care for poor children.
2. The introduction of seat constraints to prevent accidents to child passengers in automobiles.
3. The development of a behavioral pediatrics training program to improve responsiveness to children's behavioral problems.
4. The development of a chronic disorders research consortium to improve the quality and comprehensiveness of care to children.
5. The introduction of immunization programs to prevent and ultimately eradicate infectious disease.
6. The introduction of programs to introduce fluoridation in water supplies to prevent dental caries.

In each example an underlying paradigm links research to action. The sequence begins with a suspicion that a problem exists, but the significance of the problem is usually not fully understood or adequately documented. This results in attempts to estimate systematically the size and severity of the problem. As a rule, the findings suggest that some form of further action is needed to help correct it. Although ultimately an ideal response often requires large-scale programs, a more common first step is the establishment of a pilot or experimental models at the local level. When these have been shown to be efficacious, the task of implementing them on a larger scale then follows. Frequently, however, the results of preliminary evaluative studies of the pilots suggest modifications that, in turn, must be further evaluated. This iterative process, involving program staff and researchers working together, lies at the heart of action-research. The same applies when programmatic or policy changes are introduced at a state or federal level. These, too, frequently require evaluation and modification before they achieve a final satisfactory configuration. In the United States the pattern of introduction of national programs has often not been followed with careful evaluation and rarely has the action-research model of iteration been fully achieved.

In the examples to be described, not all stages of this process are illustrated. Some emphasize the principles involved at the outset of the sequence much better than others, whereas in other cases the middle and end stages are more evident. Not only do the examples that have been selected serve to illustrate the principles of action-research in child health to varying extents and in different ways, but they are also limited in another fashion that is worth noting. The examples chosen are those that, for the most part, relate research to actual programs. There are, however, many more examples of research where no such relationship exists. In many instances this is intentional because the research is of a "basic" nature. In many others, however, striking failures of implementation exist in situations where it appears from the evidence that certain programmatic steps are both justified and feasible.

Primary health care for poor children: neighborhood health centers

Beginning in the mid-1950s and continuing through the early 1960s a great many studies pointed to deficiencies in the health of children living in poverty. This was evident in a wide variety of health indexes ranging from infant mortality to the number of dental caries. At about the same time, other studies began to appear that showed striking shortcomings in the provision of primary health care to poor children. For the most part, health care for these children was provided through hospital out-patient clinics and emergency rooms. The equivalent of a private physician was rarely found. Although at no time was a strong relationship established between lack of high-quality primary health care and any of the major health status measures used, it was commonly assumed that such a relationship exists. Consequently efforts followed to develop some form of primary health-care service for poor children.

Small but well-controlled studies of the efficacy of comprehensive care for low-income families demonstrated reduced use of hospital, laboratory, and pre-scription drugs for children cared for by the continuity-comprehensive approach as compared to care provided in a tertiary-care children's hospital ambulatory service (Robertson et al., 1974).

Following this small-scale demonstration, a population-based neighborhood health center at which primary health care was provided by a team of physicians and allied health professionals was developed (Haggerty, Roghmann, and Pless, 1975). At varying intervals following their initiation, evaluation research demonstrated the effectiveness of the health centers, that is, by shifting service utilization from emergency rooms to the centers themselves. The evaluations also indicated problems in outreach, and modifications were introduced as a result.

Although none of the studies showed direct health benefits that could be attributed to the creation of the network of neighborhood health centers alone, the general impression is that this mode of service delivery was clearly preferable to any of the available alternatives at the time. Furthermore, such health centers have proliferated to a surprising degree. The failure to implement them still more widely undoubtedly reflects the political and economic realities in the period that followed. It may also be a consequence of the failure of action-research to provide more definitive evidence of their benefits.

The Rochester Neighborhood Health Center (RNHC) opened in July 1968. It was intended to meet two needs: (1) to provide more and better health care in an old, poor neighborhood; and (2) to provide a community setting for teaching primary care medicine to physicians in training. This health center was one of many emerging across the United States as a result of funds made available by the federal government as part of the War on Poverty. Plans for the center included a commitment to the same basic elements seen in the earliest models: Columbia Point in inner-city Boston and the Mississippi Delta Health Project. Both were programs developed by Geiger and Gibson of Tufts University Medical School in 1965 (Sardell, 1983), based on the pioneering models South Africa (Kark and Steuart, 1962) and the Peckham Experiment in England (Pearse and Crocker, 1943).

Of particular interest to the designers of the Rochester Neighborhood Health Center was the commitment to a team effort, involvement of the community, and the assurance that few restrictions were placed on what was considered to be boundary areas of health care (cf. chapter 9 in Haggerty et al., 1975). Unique to the Rochester situation was the concurrent organization of the research efforts involved in the Rochester Child Health Surveys (Pless, 1978a:209–26). These were initiated to define the current health needs of children in Monroe County and thereby served to provide a baseline against which changes brought about by any new programs such as the NHCs could be measured (Haggerty and Roghmann, 1975:222). Thus, the stage was set for an action-research project.

A long process of involvement with the community to determine their health needs and priorities and to develop a consumer group to promote health care, coupled with the findings of the Rochester Child Health Surveys, led to the planning of the Rochester Neighborhood Health Center. This was to provide care for the entire family, and would include special emphasis on outreach. Once the proposal was accepted, there followed a fairly difficult period of negotiation between the grantor, the Office of Economic Opportunity (OEO), and the subcontractor (the university). Although the OEO funds were not administered directly by the local antipoverty agency, Action for a Better Community, ABC had the power to approve expenditures, and all dealings by the university had to be with them (Haggerty and Roghmann, 1975:225). This arrangement was unfamiliar to the university, and some feelings of estrangement evolved as the university administration sought for safeguards against financial risk. It was not evident that the university could accept the commitment to providing medical care to the poor community. They were reluctant to share power and fiscal control with a nonuniversity agency (ABC). The faculty, who were to be the providers, and the antipoverty agency staff, who held the War on Poverty goals above fiscal or other administrative concerns, were deeply involved in the struggle. Although the negotiations resulted in agreement, they left some feelings of resentment in the community toward the university – and vice versa.

The development of collaboration with the community was a difficult and unfamiliar problem for university faculty. The terms of the OEO grant required a community board, and the faculty responsible for the development of the health centers was committed to community participation. The university was totally unfamiliar with the sharing of power with outsiders, and the community board, made up primarily of minority-group members, was less interested in the health center than in jobs, fair employment practices, and redressing old grievances.

The relations between the staff and this board were never smooth. But in retrospect the experience was useful for all parties. The input of the community into the services offered by the health center was important in meeting the perceived needs of the target population, and both staff and the university learned a little about working collaboratively with people they had never worked with before.

The university began its administration of the health center in July 1968. Research questions to evaluate the program's effectiveness had already been designed. As the health care teams began providing their services, researchers ensured that various data were gathered for analysis.

In 1971, a report describing the effect of the neighborhood health center on the use of pediatric emergency departments was published (Hocheiser, Woodward, and Charney, 1971). In this study the number of pediatric visits to emergency departments by health center area children before the center opened was compared with the number of visits by center area children nine and twenty-one months after the health center was established. The changes were compared with other child populations in areas lacking health centers. The researchers noted: "There was a 38 per cent reduction in child visits in the Health Center area to emergency departments from 1967 to 1970. In contrast, there was no change in the number of pediatric emergency department visits from the rest of the city and a 29 per cent increase in emergency department visits by suburban children" (Hochheiser et al., 1971:148).

Though the study indicated a significant decrease in emergency room use by children served by the health center, the authors warned that there were still many eligible children not utilizing health center services. The impact of the community outreach by public health nurses who were members of the center's health care teams, the importance of physical proximity, and the prevalence of entrenched patterns of health care in target areas were also evident from the research results.

To assess the community's acceptance of the health center, Hillman and Charney (1971) conducted a household interview study in 1971. The results suggest general patient acceptance. However, further analyses show that there was a significantly high percentage of "multiproblem" families in the group of satisfied patients. Unfortunately, many registered patients continued to use hospital emergency rooms or other services outside of the health center system.

Other nonempirical indicators of community acceptance were reported. The health center was never picketed, extensively vandalized, or boycotted. Articulate neighborhood individuals and groups participated in the later evolution of the Rochester Health Network. Relations with the black community were generally good; with the Puerto Ricans, they were lukewarm. "On the average, the community's view of the center appears to lie somewhere between tolerance and enthusiasm, with individual opinion ranging from hostile rage to adoration – a spectrum probably not too different from that of most patients in other systems" (Charney, 1975:232).

The "health team" approach was an aspect of the Rochester Neighborhood Health Center that many assumed had a positive effect on its utilization and effectiveness. Public health nurses were integrated into the team along with the physician and a family health assistant. A study conducted during 1971 and 1972 compared the nature of these nurses' jobs and the professional level at which they worked with a comparable group of public health nurses employed by the health department in a similar neighborhood (Charney and Mechaber, 1972). They found that the nurses at the health center were more integrated into the health team, spent more time on tasks demanding higher professional skills, and had more patient encounters than did their counterparts at the health department. The authors concluded that the differences were due chiefly to the integration of the nurses within the primary-care system.

In 1973, a report assessing the effect of the neighborhood health center on the hospital admissions of children, 1968 to 1970, was published (Klein et al., 1973). The study design allowed for comparisons between actual users of the health center, nonusers who lived in the target area, and a comparison group. During the second year of operation, the admission rate of health center users was only 33 versus 67 per thousand for nonusers and 39 per thousand for the comparison group in another poverty area of the city. Comparing the first two years, hospital days per thousand among users dropped by approximately half. Users had fewer admissions for respiratory infectious diseases and more admissions for surgical procedures than nonusers or the comparison group.

These various studies conducted by researchers from the university provided valuable information about the effectiveness of the Rochester Neighborhood Health Center. In 1975 an attempt was made to put the health center experience in perspective (Charney, 1975:226–41). In his synopsis, Charney suggested that the health center's success could be demonstrated by its continued growth and replication. The attraction of new trainees, continued involvement of the community, employment of area residents, increasing control by the community, and the presence of quality medical services in dignified and pleasant surroundings for the neighborhood, all stand as markers of its success.

One goal of the neighborhood health center movement, that the centers become focal points for social action, saw less measurable success. However, Charney suggests that the RNHC did have a potent influence on medical and planning agencies. More than three hundred neighborhood health centers were established in the United States in the 1960s and 1970s. They achieved varying success. A final analysis of this major action in child health care by research has not been completed. Action-research probably contributed a small part to the positive image and resultant replication of these centers.

Preventing motor vehicle injuries: promoting the use of seat restraints

Statistics documenting the vulnerability of child passengers in cars are plentiful and deeply distressing. Motor vehicle accidents in general have remained the number-one killer and crippler of children in the United States for more than three or four decades. Infants and small children riding as passengers are especially vulnerable to death, disability, and disfigurement, even in minor accidents and sudden stops (Reisinger and Williams, 1978). Furthermore, as Pless, Roghmann, and Algranati (1972) and others had shown, most children were not properly restrained even though appropriate devices were generally available. As a consequence, many projects evolved in the mid-1970s to educate parents about the importance of protecting children during crashes. Unfortunately, few of these efforts provided valid information about their effectiveness in changing behavior. Many had serious methodological flaws, but nonetheless most of them strongly suggested that educational approaches alone did not have a significant effect on increasing the proper use of these restraints (Pless, 1978a).

The idea of mandating the use of belts or other restraint devices through legislation was then considered. Criteria for incentive grants to foster state safety-belt laws were first published in the *Federal Register* (1974:1314). An international conference held at that time included a paper describing the results of compulsory seat-belt legislation in New Zealand (Toomath, 1977). This set the stage for establishing a more scientific basis for future efforts to persuade state legislatures to consider similar laws aimed at protecting child passengers.

The Tennessee Child Passenger Protection Act of 1977 was the first such law passed in the United States. It went into effect in January 1978 and was the subject of action-research, both prior to its initiation and subsequently. The law resulted from a campaign launched by a local pediatrician, Robert Sanders. Making use of such data as were available at the time, Dr. Sanders, who was at the time the chairman of the Accident Prevention Committee of the Tennessee chapter of the American Academy of Pediatrics, received endorsements for the proposed act from many influential professional and parapublic groups. These included the state Pediatric Society, the Tennessee Medical Association, the Trauma Committee of the American College of Surgeons, public health physicians, and the like. The details of the lobbying and the fate of the initial bill introduced in 1976 are described by Sanders (Sanders and Casey, 1979). It highlights the two major objections raised to the proposed act and the manner in which these objections were dealt with. The concerns were, first, that the law is an encroachment on the rights and individual liberties of the parent, and, second, that the restraint systems were too expensive. Although in the end the efforts were successful, the wording of the law passed was much more permissive than what was intended because of compromises that were introduced during the legislative process (Sanders, 1981).

The main compromise exempted children held in parents' arms – a dangerous practice. It also excluded children over age 4 and limited the liability to parents or guardians transporting children in their own car. Recreational vehicles, trucks, and vans were also exempted. In spite of all these limitations the law was clearly a breakthrough and was soon to be followed by many other states.

The next step in the process of action-research was to begin to monitor the effects of this law in a scientific fashion. In one study, observations of children traveling in cars were made in Knoxville and Nashville (Williams and Wells, 1981:163). The observations were made about 5 months before the law went into effect and repeated four months after it was enacted. Similar observations were made at the same times in Lexington and Louisville in Kentucky, a neighboring state where no such legislation was in effect.

In May 1980, observations were repeated in the same four cities. In the period between the two sets of postlaw observations, there had been extensive public information and educational activities concerning the law, along with some attempts at enforcement. Observations were again made at stop signs and traffic lights at exits from the same shopping centers studied in the original survey. If cars with in-state license plates stopped at these sites contained one or more children who appeared to be less than 4 years old, information was obtained from the drivers about the ages of the children and their relationship to the driver, and observations on how the children were traveling were recorded (Williams and Wells, 1981:163–64).

Observations were made of 2,111 children who met the study's criteria. In May 1980, use rates of restraints anchored by seat belts were 29 percent in Tennessee and 14 percent in Kentucky. This represents an increase in use from 8 percent prior to the law to 16 percent four months later, to 29 percent in its third year. By contrast, corresponding rates for Kentucky were 11 percent, 15 percent, and 14 percent (Williams and Wells, 1981:164). In Tennessee, communities that combined a public information campaign with the new restraint law reported a much higher compliance rate (Meyer, 1981:123).

These findings led the researchers to recommend that the law be augmented by more advocacy, enforcement, further technical development, and more parental and professional involvement. In addition, many hospitals initiated child restraint device loaner programs to stimulate their use from the earliest possible moment. Police officers carry child car seats in the trunks of their cars and provide them to those being cited in violation of the law. Charges are dismissed when the parents appear in court with proof that they have acquired a car seat for continued use. Public safety campaigns are undertaken periodically in many communities throughout the state.

Following Tennessee's pioneering example, many other states have enacted similar laws. As of July 1, 1983, all but eight states had such laws. The National Transportation Safety Board has issued guidelines for better child passenger protection and has urged all states to follow them or to strengthen existing laws as soon as possible (NTSB, 1983). The American Academy of Pediatrics has spearheaded a program called "First Ride, Safe Ride" and has succeeded in persuading many state legislatures, as well as pediatricians' own patients, to promote the use of infant car restraints. These and other efforts should soon lead to dramatically improved statistics reflecting the protection being offered to child passengers as a consequence of this example of action-research.

In this example it is apparent that the research documenting the original twin problems of serious risk to life and limb and the low rate of use of an effective countermeasure prompted one pediatrician to initiate a program of action. His efforts were buttressed by an already established pressure group (Physicians for Automotive Safety), but his own initiatives were more sharply focused. His goal was to persuade the state to enact legislation to protect children, and his success is a convincing illustration of the manner in which lobbying must be conducted to be effective. Once the initial law was passed, further research demonstrating its effects resulted, in turn, in the adoption of similar laws in most other states.

Improving responsiveness to behavioral problems among children

Although it has long been recognized that behavioral problems are commonly seen among children, it was not until the early 1960s that population-based studies provided reasonably accurate estimates of the magnitude of this problem. One of the pioneering studies of this nature was that of Lapouse and Monk (1958). They reported the results of a detailed interview with mothers of a random sample of children of primary school age. This was followed by the equally important study of Glidewell and his colleagues using a symptom inventory administered to both parents and teachers (Glidewell, Domke, and Kantor, 1963). Some years later, still more sophisticated surveys were conducted in Britain, on the Isle of Wight (Rutter, Tizard, and Whitmore, 1970), and in Monroe County, New York (Goldberg et al., 1979).

The latter is of particular interest in relation to the theme of this book, for two reasons. First, it represents a survey of pediatricians in practice. They were, in a very real sense, active collaborators in the research that defined the frequency with which these children were being seen in their practices. Second, because the study is practice-based, it has direct implications for the training of future pediatricians. This is so because it is clear that when population-based prevalence rates are compared with those found in practice settings, there is a very large discrepancy (Pless and Pekeles, 1981). It appears that a substantial proportion of children with behavior problems are not being recognized or treated by pediatricians. It is reasonable to assume further that if this is so, it is in part a reflection of the perceived inadequacies of most pediatricians in this domain.

It was in response to findings such as these that many pediatric training programs began to place greater emphasis on the development of skills in behavioral pediatrics. The most ambitious collaborative effort of this kind is the program funded by the William T. Grant Foundation, aimed at pediatric residents at eleven medical centers in the United States. Although a variety of different approaches is used at these centers, for example, with respect to the use of mandated rotations, electives, or continuous training, the major themes are clear and reasonably consistent. For example, all had to have a pediatrician as a role model for the trainees. In 1983 a four-year study of the effects of this commitment and investment was completed by Phillips et al. (1983). The design of this program of action-research involved a comparison of the eleven externally funded centers providing mandatory behavioral training, with seven others not externally funded but also providing mandatory training, and six centers not requiring such training that served as "controls." Of the residents in the centers involved in the study, 70 percent completed questionnaires at the beginning and end of the 1980–81 training year. The measures assessed attitudes regarding behavioral disorders and physical and mixed disorders, along with actual knowledge about behavioral problems.

The results show that most of the significant effects of the training in this area were seen in the second year of residency training (the PL-2 year), when the block rotation occurred. The residents in the funded programs (those involved in the action-research) demonstrated higher change scores than the nonfunded and control residents on three attitudinal measures ("competence in management," "ability to advise parents," and "future relevance") as applied to both behavioral and mixed disorders compared with physical disorders. Both funded and nonfunded residents had superior change scores when compared with the controls. In addition, two of the knowledge measures ("knowledge of resources" and "faculty interest") were superior in their change scores compared with the controls in the case of those in the nonfunded program. It was concluded that mandatory training in this area results in positive changes in attitudes and knowledge and that overall, these changes are most evident in the specially funded programs.

The investigators have also reported on the extent of behavioral pediatric training nationwide and on perceptions of barriers that preclude initiation or further development of such programs. Although it appears that there has been a distinct ''ripple effect'' arising from this initiative, in that there is a greatly increased level of interest in this problem across the country, there is still resistance to the idea of specific training in this area by many department chairmen. In part this is because the scientific base of the discipline is perceived to be thin. ''It will be a challenge for behavioral pediatrics to develop a scientific approach to the problems of interest to the field and to contribute meaningfully to the development of new knowledge'' (Friedman, Phillips, and Parrish, 1983:907). Finally, the ultimate effect of these programs on the patterns of pediatric practice or the effect on children's behavioral disturbances is as yet unclear.

This example also serves to illustrate the relationship between research that first demonstrates the existence of a problem, followed by a program intended to correct it, which is then subjected to further research to evaluate whether it has achieved success. In this instance, as in others, the main ''actors'' were closely related through personal networks. Friedman was part of the Rochester ''team'' during the period when Haggerty was chairman of a pediatric department that was promoting the idea of the ''new morbidity.'' Some of the critical studies documenting the extent of behavioral problems were done as part of the Rochester Child Health Surveys. Friedman later put together a group of training programs supported by the William T. Grant Foundation and ultimately was the one responsible for the evaluation described.

Management of chronic illness

About 10 percent of all children experience a chronic physical disorder at some time. Many experienced clinicians have for a long time had the impression that these children had a greater likelihood of experiencing serious emotional problems than their healthy peers, but it was not until the late 1950s that systematic evidence began to emerge to support this impression. Much of the early research in this field was characterized by the collaborative efforts of physicians with specialized interest in one or more of the diseases, working alongside colleagues from the social and behavioral sciences. In many instances the setting was a specialty clinic within teaching hospitals, with the implicit goal of finding ways to prevent these secondary emotional consequences. It was appreciated that children who had both physical and emotional problems were doubly handicapped in their efforts to lead a normal existence.

In the mid-1960s one of the first attempts on a reasonably large scale to study this problem was initiated in Rochester, New York. Building from the base of the Rochester Child Health Surveys, a team comprising pediatricians and a medical sociologist began to tackle this problem. The initial studies were based on a

1 percent random sample of the child population of Monroe County. Parents of these children were systematically interviewed, and those with symptoms thought to be indicative of a chronic illness were studied in greater depth alongside a matched group of apparently healthy children. This second-stage study included a series of psychological measures obtained from parents, teachers, and the children themselves to permit an assessment of emotional functioning to be made. The results provided clear evidence in support of the general hypothesis that the children with chronic illnesses were at greater risk for maladjustment (Pless and Satterwhite, 1975).

In the course of the interviews with the parents, a number of areas of dissatisfaction with the medical care provided for them were identified. This led to a further set of studies, the first of which was to examine in greater detail the practices of general practitioners and pediatricians who provided primary care for these children. To do this, a systematic sample of all physicians in the region was obtained, and detailed interviews with them were conducted (Pless, Satterwhite, and VanVechten, 1976). The results showed that although these physicians had a substantial number of children with chronic illnesses in their practices, a majority referred them to specialists for the treatment of their specific illness. This pattern varied somewhat with the condition in question, but as a general rule it was clear that, at best, primary-care physicians were only willing to share responsibility for such children rather than to assume it exclusively themselves. It was not surprising, therefore, that when asked questions about the enlistment of other services needed to provide supportive care for the child and family, for example, counseling that might help prevent the development of the emotional problems, this was rarely done in the primary-care setting.

As a consequence of these findings, two subsequent studies focused on services provided in specialty clinics to which the previous survey had shown these children were frequently referred (Kanthor et al., 1974; Pless, Satterwhite, and VanVechten, 1978). In these studies a sample of parents attending these clinics were systematically interviewed about the services they had received for their child. A detailed inquiry was made about each of eight different types of services ranging from primary care to supportive counseling. In each case, questions were asked to determine whether, in the judgment of the parent, the service had been provided and if so by whom. The findings demonstrated that as a result of the pattern of referrals from primary physicians to specialists, many of the services (especially the supportive services) needed by these families are not provided by anyone. In short, the results indicated that the patterns of responsibility for these children between the various doctors involved in their care were either divided or duplicated, or neglected. It is those that were neglected that posed the most serious problem.

In response to this finding it was decided to provide supportive services on an experimental basis through the creation of a cadre of nonprofessional helpers, "family counselors" (Pless and Satterwhite, 1972). This is again a good example of action-research in that the program in its various stages took place as the result of collaboration between investigators and practitioners, both primary physicians and specialists, and had a multidisciplinary orientation.

The counselors were selected based on personality characteristics and randomly assigned to families with children with chronic illness. Comparison of initial scores on psychological adjustment with those obtained a year after the introduction of family counselors indicated a beneficial effect in the experimental group. This program is another good example of the relative failure to implement on a more wide-scale basis the findings that have been produced through action-research in one particular setting. Although some similar examples have taken place elsewhere, for the most part this approach to the care of children with chronic illnesses has not been widely adopted.

On the other hand, one positive outgrowth of studies such as these, and of the work of Kakalik and Brewer on the establishment of regional direction centers, was the birth of the program of action-research initiated by the Vanderbilt Institute for Public Policy Studies in 1980. Entitled "Public Policies Affecting Chronically Ill Children and Their Families," this ambitious example of action-research was supported by grants from the Office of Maternal and Child Health, the Office of Special Education, and the Robert Wood Johnson Foundation (Pless and Perrin, 1985). It was developed to examine the effects of public policy on children with severe chronic illnesses and their families and to develop a national policy responsive to their needs. The project was led by the late Professor Nicholas Hobbs, a highly respected psychologist who held a strong commitment to problems of this kind. He was, no doubt, inspired by his previous success in a similar undertaking dealing with children with learning disorders.

In the first stage of the research, materials were gathered to improve public awareness of the situation of these children and their families. From the outset, in addition to a National Advisory Council composed of respected and influential individuals representing a wide variety of constituencies, a consortium of investigators actively working in this area of research was also identified. Both served to advise and guide the work of the core staff and also interacted with each other, thus again comprising an example of "action-research" as previously defined. Also involved from the outset was a collaborative group of action personnel, for example, policymakers, and those who influence policy such as program planners, providers, and consumers.

It was soon realized that the key to future improvements was the manner in which services are organized for these children. The current modalities of service delivery have been analyzed by the staff to identify gaps and overlaps and to identify successful experiments involving the reorganization of services. It was recognized that a chronic illness may or may not create a handicap for an affected child. Often the outcome is determined less by the severity of the illness as such than by the nature and availability of family support, community services, and health care. Thus, a main goal has been to prevent or diminish handicap and to enable the affected children to grow to their fullest capacity despite the illness. The emphasis on primary and secondary prevention is a recurrent theme in the policy recommendations that have emerged.

Immunization policies and practices

One of the most dramatic examples of action-research is found in the sequence of events that has led to the near eradication of a large number of important infectious diseases of childhood. At the turn of the century, deaths and serious illness from these conditions were among the most frequent afflictions of childhood. Physicians had few tools with which to combat these epidemics, and the only feasible preventive strategy relied on public health countermeasures to control the spread of existing infection. Needless to say, this had limited effects and it was apparent that more efficacious means of prevention were needed.

Investigators in laboratories combined with epidemiologists to develop and test vaccines. These efforts first met with success in the early 1920s, followed by a second wave of vaccines in the 1950s and 1960s. By 1970 most of the important contagious diseases of childhood could be prevented through immunization.

Unfortunately, throughout much of the world including parts of the United States, many cases of vaccine-preventable disease continued to appear (Pless, 1980). Obviously, vaccination programs were proving less successful than they could and should be. As a consequence, further action-research was initiated to determine where the problems lay and how they could best be corrected.

Several studies followed indicating that both public health programs and private practitioners were falling short of the mark in their efforts to prevent these diseases (Schreier, 1974). In many instances the problem appeared to be one of divided responsibility and lack of communication. Parents were frequently uncertain whether their children had been completely immunized, and few physicians had records in such a form that they could identify those incompletely protected. Nor did they have the resources to pursue these cases aggressively.

One obvious solution was to create a system of linkage of information through the establishment of an immunization registry. With the advent of computer technology the feasibility of doing this was greatly enhanced. However, few constituencies have been able to obtain the necessary cooperation between private practitioners and public health authorities to enable such a registry to be successful. An important exception took place in one public health district in Montreal,

Canada (Loeser et al., 1983). Through the registry devised by Loeser and her colleagues, it is possible to identify, on a monthly basis, all those who have fallen behind the recommended schedule of inoculations. With the cooperation of public health nurses these cases are then pursued. As a consequence, reported immunization rates have risen to a level that is generally satisfactory.

This registry is an excellent example of an action-research program in all its phases: The underlying problem – incomplete immunization – was identified initially by public health officials; it was studied further by academic investigators, who proposed and implemented the solution – the registry. Together, the investigators and the public health department assessed both feasibility and cost-effectiveness and fed the results back to the practicing physicians who contributed the essential reports. Thus reinforced, the registry has continued. The health department now fully supports the registry's operation and has been joined by another neighboring health department. The community's children's hospital serves as the focal point for these activities because that is where the computer is based.

Although the registry is a proven solution, much the same results have been obtained in states where legislation has been introduced to require children to be fully immunized before entering school. Legislation of this kind was prompted by the results of earlier small-scale studies showing that this strategy was likely to be effective (Jackson and Carpenter, 1972).

For example, in the spring of 1971 the Texas legislature enacted a mandatory immunization law for schoolchildren. Data analyzed by the Department of Health and the Texas Education Agency indicated successful compliance with immunization efforts, followed by radical decreases in reported cases between 1970 and 1973. The success of the immunization program, however, is attributed to more than just the legislation (Gee and Sowell, 1975).

Compulsory immunization laws have been in effect since the nineteenth century, when some states began requiring smallpox immunizations (Jacobson, 1905). Challenges have been usually unsuccessful and the laws have been upheld by local and state courts and the Supreme Court. With the introduction of other vaccines (poliomyelitis, measles, mumps, and rubella) the laws were extended.

By 1969, twenty-six states had enacted legislation requiring immunizations for school attendance (Jackson, 1969). At that time, the Texas Code allowed local school boards to require immunizations. As a result there was no statewide continuity in immunization efforts. However, in 1970 a measles epidemic in Texarkana, a city of 90,000 bisected by the Texas-Arkansas border, dramatically illuminated the disadvantages of this situation. In Arkansas, where immunization was mandated by law, only 27 children were stricken. By contrast, on the Texas side of the city, there were 606 victims (Schreier, 1970). In the same year, the third outbreak of diphtheria in three years occurred in a Texas city, and 22 cases

Table 8.1. *Cases of vaccine-preventable disease, Texas 1970–73*

	Number of cases reported			
	1970	1971	1972	1973
Diphtheria	234	56	41	18
Tetanus	14	10	20	10
Pertussis	437	282	185	115
Poliomyelitis	22	4	4	0
Measles	8,494	9,585	1,617	533
Rubella	8,409	4,414	1,596	1,129

of paralytic poliomyelitis were reported, two-thirds of the national total (Gee and Sowell, 1975). These outbreaks provoked public alarm.

Accordingly, the following year, with the support of the state Medical Association, the state Department of Health, and other groups, the legislature made immunizations for school children mandatory, and a companion law required immunizations for preschool children in day-care centers and other institutions. The law allows exemptions only for religious or medical reasons. It also enables the state Department of Health to make vaccines available in areas where no local provision exists. There are, however, no penalties for failure to comply. In response to a challenge in the courts in 1972, the law was upheld by the Texas Supreme Court as "a valid exercise of the State's police power" (*Leo Itz*, 1973).

Implementation of this law was enhanced by harmonious coordination between the State Board of Health and the Texas Education Agency, as well as by the substantial appropriations built into the legislation. In addition to the implementation of the school and day-care laws, there was a sustained education campaign; an Infant Immunization Surveillance program, which provided contact with parents of newborns; additional clinics; and expanded outreach. The reduction in morbidity shown is a cumulative effect of all of these programs (Gee and Sowell, 1975:24).

The Texas Education Agency also produced figures showing significant increases in the immunization levels in the state's public schools, based on a series of immunization reports from all 1,145 school districts, showing cumulative totals of official records kept on each campus – a complete count of more than two and one half million school children in Texas. The findings indicated an average rise in immunization levels of more than 15 percent from May 1972 to October 1973.

In summary, these efforts to raise the levels of immunization, and thereby lower the incidence of vaccine-preventable disease, appear to have been successful. The success rests not only on the effective collaboration between researchers and program providers but on the presence of many other highly favorable factors: public concern, a well-drafted law, cooperation among physicians, medical societies, schools, local health departments, the two responsible state agencies, and, above all, legislative support and adequate funding.

The present situation in the United States with respect to immunization provides much reason for optimism. Statistical reports document the declining rates of cases and fatalities from vaccine-preventable diseases. In short, this has been a reasonably unqualified success story. It illustrates well how a series of action-research steps has led to implementation on a large scale with the intended result.

This example may be contrasted with the picture in Great Britain, where a series of studies focused attention on the possibly harmful effects of one component of the vaccination program, which related to pertussis (*Lancet*, 1981). In spite of consistently equivocal results, the net effect of these studies has been a much less comprehensive program of immunization. Consequently, rates of a number of important diseases continue to be far higher than they are in the United States. Current high medical liability settlements for the rare complications of immunization have led one manufacturer of DPT vaccine to discontinue production, jeopardizing this very satisfactory progress.

These contrasting situations provide impressive evidence that action-research can influence government policy. It also appears, however, that for research of this kind to have an effect on government policy, no matter how well it is done or on what scale, it is necessary that the political climate be "right" and that the resources needed to effectuate the policy be available. In the case of the United States the results of the research were noted by various interested parties led by the American Academy of Pediatrics. Thus the combination of public pressure, the ready availability of reasonable means of accomplishing the target, and the political will to do so, led to eventual success.

Fluoridation

In 1931, fluoride was identified as the natural substance in domestic water supplies in areas of the southwestern United States that produced a remarkable resistance to tooth decay. Over the next ten years, research teams led by H. T. Dean studied the dental status of 7,257 children in twenty-one cities having various levels of natural fluoride in their water (Dean, 1942).

The results were unequivocal. The more fluoride in the water, the fewer dental cavities the children experienced. When the water contained approximately 1 ppm or more of fluoride, the children developed about 60 percent fewer cavities than did those who drank water with negligible fluoride content. Furthermore, at the 1 ppm level, the unattractive mottling did not occur. It was associated with levels above 2 ppm. Thus, 1 ppm of fluoride became the benchmark level. [*Consumer Reports,* 1978:2]

In spite of these findings, there was, from the outset, strong opposition to adding ''a chemical'' to community water supplies. There was also no scientific data on possible side effects. However, reassurance was provided by noting that people had been ingesting naturally fluoridated water, containing several times the 1 ppm level, since the beginning of time without any discernible side effects except mottled teeth. Eventually, a few cities decided to take the chance.

One of the earliest trials was conducted by the New York State Department of Health (Newburgh-Kingston, 1956). They devised a long-term, controlled study of a group of children who were carefully monitored by physicians. Two communities, Newburgh and Kingston, participated in the study.

Located some 35 miles apart near the Hudson River, both cities had populations of about 30,000 and were similar in racial, economic, and other demographic characteristics. Each also used reservoirs with water deficient in fluoride. One city's water supply was then fluoridated, the other not. Matched groups of children from the two cities were then followed from infancy onward, by means of comprehensive pediatric checkups to detect any side effects from fluoride. Special attention was given to growth rates, bone development, blood chemistry, the skin, the thyroid gland, vision, and hearing. Each child also received meticulous, regular dental exams. [*Consumer Reports,* 1978:2]

Newburgh's water supply was fluoridated to 1 ppm in 1944. Kingston served as the control city. Eight hundred and seventeen children were enrolled from Newburgh and 711 from Kingston. Several infants were added during each of the first three years to ensure having some children whose mothers were exposed to fluoridated water throughout pregnancy. The study went on for ten years, with a majority of the children in both groups participating through to the final examination. The findings disclosed no adverse consequences of medical significance between the two groups that could even remotely be attributable to fluoride. Differences in dental health were, however, marked: The Newburgh children experienced nearly 60 percent fewer cavities than the Kingston children.

Unfortunately, fears of side effects to fluoridation again surfaced in Newburgh, soon after the project was approved. The commissioner of the New York State Department of Health reported in the *Journal of the American Dental Association* (in March 1956) that there were complaints from Newburgh citizens:

Some protested that the fluoridated water was discoloring their saucepans. Others complained that it was giving them digestive troubles. One woman complained to her dentist that the ''fluoride water'' had caused her dentures to crack. These incidents all occurred before fluoride was added to the water supply. . . . The complaints stopped abruptly after a Newburgh newspaper criticized the town's imaginary ills. [*Consumer Reports,* 1978:3]

Doubts and questions raised regarding the safety of fluoridation continue to be presented by a well-organized and vociferous opposition. Among their claims:

Fluoride is a poison; it causes birth defects, genetic mutations, allergic reactions, cancer, and heart disease. All of these claims have been researched in depth by scientists and all have been found to be based on invalid research methods (Dunning, 1975:377–78). In 1970, the World Health Organization published a compilation of studies, offering an impartial review of the scientific literature on fluoridation. The report, "Fluoride and Human Health," concluded that no reliable evidence was found that any ill effects or symptoms resulted from drinking water fluoridated at recommended levels (WHO, 1970). Repeated analysis in countless studies has led to the same conclusion: At 1 ppm, the addition of fluoride to the water supply is a harmless, effective deterrent to tooth decay.

In spite of this, antifluoridationists have succeeded in delaying and even reversing fluoridation in several areas. At the heart of the opposition movement are well-funded national multi-issue organizations that disseminate scare propaganda throughout the country. One such group is the John Birch Society. Another was the Rodale Press, publisher of *Prevention* magazine, a frequent proponent of unproven nutritional concepts. The most active and effective group has been the National Health Federation (NHF), headed by a man previously convicted by a U.S. district court of mail-order fraud for a diagnosis-by-mail service and for the sale of electronic treatment devices for "curing" numerous disorders.

In 1963 the Food and Drug Administration released a report on the NHF that said in part:

The stated purpose of the federation is to promote "freedom of choice" in health matters. The record shows that what this frequently means is freedom to promote medical nostrums and devices which violate the law. From its inception, the federation has been a front for promoters of unproved remedies, eccentric theories and quackery. [*Consumer Reports*, 1978:4]

In 1974, the NHF launched a national campaign to crush profluoridation efforts. A doctor hired by the NHF authored a study claiming that 25,000 or more excess cancer deaths occur annually in U.S. cities that fluoridate their water. The assertion was based on a comparison of death rates for specific cancers in some counties that were fluoridated compared with others that were not (Burke, 1975). The National Cancer Institute (NCI) reviewed the study, reanalyzed the data taking into account such influences as ethnic composition of the population, geographic location, socioeconomic status, and other key risk factors, and found no differences in the cancer death rate (Hoover et al., 1976).

The doctor and his colleague followed with another study, again methodologically unsound, purporting to show that death rates in fluoridated cities were higher than in nonfluoridated areas. The NCI again reviewed and dismissed this study, by analyzing the data after taking account of other risk factors. The NHF scientists charged the NCI with concealing data and misleading the public. To check this claim, researchers from the Department of the Regius Professor of

Medicine at Oxford and the Council of the Royal Statistical Society in Britain undertook further studies. The results published in *The Lancet* (Doll and Kinlen, 1977) and *Applied Statistics* in 1977 (Oldham and Newell, 1977), both rejected any evidence of links between fluoridation and cancer.

These refutations, however, have not prevented the fluoridation opponents from using the studies as "scientific" evidence in support of their claims. They have had reports of their conclusions entered into the *Congressional Record* and disseminated to the public at strategic times. Their tactics have succeeded in raising fears, and have left the nonscientific public wary of any "scientific" findings. Consequently, in spite of the overwhelming scientific evidence in support of the safety and effectiveness of fluoridating water, many cities' ordinances to fluoridate are often defeated.

This example of the interplay between program development, research, and social change emphasizes the importance of communicating research findings to the public more effectively. It also illustrates the compromises inherent in the democratic/political process. There is some irony in that open process has the potential for disseminating misleading information. Whether it is appropriate for such public health policies to be decided upon by the public is an old dilemma. The critical role of dissemination of findings in action-research cannot be underestimated.

Discussion

The "health" of children is a concept that is surprisingly difficult to specify. On the one hand, there exists the well-known WHO definition that attempts to measure health in broad, comprehensive, and positive terms. On the other hand, because this construct is virtually impossible to operationalize, most studies view health as the opposite of disease. Thus, health becomes the absence of illness and this is one idea that links the examples cited in this chapter.

Another common theme is the notion of prevention. Children, unlike the elderly, are usually free of disease or impairment. The main task of child health is, therefore, to maintain health by preventing disease. None of the examples cited relate to the cure of disease or to the rehabilitation of the handicapped.

In the case of Neighborhood Health Centers, for example, the services provided are in the realm of "primary care." These, very broadly, are addressed at health maintenance through such activities as immunization, well-child examinations, or counseling. Primary care is, therefore, in one sense, a final common pathway for those examples where the emphasis is on prevention. The only exception to this is the case of behavior problems, where many of the intended results lie in the area of treating disturbances after they have arisen. In contrast, even in the case of chronic illness, the key thrust is toward modification of the delivery of health services in order to prevent emotional disturbances. Likewise, fluoride is intended to prevent dental decay, just as seat belts are intended to prevent damage to the head and other body parts, or vaccines are intended to prevent infectious diseases.

Another thread that runs through the examples chosen is that the problems are, in general, assessed by process measures – indicators of proximal, versus distal (ultimate), outcomes. For example, in the case of motor vehicle accident injury control programs, the key measure used is the rate of restraint utilization rather than the more salient measure, an actual reduction in the rate of passenger injuries. Similarly, the measure of "success" in the case of fluoridation is the *decision* to fluoride public water supplies, rather than the reduction of dental caries as such.

To some extent the rationale for this approach is the need to choose between efficacy versus effectiveness. In each of these instances cited, the efficacy of the intended action is assumed to have been established. For example, the research question with regard to motor vehicle accident safety, or the prevention of infectious diseases, is not whether seat restraints or vaccines have been proven to "work." Rather, based on earlier studies, it is assumed (correctly, we believe) that they do. Thus the question becomes: How can these proven measures be translated effectively and efficiently into as widespread use as is required?

The action-research question that should or could be addressed in this regard, and the one that could contribute most to a body of theory and thus add to scientific knowledge, is how decisions are made regarding the adoption of these measures. In the two examples listed above (vaccinations and seat restraints), one focus is legislators at the state or federal level. They, along with the constituencies they represent, must be persuaded by the strength of the researchers' original findings (the technology level), plus those at the next level (the applied level), to agree to introduce policies that would foster or ensure the widespread adoption of these technologies. Whether they agree or not, and what factors are instrumental in persuading them to do so, becomes the key topic for further research.

Unfortunately our skills and the resources available to us (and to most investigators working in domains such as these) do not permit an exploration of these issues at the level required. Nor does it appear that it is an area that has been well explored by others. As a consequence, it may be fair to say that the knowledge generated by this research is greater at the outset, at the basic level, than at the level of application. What has been learned about the issues surrounding how research findings are best applied to contribute to scientific knowledge is uncertain. There are still too few studies that relate the process of implementation to ultimate success at the level of program or policy.

It is difficult to glean from these examples which specific factors – if any –

have produced the most effective interplay between research and such actions in the projects described. However, although it cannot be established conclusively, personal relationships among the key actors appear to have been one major determinant. It is evident, too, that the timing and setting of the projects may have had a disproportionate influence on the action-research relationship.

Studies undertaken in the 1960s (such as the Neighborhood Health Center) were influenced by the ethos of that period. For example, the spirit of community participation and involvement extended even into the halls of academe. The setting for this project was Rochester, a community that had become "enlightened" in part through the force of the confrontations at Kodak led by the Black Power organization FIGHT. At the university level, the role of a pediatric department chairman willing to support the kind of collaborative relationships needed to make the health center concept work cannot be underestimated.

In Aaron's book (1978) *Politics and the Professors,* the conclusion is reached that research makes a relatively small contribution to government decision-making processes. In a similar analysis by Steiner, the experience with Head Start is examined. It is suggested that "it was by chance that the knowledge provided in the specialized writing of child development theorists found its way into policy, and the war on poverty was the vehicle for it" (Russell, 1980:6).

A somewhat less pessimistic conclusion is reached by Hofoss and Hjort (1981), who examined the relationship between action and research in health policy, largely drawing from Scandinavian experiences. They acknowledge that many conclude that health services research has had little or no effect. But they suggest that more emphasis should be placed on long-term, indirect effects on "the concepts, ideas and methods which shape the health service." Using these criteria, they conclude that there is evidence that research in this domain does make a difference. They go on to advocate that the effects would be improved if research was planned carefully to anticipate issues likely to be debated; if it cooperated closely with planners, rather than antagonized them; if it avoided drowning in "methodological refinements and scientific jargon"; and finally, if the job was not considered finished when a report was published, but only after various ways for "selling the ideas" had been explored.

One feature of the programs cited that may bear some relation to their success is their "network" character. Most did not begin as part of any large-scale program, nor were they isolated clinical or field projects. Rather, they were all part of larger movements of ideas and values and those who shared them. These included concern for the shortcomings of immunization levels, especially among the poor; the sensitivity of the public and the medical profession to the need for more adequate protection of child passengers; and the concern for the care of children with chronic disorders or handicaps. Thus, the projects benefited from (or may even have stimulated) these broader movements. In general, it is true that the strength of each alone drew from the extent to which one project built on others in the same field, with one investigator following the findings of others.

The dynamics of the interactions in the collaborative relationships involved are, in retrospect, hard to isolate and describe. In many respects the relationship between the "action" and the "research" was not one of collaboration in the usual sense. Rather than a close, direct relationship between program director and researcher, it was more often the case that the two (or more) main parties were isolated in time and/or space, learning of each other's work primarily through word of mouth, publications, or other forms of scientific communication.

The exceptions to this general observation were the three projects that began in Rochester in the late 1960s. As mentioned earlier, the NHC project most closely approached a traditional action-research model. Early studies by Robertson et al. (1974), and a team that included Haggerty, pointed to the promising benefits of comprehensive primary care. As a result, Charney adapted the health center model, developed by others, to the special needs of the Rochester community. Then, while serving as director, he stimulated, fostered, and encouraged further research, both evaluative and substantive. The combined effect was to broaden the network of centers within the Rochester community (from one to four within a five-year period) and to catalyze an incipient national movement in this direction.

The chronic disease studies and projects were similarly unusual. Both the initial studies and later interventions were spearheaded by the same team – one that first worked together in Rochester during the 1960s. The results of both the analytic studies and the service programs received considerable attention, leading directly to the development of a consortium of investigators with common goals and philosophy. In recent years this consortium has helped other researchers, developed common procedures, and prepared position papers on special methodologic problems in this field of inquiry. The success of this "chronic disease" movement rests heavily on the network of personal relationships that existed among a relatively small coterie of advocates with interests spread equally between research and program development.

In summary, the most effective interplay between research and action among the projects considered was the result of this network of old friends and comrades. Because many of the projects took on the aspect of uphill campaigns, it appeared that newcomers to the field were quickly attracted to the "old guard," core group by a mutual sense of being in a beleaguered, unappreciated, unrecognized minority. This was especially true for those in academic settings in departments that acknowledged only the traditional "bench sciences" and disparaged more socially oriented ventures into "the community."

In the final stages of most of the examples given, there exists a large "black box," the contents of which can only be guessed at. How and why research findings become translated into policy or large-scale programs (or, as is more often the case, fail to do so) is poorly understood. One can guess that political science, public relations, current events, charisma, and luck all play a part. Equally, even when well-designed, carefully focused targeted strategies exist, seemingly random forces still account for much of the variance of success or failure. A clear example of the latter can be found in the chronic illness area.

Two case studies

The RAND project

As the results of many studies of "unmet needs" of these children began to accumulate, all of which had as an implicit goal the intent to modify services or to create new ones to help meet these needs if necessary, various efforts to bring about changes in how health services are delivered emerged. One such process was the outgrowth of the RAND Corporation study on "Improving Services to Handicapped Children" (Kakalik et al., 1974). This project appeared to have a good chance of "success" (as defined by program evolution or change) in view of its sponsors, the federal government's Department of Health, Education and Welfare. A clear set of recommendations were formulated, the foremost of which was to establish regional direction centers to foster coordination and integration of services for these children at the regional level.

Unlike in many other such studies the investigators were sufficiently concerned about ensuring the application of their findings that they sought and secured additional funds to support the implementation strategies they judged to be most appropriate. There followed a series of steps, ranging from public meetings to media events, designed to catalyze widespread acceptance of the recommendations. In the end these well-laid plans went astray because the final step of the strategy was upstaged by Watergate and the public preoccupation with this event.

In the epilogue to a book summarizing their findings, Brewer and Kakalik (1979) describe "What happened after the research reports were filed." This highlights the experiences involved in the decision-making and implementation phases of the policy process. After detailing the origins of the project, they go on to describe their efforts to secure its success: the manner in which a dialogue was established with the sponsors in Washington, the many attempts made to maintain the attention of the key federal officials involved, the press releases, seminars, and so on, culminating in an intensified dissemination strategy. This involved incorporating the advice of experts in the field of sociology as well as those of renowned media men and resulted in a decision to produce a film documentary *(What Do We Do Now)*, which was to be shown widely but targeted on several key areas and individuals. Although the final results are distinctly encouraging, one of their key conclusions is noteworthy: "If our experiences with dissemination of results from the handicapped children's project suggest anything, it is that nearly as much time, effort, and resources need to be expended in the research utilization and policy implementation phases as in the conduct of the research itself" (p. 574). In general, the same conclusion is reached by Pless in an editorial, "Implementing Research Findings: Who is Responsible?" (1982).

The Jacobi project

One important spin-off from the growing interest in improving the care of children with chronic physical disorders is the trial conducted by Stein, Reissman, and Jessop. This is a rare example of a true experimental design with human subjects conducted under real-life circumstances. In this case the goal was to assess the value of home care as an adjunct to regular care for these children.

The importance of this service delivery program, conducted at Jacobi Hospital (part of the Albert Einstein School of Medicine) in the Bronx in the mid-1970s, goes beyond the scientific results – themselves impressive and encouraging. It illustrates as well the reciprocal relationship between the program being evaluated and the research itself. It shows how research is developed based on the values and interests of the persons and institutions involved.

In their paper, subtitled "A Case Study in the Sociology of Applied Research," Jessop and Stein (1983) describe how the challenging demands of the experimental design were able to succeed in a tough, real-world setting, combining the Bronx with the haute academe of a leading medical school. The project grew out of a growing awareness of the myriad problems associated with the care – particularly the hospital care – of children with chronic illnesses. This awareness was shared by a growing cadre of researchers in pediatrics, some parent groups, and, importantly, by the then acting chair of the department.

Pediatric Home Care (PHC), the service program already in existence, embodied many of the philosophies of the 1960s: the need for comprehensive, integrated medical and psychological services aimed at children and their families; the desirability of an interdisciplinary approach; and the wish to provide as many services as possible outside the hospital, for example, in the patient's home. The details of the pre-post experimental design used to evaluate the PHC (called the Pediatric Ambulatory Care and Treatment Study, or PACTS) are given elsewhere (Stein et al., 1982). Alongside these scientific details, however, the team also offers a fascinating glimpse into the social and political forces that had to be overcome in some instances and that, in other respects, helped render the project a success (Jessop and Stein, 1983).

Much of the impetus for the study was financial pressure on the institution during a time of fiscal crises. Although the option of lobbying for the continuation of a program many of their colleagues viewed as an "expensive frill" occurred to them, the investigators chose the research route instead. They did so for a variety of reasons: It bought time for the program while the application was pending; documenting the value of PHC might be persuasive evidence to help save it; outside peer review, if successful, would be prestigious and enhance the status of the applicants and the unit as a whole; the rigor of a trial would help make the evaluation acceptable to senior, influential department members whose support through informal institutional ties helped get the project off the ground. Finally, the funding agency was receptive to the idea of such a trial because it had implications for policy formulation and funding of service delivery programs directly and indirectly (Jessop and Stein, 1983:105).

Although the experimental design was decided quickly and without much of the conflict associated with such an approach in human research, it was only because the investigators were wise enough to anticipate objections and develop acceptable arguments to support their approach. Further, they had the foresight to establish a special ethics review committee to permit the inclusion of all children regardless of the severity of their condition. The composition of the committee, combining both senior staff members and grass-roots house staff, also contributed importantly to its success. In summary, the research design was consonant with biomedical traditions.

The authors make it clear that the research had a number of unanticipated effects on the program being studied. They had to win the support of the action team and did so by involving them in many of the decisions about how the service would be run during the research period. Regular meetings were held, but in spite of all efforts, the service team felt constrained by the project, probably because of some loss of "control." The study affected the team's ability to form a close, ongoing relationship with the families they were to serve and, in a variety of other ways, had a "debilitating effect on morale and energy" of the providers. It appeared, too, to have an impact on the quality of service given as a result of conflicts in feelings about the type and number of cases that had to be served. Because the study required, and enabled, the program to be temporarily expanded, the intimacy of the team diminished, as did the intensity of their involvement. There were, as a consequence, more staff changes than might be expected during the trial period. At the end of the study there occurred a phase of paralysis with respect to decisions and a sense of lack of autonomy on the part of the leadership. In the end, "it became a difficult task for the team to regroup and develop dynamism lost during the research period" (Jessop and Stein, 1983:112).

The experience with this program is undoubtedly typical of others involved in action-research of a similar kind. On the one hand, it points clearly to the importance of capturing a concordance of values and interests of all the actors involved to ensure the success of the undertaking from the research viewpoint. On the other hand, it is evident that the evaluation affected the program in many ways. It is therefore reasonable to ask, as the writers do, whether the goals are "adequately accomplished by a design that alters the functioning of the program? If the quality or intensity of the program is diluted, it in essence has not been given a fair chance to prove itself." This is in contrast to the more familiar paradox that arises when a new program is being evaluated and the enthusiasm and dedication of the providers result in the effects being overstated.

Summary

In the end, it must be clear that these examples from the field of child health are each imperfect illustrations of the basic concept of action-research. They are, however, perhaps typical of most present-day variations on the theme. The note struck by Kurt Lewin over fifty years ago continues to sound, but the tune today is a different one. The reality is that the concept of a closely knit team working together to do action and research simultaneously is rarely found. This is so both for scientific reasons and for less elegant, mundane reasons such as the politics of research funding and the demands of academia. Instead, there exist well-defined and amorphous networks of investigators in search of programs for study, and action programs in search of researchers to help them determine what they are doing and how well. The end result may well be the same as what was originally intended. The successes come with mutual respect, good fortune, good timing, and, above all, a favorable political climate – one that fosters such collaborations. Finally, it must be stressed that the process under consideration is a variable one. At times, research alone generates services; at other times, it is the services that stimulate the research. At all times, the manner in which the results are "sold," that is, diffused and implemented widely, remains a major, problematic issue.

References

Aaron, H. J. *Politics and the professors: The great society in perspective.* Washington, D.C.: The Brookings Institution, 1978.

Brewer, G. D., and Kakalik, J. S. *Handicapped children: Strategies for improving services.* New York: McGraw-Hill, 1979.

Burke, D., and Yiammouyannis, J. *Congressional Record,* July 21, 1975, *191* (H7172–7176).

Charney, E. The Rochester Neighborhood Health Center: Five years in retrospect. In R. J. Haggerty et al. (Eds.), *Child health and the community.* New York: Wiley, 1975, pp. 226–41.

Charney, E., and Mechaber, J. Public health nurses: Professional level of performance in a neighborhood health center compared with a health department. Mimeographed. 1972.

Consumer Reports. A two-part report on fluoridation. Reprint, July and August 1978. Mount Vernon, N.Y.: Consumer's Union of the United States, 1978, 2–5.

Dean, H. T., et al. Domestic water and dental caries with additional studies of the relationship of domestic waters to dental caries experiences in 4425 white children aged 12–14 years in 13 cities in 4 states. *Public Health Reports,* 1942, *57,* 32.

Doll, R., and Kinlen, L. Fluoridation of water and cancer mortality in the USA. *Lancet,* 1977, *i,* 1300.

Dunning, J. M. *Principles of dental public health* (2nd ed). Cambridge, Mass: Harvard University Press, 1975, pp. 367–403.

Federal Register, 1974, *39,* 1314.

Friedman, S. B., Phillips, S., and Parrish, J. M. Current status of behavioral pediatric training for general pediatric residents: A study of 11 funded programs. *Pediatrics,* 1983, *71,* 904–8.

Gee, L., and Sowell, R. F., Jr. A school immunization law is successful in Texas. *Public Health Reports,* 1975, *90*(1), 21–24.

Glidewell, J., Domke, H., and Kantor, M. Screening in schools for behavior disorders: Use of mothers' reports of symptoms. *Educational Research,* 1963, *56,* 508–15.

Goldberg, I. D., Regier, D. A., McInerny, R. K., Pless, I. B., Roghmann, K. J. The role of the pediatrician in the delivery of mental health services to children. *Pediatrics,* 1979, *63,* 898–909.

Haggerty, R. J., and Roghmann, K. J. The Rochester Health Center. In R. J. Haggerty et al. (Eds.), *Child health and the community.* New York: Wiley, 1975, pp. 222–34.

Haggerty, R. J., Roghmann, K. J., and Pless, I. B. (Eds.). *Child health and the community.* New York: Wiley, 1975.

Hillman, B., and Charney, E. A neighborhood health center: What patients know and think of its operation. *Medical Care,* 1971, *10:*336–44.

Hocheiser, L. I., Woodward, K., and Charney, E. Effect of the neighborhood health center on the use of pediatric emergency departments in Rochester, New York. *New England Journal of Medicine,* 1971, *285*(3), 148–52.

Hofoss, D., and Hjort, P. F. The relation between action and research in health policy. *Social Science and Medicine,* 1981, *15A,* 371–75.

Hoover, R. N., McKay, F. W., and Fraumeni, J. R. Fluoridated water and the occurrence of cancer. *Journal of the National Cancer Institute,* 1976, *57,* 757–68.

Jackson, C. L. State laws on compulsory immunization in the United States. *Public Health Reports,* 1969, *84*(9), 787–89.

Jackson, C. L., and Carpenter, R. L. Effect of a state law intended to require immunization of children. *Health Services Report,* 1972, *87,* 461–66.

Jacobson v. The Commonwealth of Massachusetts, 197 US 11, 25 S. Ct. 358, 49L, Ed. 643, Ann. Cas. 765 (1905).

Jessop, D. J., and Stein, R. E. K. A service delivery program and its evaluation – A case study in the sociology of applied research. *Evaluation and the Health Professions,* 1983, *6*(1), 99–114.

Kakalik, J. S., Brewer, G. D., Dougharty, L. A. et al. *Improving services to handicapped children.* Santa Monica, Calif.: RAND Corp., 1974.

Kanthor, H., Pless, I. B., Satterwhite, B., and Myers, G. Areas of responsibility in the health care of multiply handicapped children. *Pediatrics,* 1974, *54,* 779–85.

Kark, S. L., and Steuart, G. W. *A practice of social medicine.* Edinburgh: E & S Livingstone, 1962.

Klein, M., Roghmann, K., Woodward, K., and Charney, E. The impact of the Rochester Neighborhood Health Center on hospitalization of children, 1968–1970. *Pediatrics,* 1973, *51*(5), 833–39.

Lancet. Vaccination against whooping cough (editorial). May 23, 1981, pp. 1138–39.

Lapouse, R., and Monk, A. An epidemiological study of behavioural characteristics in children. *American Journal of Public Health*, 1958, *48*, 1134.

Leo Itz et ux. v. Penick et al., 493 S.W. 2d 506, Texas sup ct (1973).

Loeser, H., Zvagulis, I., Hercz, L. et al. The organization and evaluation of a computer-assisted, centralized immunization registry. *American Journal of Public Health*, 1983, *73*, 1298–1301.

Meyer, R. J. Save that child: Children and automobile restraints (editorial). *American Journal of Public Health*, 1981, *71*(2), 122–23.

National Transportation Safety Board. Safety study: Child passenger protection against death, disability, and disfigurement in motor vehicle accidents. Washington: D.C., September 7, 1983.

Newburgh-Kingston caries-fluorine study, XIV. Combined clinical and Roentgen-graphic dental finding after 10 years of fluorine experience. *Journal of the American Dental Association*, 1956, *52*, 3.

Oldham, P. D., and Newell, D. J. Fluoridation of water supplies and cancer – a possible association. *Applied statistics – Journal of the Royal Statistical Society*, Series C, 1977, *26*, 125–36.

Pearse, I. H., and Crocker, L. H. *The Peckham Experiment, a study of the living structure of society*. London: George Allen & Unwin, 1943.

Phillips, S., Friedman, S. B., Smith, J., and Felice, M. E. Evaluation of a residency training program in behavioral pediatrics. *Pediatrics*, 1983, *71*, 406–12.

Pless, I. B. Child health and the community: The Rochester child health studies 1966–1977. Proceedings of a workshop on the evaluation of child health services: The interface between research and medical practice. Bethesda, Md.: J. E. Fogarty International Center, National Institutes of Health, 1978. (a)

Pless, I. B. Accident prevention and health education: Back to the drawing board? *Pediatrics*, 1978, *62*:431–35. (b)

Pless, I. B. Current morbidity and mortality among the young. In S. B. Friedman and R. A. Hoekelman (Eds.), *Behavioral pediatrics: Psychosocial aspects of child health care*. New York: McGraw-Hill, 1980, pp. 39–57.

Pless, I. B. Implementing research findings: Who is responsible? An editorial commentary. *Canadian Medical Association Journal*, 1982, *126*, 345–46.

Pless, I. B., Roghmann, K. J., and Algranati, P. Prevention of injuries to children in automobiles. *Pediatrics*, 1972, *49*, 420–27.

Pless, I. B., and Satterwhite, B. Chronic illness in childhood: Selection, activities and valuation of non-professional family counsellors. *Clinical Pediatrics*, 1972, *11*, 407–10.

Pless, I. B., and Satterwhite, B. B. Chronic illness. In R. J. Haggerty, K. J. Roghmann, and I. B. Pless (Eds.), *Child health and the community*. New York: Wiley, 1975, pp. 78–93.

Pless, I. B., Satterwhite, B., and VanVechten, D. Chronic illness in childhood: A regional survey of care. *Pediatrics*, 1976, *58*, 37–46.

Pless, I. B., Satterwhite, B., and VanVechten, D. Division, duplication, and neglect: Patterns of care for children with chronic disorders. *Child: Care, Health and Development*, 1978, *4*, 9–19.

Pless, I. B., and Pekeles, G. Applications of health care research to child health services; a problematic relationship. *Israel Journal of Medical Sciences*, 1981, *17*, 192–200.

Pless, I. B., and Perrin, J. Chronic childhood illness: The commonalities among conditions. In N. Hobbs, and J. Perrin (Eds.), *The constant shadow*. San Francisco: Jossey-Bass, 1985.

Porter, P. Personal communication to R. J. Haggerty, 1985.

Reisenger, K., and Williams, A. F. Evaluation of programs designed to increase the protection of infants in cars. *Pediatrics*, 1978, *62*(3), 280–87.

Robertson, L., Kosa, J., Heagerty, M. C., Haggerty, R. J., and Alpert, J. J. *Changing the medical care system: A controlled experiment in comprehensive care*. New York: Praeger, 1974.

Roghmann, K. J., and Charney, E. The impact on the utilization of emergency room services. In

R. J. Haggerty, K. J. Roghmann, and I. B. Pless (Eds.), *Child health and the community*. New York: Wiley, 1975, pp. 242–52.

Russell, A. Building a bridge from research to action: The High/Scope Foundation's Policy Center for Young Children. *Carnegie Quarterly,* 1980, *28*:5–7.

Rutter, M., Tizard, J., and Whitmore, K. *Education, health and behavior.* New York: Wiley, 1970.

Sanders, R. S. Legislative approach to auto safety: The Tennessee experience. The Twelfth Ross Round Table on critical approaches to common pediatric problems. Seattle, Washington, March 29 and 30, 1981.

Sanders, R. S., Casey, E. L. The Tennessee child passenger protection act: Origin, legislative success, and national impact. Proceedings of the Twenty-Third Conference of the American Association for Automobile Safety. Louisville, Kentucky. October 4–6, 1979.

Sardell, A. Neighborhood health centers and community-based care: Federal policy from 1965 to 1982. *Journal of Public Health Policy,* December 1983, 485.

Schreier, H. A. Sounding board: On the failure to eradicate measles. *New England Journal of Medicine,* 1974, *290,* 803–4.

Stein, R. E. K., Reisman, and Jessop, D. J. A non-categorical approach to chronic childhood illness. *Public Health Reports,* 1982, *97,* 354–62.

Toomath, J. B. Compulsory seat belt legislation in New Zealand. Presented at the Sixth International Conference of the International Association for Accident and Traffic Medicine. Melbourne, 1977.

U.S. Department of Health, Education and Welfare. Annual summary for the United States. Births, deaths, marriages, and divorces. Public Health Service. National Center for Health Statistics. Monthly Vital Statistics Report, 1975, *24*(13), 2–12.

Williams, A. F., and Wells, J. K. The Tennessee child restraint law in its third year. *American Journal of Public Health,* 1981, *71*(2), 163–64.

World Health Organization. Fluoride and human health, 1970.

9   Community mental health: developments in the United States

Gerald L. Klerman

Introduction

Community mental health as a field of research and action emerged in North America and Western Europe after World War II. The field grew rapidly and reached the proportions of a social movement in the 1960s. To refer to community mental health as a ''social movement'' signifies not only that there was professional and scientific activity but that its ideas and goals had gained substantial support in public circles, particularly among governmental policymakers.

Psychiatry, as a medical specialty, began in the late eighteenth and early nineteenth centuries in the asylums, the forerunner of today's public mental institutions. Until the early part of the twentieth century, psychiatry was almost exclusively concerned with patients with ''lunacy'' and ''insanity,'' conditions that today would be called psychotic illnesses, and that were often medically disabling and socially incapacitating. In the early part of the twentieth century, the scope of psychiatry was expanded to include patients with psychoneuroses and personality disorders being seen by practitioners in urban settings and in psychiatric units of general hospitals.

After World War II, there was a marked further expansion in the scope of mental illness and mental health, and in the range of settings in which psychiatrists and other mental health professionals worked. Much of this expansion occurred under the aegis of ''community mental health.''

The field of community mental health was to encompass a range of concepts and programs, including: new techniques for treating individual patients; reform of institutional care in mental hospitals; new forms of community services; and major revisions of public policy regarding mental health and mental illness.

During this period, two new professional fields – social psychiatry and community mental health – emerged within mental health, and their ideas became major forces for change within the social sciences, the mental health professions, and public policy. The early developments of the field occurred during and after

236

World War II through a number of innovative local projects, and later their adoption as federal policy in the United States involved close collaboration between researchers in the social and behavioral sciences and "action" professionals in psychiatry, law, and public administration.

After considerable optimism and program expansion in the 1950s and the 1960s, we are now in a period of retraction of public support, restriction in fiscal appropriations, and loss of professional consensus. The close collaboration of social science research and program development characteristic of the previous period has almost completely disappeared.

The time is, therefore, propitious to review these developments in mental health in general, and to assess the role of research and action, in particular. This chapter will review the background and development of community mental health in the United States. Although a major focus of this volume is on the needs of children and adolescents, these populations will not be discussed in great detail in this chapter, but rather as part of the larger developments in U.S. mental health services.

Interaction, collaboration, organization, and integration between research and action and community mental health

Rapoport, in the introductory chapter to this volume, has described the general relationships between scientific research and societal action. In the forty-to-fifty-year history of community mental health, the degree of integration of research and action has varied. Different types of interaction, collaboration, and organizational integration have marked different periods, and the advantages and disadvantages of these arrangements merit continued discussion.

As shown in the accompanying figures, there have been four types of organizational integration between research and action in community mental health.

Type 1: The "pure" research ideal

In the late nineteenth century, the ideal of "basic" research appeared and the distinction between basic and applied research was accepted. Thus, the researchers and the action professionals function in separate organizations. The researchers are usually in academic centers but may also be in research institutes sponsored by government, industry, or foundations. In the "pure" research ideal, information is expected to flow from the researchers to the action professionals (see Figure 9.1). Communication takes place through publications, reports, conferences, and consultations.

Basic researchers often insist that the long-term social benefit from their research derives from minimum societal interference and maximum autonomy. It

Figure 9.1. Pure research ideal. (In each of the figures in this chapter the attempt is made to display the organizational relationships between individuals and groups involved in research and in action and the flow of communication and information. The solid lines indicate formal organizational boundaries. The broken lines indicate less formal boundaries within a formal organization, such as a research unit with a hospital. The arrows indicate the direction of communications; the modes of communication include written or verbal exchange of information.)

is claimed that the "splendid isolation" of pure research will contribute, in the long run, to the greater social good.

An example of this benefit occurred in the research and action experiences at Yale University in New Haven, Connecticut. For many years, social scientists had conducted extensive field research on the community organization and social stratification within the New Haven community. After World War II, Redlich, a psychiatrist, and Hollingshead, a sociologist, collaborated in an extensive survey of treated prevalence of mental illness in the New Haven area. This research demonstrated an inverse relationship between social class and the prevalence of serious mental disorders, particularly schizophrenia. Their publications, particularly *Social Class and Mental Illness* (1958), had a powerful impact on theory and practice. Action programs were designed to correct the inequity of access to treatment and the presumed causal relationship between low social class and an increased risk for mental illness. Later, Redlich was influential in the founding of the Connecticut Mental Health Center, and as its first director, implemented community programs based upon his previous research (Redlich et al., 1966; Klerman, 1969). In the Yale–New Haven example, one individual, Fritz Redlich, served as a link between the research carried out in the 1940s and its implementation into action in the mid-1960s.

One of the limitations of the "pure research" ideal is the long time often required for the impact of research on action. Frequently, the individuals involved change over time. The integrated research-action model that emerged after World War II hoped to facilitate this interaction and to accelerate the pace of application of research findings into social change.

In the New Haven experience, the impact of research on action took place over a number of decades, during which time most of the actors in both the research and action programs changed. Even after the retirement of Redlich, an active research program in community epidemiology continues, led by Myrna Weissman, Ph.D., and Jerome Myers, M.D., working in parallel with but organizationally semi-autonomous from the action leadership of the Connecticut Mental Health Center under its director, Borus Astrachan, M.D.

Type 2: Feedback between action and research

The pure research ideal has been criticized as being only partially related to actual practice in social policy in general health and mental health. It has been pointed out by many observers that the flow of information is, in actuality, both ways.

Figure 9.2. Feedback between research and action.

The identification of questions for which research is desirable often flows from pressing clinical or social concerns. For example, in mental health: "Are there adverse effects in the social organization of mental hospitals?" "How does poverty influence access to mental health services?"

After World War II, a major action-research goal was to facilitate research-action collaborations in the hope of stimulating new knowledge and also of increasing rate of feedback to contribute to social change. One example of this relationship occurred in the efforts in the Stirling County Project in Nova Scotia, where simultaneous with and parallel to the extensive epidemiologic studies undertaken by A. H. Leighton and his associates, the local community established a community mental health program (Leighton, 1963, 1982). The early hopes that the epidemiologic research and the community mental health service programs would be highly integrated were not realized. Leighton has written a detailed description of the ways in which these feedback experiences were impeded by different goals and values (Leighton, 1982).

As action programs are planned and implemented, their experience poses questions for further research. Usually, the new research is "evaluation research" in which the questions for investigations are concerned with the functioning and outcome of the action program. However, questions for "basic" research may also emerge when the outcomes of programs do not follow expectations or challenge theoretical assumptions. For example, in the mental health field, deinstitutionalization has been followed by community rejection of mental patients and neighborhood resistance to the creation of community-based residential facilities. New forms of chronicity of mental illness have emerged in community settings that were counter to the theoretical assumptions of community psychiatry and extrapolations from the findings of social psychiatric research conducted in the 1950s and early 1960s.

Type 3: The action-research ideal

In this ideal, organizational integration of research and action is at a maximum. The researchers and the planners and implementers of action programs are within one organization whose leadership facilitates and integrates the action-research relationship. This ideal emerged in anthropology before World War II, and was prominent in the writings about interdisciplinary research after World War II, as described by Rapoport in Chapter 1 of this volume.

Figure 9.3. Integrated action-research ideal.

In the 1950s and 1960s, this model was widely applied in mental health, especially in efforts at institutional reform of mental hospitals (Price and Politser, 1980). For example, Drs. Overholzer and Stanley, superintendent and deputy superintendent respectively at St. Elizabeth's Hospital, invited a young social psychologist, Erving Goffman, to undertake a study of the social organization of the hospital with the explicit intent of using his observations as guides to institutional reform (Goffman, 1961).

Another example of this ideal was the collaboration between Maxwell Jones and Robert Rapoport in the evaluation of the "therapeutic community" efforts aimed at the rehabilitation of individuals with severe social incapacity due to personality problems (Jones, 1953).

In another example, the Russell Sage Foundation supported efforts at the Massachusetts Mental Health Center involving induced change in the social organization of mental hospitals, and quasi-experiments to transfer chronic mental patients from the state hospital to intensive treatment centers. Milton Greenblatt, M.D., served as the director of research with the support of Dr. Harry C. Solomon, superintendent, and Dr. Robert Hyde, assistant superintendent, of the Massachusetts Mental Health Center, and Commissioner of Mental Health Dr. Jack A. Ewalt (Greenblatt, York, and Brown, 1955). The research team included a number of social scientists – Richard Williams, Daniel Levinson, and Elliott Mishler (Greenblatt, Levinson, and Williams, 1957 – and the reports of their research findings appeared in a number of volumes that were influential in the subsequent activities of the Joint Commission on Mental Health and Mental Illness.

Type 4: Differentiated and coordinated complex organization

Complex systems for interaction between research and action have evolved in large health and social welfare agencies at the state and federal level. Within such agencies, there are usually semiautonomous units for research, policy planning, and program evaluation, and for the management and direction of various programs. These components may be coordinated and directed at different levels of leadership (i.e., Commissioner of Mental Health, Secretary of Health and Human Services, Medical Director of the VA). The impetus for these arrangements come not only from the size and complexity of large organizations, particularly governmental agencies, but also because of attempts to minimize conflict of interest, often based on previous research on the nature of organizations and often conflicting theoretical assumptions held by different groups within the agency.

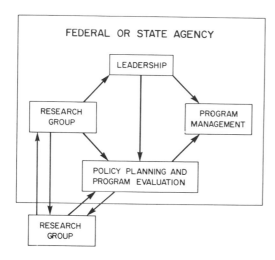

Figure 9.4. Differentiated and coordinated complex organization.

For example, during World War II the United States Army established a research unit of social scientists who were influential in advising the military leadership on training and morale. The army research undertaken to evaluate mental health services during World War II played an influential role in modifying the ways in which combat reactions were handled during the Korean and Vietnam wars with dramatic reduction in the incidence of combat-related psychiatric casualties (Glass, 1955).

Currently, the differentiated and coordinated complex type of relationship predominates particularly in public institutions, but also in general hospitals and other large institutions where mental health services are delivered.

Historical background

Although the major activity in community mental health occurred after World War II, it is important to place these endeavors into the appropriate historical context.

The influence of Adolf Meyer

The theoretical approach basic to social psychiatry and community mental health is the legacy of Adolf Meyer (Klerman, 1979). The Flexner Report (Flexner, 1910), which reported on the state of medical education, used as its model the curriculum of Johns Hopkins University, which was committed to creating the first modern American medical school. William Welch, the dean and professor of pathology, was the architect of changes at Johns Hopkins along with Osler, Halsted, and the other greats of the Hopkins faculty. Adolf Meyer helped create the first major university teaching center in psychiatry in North America.

There is a paradox in this. Meyer, who was Swiss, was brought to Johns Hopkins because of his success in neuropathology. Meyer transcended his cultural and professional background and developed a uniquely American approach to psychiatry based upon his interpretation of Darwin's theory of evolution and the application to psychiatry of the tenets of pragmatism. His view of psychobiology was one in which understanding of mental illness was to be found in research on life experience and social context rather than exclusively in biological laboratory experimentation.

His students became the leading academics in the United States. However, the impact of Meyer's ideas was not fully felt until after World War II. Meyer had given only the broadest outline of the important role of experience for the development and treatment of mental illness. His students carried his ideas forward into various areas.

1. The child guidance movement of 1920 bore his influence. With the creation of these clinics there was a renewed interest that early intervention would correct neurotic habits and prevent the emergence of schizophrenia, delinquency, and other serious adult disorders. Meyer's views and theories predominated in the practices of the first child guidance clinics. William Healy began the Institute for Juvenile Research, which became the model for future guidance clinics.
2. His work on dynamic psychotherapy with Morton Prince later bore fruit in the pioneering studies of psychotherapy by Jerome Frank (1973).
3. The Baltimore-Washington area became the locus of new social psychiatric ideas. In the period before and during World War II, Hopkins and the Washington-Baltimore area were the loci of great intellectual ferment with the infusion of insights from anthropology, sociology, and the other social sciences into psychiatry and psychology. These ideas became crystallized in Sullivan's interpersonal theory of psychiatry (Sullivan, 1953). Sullivan (1953) and Fromm-

Reichmann (1960) and their associates at the Chestnut Lodge and Sheppard and Enoch Pratt hospitals initiated a psychotherapeutic approach to schizophrenia.
4. Among the most lasting contributions of Meyer was the vision of a social epidemiology of mental illness. Lemkau, Tietze, and Cooper (1942), Pasamanick, Scarpitti, and Dinitz (1967), Srole, Langner, Michael et al. (1962), and others amplified Meyer's general approach to identify social factors that generate mental illness and mental retardation in specific communities.
5. In public health, Meyer's influence was equally powerful, but here, too, it stands in danger of being forgotten. In 1913, he proposed the blueprint for a mental hygiene clinic for the area near the hospital, and this succinct plan captures the essence of today's community mental health center program.

I consider it of the greatest importance that the clinic make itself responsible for the mental health of a fairly well circumscribed unit of population, so as to make possible studies of the social situation and of the dynamic factors which lead to the occurrence of mental derangements which must be attacked for purposes of prevention. [Meyer, 1951]

These efforts of Meyer's took place in a specific historical context. The decades before World War I, during which the progressive movement was at its height, had an influence not only in mental health but also in child welfare development of public health approaches and in the emergence of psychology, sociology, and anthropology as distinct academic influences (Klerman, 1979).

There is an important link between American developments and those in the United Kingdom. Aubrey Lewis, the dominant leader in English psychiatry after World War II, had come to the United States as a visiting fellow in the early 1930s, where he came under the influence of Adolf Meyer (Lewis, 1934). In his influential papers on depression published between 1933 and 1935, Lewis states that his intent was to apply to the concept of manic-depressive insanity and endogenous depression, the ideas of Adolf Meyer, and to modify the purely disease-entity view associated with Kraepelin for depression, as Adolf Meyer himself had done for dementia praecox. After World War II, when Lewis became head of the Institute of Psychiatry at the Maudsley Hospital, one of his major decisions was to create the Medical Research Council (MRC) Social Psychiatry Research Unit, out of which has come the influential work of Wing, Brown, Shepherd, Rutter, Kendell, and a generation of English epidemiologists and social psychiatrists.

Child guidance movement

The experience of the child guidance movement provided one of the important links between the developments before World War I and the community mental health activities after World War II. Stimulated by the thinking of Adolf Meyer and the impact of Freudian theories of childhood development, a number of foundations, notably the Rockefeller Foundation and the Commonwealth Fund, provided money for the creation of child guidance clinics in local communities.

These clinics provided early intervention with the hope not only of reducing distress and difficulties in childhood but of preventing the later onset of adult disorders, particularly schizophrenia. These clinics were multidisciplinary, involving close cooperation of psychiatrists, psychologists, and social workers. Many current practices on child therapy, family evaluation, family therapy, and consultation with the school were first developed in these clinics. The American Orthopsychiatry Association was formed by its professionals, and for many decades had been the leading interdisciplinary forum for mental health professionals concerned with early intervention, prevention, and community activities.

Experience during World War II

The World War II experiences of the Selective Service and the U.S. armed forces had an important impact on postwar developments. The Selective Service System rejected large numbers of young men for psychiatric reasons; in fact, psychiatric diagnoses, including mental retardation, accounted for the largest proportion of nonacceptance. After the war, the scientific and military justifications for the rejections were criticized and the validity of the diagnostic procedures was questioned. Nevertheless, the publicity given to the high rates of psychoneurosis, personality disorders, and psychosomatic problems focused public attention on mental health problems and supported efforts to obtain more information on the rates of psychiatric disability and to implement interventions (Menninger, 1963).

In the U.S. Army, a group of talented social scientists was organized (Stouffer et al., 1949). Using the best available sampling methods, survey techniques, and statistical analyses, this group conducted a wide range of studies and developed neuropsychiatric screening questionnaires to relate neurotic symptoms to combat stress and morale problems. These scales were the forerunners of the impairment scales used in community surveys after the war.

Neuropsychiatric specialists were widely dispersed in the military and contributed clinical description and documentation of mental disorders related to military service and combat, such as combat fatigue, transient functional psychoses, dissociative states, and stress reactions. Whereas the rates of psychoses in the military remained relatively stable, the rates of psychoneuroses and personality reactions fluctuated and were related to combat and other acute stresses (Grinker and Spiegel, 1945; Glass, 1958; Dohrenwend and Dohrenwend, 1969). The observations were extended to the reactions of prisoners exposed to the extreme deprivation in concentration camps.

The observation that rates of psychiatric reactions varied in relation to combat stress was of theoretical and practical importance. These psychiatric reactions occurred in young men for whom preexisting disability factors would seem to have been minimized by premilitary psychiatric screening. From today's vantage point, these screening methods were far from ideal. However, for the post–World War II phase, the experience was highly important. The planners of epidemiologic research and community mental health in the post–World War II period were impressed by the experience of the Selective Service and the military. Since predisposing vulnerability and concurrent mental and physical illness had been screened out, it seemed reasonable to conclude that precipitant stress, rather than predisposition or vulnerability, was the major factor in psychiatric illness. In the post–World War II decades, "stress" became a major unifying concept in social psychiatry and community mental health. Poverty, urban anomie and alienation, rapid social change, and low social class became the civilian equivalents of the stress of organizational life in the military and the threat of death in combat.

The post–World War II experience, 1945–1960: the golden era of social psychiatry

In retrospect, the two decades immediately after World War II were a "golden era" (Weissman and Klerman, 1978). New ideas had been developed, particularly the concept of stress, and a cadre of psychiatrists, psychologists, and social scientists reentered civilian life with enthusiasm and vision that these ideas could be applied to reforming society. Their vision was supported by public response, which made large sums of money available and supported a national mandate for change in mental health.

Social psychiatry emerged as a new academic discipline concerned with understanding the role of social factors in the genesis and maintenance of mental illness, and also in stimulating reforms of mental institutions, facilitating new community-based mental health services, and increasing the access of disenfranchised populations to services (Mechanic, 1978).

The concept of "mental health" gained popularity. This concept signified that the scope of concern was greater than mental illnesses, in general, and psychotic illness, in particular. It is significant that the congressional legislation created the National Institute of Mental Health (NIMH), not a National Institute on Mental Illness. Thus, U.S. public policy at the highest level enunciated a broadened goal and this legislation itself represented one of the first achievements of the new approach.

Social epidemiologic studies

After World War II, the experience gained by the military and the growing public awareness of the high prevalence of mental illness prompted new epidemiologic studies in the civilian population. When the National Institute of Mental Health was created in the legislature in 1946 and became operational in 1949, there was financial and policy support for research.

The studies included:

1. The Midtown Manhattan survey by Rennie, Srole, Langner, and the Cornell group, which assessed the impact of urban life on mental health by interviewing more than 1,000 adult residents, selected by probability sampling in midtown Manhattan (Srole et al., 1962).
2. The Hollingshead and Redlich study of treated prevalence in New Haven, Connecticut (Hollingshead and Redlich, 1958). This study established social class as an important determinant of treated mental illness, particularly of schizophrenia, results that were replicated by Myers and Bean's (1968) follow-up of the sample ten years later.
3. The nationwide survey of attitudes toward mental health by Gurin, Veroff, and Feld (1960) at the University of Michigan Survey Research Center, in which more than 2,000 adult Americans also selected by probability sampling were interviewed.
4. The cross-cultural studies of A. H. Leighton et al. after Leighton's research of the Japanese-American internees in California during World War II and studies undertaken in the 1950s in Nigeria (Leighton, 1963), northern Canada, and southwestern United States.
5. The Stirling County study (D. C. Leighton et al., 1963) assessed the impact of social and economic change on the mental health of a previously stable community in Stirling County, Nova Scotia.

These studies reported high rates of mental impairment. For example, the Manhattan study found that only 19 percent of the subjects were free of significant symptoms and that 23 percent were substantially impaired (Srole et al., 1962).

With some exceptions, the studies conducted during this period had certain similarities. They decided against using existing psychiatric nosology and substituted measures of overall mental impairment for traditional diagnostic categories (MacMillan, 1957). Out of an awareness of diagnostic unreliability, the use of general impairment scales rather than diagnostic judgments made it easier and more economical to execute surveys. Highly trained psychiatrists were not required to make diagnostic judgments. Unreliability of diagnosis and nosological disputes could be avoided.

These studies used impeccable methods of sampling, paying attention to the representativeness of the sample selected for interviews and to the rate of response. They demonstrated social factors as causal to impairments of mental health (Mechanic, personal communication).

Research and action in mental hospitals

The research and action agenda of social psychiatry also included a focus on mental hospitals, particularly public mental hospitals. Almost immediately after the creation of the state mental hospital in the late eighteenth and early nineteenth centuries, numerous surveys, public commissions, and journalistic accounts had documented abuses, limitations of space and staff, and unsanitary and inhumane procedures in these institutions.

What was novel about the post–World War II efforts was the recruitment of social scientists into this agenda. A number of influential collaborations occurred between psychiatrists and social scientists. These included:

1. The Stanton and Schwartz study at Chestnut Lodge Hospital, Rockville, Maryland, which was published in the classic volume *The Mental Hospital* (Stanton and Schwartz, 1954).
2. Goffman's observations at St. Elizabeth's Hospital led to his concept of "total institutions" (Goffman, 1961).
3. Wing and associates in the United Kingdom investigating the adverse effect of understimulation and social isolation in mental hospitals upon the clinical course and outcome of schizophrenia (Wing, 1970).
4. Studies in Massachusetts at the Massachusetts Mental Health Center and Boston State Hospital led by Greenblatt (1955, 1957).
5. The efforts at Belmont, England, on social rehabilitation of individuals with chronic personality disorders out of which came the concept of therapeutic milieu, and the collaboration between Maxwell Jones (1953) and a group of social scientists, notably Robert Rapoport (1960).

These research efforts were seldom of the "pure" nature. The researchers were often personally close to the psychiatric administrators and ideologically committed to reform and innovation. Most of these reforms and innovations had begun in Western Europe. The "open door" policy, day treatment programs, therapeutic community, and nonrestraint were pioneered in the United Kingdom, Scandinavia, and France. As news of these innovations diffused into the United States, a number of American foundations played an influential role in catalyzing change, notably, the Milbank Memorial Fund, the Russell Sage Foundation, and the Commonwealth Fund. The Milbank Memorial Fund sponsored conferences and gave grants toward the development of mental health epidemiology and to support action programs, such as the Hudson River Project led by Ernest Gruenberg. The Russell Sage Foundation supported the work of Greenblatt and associates in Massachusetts. The Commonwealth Fund paid for visits by superintendents of mental hospitals and commissioners to the United Kingdom to learn the action programs for reform.

One of the popular reforms in mental hospitals was the adoption of the "therapeutic community" (Klerman, 1960; Rapoport, 1960). This technique relied heavily on small groups, not for traditional psychotherapy but as arenas for the discussion between patients and staff, regarding the progress of individual patients and the social organization of the unit. This technique was developed by Maxwell Jones for individuals suffering from personality disorders. It was applied in the United States in the early 1950s and used vigorously in the treatment of schizophrenics by Wilmer in the United States Naval Hospital in Oakland and by Artiss at the Walter Reed Army Hospital in Washington, D.C. These techniques were then rapidly accepted by the staffs of psychiatric units in general hospitals through the 1960s.

The study of mental hospitals was a vigorous area of academic and research endeavors by social scientists and psychiatrists in the 1950s and early 1960s; such collaborations are almost completely nonexistent today and there is very little interest in mental hospitals. A number of factors contributed to this disengagement between social scientists and psychiatrists and other mental health professionals. The increasing politicizing of community mental health during the Nixon administration was one factor. Another factor was the professional conflicts, predominantly within psychiatry, but also within psychology, as to the theoretical and social basis for the rapid expansion of community mental health services (Borus, 1978; Wolfe and Astrachan, 1985). At the same time, the intellectual climate within sociology, anthropology, and social psychology has become "antipsychiatric" with the influence of labeling theory. Szasz (1974), Rosenhan (1973), and Scheff (1966) challenged the validity of the concept of mental illness and the legitimacy of applying the medical model to personal problems and social issues.

Innovations in community mental health services

Soon after attempts were made to reform the internal functioning of mental hospitals, efforts were made to provide community-based programs for the aftercare of discharged patients. With the decision to reduce the duration of hospitalization, it became desirable to prevent rehospitalization of discharged patients. For example, by 1954, in the United States, before the introduction of the new drugs, the average duration of hospitalization was six months. This was in contrast to the period before World War II, when the average duration of hospitalization was one to two years. These efforts accelerated after 1952–54, following the introduction of the new psychopharmacologic agents. With the drug-induced reduction of psychotic symptoms and behavior, discharge into the community became more feasible, and duration of hospitalization was further reduced.

Aftercare programs were developed. Notable in these efforts was the comprehensive program at the Hudson River Project, New York, funded by the Milbank Memorial Fund, and under the leadership of Ernest Gruenberg. This project was aimed at developing links between the hospital and the community, with the goal of reducing the prevalence of social breakdown syndrome and other manifestations of chronicity (Gruenberg, 1967). Even before the impact of the new drugs, Gruenberg was able to demonstrate that rehospitalization rates could be reduced, and the prevalence of chronicity (social breakdown syndrome) decreased.

Along with programs for aftercare, a number of projects attempted to prevent hospitalization by providing community-based alternatives. Day hospitals, first developed in Moscow, were extended in London (Bierer, 1951). The first day hospital in the United States was developed in Boston at the Massachusetts Mental Health Center, and controlled studies (Zwerling and Wilder, 1964) demonstrated that up to 80 percent of acutely ill patients who might otherwise require hospitalization could be treated effectively in a day treatment program.

Another important innovation was home treatment by public health nurses. In a well-designed study, Pasamanick and associates (1967) demonstrated the efficacy of home treatment whereby public health nurses using medication and social therapeutic techniques could prevent hospitalization and reduce the secondary effects of hospitalization on families, particularly on children.

It is significant that day hospital programs and the home treatment programs, though their value is confirmed by controlled studies demonstrating efficacy, have not been widely adopted. In large part, this is because of the reluctance of insurance companies to provide coverage for these treatments.

During this period, a large number of innovations were developed and evaluated by systematic research, often using quantitative assessments of outcome and comparison and control groups. Social science researchers played an active role in these efforts (Fairweather and Tornatzky, 1977).

Lindemann and Caplan

Through the 1940s and 1950s, Eric Lindemann was formulating the theoretical basis for community mental health programs at the Massachusetts General Hospital and Harvard School of Public Health. Lindemann emphasized the role of community caretakers in providing a social network to support patients and their families (Satin, 1982). He pioneered the practice of mental health professionals moving out into communities. He expected these efforts to have long-term preventive impact. Some of these ideas were developed from the West End project in Boston. The research, which was conducted with the collaboration of social scientists such as Herbert Gans and Marc Fried, detailed the impact of urban relocation in a working-class community, and had considerable influence in the planning fields as well as psychiatry. Lindemann also expanded his experience with consultation in emergency units and in medical services to the concept of community consultation and education. He organized the Wellesley Human Relations Center, the first community mental health service in the United States.

Lindemann was later joined by Dr. Gerald Caplan, who had served in the British Army during World War II and worked at the Tavistock Clinic, where a number of psychoanalytically oriented social interventions were being developed. Caplan developed a comprehensive educational training and research program, first at the Harvard School of Public Health, and later at the Laboratory of Community Psychiatry at the Massachusetts Mental Health Center (Caplan, 1964, 1970). Under Caplan's leadership, the laboratory became an important center for the training of clinicians in techniques of consultation and community action, and in developing a cadre of administrators and leaders who were to play important roles in implementing the federal program of community mental health centers (Davis, 1978; Schulberg and Killilea, 1982).

During this period, a utopian vision emerged that community mental health could not only provide services to patients but might provide the basis for a public health approach to primary prevention of mental illness. The main intervention for the preventive efforts was seen as restructuring of communities and neighborhoods through the extensive application of the techniques of consultation and mental health education.

By the end of the 1950s, a theoretical structure for community mental health had been developed and applied in a number of important projects in hospitals and communities. The groundwork was laid for a federal program to extend these ideas and programs to the nation at large, particularly to segments of the population that, because of economic, social, and geographical barriers, lacked access to needed mental health services.

Federal action for community mental health: 1960–1984

During the brief period between 1960 and 1965, a significant shift occurred in U.S. mental health policy. With the election of President John F. Kennedy, the federal government enunciated a national program for community mental health centers, which represented the first federal commitment to direct service.

In colonial times, public policy for mental health in the United States placed responsibility for mental health services at the local community level. In the mid-nineteenth century, this responsibility shifted from local communities to the states, with the advocacy of Dorothea Dix and the creation of state mental hospitals (Grob, 1973). For more than a century thereafter, the responsibility for mental health services was with the states (Mechanic, 1980).

Federal involvement in mental health began after World War II with the creation of the National Institute of Mental Health. The federal responsibilities were exclusively in funding of research and of training for mental health professionals. By the mid-1960s, a significant change in public policy had emerged with the authorization of the community mental health centers program and enumeration of·the goal of two thousand centers to be established throughout the network providing comprehensive services to all citizens (Foley and Sharfstein, 1983).

Joint Commission on Mental Health and Mental Illness

Mental health concerns at the community and state level reached national attention in 1955, when Congress created the Joint Commission on Mental Health and Mental Illness. This commission was a landmark in public policy.

The commission operated over five years, led by Jack Ewalt, M.D., superintendent of the Massachusetts Mental Health Center and professor of psychiatry at Harvard. Many social scientists were involved in this commission. Its final report, *Action for Mental Health,* appeared in 1961 focusing on the psychotic patient, and proposed creating small mental health hospitals as alternatives for patients otherwise destined for large public mental hospitals.

A major impetus to the creation of the commission was public concern over the rise in numbers of patients in public mental hospitals. In 1955, projections were that if the then current rate of increase of patient populations was to continue, by 1980 there would have been more than 1 million patients in public mental hospitals; and the cost of constructing the facilities for custodial care would have been 2 billion dollars (by 1950 dollars). There were numerous journalistic reports about the poor quality of treatment, high death rate due to infection, malnutrition, poor sanitation, and other abuses. This campaign had been led by outspoken journalists, particularly Albert Deutsch. Reform was also supported by public reaction to the film *The Snake Pit,* starring Olivia De Havilland.

As it turned out, these dire predictions did not come about. By 1961, the year of the report *Action for Mental Health,* the number of patients in state hospitals, VAs, and county hospitals began to drop.

The professional leaders and public policy administrators could not have been aware in the late 1950s of the impact of these changes. They were motivated by the immediate need to deal with the public concern about the increasing numbers of patients in mental hospitals and the quality of care and treatment. Moreover, there was a pressing need for the development of mental health services for urban populations, who, because of lack of economic resources and other factors, did not have access to needed mental health services.

President Kennedy's message to Congress on mental health and mental retardation

In 1961, President Kennedy issued his address to Congress on mental health–mental retardation. This was the first presidential address devoted to mental health and reflected his personal and his family's interests and his response to the impact of the joint commission. It called for "returning psychiatry to the mainstream of medicine" and was the beginning of major federal programs for services to mental health and mental retardation. The Kennedy address represented the first enunciation of policy for federal involvement in community services. The initial resistance from the American Medical Association and other groups to increased federal involvement resulted in the approval of funding for construction, followed in 1963 by passage of the staffing act.

The NIMH comprehensive community mental health centers program

The period of the mid-1960s was one of great optimism and activity as large amounts of federal money were made available. The first phase of federal allocations was for planning and development. Grants were made to the states for planning and initiation of programs in retardation and in mental health.

Due to the involvement of the Kennedy family in problems of mental retardation (prompted by the mental retardation difficulties of one of their children), considerable impetus was given to political activity by parents of the mentally retarded. In many states, programs for the mentally retarded were separated from those of mental health, and either separate departments of mental retardation were established or they were implemented through semiautonomous divisions in departments of education or public health.

In the mental health field, federal regulations mandated catchmenting a list of essential services. It is significant that the federal regulations promulgated by NIMH went far beyond the recommendations in *Action for Mental Health* or the congressional language. *Action for Mental Health* was directed primarily at creating alternatives to the state mental hospital for patients with psychotic illnesses and attendant serious disability. When the federal regulations were promulgated, the priority given to the acutely psychotic and chronically mentally ill was mixed with program objectives for care of children, drugs and alcoholism, the elderly, consultation, and education and prevention. Thus, there was no regulatory requirement that priority be given to formerly psychiatric or disabled patients discharged from state mental hospitals during the deinstitutionalization program. Only a minority of community mental health centers directed significant proportions of their resources to the needs of this population, the public health intent of catchmenting.

The NIMH regulations also required appointment of citizen advisory boards, which later became a mandate for citizens' control and restriction of professional authority. One consequence of this was the disaffiliation between many community mental health centers and academic institutions, further weakening the research tie.

Many community boards set priorities other than clinical services. In inner-city urban areas where black and Hispanic populations were in the majority, the community mental health center programs were seen as opportunities for employment and for political power. The policy of local community control resulted in a high degree of variability in priorities given to various populations (Klerman, 1969). Thus, in some communities, emphasis might be given to the certain needs of children; whereas in other communities, the needs of chronic patients were emphasized.

Mental health of children

At first, these programs were applied mainly to the needs of adults, particularly psychotic adults whose needs had been highlighted by the joint commission's report. Concern was increasingly expressed through the 1960s about the needs of children, and a Commission on the Mental Health of Children was created. At the same time, the Carnegie Council underwrote a number of studies of the impact of the social environment, particularly the economic disadvantage on the health, social, and educational achievements of children. These reports called for significant commitment of resources to the educational and health needs of children. Public policy response, however, was not forthcoming and most of these recommendations were not implemented.

However, Congress did appropriate special funds for programs for children treated by community mental health centers. Although the amount of these funds was relatively small, they did represent an acknowledgment of the special needs of children.

Related federal programs

During the period 1960–65, a number of important national policy decisions were made that had consequences for mental health service programs. Some were made by the federal government, and others by the states. The federal decisions included the community mental health centers program and the creation of Medicare and Medicaid.

The Medicare/Medicaid legislation represented the entrance of America into the modern welfare state. The United States had lagged behind Western European and other industrialized countries in providing national financing for medical care. The Medicaid and Medicare legislation initiated a period of rapid growth in medical services and inflation in medical costs.

The percentage of the GNP devoted to health began to rise, so that by 1980 it was more than 10 percent of the gross national product. Although this was a period of great expansion in mental health services, the percentage of the health dollar devoted to mental health has not changed significantly in more than twenty-five years. Although the percent of the GNP devoted to health has increased, the percentage of the health dollar for mental health has remained constant at about 15 percent. Thus, the growth in mental health services and utilization has been in parallel with the large expansion of health services and health expenditures, in general, in the United States.

The main impact of Medicare has been on the health and welfare of the elderly, with significant improvement in their longevity, access to medical care, and in increased utilization of hospitalization and medical services. Many elderly patients with mental illness who are primarily admitted to public mental hospitals were sent to nursing homes from general hospitals or community agencies.

In addition, the Medicare/Medicaid legislation helped create the proprietary nursing home industry. The growth of nursing homes has significant impacts on mental health services. First, a significant percentage of patients over 65 in public mental hospitals were transferred to nursing homes. Second, this transinstitutionalization has contributed to the decrease in numbers of patients in public mental hospitals. Third, Medicaid paid for medical services for the indigent, and many discharged mental health patients were eligible for Medicaid, which contributed to the deinstitutionalization policy decisions.

In the 1960s and 1970s, deinstitutionalization was adopted as policy by most states. Although a state governmental policy, its adoption was spurred by a number of federal efforts. The leadership at the federal level, particularly at NIMH, strongly pushed the development of community mental health centers, in part with the hope of providing effective alternatives for mental hospitalization. A number of federal income transfer programs (Medicaid, food stamps, and increases in Supplemental Security Income/Disability) provided federal funds to assist the state in the costs of deinstitutionalization. Without these federal funds, the state's deinstitutionalization programs could not have been put into effect. Thus, the federal policy decisions contributed to the decisions by the states to implement deinstitutionalization.

The social and political context

These state and federal programs were part of a larger set of social programs undertaken during the Kennedy and Johnson administrations. These programs included the War on Poverty, Operation Head Start, civil rights legislation, manpower training programs, and the community action activities of the Office of Economic Opportunity (OEO). One explicit goal of these programs was to develop neighborhood organizations and other local political power bases, often in competition with and as alternatives to state, county, and municipally elected authorities. Many of these programs derived from the conviction that the federal government was more responsive to the needs of disenfranchised groups – the elderly, the poor, and blacks, Hispanics, and other minorities – whereas state and local municipal governments were politically conservative. These new federal programs bypassed state and local authorities to create neighborhood and community-based programs. The neighborhood health centers, the child health programs, and the community mental health centers were part of this general social-political policy.

The Nixon administration: presidential opposition and political struggle

Following the election of President Nixon in 1968, attempts were made to eliminate the NIMH community mental health center programs, with the rationale that the programs had proven a successful demonstration, and when this failed, the Nixon administration mandated significant cutbacks. Since the Congress was controlled by Democrats, congressional efforts thwarted these efforts of the Nixon administration. Nevertheless, considerable energy on the part of the community mental health program went into lobbying efforts to maintain the federal role and prevent funding cutbacks and program restrictions. The community mental health centers became increasingly involved in local, state, and federal politics.

The Carter administration: hope for rejuvenation

The election of President Carter in 1976 promised to reverse these trends. While governor of Georgia, Carter had taken the initiative to reform the state's mental health system and had gained considerable acclaim for furthering community services and for creating special programs in drug and alcohol abuse. His wife, Rosalyn, was active in the National Association for Mental Health even before the 1976 presidential campaign. Dr. Peter Bourne, a psychiatrist, was active in the reforms in Georgia and as a close personal friend of the Carter family was an influential member of the Carter inner circle in the first years of the administration.

One of President Carter's first acts in January 1977, soon after taking office, was to create the President's Commission on Mental Health. The honorary chairperson of the commission was Mrs. Carter, and numerous academics, researchers, and citizen leaders were appointed to the commission or to serve on various task forces and advisory panels.

There was hope for rejuvenation of the federal programs in community mental health, especially after the years of opposition and conflict during the Nixon administration. The matching-funds formula adopted by the Congress for the community mental health programs called for a phasing-out of federal funds to individual centers after seven years. The expectation had been that federal funds would be replaced by appropriations from state and local authorities or, more significantly, by third-party reimbursements. However, the experience through the 1960s and 1970s did not fulfill this expectation, and many community mental health centers were under considerable financial pressure. The creation of the

President's Commission on Mental Health offered the possibility that the federal government would reverse the declining match provision and/or provide funds via national health insurance.

The other hope raised by the election of President Carter was for the enactment of national health insurance. The United States came close to a system of national health insurance in the years 1977–78. President Carter had run for office with the promise of national health insurance as part of his platform. The administration's proposals for national health insurance included various benefit packages to cover inpatient and outpatient mental health services; and some of the proposals gave priority to those services delivered through organized programs, such as federally mandated community mental health centers.

Unfortunately, the combination of political struggles between President Carter and Senator Edward Kennedy for leadership of the Democratic party plus the declining economic situation in the second half of the 1970s resulted in the failure to enact a program for national health insurance, and the hopes that the community mental health center programs would be placed on more secure financial grounds ended. The final recommendations of the President's Commission on Mental Health did not call for continuing federal support of individual centers, but reiterated the policy of declining match.

By the end of the 1970s, more than six hundred community mental health centers had been initiated with federal funds; well over 50 percent of the population were served by a federally supported center. In 1979, Congress passed the Mental Health Systems Act, which was the major legislative effort to implement the recommendations of the President's Commission. This act had barely been in operation when the election of Ronald Reagan as President in 1980 resulted in new legislative and budgetary proposals that together ended the era of direct federal support for community mental health services.

The election of Reagan in 1980: the end of federal leadership in community mental health

The Reagan administration enacted the system of block grants whereby direct funding of community mental health centers, alcoholism programs, and drug abuse programs has been discontinued; the states receive block grants for these activities, but at a reduced level of support.

Since 1981, the community mental health centers have engaged in frantic efforts to secure their financial sources. Very few community mental health centers have closed, but the scope of local programs has been greatly reduced. Consultation and education has declined, in fact, has almost disappeared. Many of these changes were evident in the late 1970s but have accelerated since 1980 and the statutory and appropriation changes following the election of Mr. Reagan. The centers are increasingly led by nonpsychiatric professionals, clinical psychologists and social workers. Involvement by psychiatrists and other medical personnel has decreased. Many of the centers have adopted an antidiagnostic and antimedication ideology. The provision of services for the chronically mentally ill is highly variable.

In spite of these adverse political and financing developments, it is impressive to the extent to which leadership has emerged at the state and local level. Very few community mental centers have been closed down. Alternative sources of financing have been arranged, including various mixtures of state and municipal grants plus reimbursements from third-party insurers. The scope of community mental health problems has often been reduced with increasing attention being given to the medical, psychiatric, and social service needs of the large numbers of deinstitutionalized patients now living in various communities. Consultation and education efforts have also been severely cut, except where reimbursements have been worked out with local school systems or other agencies. The full impact of these changes in federal support have yet to be seen. Nevertheless, although the federal program of comprehensive community mental health centers being supported by NIMH grants has come to an end, community mental health services have become an integral part of the mental health system at state and community levels.

Assessment

How can we assess these events?

My assessment will be divided into two components:

1. The achievements and limitations of the community mental health movement.
2. The relationship between research and action, the focus of this volume.

The achievements and limitations of the community mental health movement

Assessing the achievements of the community mental health movement depends on the vantage point to be chosen and the nature of expectations. Viewed from the state of mental health services immediately after World War II, highly significant progress has been made in the development of community-based services, in increasing utilization, and in promoting access to services, particularly by previously disenfranchised groups. However, viewed from the hopes and goals of the 1960s, the 1980s are a time of pessimism and discouragement (Dorwart, personal communication).

Nevertheless, the evidence indicates a high degree of programmatic achievement (Price and Smith, 1983). Many of the goals of the community mental health movements have been furthered. The locus of psychiatric care is no longer in the large public institutions but is increasingly in community facilities. The role of public institutions has been greatly diminished. In 1955, almost all mental health services were provided through state, county, and VA hospitals. Today these institutions represent the minority, even of inpatient admission.

The system has become increasingly pluralistic in its organizational and fiscal auspices with mixtures of governmental and private enterprises, including for-profit organizations. The psychiatric units in general hospitals have expanded greatly, so that they are now the main locus of inpatient care. A new type of facility, the community mental health center, has been established and most centers have managed to survive the legislative attacks and fiscal cutbacks of the Reagan administration. At the community level, various mixtures of program and funding support have contributed to innovative efforts to sustain these facilities and programs.

Most important, there has been a marked expansion in utilization of mental health service (Klerman, in press). There has been almost a tenfold expansion of utilization of mental health professional services since 1955 (Klerman, 1982). This expansion in services has not occurred as a result of comparable increase in incidence and prevalence of mental disorders, but rather because of the availability of a variety of services funded by governmental, insurance, and private sources (Borus and Hatow, 1978; Borus et al., 1979).

Correspondingly, with an increase in overall acceptance, the gap in access between upper and lower social economic groups, between the elderly and young, and between minorities and the white majority, has considerably lessened, but not completely disappeared (Mollica, in press). The social class differentials in utilization documented by the research of the 1950s has greatly diminished. The programs have resulted in considerable success, however, in terms of the program goals of increased access, increased availability of services, and reductions of barriers due to income, class, age, and race (Klerman, in press).

Although these are substantial achievements, they did not fulfill the hopes and expectations of the early 1960s (Borus, 1978). The United States has not instituted a national health insurance program and, given the political and economic climate, is unlikely to do so in the near future. At this moment, claims for prevention efforts (especially for primary prevention) are still premature and unsubstantiated for evidence of efficacy.

In its application, deinstitutionalization has become a policy failure and a human tragedy (Mollica, 1983). The hopes for community acceptance of the deinstitutionalized chronically mentally ill have not been fulfilled. The local communities and states have not been able or willing to appropriate the funds necessary to provide adequate residential facilities. The declining availability of low-cost rental housing has contributed to an increase in the homeless populations in large urban areas. Substantial percentages of the homeless have diagnosable mental illnesses and histories of hospitalization (Bassuk, 1984). Interestingly, when homeless mentally ill are polled as to their desire to return to state hospitals, the majority assert that their current lives, however dismal they may appear from the viewpoint of mental hospitals, are better than they would anticipate it to be were they institutionalized.

Although the patient population in public hospitals has decreased dramatically, only very few public mental hospitals have closed. Moreover, the state funds have not always followed the patients into the community, and the largest segment of state budgets for mental health still supports institutional care rather than community programs.

The hopes that community control of mental health services would improve quality and increase community acceptance of mental illness, similarly proved naive and unrealistic. In the absence of a national mandate for priorities, high variability of programs occurred, and quality control of services and fiscal management proved difficult.

As regards the chronically mentally ill, the group whose plight initiated professional reform and public humanitarian concern in the 1950s, the policy debate has come full circle. Whereas in the 1950s journalistic exposé focused on the plight of the institutionalized mentally ill, in the 1980s the press and TV focused on the plight of the deinstitutionalized homeless mentally ill.

Action for Mental Health in 1961 envisioned a network of community-based facilities to provide alternatives for the state hospitals. The state hospital population has been greatly diminished, particularly through deinstitutionalization efforts. However, alternative community residential facilities and service programs have not been implemented. In recognition of this, NIMH initiated a community support program in the mid-1970s to encourage the states to create categorical programs for the chronically mentally ill, a tacit recognition that the community mental health centers program was not meeting these needs.

A period of time is required to place these decades into perspective, but it should not be concluded that the community mental health efforts were failures. Viewed in terms of the status of mental health services in the late 1940s, considerable progress has been made. However, viewed in terms of the high hopes and expectations of the 1960s, the limitations and shortfalls appear discouraging. Community mental health programs may have failed to achieve all their goals, but compared to the 1940s, immense progress has been achieved toward expansion of services, increase in utilization, decrease in barriers to access, and greater availability of community-based services.

Relationship of research to action in community mental health

The limited collaborative relationship between research and community mental health action since the late 1960s represents a major disappointment for those involved in the social psychiatric innovations of the 1950s that initiated many of these action programs.

Although program evaluation was listed by NIMH as one of the essential services for community mental health centers, the funds available for evaluation efforts were minimal.

At the federal level, there was a congressionally mandated 1 percent set aside for evaluation funds, but efforts to assess the community mental health center programs at the national and state level never fully assessed their clinical or community impact (Musto, 1975; Klerman, in press). The evaluation methodology applied in the mid-1960s and the 1970s derived largely from the experience in the Department of Defense. A number of political scientists, policy analysts, and economists, many of whom had worked with Secretary Robert S. McNamara and his associates in the Department of Defense during the 1960s, and at the RAND Corporation, implemented a congressional mandate for 1 percent of program funds to be set aside for evaluation. However noble the intent of this legislation, in practice the evaluation efforts facilitated the creation of a mini-industry of research institutes and consulting firms involved in competing for contracts and bidding on Requests for Projects (RFPs).

During the Nixon administration there was open antipathy and hostility between the evaluation professionals in the Office of the Assistant Secretary for Program Policy and Evaluation, and the leadership in the Public Health Service and NIMH. The goals of evaluation programs, the process of awarding of contracts, and the modes of publication and dissemination became embroiled in political controversy between the higher levels of the executive branch, particularly the White House and the Office of Management and Budget (OMB), and senior appointees in the Department of Health, Education and Welfare (HEW).

Where evaluation efforts were successful, they documented the extent to which the goals of the federal program had been achieved. Survey methodology demonstrated that the centers were opened in the priority areas, particularly rural, inner-city, and poverty communities. Evidence was generated of increased community participation in decision making through advisory committees and community boards. Relatively less data were available as to the characteristics of the population served. Practically no data were available on the follow-up of individuals served and their outcomes in areas of psychiatric symptomatology, rehospitalization, social adjustment, employment, financial independence, and other relevant outcomes. No systematic studies were available to assess the efficacy of these programs in bringing about change, or to estimate cost-benefit and cost-effectiveness analyses.

On the other hand, the Congress, through the General Accounting Office (GAO), undertook a number of evaluation studies. The Congress, dominated by liberal Democrats, was intent on preserving the community mental health program and other health and social programs initiated in the 1960s. The evaluation results for neighborhood health centers, Head Start, and child health programs were used as a political process to attack or protect community programs.

These political struggles around evaluation at the federal level were replicated at state and local levels. There was very little incentive for program administrators, state commissioners, or directors of local centers to assess program effectiveness.

NIMH had funded a number of computer systems, notably the MSIS (multistate information system) based at Rockland State Hospital in New York, in an attempt to develop a management information system that used new technology. It was hoped that these new technologies would facilitate program monitoring and improve patient care. Only a few states participated in this effort, and the capacity of the states and the local communities to document adequately the nature of services provided, let alone measure cost-efficiency or outcome, was negligible.

During this period there was considerable professional controversy, particularly within psychiatry, as to the scientific value of the community mental health centers program. Only a minority of medical school departments of psychiatry participated actively in these programs. In a number of instances, often in minority neighborhoods, notably at Temple University in North Philadelphia and Albert Einstein College of Medicine in the Bronx, New York, conflicts erupted between advocates of community control and the mental health professionals. Similar tensions emerged in New Haven at the Connecticut Mental Health Center, although to a lesser extent, and also in Boston between Boston University and the Roxbury community.

These professional tensions between communities and university medical centers combined with NIMH regulations calling for community control resulted in the disaffiliation of most medical schools from the NIMH community mental health centers program.

With the advent of federal programs in community mental health, research activities became increasingly involved in evaluation. With the exception of a handful of centers, notably in Boston and New Haven, social scientists and other researchers did not participate in program evaluation of individual centers. Where management information systems were set up using computer technology, first priority was usually given to fiscal management, billing, reimbursement, and personnel, and only secondarily to maintaining records of admissions, patient characteristics, and outcomes.

At the federal and state levels, these evaluation efforts embodied the differentiated but coordinated model (see Figure 9.4). The program administrators wished to break the close bond between research and action that had characterized the 1950s and the 1960s. They were suspicious of the alliance between researchers and program managers and felt that this constituted a "conflict of interest" and a breech of "objectivity." Particularly during the Nixon administration, evaluation efforts were guided by politically appointed policy administrators, who were often ideologically hostile to the community mental health center programs. Thus, a triangle was established between policy executives appointed by a hostile administration, program managers at NIMH and in community programs, and evaluation researchers caught between these conflict-ridden and opposing groups.

Prospects for the future

We have now come to the end of the community mental health movement. Academic social psychiatry, which provided the theoretical and scientific foundation for community mental health, is in a period of intellectual and professional decline. Social psychiatry in North America and Western Europe became associated with radical critiques and antipsychiatry. The action component – the community mental health center movement – has receded into the background with the political success of the conservative Reagan administration. These political events demonstrate the close affiliation between community mental health programs and a liberal definition of government policy. Without continued political support at the national level, the community mental health movement has come to an end.

Looking to the future, there are a number of important research developments that offer hope for new beginnings (Mechanic, 1978; Mechanic, personal communication). Psychiatric epidemiology has become revitalized and has broadened its scope beyond the assessment of mental impairment to the development of indexes of rates for individual disorders (Sartorius, 1977; Weissman and Klerman, 1978). In addition, the scope of relevant risk factors for mental illness has expanded beyond the social epidemiologic concerns of the 1950s and the 1960s, and the field of genetic epidemiology has become a vital force in psychiatric research.

Mental health economics is also emerging as an important area of research whose findings have important policy implications as all modern industrialized nations struggle to develop a rational formula for the allocation of scarce resources. As the percentage of the gross national product devoted to health increases in almost all industrialized nations, pressures mount for control of costs and expenditures, and research on health economics, in general, and mental health economics, in particular, is gaining increasing momentum, and showing greater theoretical and empirical sophistication (McGuire, 1985; Sharfstein, in press).

The technique of the randomized controlled trial, initially perfected for the assessment of drug treatments, is increasingly being applied to psychosocial interventions. A large number of randomized trials have been conducted and others are under way to assess psychotherapy, whether individual, family, or group. Interestingly, the randomized controlled trial has been applied to the assessment of large-scale organizational changes, such as day hospitals, continuity of care, financing mechanisms, and educational efforts.

At the moment, the "action" implications of these new research efforts in epidemiology, mental health economics, and assessment of efficacy of interventions are not clear. There is no new "movement" on the horizon with broad goals and optimistic worldview that characterized the community mental health movement. The development of such a new vision probably awaits change in the political and economic climate; such visions in mental health have usually been associated with periods of social and political change, as in the Enlightenment of the late eighteenth century in Western Europe and North America, the Jacksonian era in the United States, and the progressive era before World War I in the United States.

References

Bassuk, E. The homelessness problem. *Scientific American, 1984, 251,* 40–45.

Bierer, J. *The day hospital: An experiment in social psychiatry and psychoanalytic psychotherapy.* London: H. K. Lewis, 1951.

Borus, J. F. Issues critical to the survival of community mental health. *American Journal of Psychiatry, 1978, 135,* 1029–35.

Borus, J. F., Anastasi, M., Casoni, R., Dello Russo, R., Di Mascio, L., Fusco, L., Rubenstein, J., and Snyder, M. Psychotherapy in the goldfish bowl: The role of the indigenous therapist. *Archives of General Psychiatry, 1979, 36,* 187–90.

Borus, J. F., and Hatow, E. The patient and the community. In J. C. Shershow (Ed.), *Schizophrenia: Science and practice.* Cambridge: Harvard University Press, 1978.

Caplan, G. *Principles of preventive psychiatry.* New York: Basic Books, 1964.

Caplan, G. *The theory and practice of mental health consultation.* New York: Basic Books, 1970.

Davis, H. R. Management of innovation and change in mental health services. *Hospital and Community Psychiatry, 1978, 29,* 649–58.

Dohrenwend, B. P., and Dohrenwend, B. S. Etiological leads from epidemiological studies. In B. Weiner (Ed.), *Social status and psychological disorder: A casual inquiry.* New York: Wiley, 1969, pp. 9–31.

Fairweather, G., and Tornatzky, L. G. *Methods for experimental innovation.* Elmsford, N.Y.: Pergamon Press, 1977.

Flexner, A. *Medical education in the United States and Canada.* New York: Carnegie Foundation, 1910.

Foley, H., and Sharfstein, S. *Madness and government.* Washington, D.C.: American Psychiatric Press, 1983.

Frank, J. D. *Persuasion and healing: A comparative study of psychotherapy.* Baltimore: Johns Hopkins University Press, 1973.

Fromm-Reichmann, F. *Principles of intensive psychotherapy.* Chicago: Phoenix Books, 1960.

Glass, A. Principles of combat psychiatry. *Military Medicine, 1955, 117,* 27.

Glass, A. J. Observations upon the epidemiology of mental illness in troops during warfare – Proceedings from the Symposium on Preventive and Social Psychiatry. Sponsored by the National

Research Council and Walter Reed Army Institution of Research. Washington, D.C., 1958, pp. 185–88.

Goffman, E. *Asylums*. New York: Doubleday, 1961.

Greenblatt, M., Levinson, D. S., and Williams, R. W. *The patient and the mental hospital*. New York: Free Press, 1957.

Greenblatt, M., York, R., and Brown, E. L. *From custodial to therapeutic care in mental hospitals*. New York: Russell Sage Foundation, 1955.

Grinker, R. R., and Spiegel, J. P. *Men under stress*. New York: McGraw-Hill, 1945.

Grob, G. N. *Mental institutions in America: Social policy to 1875*. New York: Free Press, 1973.

Gruenberg, E. Can the reorganization of psychiatric services prevent some cases of social breakdown? In A. B. Stokes (Ed.), *Psychiatry in transition, 1966–67*. Toronto: University of Toronto Press, 1967.

Gurin, G. J., Veroff, J., and Feld, S. *Americans view their mental health: A nationwide interview study*. New York: Basic Books, 1960.

Hollingshead, A. B., and Redlich, F. D. *Social class and mental illness*. New York: Wiley, 1958.

Jones, M. *The therapeutic community*. New York: Basic Books, 1953.

Klerman, G. L. Mental health and the urban crisis. *American Journal of Orthopsychiatry*, 1969, *39*, 818–26.

Klerman, G. L. Staff attitudes, decision-making and the use of drug therapy in the mental hospital. In H. C. Denber (Ed.), *Therapeutic community*. Springfield, Ill.: Thomas, 1960.

Klerman, G. L. The impact of psychopharmacology on the mental health service system. In W. R. Gove and G. R. Carpenter (Eds.), *The fundamental connection between nature and nurture*. Lexington, Mass.: Lexington Books, 1982.

Klerman, G. L. The psychobiology of affective states: The legacy of Adolf Meyer. In E. Meyer and J. Brady (Eds.), *Research in the psychobiology of human behavior*. Baltimore: Johns Hopkins University Press, 1979, pp. 115–31.

Klerman, G. L. Trends in utilization of mental health services: Perspectives for health services research. *Medical Care*, in press.

Leighton, A. H., Lambo, T. A., Hughes, C. C., Leighton, D., Murphy, J., and Macklin, D. B. *Psychiatric disorders among the Yoruba*. Ithaca, N.Y.: Cornell University Press, 1963.

Leighton, A. H. *Caring for mentally ill people*. Cambridge University Press, 1982.

Leighton, D. C., Harding, J. S., Macklin, D. B., et al. Psychiatric findings of the Stirling County study. *American Journal of Psychiatry*, 1963, *119*, 1021–26.

Leighton, D. C., Harding, J. S., Macklin, D. B., et al. *The character of danger: Psychiatric disorders and sociocultural environment*. Vol. 3: *The Stirling County Study*. New York: Basic Books, 1963.

Lemkau, P., Tietze, C., and Cooper, H. Complaint of nervousness and the psychoneuroses. *American Journal of Orthopsychiatry*, 1942, *12*, 214–23.

Lewis, A. Melancholia: A historical review. *Journal of Mental Science*, 1934, *80*, 1–42.

MacMillan, A. M. The health opinion survey: Technique for estimating prevalence of psychoneurotic and related types of disorders in communities. *Psychological Reports*, 1957, *3*, 325–39.

McGuire, T. G. Economics of mental health. In G. L. Klerman (Ed.), *Psychiatry: A textbook* (Vol. 6). Philadelphia: Lippincott, 1985.

Mechanic, D. Prospects and problems in health services research. *Milbank Memorial Fund Quarterly/Health and Society*, 1978, *56*, 127–39.

Mechanic, D. *Mental health and social policy*. Englewood Cliffs, N.J.: Prentice-Hall, 1980.

Mechanic, D. The contribution of sociology to the understanding of mental disorder. Paper presented at World Congress of Psychiatry, Vienna, 1982.

Menninger, K. *The vital balance*. New York: Viking Press, 1963.

Meyer, A. *Collected papers* (Vol. 6). Baltimore: Johns Hopkins University Press, 1951.

Mollica, R. F. From asylum to community: The threatened disintegration of public psychiatry. *New England Journal of Medicine*, 1983, *308*, 367–73.

Mollica, R. F. Trends in mental health, social class and psychiatric practice: A major revision of the Hollingshead and Redlich's treatment model. *American Journal of Psychiatry*, in press.

Musto, D. Therapeutic intervention and social forces: Historical perspectives. In S. Arieti (Ed.), *Handbook of American psychiatry* (Vol. 2). New York: Basic Books, 1975.

Myers, J. K., and Bean, L. L. *A decade later: A follow-up of social class and mental illness*. New York: Wiley, 1968.

Pasamanick, B., Scarpitti, F. R., and Dinitz, S. L. *Schizophrenics in the community: An experimental study in the prevention of hospitalization*. New York: Appleton-Century-Crofts, 1967.

Price, R., and Politser, P. *Evaluation and action in the social environment*. New York: Academic Press, 1980.

Price, R. H., and Smith, S. S. Two decades of reform in the mental health system (1963–1983). In E. Seidman (Ed.), *Handbook of social intervention*. Beverly Hills, Calif.: Sage, 1983.

Rapoport, R. N. *Community as doctor*. London: Tavistock, 1960.

Redlich, F. C., Klerman, G. L., McDonald, R., and O'Connor, J. F. The Connecticut Mental Health Center. A joint venture of state and university in community psychiatry. *Connecticut Medicine*, 1966, *30*, 656–62.

Rosenhan, D. On being sane in an insane place. *Science*, 1973, *197*, 250.

Sartorius, N. Priorities for research likely to contribute to better provision of mental health care. *Social Psychiatry*, 1977, *12*, 171–84.

Satin, D. *Eric Lindemann*, Pioneers in American Medicine Series. Francis A. Countway Library of Medicine, Boston, 1982.

Scheff, T. *Being mentally ill: A sociological theory*. Chicago: Aldine, 1966.

Schulberg, H. C., and Killilea, M. (Eds.). *The modern practice of community mental health*. San Francisco: Jossey-Bass, 1982.

Sharfstein, S. S. Financial incentives for alternatives to hospital care. *Hospital and Community Psychiatry*, in press.

Srole, L., Langner, T. A., Michael, S. T., Opler, M. K., and Rennie, T. A. C. *Mental health in the metropolis*. New York: McGraw-Hill, 1962.

Stanton, A. H., and Schwartz, M. S. *The mental hospital*. New York: Basic Books, 1954.

Stouffer, S. A., Lumsdaine, A. A., Lumsdaine, M. H., et al. *The American soldier: Combat and its aftermath* (Vol. 2). Princeton, N.J.: Princeton University Press, 1949.

Sullivan, H. S. *The interpersonal theory of psychiatry*. New York: Norton, 1953.

Szasz, T. *The myth of mental illness*. New York: Harper & Row, 1974.

Weissman, M. M., and Klerman, G. L. Epidemiology of mental disorders. *Archives of General Psychiatry*, 1978, *35*, 705–12.

Wing, J. K., and Brown, G. W. *Institutionalism and schizophrenia: A comparative study of three mental hospitals, 1960–1968*. Cambridge, Mass.: Harvard University Press, 1970.

Wolfe, H. L., and Astrachan, B. M. Community mental health services. In G. L. Klerman (Ed.), *Psychiatry: A textbook* (Vol. 6). Philadelphia: Lippincott, 1985.

Zwerling, I., and Wilder, J. F. An evaluation of the applicability of the day hospital in treatment of acutely disturbed patients. *Israel Annals of Psychiatry*, 1964, *2*, 162.

10   Reconsidering action-research

Robert N. Rapoport

Reviews of the eight fields relating to children, youth, and families have presented us with a rich harvest of observations and analyses. The reviews were based on the mature perspectives of authorities, who chose their cases strategically rather than statistically to illustrate their considered views.

The contributors do not speak with one voice about action-research – except to reaffirm that it is not a single entity with homogeneous philosophy and methodology. Rather, it is what Maughan and Rutter call a "family of approaches." Collaborations between behavioral scientists and action agencies have been conducted at various levels. There are many models for collaboration, and many styles of working and of drawing and disseminating conclusions. Many problems have been identified in the experiences reported, and some fiascos. At the same time, there were many striking successes, and many constructive lessons for the future. There is a strong desire for more and better interplay between knowledge and action, theory and practice – what the Greeks call "praxis." This should be approached in an informed manner – reinventing only where constructive to do so. To this end, the contributions will be sifted twice – first, to summarize the main points field by field; and second, to provide answers to the questions posed at the end of the introductory chapter.

Education

Barbara Maughan and Michael Rutter note that research in education, as in other fields, has contained an important strand with the twin concerns characteristic of action-research – using knowledge to change the world and studying the changes to increase knowledge. Also, as in the other fields, there has been a variety – what they call a "family of approaches" – having these characteristics, and the scale of the efforts has ebbed and flowed with political vicissitudes.

The seven programs discussed – *preschool education, Head Start, Educational Priority Areas, Parent Child Development Centers, Perry Preschool Program, parent-teacher collaboration,* and *school influences and improvement*

266

projects – represent an evolution of theory and practice with elements of similarity on both sides of the Atlantic. They have shared a concern with overcoming disadvantage, and similar lessons have been learned about strategy, methodology, and techniques of action-research.

The preschool education project and the Head Start project highlighted the importance of sensitizing researchers to the need for distinguishing between short-term and long-term effects. When early positive results gave way to intermediate signs of backsliding in the students' performances, critiques of the program proliferated reflecting the persuasion of the critic: inherent racial inferiority, insufficient follow-through, insufficient attention to working with ecological (e.g., familial) influences, futility of massive federal programs, and so on. Subsequently, with another wave of follow-ups, and even more trenchantly with the follow-up-cum-cost-benefit analysis of the Perry Preschool Program, a different picture emerged restoring confidence in the suggestion that, in some circumstances, there might be lasting indirect benefits from early intervention. As educational programs represent universal services with long time-frame perspectives whereas research projects tend to be selective and of short duration, time-frame issues are crucial for interpretive analysis.

The Parent Child Development Center program in the United States and the Educational Priority Area program in Britain have in common that even well-conceived projects are vulnerable to the vicissitudes of political and intellectual changes. The very size of the American program was its Achilles' heel in that the attack on expensive programs accompanying change of government made it a highly visible target. In the case of the American project, intellectual changes played a part too. There was much disenchantment with theories and programs oriented to the critical importance of specific early experiences such as those associated with the mother-infant relationship. This focus was thought to distract attention from structural factors. The British project did not suffer this particular disadvantage – if anything, it was seen as having the obverse bias. However, it, too, suffered a shortage of financial resources and a change of government, and it experienced another set of difficulties. Led by a university-based director, the project enjoyed good collaborative relationships with central government leaders. However, at the local level there was much variation in the relationships developed with teachers. The researchers emerged with the conviction that the teachers' orientation to the intervention and the associated research was pivotal, and considerable information about the difficulties in securing the kind of standardized commitment required by a large-scale intervention design. Teachers are not always interested in research, and even where they are, they may have their own ideas as to the experimental intervention. The observed results were therefore equivocal, and here, too, critics of the study attacked it from their specific standpoints, among which was the view that action-research of this scale was unfeasible. Maughan and Rutter observe that in such complex undertakings it is particularly difficult for a single project to contain all of the skills required for conceptualization, design, implementation, analysis, and policy recommendation.

In the two other British projects described – the one led by Tizard and the other by Rutter – a high degree of collaboration was sustained at the grass-roots level. Where elements in the research strategy required a departure from classical axioms of experimental methodology, the investigators made the necessary adaptations and sought to take the possible implications into account in their analysis rather than shying away from the whole enterprise on that account. In the last-described project, which had the desired iterative quality of a long-term action-research enterprise, different styles of research collaboration were used at different stages of the work. The cumulative effect was particularly valuable in the context of the action-research goals – to increase understanding of child development through a study of the changes, as well as to apply state-of-the-art knowledge of child development to the design of innovations.

Youth employment/unemployment

Richard Price and Celeste Burke begin by noting that there has been ambivalence in our society about youth employment. Conflicting attitudes, theories, and research findings have fed prevailing uncertainties about whether work is a good thing for young people, at what age and under what conditions, and about who might be responsible for doing what about it. Nevertheless, a number of programs have emerged to facilitate youth employment because, however uncertain attitudes might have been toward the various forms of employment, there has been a fair degree of unanimity about the undesirability of unemployment, particularly for young people when they leave school.

Price and Burke identify three intervention strategies: (1) changing the distribution of positions available to youth; (2) changing the distribution of youth available to fill positions; and (3) changing the allocation rules for matching people to positions.

For each intervention strategy, Price and Burke describe a program initiative that has been associated with research. The three projects are the *Youth Entitlement Demonstration,* the *Work Maturity* program, and the *Job Track* program. They note that there is a pervasive tendency for tensions to develop between researchers and intervention agents, however much they value the collaboration. The factors making for endemic tensions in the collaboration include differences in values, differences in time perspectives, and differences in specific expertise and the manner of exercising it. Price and Burke argue that the constructive management of these tensions can go beyond simply making it possible to conduct action-research, it can contribute to the creative adaptations that are necessary as each project seeks to develop new and effective ways of dealing with youth issues in specific situations.

The Job Track projects illustrate their point. An innovative program that was found to work on initial evaluation was nevertheless difficult to sustain because it was considered cost-inefficient. In the next stage of the work – distinguishing the Olympus Research Center's approach from a crude evaluation study and bringing it into the action-research fold – the concentration was on process rather than only outcome, and the research team came up with program recommendations that proved to be both effective and cost-efficient. The eventual success of the program was based on three principles: using regular rather than specialized (costly) staff; getting the right balance in the young person's stipend of allowance for the job search and also in getting the right mixture of difficult-to-place and placeable youth; and, finally, working at an interactive process-oriented approach to the action-research collaboration. These principles were developed in the course of the work. The conclusions – that programs must be robust, that is, workable within the agency's own role capacity, and financially defensible – were useful contributions to the theory of innovations for youth.

The other projects described illustrate how differences in values, in time perspectives, in local versus cosmopolitan knowledge, and between the requirements of analysis and those of implementation, may play their part in generating specific tensions. Nevertheless, they argue that under favorable conditions, creative developments of thought and action may be stimulated that might not have emerged without the tensions. Price and Burke believe that action-research in the youth employment field can develop where there is a dialogue between researchers and action agencies. Building new projects on what we have learned should help partnerships to develop new programs and to increase our understanding of the place of work in the lives of youth.

Juvenile justice

Leslie Wilkins concentrates on the criminal justice branch of the field rather than on those branches focusing on social justice and child welfare in relation to the law, and discusses six projects: the *Cambridge-Sommerville project*, the *Massachusetts Alternative*, the *Highfields experiment*, *Mobilization for Youth*, the *Chicago Area project*, and the *California Probation Subsidy Bill*. Even in the juvenile delinquency subfield, Wilkins considers that there are some distinctive problems in that the definitions of which particular children are in focus and what particular goals are salient are ill-defined and have continuously shifted with political, professional, and ideological currents in society. Criminologists work in an environment that is, in his term, ''muddled'' (though this is often glossed over in formal reports), and muddle has been very much a part of action-research in this field. Nevertheless, there has been an evolution of policy and practice in the field that has been influenced to some extent by research. At each stage research has played a role, though not always the one envisioned by the researcher, and Wilkins expects that research will have a role in moving the field forward.

As in other fields, there was an increase in the number of research projects in the 1960s, peaking in the early 1970s. The first phase in the evolutionary set described by Wilkins began before World War II and continued after it into the 1970s. The Cambridge-Sommerville project is the marker for this stage. A key characteristic was the orientation to individuals at risk for delinquency as characterized by personality disorders. Accordingly, psychological counseling was given to those at risk in the community, and their progress through life was compared with a ''normal'' control group. Here again the short-term versus the long-term perspective was important, though findings were the reverse of those in the Head Start studies. Initial findings were equivocal, but at the thirty-year follow-up it was clear that the intervention group did worse than the controls on most of the indicators. True, all those selected were high-risk individuals, but the inevitable conclusion was that the interventions were at best insufficient, and at worst counterproductive. Negative findings can, of course, be important to progress. In this case they contributed to the decline of the individual therapy approach to delinquency prevention. It is still under discussion, however, whether the negative findings reflected a defect of the therapeutic method, or something else, for example, a secondary consequence of the dependency relationship. In the absence of an adequate body of research on intervention, such discussion remains speculative.

The next phase, emphasizing *social* interventions, is illustrated by two projects, the Massachusetts Alternative, and the Highfields experiment. The first was, in a sense, an experiment of nature in that a new administrative arrangement emerged inadvertently through the introduction of a discharge procedure based on a misreading of the director's memorandum. The director, noting that the new procedure seemed to work in that there were few complaints, embraced it as an advance in administrative treatment. His attempt to understand what was happening took the form of consultative work with Maxwell Jones, who had conducted action-research in England aimed at reforming custodial mental hospitals.

The Highfields experiment used a therapeutic-community approach also influenced by Maxwell Jones's work. This approach contrasted with the more harsh and punitive regimes of the typical reformatory exemplified by Annandale. The idea of developing a project to compare the effects of Highfields and Annandale became the core of a quasi-experimental study, with an attempt at random assignment of cases to the two units. In the end the purity of the design broke down because judges and other participants in the collaborative relationship acted less in response to the dictates of science than the requirements of practice as they interpreted it.

Although both projects were instructive, neither was conclusive, and it would have taken powerful data indeed to stem the inevitable swing away from more ''open'' policies. Although both the Massachusetts Alternative and Highfields were less costly than long-term incarceration, there were too many ambiguities in the interpretation of how they worked to demonstrate any other kind of superiority. There were too many residual problems in the outcomes themselves for these innovations to be regarded as satisfactory solutions to the prevention and treatment of delinquency, but some features of the projects have remained in operation and these interventions have had an impact in a general way upon the development of theory and the direction of reformist thought.

There were similar equivocal experiences with other ''social interventions,'' such as Mobilization for Youth and the Chicago Area project. Accordingly a new emphasis gradually emerged – away from the delinquent or potential delinquent as the central figure of analysis, toward other factors in the total situation. It was seen as necessary to develop a more complex analysis that could focus independently on any of four kinds of data, namely that concerning (1) the actor; (2) the act; (3) the environment; and (4) the decision makers in the system. Only a small proportion of criminal acts is identified and an even smaller proportion traced to the acts' perpetrators. The problem of what to do about crime and the problem of what to do with that small proportion of delinquents who were identified came to be seen as independent issues.

When it was believed that the way to deal with crime was by treatment of offenders, action and associated research based on the therapeutic or medical model were in vogue. When this model was abandoned, there was a revival of the idea of ''just desert'' and the concept of individual rights and responsibilities. As a corollary there was the application of punishment appropriate to the gravity of the offense actually committed, rather than according to the potential in future to avoid offenses if the perpetrator were subjected to intervening treatment of some kind.

To illustrate how a new emphasis may affect the type of action-research that emerges, Wilkins selects the California Probation Subsidy Bill, which is then traced from an initial abortive phase to its final enactment. Research played a role in this through identifying some of the sources of support for and barriers against subscribing to the concept.

In conclusion, Wilkins notes that much of the work in the juvenile justice field has diverged from the ideal model of action-research, and many changes that occurred were as a result of larger social processes, including the famous muddling through of piecemeal social planning in an open society. However, he believes that there has been much learned in these experiments and much that could be learned using an action-research approach in future, particularly about how to reduce crime and deal with offenders. To do so satisfactorily, however, and to make the effort a more cumulative one from the scientific point of view, the researcher should take a more active collaborative role in the development of new programs, rather than a relatively passive servicing or "hired hand" role.

The social services

Sheila Kamerman and Alfred Kahn, in reviewing this vast field of social problem interventions, choose examples from two discrete domains – personal social services, and income transfers (maintenance).

Three projects are analyzed to illustrate their points:

Project Redirection is an example of a small, network-type research development project in the human services area. It aimed to develop and demonstrate an innovative approach to teenage mothers. In contrast, a second project in the income maintenance field (*SIME-DIME*) was a large/scale experiment based on predetermined hypotheses and using structured methodologies. There was relatively little initial interest in learning more about the processes of human services use. The third project analyzed was the *Services integration* initiative – emanating from the Secretary of Health, Education and Welfare and based more on organizational assumptions of practice-knowledge than formal social science theory.

They note that projects vary in terms of many dimensions expressing the diversity of situations in which action agencies and researchers interact. Projects differ in their disciplinary mixes, their status composition and structure, their primary and secondary task definitions, scope and experiences of project development. Because research as such may play such a varied role in relation to large-scale intervention programs, Kamerman and Kahn consider the paradigm of action-research developed in small-scale agency settings to be inadequate.

Project Redirection used an inductive approach to develop and test hypotheses in the field; the second (SIME-DIME) started with a hypothesis and a well-designed field experiment to test it, proceeding thereafter to explore interesting serendipities. The third (services integration) started with a commitment to a predetermined outcome and proceeded to take action wherever possible to produce movement presumed to be in the desired direction, examining the correspondence between assumption and experience only after the fact.

In Project Redirection, the field of teenage pregnancy has been intractable, the problem growing despite an array of preventive intervention programs. In this context even modest results have been accepted as positive, and qualitative understandings welcomed – for instance, on the dynamics of an innovative role, the Community Woman.

In the income maintenance (SIME-DIME) experiment, "hard" quasi-experimental findings about the effects of income maintenance strategies on labor force participation were produced but nevertheless disregarded partly because of a serendipitous finding about the negative impact of the program on marital stability. There had been a change in the political atmosphere that sensitized legislators to any excuse for rejecting centralized economic interventions.

The services integration effort illustrates not only how a concept generated at the top from an abstract concept may be very differently interpreted in different contexts, but that even where the desired organizational effect is achieved, it may be counterproductive in its impact on clients. Organizational efficiency and client service cannot be assumed to be identical.

Kamerman and Kahn conclude with the exhortation to bear in mind the complexity of the connections between research and action, particularly in large-scale national and international programs. Those who seek simple connections are likely to be unrealistic and may not appreciate the varieties of phenomena involved. Those who are more sophisticated yet seek to develop connections in an informed manner must find ways to overcome a range of obstacles to achieve either practical or scientific goals, let alone both simultaneously. Problems of status differences, communication difficulties, organizational complexities, methodological issues, and financial continuities are some of the salient ones. Flexibility and readiness to see and learn from what actually happens is as important as technical competence in testing hypotheses if the researcher is to make the most of results emerging from a project. For this the action-researcher of the future should cultivate the quality of *disciplined alertness*.

Family dynamics

Hamilton McCubbin, David Olson, and Shirley Zimmerman delineate three major arenas in the family research field within which they select projects for discussion: the *family policy arena,* the *family therapy arena,* and the *family stress arena.*

In the family policy arena, examples discussed in relation to family impact analysis overlap with those discussed by Kamerman and Kahn in the chapter on the social services. However, there are differences in focus. Kamerman and Kahn concentrate on the analysis of the interplay between research results and policy, noting that given the finding that income maintenance was correlated with a rise in divorce, there was little chance of the program being supported by a conservative government seeking to reduce centralized programs. McCubbin and his colleagues carry the analysis toward family dynamics issues and observe that in this sample the increase in divorce might well have reflected an enhanced capacity to choose more satisfactory options. This is supported by data revealing enhanced self-esteem and lowered alcohol consumption among the separated spouses. This kind of "family morphogenesis," they argue, is at least hypothetically favorable for the children.

Other program evaluation studies in the policy arena are examined for attempts to understand family issues that go beyond a simple summative evaluation. However, many problems emerge in attempting to think of research in the policy arena as collaborative. At best, research on a macroscopic social policy issue should be seen as *potentially* applicable, with many intervening variables including the efforts of the researchers themselves at dissemination, public relations, and advocacy. At worst, the research enterprise may be futile as family issues become grist for political and ideological mills.

In the therapy arena one finds that research and action are frequently conducted by the same person – the "scholar therapist." A number of family therapy schools have built up conceptual positions in this way. The authors note that where the researcher is also the proponent of a particular action approach, the character of the work over the past two or three decades has been to integrate and refine the postulated models rather than to create new breakthroughs. Nevertheless, research has contributed to improving effectiveness of family therapy *within* schools, and the family therapy arena as a whole has contributed to family science by providing information on how different types of families function and how they change. Olson's Circumplex Model is presented as a device with which therapists can identify and standardize variables with which they work, for example, the capacity for cohesion, adaptability, and communication. Its application potentially enhances family therapy by allowing comparative analyses to be made on different kinds of effort to improve family functioning.

The third arena, family stress research, is one in which McCubbin and his colleagues have written extensively. They distinguish between normative and catastrophic types of stress and identify situations in which the "pile-up" of stresses can overpower family coping capacities. As an example of the action fields in which this kind of analysis has been used, McCubbin and his colleagues discuss contract research for the Department of Defense. Contract research differs from consultancy work in that the consultant is more likely to emphasize the firmness of the knowledge already available to apply, whereas the researcher is more likely to emphasize knowledge deficiencies. It is the need to know more that triggers sponsorship of research to feed back results as available.

Contract research is commissioned not only by government bodies but by churches, education institutions, and other community agencies. Although this type of work has been productive for both theory and policy – as illustrated in the Minnesota program of research on military families – it is also prone to constraints emanating from the general ethos. McCubbin and his colleagues describe this through comparing the conditions they experienced in researching the same substantive area in "open," "developing," and "closed/controlling" eras of research commissioned by the Department of Defense. They emphasize the importance to scientific development of maintaining academic freedom while accepting the need to exercise certain controls in some collaborative relationships.

Family support systems

Edward Zigler and Heather Weiss, in their review of recent programs designed to support child and family development, argue for the establishment of a new balance. The naive optimism of some of the efforts immediately following World War II led to disillusionment in some quarters, but there is in fact a "substantial legacy of hard-won knowledge about how to design, implement, and evaluate interventions for children and families," and this as well as a degree of skepticism should be kept in mind.

Examining four major programs in higher magnification, they draw some concrete conclusions about what has been learned and where we are going. The *Head Start program,* the *Yale Child Welfare Research Program,* the *Brookline Early Education Project,* and the *Child and Family Resource Program* all offer lessons, and together they provide a sense of progression in the evolution of the field.

In the 1960s, when Head Start was born, the political pressures were the obverse of those operating today. Rather than recoiling under the impact of retrenchment and cutbacks, researchers were pressed to take positions before they felt they were ready in a rapidly expanding field. Some, who colluded with the calls to "think big," suffered the consequences when there was disappointment with apparent promises. Fortunately, there was a core of more tentative experimentation on a wide range to develop solutions through experience. While this created the problem of comparing disparate experimental inputs, it did provide a number of lessons and, in some instances, some persuasive demonstrations. The authors describe this development from the inside, complementing the descriptions presented by Maughan and Rutter. They conclude that one of the important lessons learned, other than the already mentioned one of alertness to the need to handle political pressures on the researcher, include the need to enlarge the focus both of intervention and of evaluation from the child to its family. Furthermore, it became increasingly apparent that social support plays a crucial role in family well-being. They note that the Head Start intervention itself, as well as requiring extension through time, showed the importance of a multilateral partnership model. The intervention, originally thought of as primarily didactic in character, came increasingly to be seen as a form of social support as well, and from the whole experience comes an emphasis on the importance of building family strengths and supports.

Zigler and Weiss draw from the Head Start analysis the point that individual life-span perspectives must be combined with family life-cycle perspectives for maximum effectiveness. This contrasts with the tendency in monodisciplinary analyses to emphasize one or the other. On the outcome side, the use of IQ as an exclusive outcome measure needs to be expanded to use a broader set of variables.

In the discussions that have emerged from the Head Start program, there have been not only theory-building and program development implications, but a broader benefit in the use of the model for a wide range of social support innovations in the community. In addition, the effort to introduce experimentally adequate methods into a dynamic real-life situation has led to an increased appreciation of the importance of using qualitative analysis in conjunction with quantitative analysis. The quest is for understanding not only whether or not a program works in terms of some bottom-line numerical statement, but in understanding how it works – or could be made to work better. Joining the two forms of research and analysis can lead to a mutually reinforcing effort to strengthen understanding.

Both the Yale Child Welfare Research Program and the Brookline Early Education Project confirm these trends and insights, with different designs, different professional personnel, and different auspices. Focuses have been moving from the individual child to the family, and from the family in isolation to the family in ecological context. Intervention emphasis has shifted from more directive professional action to the emphasis on enabling the child and the family to handle their own problems.

The Child and Family Resource Program built further on the idea of strengthening family support services and sought to reduce fragmentation in such services via multiservice neighborhood centers. Intensively evaluated by the General Accounting Office and by Abt Associates, further reinforcement has emerged for the trends detected in analyzing the previous studies. Additional demonstration was achieved, moreover, of how careful ethnographic analysis in conjunction with quasi-experimental designs can enrich theory and practice. The eleven programs evaluated had similar outcome scores as far as successful achievement of two program goals – individuation of services and establishment of a network for coordinating social support services. Ethnographic analysis revealed that one of the mechanisms for achieving this effect was the establishment of a "system of interlocking directorates" among the agencies. In addition, ethnographic analysis located in the paraprofessional role both the key human resource capacities and the need to counter their vulnerability by improved training and supervision. In addition, the ethnographic analysis identified a series of built-in dilemmas, the resolution of which would affect outcome – for example, between social service and child development goals, between working mothers' needs and domestic needs of the child, between service provision for those with special needs and service provision for parents generally, and between family needs on the local scene and those recognized in the larger national program. Balancing these in-built conflicts is helped by knowing their characteristics.

Zigler and Weiss consider this to be an auspicious time for action-research on family support because practitioners and researchers each have a substantial amount to bring to and to gain from such a partnership. We are now more aware than previously of some of the pitfalls – for example, of the need for an open-minded approach to evaluation rather than the "trapped" variety where administrators cannot afford to have any outcome that may run counter to what they are committed to in advance. Another lesson is the need to combine various types of analysis and various indicators of outcome adequately to assess an intervention. Action-researchers are now aware of the fact that the kind of expertise required goes beyond that provided in conventional methodological training within the academic disciplines. Such multidimensional expertise is being cultivated in centers such as the Bush Centers, and in the Congressional Science Fellowship program.

Child health

Barry Pless and Robert Haggerty note that much of the progress in the child health field attributable to interaction between research and practice has arisen out of an impression of problems in practice, for which research has suggested solutions. Local experimentation using research principles characteristically leads to policy recommendations for application on a larger scale. This becomes part of a movement in which research plays a necessary but not a sufficient role in the improvement and dissemination of the program. They analyze six examples: *neighborhood health centers* (in response to the primary-care needs of poor children); *seat restraints* (in response to the high accident rates in automobiles); the *behavioral pediatrics program* (in response to the need to increase doctors' sensitivity to children's behavior problems); a *chronic disorders research consortium* (in response to the need to develop new policies to help chronically disabled children); *immunization* (in response to the high rates of infectious diseases); and *fluoridation* (in response to the high rate of dental caries). Two projects in the chronic diseases research consortium are examined in higher magnification – the RAND project, and the Jacobi project.

Each of these examples shows the loose-knit pattern of development that has occurred in the child health field. An experiment in Tennessee is copied in other states following research that evaluates the program and points to ways of improving it; an experiment in England in community health centers was developed in South Africa and adapted to meet primary-care agenda in the poverty program in America; a survey in Rochester demonstrating the link between chronic illness in children and subsequent psychological maladjustment together with a study of physicians indicating their reluctance to take on exclusive care responsibility for such children led to the formation of a chronic illness research consortium that had as its goal the development of improved policies and services. A similarity between Pless and Satterwhite's concept of "family counselors" as an innovative nonprofessional role that might provide the supplementary care required and Nicholas Hobbs's interest in the French *educateur* role as a supplementary educational counselor for children with learning disorders brought in a strong representation from Vanderbilt University from which the consortium grew. Immunization and fluoridation provide additional examples of the interplay between research and action, with growth occurring via a loose-knit movement.

Aside from the fact that advances in medicine have often occurred in this way, Haggerty and Pless point out some distinctive elements to the child health field. The emphasis is on prevention rather than cure, and outcome measures are of "proximal" rather than "distal" effects. In the examples cited, the emphasis has been less on discovering whether a given measure works (efficacy) – that tends to have been established in basic research – but rather on how to get these proven measures translated into use (effectiveness). Although action-research seems to have arisen in this field around implementation problems, there is still a need for a better understanding of the implementation process. Opinions differ as to how much and in what way research influences policy and practice in this field, and even the most optimistic proponents deplore the maladroitness of many of the attempts at relevance. To the extent that there has been cumulative effectiveness, it has been due to the networking of a relatively small number of dedicated behavioral pediatricians, exchanging information and results, providing personal-professional support and encouragement, and advocating their convictions of the importance of behavioral sciences in pediatrics.

In the case studies cited, particularly the Jacobi case, Pless and Haggerty indicate some of the factors associated with conducting a multidisciplinary, multistage project other than those dictated by the research design. The project can serve or subvert various other functions, including public relations, team solidarity, and client relations. And, the action research project has a life cycle that may or may not articulate with the needs and capacities of the service staff.

Pless and Haggerty conclude that the classical Lewinian model of action-research is a sound conception but as a working model is probably unrealistic in today's world. Action-research may arise and develop in different ways, with variations in the role relationships between researchers and service providers, and the dissemination of the results of their collaboration may require additional inputs beyond the traditional roles of either.

Community mental health

Gerald Klerman begins by setting out a typology of interrelationships between research and action in the mental health field. His Type 1 interaction is the simplest and least troublesome: Researchers do their work in their laboratories and mental health practitioners apply the knowledge in their clinical settings. His Type 2 model is an interactive one: The researcher learns from the practitioner as well as vice versa, but they work in different settings. Type 3, which he calls the action-research ideal, is one in which not only do the two parties seek to learn from one another's activities, but they are contained within a single project structure, generally under the leadership of a coordinator. Type 4, the "differentiated and coordinated complex" model, pertains to macroscopic programs, generally of a national character. There are various participating groups at different levels, with a higher degree of specialization of function.

As Klerman traces the development of the community mental health field from its pre–World War II roots to the present, it is apparent that there was an evolution from a situation in which Type 1 interaction was the dominant form to a situation in which Type 4 was dominant – the Golden Age of Social Psychiatry in the 1950s and 1960s. Collaborative projects and programs flourished in many areas – social epidemiology, mental hospital research, community mental health programs, and eventually, following the publications of the Joint Commission on Mental Health and Mental Illness, the development of a network of community mental health centers. This was an era of growth in federal programs, with a wide range of association research efforts from basic research to the most differentiated complex model of action-research.

Klerman conducts us through the implications for the community mental health movement of changes of administration from Kennedy/Johnson through Carter and Nixon to Reagan. There is a sense of the inevitable pendulum swing. Curtailment of federal programs and the return of mental health responsibilities to the states has produced a new round of social problems calling for research relevant to action, but the very cuts that have been associated with deinstitutionalization have curtailed resources available for research. Though most of the community mental health centers have survived, they have had to work very hard for it and to change their role. This is not necessarily bad, because it is recognized that the threat to survival can stimulate new programs. However, the burgeoning demand for services has not, in recent years, been accompanied by new action-research. Rather, it has been based on established principles. Neither the financial support nor the scientific curiosity that has driven research initiatives in the past have been conspicuous. There was specialization during the growth of the complex-differentiated programs, for example, in program evaluation and policy analysis. However, the risk now is of fragmentation. Differentiation has led to specialists in economics, genetics, or computerization concentrating on their own specific realms, with little knowledge or interest in the others' domains. A new range of psychotherapies has evolved and established itself in the community independently of psychiatry.

In his conclusion, Klerman raises the question of whether it will require another period of turbulence such as that associated with World War II and its aftermath to throw up some innovative approaches comparable to those of the Golden Age of Social Psychiatry, and what they might be.

Issues

The ten questions

Ten questions were posed at the end of the introductory chapter. In the chapters that followed, many answers were suggested – directly and indirectly. No consensus was sought or imposed. The suggested answers that follow may be thought of as a semiconsensus, which most of the contributors agree partially. In this way the ifs and buts of a committee formulation are avoided. The answers presented, whatever else they may be, are clear. If they are arguable, so much the better. This is the path of progress.

1. *What is action-research today?* Action-research is a "family of approaches" having at its core the joining together within a project or program two agenda: to advance an action program through the use of scientific knowledge, and to advance knowledge through studying the workings of the action program.

The family metaphor is useful, though, as with metaphors generally, it should not be pushed too far. Like the family, the nuclear partnership may take many forms – according to the disciplinary culture, the structure, and the context of the particular project. Like families, projects have a variety of extensions and connections in the larger environment in which they function. And, like the field dubbed "famology," action-research is multidisciplinary, integrated by a shared substantive focus and a shared value orientation. In this case, the shared value orientation is in the area of doing something to benefit children, youth, and families. Like families, specific action-research teams vary in their closeness, harmony, and longevity.

The modern action-research project is distinguished from its predecessor by a higher degree of methodological sophistication, and the employment of "appropriate" methodologies to the different phases of the project rather than expecting that an omnicompetent researcher can conduct all phases: exploration, design, intervention, evaluation, and dissemination.

2. *What is the relation between action-research and other approaches seeking to link theory and practice?* Action-research in its multidisciplinary character is both broader than the others and narrower.

It is broader in that it embraces many of the specialist approaches that have evolved to link research and action, though the latter tends to have a different character when used independently. For example, program evaluation when used independently tends to be conducted with minimal collaborative interaction between researcher and action agent, and to be summative in character. In the action-research context, program evaluation is often "formative" in character, with researcher and action agent seeking a higher degree of interaction in an iterative manner. Independent program evaluations may be process-oriented, but when evaluation is part of an action-research project, it is intrinsically so, characteristically taking as great an interest in the "how and why" of an observed outcome as it does in the "bottom line" of efficacy and cost-efficiency.

Policy analysis, too, may be a component of action-research or conducted independently. When it is conducted independently, its practitioners tend to operate in public arenas such as the mass media, advocacy campaigns, and legislative committees. Though some action-researchers, like Eric Trist, have engaged with large-scale systems, their more general penchant is toward smaller-scale systems, in which generic policy issues may be addressed.

A closer relationship, sometimes amounting to identity, is seen with the family of approaches termed "social intervention," "social experimentation," and "social engineering." The distinctive element in the approaches we categorize as action-research is the abiding interest in learning *from* the application of the social/behavioral sciences as well as contributing to the pressing concerns of an action agency. This does not mean that action-researchers do not emphasize practical benefits; nor does it mean that program evaluators or social engineers disdain conceptualization – witness the work of Peter Rossi and Howard Freeman. It is a matter of emphasis, and to some extent of labeling.

3. *What conditions give rise to an action-research project?* Action-research projects may arise under various conditions, particularly where there is conspicuous social change and reorganization. Three mechanisms are recognizable, and projects are more likely to arise when two or more of them coalesce: agency thrust, researcher thrust, and external pressure.

Agency thrust occurs when an agency develops its program to where it is felt that a research input would be beneficial. In some cases, the agency thrust comes early in its development (e.g., where there is an innovation, perhaps by a charismatic leader, and the wish to understand better how it works and make it more widely known); in others the thrust comes late in the agency's organizational career (e.g., where there has been a routinization and there are problems or a need for a new image or sense of mission). Characteristically, this type of project begins with a presenting problem. The agency approaches a researcher on the grounds of some combination of rationales: *time* (the action persons are too busy giving service to do the research), *expertise* (the action agents' sphere of expertise is not in research), *deadlock* (outside help or perspectives are needed to break through an impasse), *legitimation* (research by an external agency is more credible, particularly where there are evaluative elements). As Zigler and Weiss noted, it is important that the agency concerned not be so "trapped" in its approach that it cannot afford to entertain research results that may run counter to its expectations.

Researcher thrust occurs when a researcher has an idea or theory that he sees as capable of being developed through collaboration with an action agency. This may be associated with a variety of approaches, among which the following are familiar types: the *researcher-entrepreneur* may take an initiative if he sees that he can further his line of research through collaborating with an action agency. This type of researcher, located in a clinic, university laboratory, or research institute, tends to be dedicated to a particular line of theoretical or methodological work, for example, stress-resistance, family dynamics, or moral development, and will work in various situations to pursue the development to which he is committed. This differs from the *research opportunist,* who has certain skills available for deployment and will take an initiative wherever an opportunity makes itself apparent. This sort of research generalist may work not only in various settings but also on various topics with less continuity than the researcher-entrepreneur. The *scholar-activist* differs from the two previous types in that the primary force impelling him to join forces with an action agency is the possibility that the products of his work will be used to help someone or to change the world somehow.

External pressures are also of several types. *Mandated* program evaluation may give rise to action-research via program evaluation. *Social ferment* is another situation giving rise to action-research. Social ferment can vary: it may be a general sense of malaise (in the context of which projects may arise oriented to a theme such as youth alienation, marital discord, or gender inequity), or it may be more acute as in "public uproar" or "moral panic," as have been associated with homelessness, family violence, or vandalism.

These are characteristic though not exhaustive conditions giving rise to action-research, and there are various combinations and mixed types.

4. *Forms of collaboration?* Parity is the most desirable condition of collaboration – that is, the form in which neither the action agent nor the researcher is treated as superior to the other or has power over the other.

In reality, of course, there are many forms and gradations of status ranking that intrude on a collaborative relationship, even where it seeks parity. For example, there may be differences in responsibilities assigned in the situation – such as for treatment of patients, for care of children, or for production of reports. There are the social realities of professional status-ranking that in some situations allocate higher status to one or the other party – for example, the difference between a university professor and a primary-school teacher, or a medical clinic director and a sociology graduate student. In complex projects there may be parity relationships at various levels – with "generals talking only to generals," and so on. Where status *dis*parity becomes a loaded issue, it has to be dealt with so that appropriate adaptations can be made to use available resources in the best way possible. Parity, it should be stressed, does not mean identical matching. Women do not always and exclusively communicate best with other women, blacks with other blacks, manual workers with other manual workers, older people with their age-mates, and so on. Facilitating communication between researcher and action agent has much to do with attitude and the capacity to develop trust. It is easier to indicate what is to be avoided than to give prescriptions as to how this should be done:

The action agent should not be so much in control (financially or in power terms) that the researcher is constrained to find results pleasing to the sponsor even if at the expense of the data.

The researcher should not, conversely, have such rank or power that the subjects and collaborators in the project feel obliged to please him or to produce the results he hypothesizes.

The researcher and action agent should not be merged – that is, one person doing both. Though role merging is feasible, this model entails difficulties in objectivity, in competence, in credibility, and in allocating priorities. Though there are advantages in the work of the scholar-therapist, clinical-researcher, researcher-advocate, individuals merging these roles tend to be biased one way or the other, to be more competent at one than the other, and to give priority to one or the other set of activities. As McCubbin, Olson, and Zimmerman indicated, in the family therapy field, researcher-practitioners (scholar-therapists) tend to contribute to refinements – rather than to breakthroughs – within the "schools" of thought with which they work. The Freuds of this world are few and far between, and the most valuable application of the merged role model seems to be in the exploratory stages of a project, for hypothesis development.

Developing a collaborative relationship between a researcher and an action agent in large-scale organizational settings should not be assumed to attend to all of the other relationships required for a successful project – even if the collaboration is at the very top. This was seen in the Educational Priority Areas program described by Maughan and Rutter, and in the services integration program described by Kamerman and Kahn.

Merged roles and macroscopic partnerships are possible, but they present special, often formidable, problems. The Goldilocks story with its parable of the three bears seems appropriate: The large-scale macro project may be "too big" for an effective action-research project (given all the stipulations), and the clinical-researcher model may be "too small" for other than setting up or fine-tuning an established activity. The collaborative-interactive parity partnership, difficult as it is to achieve in practice, seems to have the best chance to be "just right."

5. *How can such a disparate relationship be managed?* A simple answer to this is "with difficulty." Coupling representatives of any two subcultures presents difficulties and gives rise to tensions. However, there are attractions in the potential complementarities, and the tensions can be identified and managed. In the best situations they can even trigger creative new possibilities.

As Price and Burke illustrated, the right balance of tensions can produce breakthroughs in thinking along with solutions to tricky field problems. In their analysis of the Job Track project, the joining of forces between researchers and innovative agencies in relation to a threatened program led to a viable innovative approach. Without the collaboration, an attractive but uneconomic innovative program might have collapsed and the "baby might have been thrown out with the bath water."

Complementarity and trade-off are important concepts in thinking about the character of the relationship. It is important to recognize explicitly the differences and work out a way to contain them. Partnerships are often begun on the basis of an initial impression of shared values but insufficient attention to the differences. Unless these, too, are recognized, there may be disenchantment.

It is useful to rehearse possible outcomes to a collaboration. The action agency must accept, at least in principle, that the findings may be negative as well as corroborative of what they are doing. This is difficult to accept in practice, however much it may be endorsed in the abstract. Awareness of the ways in which negative findings may themselves be productive can help, as Wilkins and others have indicated, a potentially rewarding orientation is alertness to serendipities or unexpected results.

Some principles are:

Recognize both overlap and differences in the contributions of the two parties, and their implications for the planned work.

Consider elements of complementarity and trade-offs.

Recognize that different capacities may be required at different stages of a project, and different work patterns. Accept that these require constant renegotiation and legitimation in the framework of the original understanding.

Identify other parties whose cooperation is required – beyond the nuclear partnership. In multilevel organizations, this can become complicated and deliberate choices should be made about how much effort should be spent on gaining collaboration and in what quarters.

Consider possible "bottom line" outcomes in advance. Explicate who gets what out of the collaboration. Practical issues are publication rights and credits, financial underpinning, access to institutional roles and career opportunities. Although they should not become obsessive, they must be recognized as elements in the relationship. It is important to establish the "umbrella" of shared values and ethical principles in embracing the various difficulties and differences and confirming that they are of secondary importance.

6. *How can continuity be maintained?* The first requirement is to recognize that there will be continuity problems and that these problems are multifaceted. The ideal action-research project requires an iterative process through a cycle of phases, which some observers have argued should span several years. Problem definition, fact finding, goal setting, intervention, evaluation, and dissemination are all involved – they are time-consuming, expensive, engage many kinds of people and skills, and involve a consideration of long-term as well as short-term outcomes.

Some continuity elements can be encompassed in an initial contract between researcher and action agency. However, not even the best-laid plans and most exquisitely thought-through agreements between the collaborators can guard against changes in environmental conditions such as change of political personnel and priorities. Excellent projects have foundered on this kind of change, as several contributors have noted (although, conversely, some mediocre projects have soared to success when caught up in favorable currents).

Continuity of funding support may be facilitated by anticipating the need for follow-through work. Funding bodies are often prepared to support such work, conditional on satisfactory interim results. Awareness of differences in short-term versus long-term outcomes affects project planning and interim analyses. Awareness of the issue of discontinuities *within* a project – for example, between specialists from phase to phase – can alert project directors to the need for efforts specifically to assure communication across the transition points.

Maintaining continuities in the action program may be achieved by the provision of a self-perpetuating element. Research personnel from a specific project may train their action personnel to continue to monitor results. "Action-learning," as Gareth Morgan and his colleagues call it, seeks to create systems able to learn from their own experience and to modify their structure and design to reflect what they have learned. This seems to have happened in some of the community mental health fields and in some of the social services. Building on results of an action-research project may be facilitated by various combinations of parties associated with the project – trustees, advisors, governors, stakeholders.

One observation that has emerged in several of the contributions is the idea that continuity can be maintained even where there are discontinuities in sponsorship, in the collaborative relationship, in the field situation, and in finance.

This is, of course, one of the functions of publication and of professional associations; but as action-research is multidisciplinary, and as new topics may not have generated formal associations, the informal mechanisms of networking and consortia-formation are important.

7. *How can both generic and specific elements in the action-research situation be taken into account?* A bi-focal perspective is required, seeing the general in the specific and vice versa. The classic Lewinian parable "nothing is as practical as a good theory," touches on this idea. There are two parties to this: the action agent, or social entrepreneur, and the researcher.

Many social entrepreneurs emphasize the unique elements in their intervention, and stress the importance of sympathetic immersion in the experience to really understand it. On the one hand, a research task is to place the action in its proper perspective; to see its generic elements may require distancing or "objectification" of the phenomenon being studied. Too much pressure in this direction may constitute what Kamerman and Kahn refer to as a "trap" for the researcher, distracting him from engagement in the immediate situation. Aside from the harm this could do to the scientific task of detailing the specifics, it could affect the morale of those whose lives are wrapped up in the particular situation, or the quality of their relationship with the researcher.

On the other hand, too great immersion in specifics may lead to "not seeing the wood for the trees." This hampers the task of generalizing, without which neither the scientific task nor the task of propagating what is beneficial in the action program proceeds satisfactorily.

8. *How can the impact be maximized?* New methods of maximizing the impact of action-research results should be encouraged. Professional academic constraint on self-publicization is appropriate, but there is an equally appropriate need to disseminate results.

Everyone working in these fields is aware of instances where exemplary action programs go unnoticed, and excellent research reports gather dust on the shelves of those with power or influence. Promising collaborations may fail to gain momentum toward their hoped-for synergistic takeoff point because of lack of external support, which in turn may partly reflect a communication failure.

Efforts to overcome these difficulties can take several forms. Networks and consortia of like-minded colleagues, embracing a range of disciplines, is one device. Informal colleague networking builds up "interest groups" for mutual support and exchange of information. Wasteful duplication of effort can thus be avoided and a committed audience for new results assured.

Another device, which has grown tremendously since the earlier action-research era, is the use of public relations and advocacy groups. Although academic norms disdain popularization, public relations agencies make it their special contribution. Those public relations agencies that emphasize communication, as distinct from persuasion or image-building, can function as effective allies with the action-research partners. The same is true for responsible advocacy groups. Those that are based on seeking the effective use of scientific knowledge, as distinct from the pressing of a particular position whatever the evidence, can be effective partners in the dissemination of action-research results.

9. *What conditions favor successful action-research?* The conditions favoring successful action-research can be identified as follows:

Successful action-research occurs when there are reciprocal needs (i.e., the researcher for access to otherwise unavailable data or subjects; the action agency for information, documentation, or increased understanding).

Successful action-research occurs when there are effective devices for negotiating contractual arrangements between the parties in the collaboration – recognizing their diverse goals and institutional structures.

Successful action-research occurs when sound results are obtained: using an appropriate research design and methodology, skillful techniques for gathering qualitative and quantitative data, and analysis that links the results to the interests of the parties concerned.

Successful action-research occurs when effective devices are employed to communicate results – both internally through feedback to those involved, and externally.

Successful action-research occurs when there is a recognition in the larger environment of its relevance. This is not entirely a matter out of control of the action-researchers, though many of the large-scale political and economic factors may be at any given time. Attention to creating a set of individuals or organizations capable of mediating between the project and the larger social environment is one useful device.

Successful action-research occurs when a self-perpetuating process is developed out of the momentum generated by the project. This may be done in various ways: through developing dedicated networks to carry on the work in various sites, by incorporating into the research site a capacity for ''action-learning,'' or by spawning new activities based on what has been learned in the course of the project.

Good research sometimes does not get used, whereas poor research is sometimes effective. This leads to the conclusion that the direction of effort should be toward seeing to it that good research is both done *and* used.

10. *What is the future of action-research?* If action-research did not exist, it would have to be invented. However, in view of our awareness of its past difficulties as well as its achievements, we need a new genre of action-research. This is the more so because of the image problem that is the result of past experiences. Some see the idea of action-research as an impossible dream, an unfeasible model, an old idea that has been tried and discarded. On the other hand, there is an

increased recognition that mutual withdrawal of researchers into academic settings and practitioners into routinized action can be sterile, and is not the best way to meet the human needs facing us.

The need for a vibrant relationship between researchers on the one hand and action agencies on the other is as great as ever, if not greater. A new generation of social problems has emerged for the solution of which existing research knowledge and methods have a potential use. Activists are evolving experimental solutions which would benefit from better understanding and evaluation. A new generation of researchers is emerging with better training than its predecessors, and with high motivation to look outside the academic pastures for opportunities to deploy its skills.

All of these factors lead to a positive outlook – ranging among the contributors from those who see action-research approaches as having a modest contribution to make, to those who see the present time as an auspicious one for this approach, and the approach itself as not only commendable but essential. What now?

From the *old* idea of action-research we shall want to keep the conception of a multidisciplinary interactive collaboration in a multistage cycle of research and action yielding improved practice *and* increased knowledge. What is *new* is both a greater awareness of the difficulties in achieving this ideal, and a greater sophistication in applying specialist skills to various parts of the process.

Specialist fields have taken over parts of the old action-research model and developed them separately – for instance, evaluation, policy analysis, dissemination. Although the need for specialism remains, and specialist competence will continue to be valued, the need for new integrations is also being reaffirmed.

Rather than a single model of action-research, differently expressed in different "schools," there will be a set of approaches cooperating in the interactive connections between action agents and researchers. According to the scope of the project, the nature of the problem, the resources available, and the possibilities in the situation, different combinations of these approaches to action-research are likely to emerge. None will have a claim to being the exclusive or the best approach to problem solving or knowledge building. On the other hand, they will share an appreciation of the action-research approach as useful, not only to "do good" but to enrich social science by engaging with important issues.

Some of the hazards and difficulties in the past were due to poorly developed social science; some, to poorly managed collaborative-interactive work; and some, to grandiose expectation. The new action-research will emphasize grass-roots activity – with collaboration in small teams with personal commitment and face-to-face working relationships. This will present its own problems of execution, implementation, and dissemination. One strength of the face-to-face collaboration is its personal commitment; but this also entails potential problems in the reliance a project has on the individuals getting along with one another. Another strength is its manageability, with a smaller number of people, and fewer levels of organization. On the other hand, this smallness of scope presents problems of discerning the generic in the specific, and of making an impact on a wider set of relevant agencies.

New devices exist for dealing with these problems. There are agencies skilled as intermediaries between small organizations and the larger political, economic, and professional organizations. There are public relations and advocacy organizations skilled at dissemination. There are networks, consortia, interest groups, and other linking bodies that allow particular projects to be joined to a larger movement without being submerged in a large-scale bureaucratic system. Professionals who operate action agencies are more likely now to be sophisticated in the social sciences, making for a better bonding with social research collaborators should opportunities arise. Social researchers are more open to nonacademic research opportunities than previously, given the current demographic and institutional situation. Some foundations have taken up the idea of a new generation of action-research and, as with the William T. Grant Foundation, see the approach as helpful in encouraging innovations and in shortening the time span between knowledge building and its application.

We are in a phase where a closer relationship is being called for between the research and action "dancers" – and there are many invitations out to come closer. It is important to renew the idea of action-research and to encourage this intimacy. It is important for social science – in keeping the field more relevant and therefore more valid scientifically; and it is important for the action agencies in that through research and analysis they may be able to do what they are doing more effectively.

Action-research is a *family* of approaches, which can help to evolve the kind of society that will benefit all our children, youth, and families.

Contributors

Anna Celeste Burke is a researcher at the Institute for Social Research, the University of Michigan. She is a staff member of the Michigan Prevention Research Center studying the impact of work and work transitions on the health and mental health of workers. At this center she is also engaged in the design, development, and evaluation of interventions related to employment. She has advanced degrees in both social work and sociology from the University of Michigan.

Robert J. Haggerty is President of the William T. Grant Foundation. He is also Clinical Professor of Pediatrics at Cornell University Medical School, where he administers the Robert Wood Johnson Foundation's Academic General Pediatrics Program. He is editor of *Pediatrics in Review,* and a member of the Institute of Medicine. He was formerly a Roger I. Lee Professor of Health Services at the Harvard School of Public Health and Chairman of the Department of Health Services (which included Maternal and Child Health Services), co-editor of *Pediatrics,* and, before that, Professor and Chairman of the Department of Pediatrics, University of Rochester School of Medicine and Dentistry. His initial faculty experience was at Harvard Medical School Children's Hospital Medical Center, Boston, Massachusetts, where he developed a training and research program in general pediatrics. He is President (1984–85) of the American Academy of Pediatrics. His interests are in clinical issues of general pediatrics, delivery of health care to children, behavioral pediatrics, and continuing education for the practice of pediatrics.

Alfred J. Kahn is Professor (policy and planning) at the Columbia University School of Social Work, co-director of the Cross National Studies Research Program, and chair of the School's doctoral program. Author of some twenty books and two hundred professional papers and chapters in other volumes, he has held many consultant and advisory positions and professional association offices. He has chaired the Committee on Child Development Research and Public Policy of the National Research Council/National Academy of Sciences. Most recently he co-authored, with Sheila B. Kamerman, *Income Transfers for Families with*

290

Children (1983) and *Helping America's Families* (1982). He also is author of *Theory and Practice of Social Planning* (1969) and other books on policy, social work, and the personal social service.

Sheila B. Kamerman is Professor (policy and planning) at the Columbia University School of Social Work and co-director of the Cross National Studies Research Program. She is the author of some twenty books and about one hundred articles or chapters in books. She has served on numerous national task forces and advisory committees, including the Economic Policy Council of the United Nations Association of the United States and the Committee on Child Development Research and Public Policy of the National Research Council/National Academy of Sciences, and chaired that committee's Panel on Work and Family Life. In recent years, she has co-authored, with Alfred J. Kahn, *Maternity Policies and Working Women* (1983) and *Child Care, Family Benefits and Working Parents* (1981). She is author of *Parenting in an Unresponsive Society* (1980) and *Meeting Family Needs: The Corporate Response* (1984).

Gerald L. Klerman is George Harrington Professor of Psychiatry at Harvard Medical School. He also serves as the Director of the Stanley Cobb Laboratories for Research at the Massachusetts General Hospital and as the Director of the Harvard Program in Psychiatric Epidemiology. His main professional activities involve research and teaching in clinical psychiatry with emphasis upon depressed and related affective disorders, their epidemiology and treatment, and the evaluation of mental health programs and treatments, especially psychopharmacology and psychotherapy. Over the years, Dr. Klerman has been the recipient of a number of professional awards honoring his prolific contributions to the mental health field. Currently, he is serving on the Editorial Board of the *Archives of General Psychiatry, Social Psychiatry,* and *Hospital and Community Psychiatry.*

Barbara Maughan is a Senior Research Officer in the Medical Research Council Child Psychiatry Unit. She entered research after some years in social work and social administration. Her research has largely focused on educational issues, and she was a joint author, with Michael Rutter and others, of *Fifteen Thousand Hours.*

Hamilton I. McCubbin is Professor of Family Social Science and Director of the Family Stress, Coping, and Health Project at the University of Minnesota in St. Paul. He is a member of the National Council on Family Relations, the American Family Therapy Association, and the National Association of Social Workers. He has served as both editor and co-editor of special issues for the *Journal of Primary Prevention, Family Relations,* and *Marriage and Family Review.* He is also a member of the Board of Editors for the *Family Systems*

Medicine journal, and is serving as an associate editor for the *Journal of Family Issues, Journal of Marriage and the Family, Human Relations, Family Studies Yearbook, Wellness Perspectives,* and *Trauma and Its Wake.* In addition to his journal publications, he has written the following books: *Social Stress and the Family; Stress and the Family: Coping with Catastrophes; Stress and the Family: Coping with Normative Transitions; Family Stress; Coping and Social Support; Marriage and Family: Individuals and Life Cycles;* and *Families: What Makes Them Work.*

David H. Olson is Professor, Family Social Science, at the University of Minnesota. He is a licensed consulting psychologist and Fellow in the American Association of Marriage and Family Therapists (AAMFT). He is Associate Editor or on the Advisory Board of eight journals including *Journal of Marriage and the Family, Family Process, Journal of Marriage and Family Therapy, American Journal of Family Therapy,* and *Family System Medicine.* His books include *Treating Relationships, Power in Families,* eight volumes of *Inventory of Marriage and Family Literature, Family Inventories,* and *Families: What Makes Them Work.*

I. Barry Pless is Professor of Pediatrics and Epidemiology at McGill University, from which he graduated in 1958. He did pediatrics training at McGill and then spent two years as a Fellow in Ambulatory Pediatrics at Harvard, followed by two years in the United Kingdom as a Milbank Memorial Fund Trainee in Social Pediatrics. He joined the Department of Pediatrics at the University of Rochester in 1967 and returned to McGill in 1975. He has been the recipient of a National Centre for Health Services Research Career Award, and a Milbank Memorial Fund Faculty Fellowship, and is currently a National Health Scientist, Health and Welfare, Canada. Dr. Pless is the co-author of three books and more than sixty scientific publications related to community pediatrics. He is the Director of Community, Developmental and Epidemiological Research at the Montreal Children's Hospital.

Richard H. Price is Professor of Psychology and Faculty Associate in the Institute for Social Research at the University of Michigan. He is also Director of the Michigan Prevention Research Center. He received his Ph.D. from the University of Illinois. He is the co-editor of *Evaluation and Action in the Social Environment.* His research interests center on the topics of work and mental health and the organization of care.

Robert N. Rapoport is Director of the Institute of Family and Environmental Research, London. A social anthropologist, he received his M.A. from the University of Chicago in 1949 and Ph.D. from Harvard University in 1951. His dissertation, published as a Peabody Museum Monograph, was on "Changing

Navaho Religious Values.'' As Field Director of Alexander Leighton's study of the epidemiology of mental illness in Nova Scotia from 1951 to 1954, he was co-author of *People of Cove and Woodlot,* and taught at Cornell University. Following this, he made a study of Maxwell Jones's pioneering therapeutic community at Belmont Hospital, England, and published *Community as Doctor* (1961). At the Tavistock Institute he published *Mid-Career Development* (1970) and numerous academic papers on the relation between career and family life. In 1971 he and Rhona Rapoport founded the Institute of Family and Environmental Research and co-authored *Sex, Career and Family, Dual Career Families* (and *Dual Career Families Re-examined*), *Leisure and the Family Life Cycle,* and *Fathers, Mothers and Society,* and co-edited *Families in Britain.* Dr. Rapoport was Vice-President for Program at the William T. Grant Foundation between 1981 and 1983, and is currently Senior Consultant for Action-Research.

Michael Rutter is Professor of Child Psychiatry at the Institute of Psychiatry, London, England; Honorary Director of the newly established Medical Research Council Child Psychiatry Unit; and consultant psychiatrist at the Maudsley Hospital. During the academic year 1961–63 he worked on a research Fellowship studying child development at the Department of Pediatrics, Albert Einstein College of Medicine, and during 1979–80 he was a Fellow at the Center for Advanced Study in the Behavioral Sciences, Stanford, California. He is an Honorary Fellow of the British Psychological Society and the American Academy of Pediatrics, and an Honorary Member of the American Academy of Child Psychiatry – reflecting his strong interdisciplinary interests. His research activities include stress resistance in children, developmental links between childhood and adult life, schools as social institutions, reading difficulties, interviewing skills, neuropsychiatry, infantile autism, and psychiatric epidemiology. His publications include some 22 books, 54 chapters, and more than 159 scientific papers. Among his awards is the C.B.E. for services to the field of child psychiatry. As a researcher and teacher, he is particularly interested in building bridges between knowledge of child development on the one hand and clinical child psychiatry on the other, and in considering the policy and practice implications of empirical research findings.

Heather Weiss is Director of the Harvard Family Research Project, a foundation-supported effort to examine evidence on the effectiveness of family support programs. She obtained her doctorate from the Harvard Graduate School of Education. She served as director of research and fieldwork for the Comparative Ecology of Human Development Project at Cornell University, and as director of the Yale Family Support Project. She is a former Fellow of the Yale Bush Center in Child Development and Social Policy and co-author of a research guide to family support programs.

Leslie T. Wilkins is a Research Professor (Emeritus) at the State University of New York, Albany, where he was a member (one-time Chairman) of the Faculty of the Graduate School of Criminal Justice. Prior to that he was Dean of the School of Criminology at the University of California at Berkeley. In Britain, he was Deputy Director (Research) in the Home Office, and in 1964–65, Senior Advisor with the United Nations. He has received many awards, including the Francis Wood Prize of the Royal Statistical Society, The Sutherland Award of the American Criminological Society, and the Durkheim Award of the International Society of Criminology. He is the author of more than a dozen books and over two hundred articles. Among his books are an early work with Hermann Mannheim, *Prediction Methods in Relation to Borstal Training* (1955), *Social Deviance* (1964) – in which he set forth his theory of deviation amplification – and *Consumerist Criminology* (1984), wherein he adapts Ralph Nader's theory of consumerism to the demand for punishment of offenders.

Edward Zigler is Sterling Professor of Psychology at Yale University, where he also serves as Director of the Bush Center in Child Development and Social Policy and as head of the Psychology Section of Yale's Child Study Center. From 1970 to 1972 he was the first Director of the Office of Child Development and Chief of the U.S. Children's Bureau. He currently serves as a consultant to numerous government agencies and testifies regularly before various congressional committees on social policy issues concerning America's children and families. His many honors include chairing the Fifteenth Anniversary Head Start Committee and receiving the American Psychological Association Award for Distinguished Contributions to Psychology in the Public Interest. He has recently been selected to receive the American Academy of Pediatrics' Aldrich Award. Current publications include books on child abuse, mental retardation, and cognitive development.

Shirley L. Zimmerman is an Associate Professor in the Department of Family Social Science at the University of Minnesota. She teaches family policy courses, and holds an adjunct associate professorship with the Minnesota Family Study Center at the university. She is the present chair of the Minnesota Governor's Council on Family and Children, and a past recipient of a National Institute of Mental Health postdoctoral fellowship in a Family Impact Analysis Training Program. She is the author of numerous articles on family policy and has conducted extensive research on related topics.

Name index

295

Subject index